# From Studies to Streams

**Comparative Policy Evaluation Series**
Ray C. Rist, series editor

*Program Evaluation and the Management of Government*
edited by Ray C. Rist

*Budgeting, Auditing, and Evaluation*
edited by Andrew Gray, Bill Jenkins, and Bob Segsworth

*Can Governments Learn?*
edited by Frans L. Leeuw, Ray C. Rist,
and Richard C. Sonnichsen

*Politics and Practices of Intergovernmental Evaluation*
edited by Olaf Rieper and Jacques Toulemonde

*Monitoring Performance in the Public Sector*
edited by John Mayne and Eduardo Zapico-Goñi

*Public Policy and Program Evaluation*
by Evert Vedung

*Carrots, Sticks, and Sermons:*
*Policy Instruments and Their Evaluation*
edited by Marie-Louise Bemelmans-Videc,
Ray C. Rist, and Evert Vedung

*Building Effective Evaluation Capacity*
edited by Richard Boyle and Donald Lemaire

*International Atlas of Evaluation*
edited by Jan-Eric Furubo, Ray C. Rist, and Rolf Sandahl

*Collaboration in Public Services: The Challenge for Evaluation*
edited by Andrew Gray, Bill Jenkins, Frans Leeuw, and John Mayne

*Quality Matters: Seeking Confidence in Evaluation, Auditing, and Performance Reporting*
by Robert Schwartz and John Mayne

# From Studies to Streams

Managing Evaluative Systems

Comparative Policy Evaluation
Volume XII

# Edited by Ray C. Rist & Nicoletta Stame

Transaction Publishers
New Brunswick (U.S.A.) and London (U.K.)

First paperback printing 2011
Copyright © 2006 by Transaction Publishers, New Brunswick, New Jersey.

All rights reserved under International and Pan-American Copyright Conventions. No part of this book may be reproduced or transmitted in any form or by any means, electronic or mechanical, including photocopy, recording, or any information storage and retrieval system, without prior permission in writing from the publisher. All inquiries should be addressed to Transaction Publishers, Rutgers—The State University, 35 Berrue Circle, Piscataway, New Jersey 08854-8042. www.transactionpub.com

This book is printed on acid-free paper that meets the American National Standard for Permanence of Paper for Printed Library Materials.

Library of Congress Catalog Number: 2005041934
ISBN: 978-0-7658-0287-3 (cloth); 978-4128-1837-7 (paper)
Printed in the United States of America

Library of Congress Cataloging-in-Publication Data

From studies to streams : managing evaluative systems / Ray C. Rist and Nicoletta Stame, editors.
    p. cm.—(Comparative policy evaluation series ; v. 12)
    Includes bibliographical references and index.
    ISBN 0-7658-0287-2 (cloth : alk. paper)
    1. Policy sciences—Evaluation. 2. Administrative agencies—Evaluation. 3. Public administration—Evaluation. I. Rist, Ray C. II. Stame, Nicoletta. III. Series.

H97.F765 2005
320.6'72—dc22

2005041934

# Contents

Introduction: Streams of Evaluative Knowledge  vii
   *Nicoletta Stame*

## Part 1  Channelled Streams of Evaluative Knowledge

1. The "E" in Monitoring and Evaluation—Using Evaluative Knowledge to Support a Results-Based Management System  3
   *Ray C. Rist*

2. How Evaluation Can Help Make Knowledge Management Real  23
   *Burt Perrin*

## Part 2  Information Systems at Work for Evaluation

3. Management of Evaluative Knowledge in National Health: Some Comparative Observations  49
   *Markus Spinatsch*

4. Organizing Knowledge: Evidence and the Construction of Evaluative Information Systems  65
   *Peter Dahler-Larsen*

5. Managing Evaluations in the Netherlands and Types of Knowledge  81
   *Frans L. Leeuw*

6. Implementing Results-Based Management  97
   *Per Oyvind Bastoe*

## Part 3  Thematic Evaluations and Their Uses

7. Complex Policies and Evaluative Streams of Knowledge  113
   *Nicoletta Stame*

8. Evaluating Knowledge about the Instruments of      129
   Government: The Canadian Federal Experience
   *Pearl Eliadis and Donald Lemaire*

9. Why Evaluations Sometimes Can't be Used—           147
   and Why They Shouldn't
   *Jan-Eric Furubo*

**Part 4   Strategic Budgeting and Streams of Knowledge**

10. Evaluation Use and Information Communication Technology:   169
    What is the Real Issue?
    *Yoon-Shik Lee*

11. Evaluative Information in the Norwegian Ministries      187
    *Marit Stadler Waerness and Ragnhild Øvrelid*

12. Evaluation Knowledge for Strategic Budgeting            215
    *Xavier Ballart and Eduardo Zapico*

**Part 5   Multi-Study Evaluation and the Learning Organization**

13. Evaluation, Knowledge Management, and Learning:         235
    Caught between Order and Disorder
    *Kim Forss and Claus C. Rebien*

14. Patterns of Evaluative Knowledge Creation and           251
    Utilization within the World Bank
    *Mita Marra*

**Postscript**
Theory of Knowledge and Use of Evaluation:                  271
Popper's Relevance for the Concept of Streams
of Evaluation Knowledge
   *Olaf Rieper*

Conclusion: A Brief Critique                                283
   *Ray C. Rist*

List of Contributors                                        287

Index                                                       291

# Introduction
# Streams of Evaluative Knowledge

*Nicoletta Stame*

This volume looks at the current world of evaluation through the prism of a metaphor, that of the "stream," meaning that evaluations no longer come anymore in single studies, but more often draw their material from a continuous flow of information that is nowadays facilitated by the ICT (Information and Communication Technologies). The authors reflect on the various shapes that such a stream may take, on the chemical composition of the water, and its potential uses: Drinking? Washing? Hydraulic power?

As with all metaphors, it has been created because a new phenomenon arose for which we have no specific concept, and it may be contested as to how suitable it is for what it was intended to accomplish. Once the metaphor was launched on a rainy day in a nicely rehabilitated ex-granary on the wharf of Copenhagen (May 2002), the authors were thrilled with the idea as it helped them understand what they were dealing with, and they embarked on this joint adventure. Each of them analyzed the stream from a different perspective: some looked at it from a bridge, others observed it irrigating their yards.

The result is a new navigation map that aims at helping evaluators and stakeholders understand when they can best benefit from flowing with the stream, when they would rather resist it and, above all, how they should learn to channel it.

### Why Streams?

We have detected many reasons for the emergence of streams. In the first place, there are limitations in single studies. Little can be learned by a single study if it is not supported by other findings (Perrin). They are expensive. They are repetitive: time and again they find out the same things, and it is foolish to have to repeat them just because of the administration's amnesia (Furubo); and they rarely produce new and relevant knowledge. According to Furubo, many single evaluations are irrelevant because they do not question the policy instruments and the relationship between means and goals, but only implementation. It is a kind of vicious circle: the evaluators limit themselves to evaluating the implementation of an instrument, and their evaluation cannot be used for policy decisions (with the apparent paradox: evaluation are more relevant where decisions are more trivial and less relevant where fundamental policy decisions are taken).[1] They are frequently untimely: as Rist stresses, "evaluation is appropriate at all phases and should not be restricted to an after-the-fact situation."

In the second place, there are new information needs that a single study cannot meet. Results based government studies require a continuous flow of data in order to be able to redress existing policies and programs on a real-time basis (Rist, Bastoe). New public management philosophies of public administration require a larger scope of evaluation in order to arrive at budgeting decisions (Furubo, Waerness, Øvrelid). Development policies, based on such principles of the "new paradigm" as ownership, coherence, partnership, results-orientation, need to focus on the coordination among the recipients' own priorities and the assistance policies (Bastoe). Evidence-based policy requires a larger basis for its generalizations (Spinatsch). New evolution areas, like complex policies and multi-layer governance arrangements (Stame, Leeuw), require a comparative analysis across different tools and across the public sector in order to overcome knowledge silos impediments or "institutional barriers to knowledge" and to move "from individual bits of knowledge about individual instruments to broader categories, namely information, capacity building, economic instruments ... rules and organizational structure" (Eliadis-Lemaire).

In the third place, new ICT resources are available that make the new tasks less daunting. The new ICT conveys much information that might be utilized for evaluation (data on performance, evaluation reports, policy analyses, administrative data, national statistics). Knowledge management (KM) systems, organizational memory and many other devices have been worked out, but it is not self-evident as to "how can one translate information into useful, practical knowledge that can be applied on a timely basis here and now in the real world" (Perrin). In fact, sometimes there is just an overload of it (Spinatsch speaks of health information systems that try to help potential users in their own search for the knowledge they need). Moreover—as Perrin suggests—it may be better to rely on the Internet for continuing a search, rather than to begin with it. As Lee points out, beyond being a "promoter" of evaluation use, the role of ICT can be that of a "demoter" or of an "onlooker."

All in all, the perspective of a "knowledge society" is seen to have gained center stage (Lee, Waerness, and Øvrelid), with new roles being attributed to knowledge activities (among which are evaluations) and with more knowledge infused in organizations, even if reality rarely seems to stand up to this ideal.

## What Kind of Streams

The problem with streams of water is that they have to be channelled, and there are many ways of doing this—with rigid embankments, or with more permeable sides. Similarly, the problem with the amount of knowledge is that it, too, has to be managed, and there are various ways of storing it (Nutley et al., 2002; Spinatsch; Lee). But when it comes to the way evaluators can swim in the stream of knowledge, other factors have to be considered: evaluation has the specific aim of improving social policies and public sector function, and it serves many constituencies (commissioners, implementers, stakeholders, the public, etc.). Thus, evaluators have to enter the stream, play with existing KM systems or help create new knowledge kits, in order to produce information that can be utilized in specific situations, with specific evaluation concerns: what we call "evaluative knowledge."[2]

We have identified different streams of evaluative knowledge by crossing two variables that are consistent with the evaluation function. Streams of evaluative knowledge may or may not share the characteristics of being channelled (yes/no) and of being composed of evaluations only or of being a mix of kinds of information.

As for their nature, streams of evaluative knowledge may be "channelled" or "un-channelled." This variable refers to whether or not knowledge has already been managed in a systematic way. "Channelled" refers to an information system that is already in place, as a kind of knowledge management; "un-channelled" means there is no such system. The positive aspect with "channelled" is that one can get it at once without making an effort, which no single evaluator could sustain. The negative aspect is that it has been done by someone else with other interests, perspectives, and/or biases, which means that the evaluator has to work out ways of dealing with it, from the selection of data storing criteria to the utilization of data. The opposite holds true when the stream is "un-channelled": the evaluator will be confronted by an amount of data that he/she has to master, and he/she will have to work out approaches for doing so.

As for their internal composition, they may be made of "evaluations only," or there may be an "information mix," composed of evaluations and other kinds of knowledge (statistical, administrative data, research, etc.). This variable refers to the scope of knowledge that can be utilized for evaluation and alludes to the fact that various kinds of information enter decision making, not only single study evaluations. If the streams are composed mainly of evaluative studies it may be easier to use them for evaluation; if they are composed of different pieces of information the evaluator will have to work harder at discerning what can be utilized.

Crossing these two variables, we have detected four main types of streams.

## Table I.1
## Types of Streams of Evaluative Knowledge

|  |  | Type of information components | |
|---|---|---|---|
|  |  | Evaluative knowledge only | Mixed kind of information |
| Nature of stream | Channelled | *1. Syntheses*: Ways of pooling together evaluations and single studies | *2. Information systems*: Information of different kinds (evaluations included) has been organized in KM systems |
|  | Un-channelled | *3. Mandated evaluations*: The evaluation function pools together evaluations mandated by law for strategic budgeting | *4. Multi-study evaluations*: The evaluator selects different kinds of information according to his/her approach to the evaluation of complex policies |

Each type may include many instances:
1. *Syntheses*. These are channelled streams composed of only evaluative studies. They differ as for the aims of the study, the approach followed, and, consequently, their intended use:

   - *cluster evaluations*: "identifying learnings across a range of projects that share some similarities, as well a number of differences" (Perrin).
   - *thematic evaluations:* "typically explore a common theme (e.g., employment of women) across a usually larger number of projects than are included in a cluster evaluation" (Perrin).
   - *syntheses of existing studies*: "collectively considering the findings and implications arising from a finite number of existing studies, such as recent evaluation and research studies that an agency or department has carried out or commissioned or otherwise has at its disposal" (Perrin).
   - *systematic reviews*: "going beyond one's own sources of information, to identify what can be learned from a review of pre-existing evaluations and other sources of information from a variety of sources and jurisdictions. A review potentially can draw upon a wide range of information from *anywhere*" (Perrin).
   - *good practices systems*: "a good practice can be defined as anything that works in some way, whether fully or in part, and that may have implications for practice at any level elsewhere" (Perrin). A variant of this is syntheses of "lessons learned" (Bastoe).

2. *Information systems*. These are channelled streams containing different kinds of knowledge. Dahlen-Larsen defines information systems as "a recipe for the selection, organization and retention of large amounts of information." It is therefore necessary to distill evaluative knowledge from the rest, in order to make it usable, in various ways (instrumental, cognitive).

- *Performance-based M&E systems*: "Performance-based M&E systems provide information on performance and movement toward outcomes and goals," while traditional M&E focuses on the monitoring and evaluation of inputs, activities, and outputs, i.e., project or program implementation. It is this linking of both implementation progress, with progress in achieving the desired objectives or goals (results) of government policies and programs, that makes performance-based M&E most useful as a tool for public management. Implementing this type of M&E system allows the organization to modify the implementation processes and to make adjustments in order to more directly support the achievement of desired objectives and outcomes (Rist).
- *Checklists of quality indicators*: Information systems that refer information on specific policies to quality standards (Leeuw on schools, Dahlen-Larsen on health systems).
- *Databases on single policies or instruments*: Large-scale datasets including statistical data, longitudinal data of given social groups, case studies, etc., which are continuously updated (see, for example, the Offender's index of Netherlands, Leeuw).
- *Observatorie*: "They do not produce any data themselves but ... their mission is to bring together, prepare and disseminate existing statistical data to monitor [specific policy problems] trends in order to improve the knowledge about the [issue] (Spinatsch).

3. *Mandated evaluations for strategic budgeting*. This is a non-channelled stream, put together by an evaluation unit or function in cases where evaluation is mandated for strategic budgeting.
4. *Multiple study evaluations*. Because of a complex evaluation arena (a policy, a mix of instruments, a multi-intervention site, etc.) evaluations bring together pieces of knowledge from different sources in various forms of triangulation, comparison, longitudinal studies, etc. An instance of this is *"realistic syntheses"* in which the "main focus should be [in Pawson's words], to develop 'a tailored, transferable theory' that indicates that 'this programme works in these respects, for these subjects, in these kinds of situations'" (Perrin).

## A New World for Evaluators and Their Partners: Continuities and Change

Looking at the evaluation enterprise through the stream metaphor, the authors have observed many changes going on in the new landscape. These changes, of course, differ both for the kind of stream, and for the way of utilizing the various streams in different contexts.

The main difference between single studies and streams relates to the actors involved. In single studies we have:

- a commissioner of the evaluation (program decision maker, program manager, stakeholders)

- an evaluator, who collects data (direct: surveys, focus groups, interviews; indirect: monitoring data) purposefully, interacts with stakeholders, and writes a report, which is a new document (the study)
- the user: the intended user (the commissioner), other stakeholders (beneficiaries, civil society, NGOs), the public.

In streams we have:

- an existing body of information already in place, encompassing statistics, researches, and administrative data, some of which may provide evaluative knowledge. This information may be retrieved and stored in KM systems organized according to different strategies (Spinatsch distinguishes between synthesizer and broker strategies)
- a commissioner who may have given some input for the tapping of a certain amount of water of the stream (Dahlen-Larsen)
- an evaluator who makes sense of existing data, and specializes in selecting them, developing different modes for knowledge management (Spinatsch: processing, networking) and applying different mixes of tacit and codified knowledge (Marra, Forss and Rebien); sometimes before looking for new ones (as in the syntheses, Perrin), at other times as a way of testing one's theory. Evaluators' roles are crucial in helping frame evaluative criteria and standards. (Dahlen-Larsen)
- a user who may either be guided by the evaluator or who may have direct access to it (as in access to school tables, Leeuw).

Sometimes, the new environment of streams allows evaluators to rethink issues that had been prominent in the single study era. Take, for example, the uses of evaluation.[3] Indeed, evaluation use had been the previous focus of the authors when planning the work for this book (see also Rieper). They realized that there was something new going on in the way evaluations were received and managed, but they believed that the debate on evaluation use was stuck, even in its latest incarnation as "influence" (Kirkhart, 2000), because it was intertwined with an evaluation perspective that was going to disappear from sight. Then came the perception that the enduring interest for use could gain from taking into consideration the new objects: the stream instead of the single study. Aiming at instrumental use is understandable, even if it rarely happens with single studies; cognitive use, which was indeed found to be more common even with single studies,[4] is well suited to the stream of knowledge (Leeuw, Stame). And, even more so than with single studies, evaluations are not the only type of information feeding the decision-making process (Furubo, Waerness and Øvrelid). However, some information systems are precisely created in order to improve the "here and now" use of evaluation data (Rist, Bastoe). Rist notes that single studies can be useless if they come too late, while performance-based M&E systems allow "real time" use of evaluation by public sectors managers. Thus, with the mind always aware of the alternative between looking for instrumental use and realizing that cognitive use is an intrinsic part of evaluation, we wanted to inquire as to whether the streams of knowledge could allow for different kinds of uses.

Similarly, the linear model of the program cycle (where evaluation is being located after result and before feedback) was already under attack within the single studies, thanks to evaluation approaches that had promoted formative evaluations, process use, and contextual redefinition of program goals. But now, as Perrin states, "with information increasingly coming in the form of streams, evaluation increasingly is being used as a process rather than a product.... This, in turn, highlights the need for a learning approach to evaluation, where the emphasis is on understanding the reasons why something works or not, and on suggesting ideas and potential approaches to consider." This idea is reinforced when seen from the learning organization perspective. As Forss and Rebien state, "the important learning events occur in preparatory meetings, in procedures of data collection, through joint analysis of achievements, and in the search for data from other sources, benchmarking and comparative analysis...the extended evaluation process itself can be viewed as a stream of information, which is gradually—through many processes—converted into knowledge."

At other times, streams bring about completely new issues, such as the abundance, not the scarcity, of available data. Apart from the risk of being drowned in it, if one lacks the ability to swim (Lee talks of the need for ICT literacy), it has become more and more ironic to justify a poor quality evaluation by saying that "the data were not available."

Perhaps the most interesting thing to note is how ideas and concepts worked out in the era of the studies got new fresh air with the streams, and became more productive, for better or worse, depending on the evaluator's and stakeholders' needs and inclinations. In fact, streams do not seem to drag new approaches to evaluation, but they certainly offer the previous approaches new opportunities to expand and to be operative. On the one hand, the movement for evidence-based policy, with its insistence on objective and consistent findings, has thrived on the possibility of collecting experimental designs across the board,[5] thus helping it get out of its trade-off between internal and external validity.[6] On the other hand, it is surprising how widespread an approach theory-based evaluation has become, expanding its turf from community-based social programs to whatever kinds of interventions and public sector functions (Stame, Ballart and Zapico, Leeuw). Having stressed the importance of understanding program theories and change models, theory-based evaluation seems better suited to answer questions as to why something happened in complex situations of multi-layer governance, in cases of mixed policy tools and of policies tackling multi-dimensional problems.[7] This advancement has certainly benefited from the work of Carol Weiss on social programs and Ray Pawson (2002b) on realistic syntheses, which many authors take as their compass.

## How This Volume is Organized

The book is divided into five parts, the first two parts of which start from the channelled streams end. Part 1 looks at them from a general point of view, with the two chapters presenting a vast landscape of what exists, articulated into the different forms of streams, their nature, logic, and working, hence the challenges they give evaluators. Part 2 is devoted to specific kinds of informative systems, referred to as policy domains (health, criminal justice, education, development), and the ways evaluators have managed them.

The following three parts then start from the opposite end, that is, the need for streams and how they are created and utilized in different situations. Each chapter takes stock of a specific issue, and presents one or more case studies dealing with how different kinds of streams have been used. Part 3 is devoted to case studies of thematic evaluations (policy instruments, "broad goals" policies, domain policies). Part 4 examines the requirement of strategic budgeting in new systems of governance that are decentralized and mandate evaluation across the board. Part 5 is particularly focused on the way organizations can learn from multi-study evaluations.

## Findings

In Part 1, we navigate across the channelled streams, be they drawing their water from evaluations only, or from mixed sources; and we become better acquainted with them. The main issues here refer to orienting these systems toward producing the kind of evaluative information needed by concerned parties such as governments and stakeholders.

Rist offers an account of how to create information systems suitable to a result based government, one that concentrates on outcomes and that needs to get timely information based on an assessment of why something worked or did not work. The evaluator concern here is for designing ways for "the near continuous production of evaluative knowledge," that through "reporting on 'how well' governments are doing compared to real or desired criteria" may help numerous parties to "participate in the 'business of government' and make suggestions on how to improve performance." The design of such a system should take into consideration the complementarity of monitoring and evaluation (monitoring which indicates how far results have been achieved; evaluation which tells whether or not they have been achieved), and serve the needs of vertical interdependence (allowing for a flow of information across levels, making linkages between projects, programs, and policies) and of horizontal interdependence (allowing management to manage in a web of relationships, shared responsibilities, and mutual accountabilities).

Perrin, as the title of his chapter denotes, looks at knowledge management (KM) systems and their claim to provide useful and timely knowledge, and tries to assess how evaluation can make KM systems live up to their promise.

Introduction  xv

In so doing, he reminds us of the tradition of evaluation syntheses, which may be considered forerunners of the actual movement for KM.[8] Different purposes can be served by the various types of syntheses, and syntheses can be composed of different kinds of information. Driving us along the various kinds of syntheses Perrin then shows how syntheses turned into information systems, what evaluative information the latter retained, and what should be added to the KM systems to make them work. Thus, Perrin introduces us to the main distinction between, on the one side, syntheses that aim at finding out what works everywhere (as in the integrative syntheses that are based on the principle of finding out what is most successful with the intention of applying it everywhere, also found in the idea of "best practices") and, on the other side, those that aim at finding "what works better where" (as in the realistic syntheses, which are oriented to the context and to the various combinations of multiple tools, and, therefore, may qualify as "good practice").

In Part 2 we see how some of these channelled streams work, and what are the stakes for evaluators and stakeholders.

Two chapters are devoted to the health system (a domain in which the need for systematic data collection has been prominent for a long time), in order to identify needs, the results of medical treatment, and the performance level according to quality standards. Perhaps this is the field in which random assignment trials have most thrived, and the one that has offered an example for others to follow. Beyond describing what information systems are like, both chapters focus on their uses for evaluative purposes. Spinatsch reviews several national health observatories, and distinguishes them according to strategies for getting access to data: (a) the synthesizer strategy, which relies on data already collected and intended for comparisons between different indicators; and (b) the broker strategy, which leaves it up to the user to decide what may best fit his/her needs. These strategies, in turn, correspond to ways of managing knowledge: the processing mode, making greater use of explicit knowledge vs. the networking mode, which is more focused on tacit knowledge. These distinctions help Spinatsch discuss ways of working with some specific platforms and information systems, presenting the advantages and disadvantages of each.

Dahlen-Larsen enters into the "very construction and design of information systems" and analyzes crucial factors—social, organizational, and technical—that have to be taken into consideration for building them, based on case studies of two Danish information systems, an accreditation system and a quality checklist (the "Indicator project"). The cases show that practical problems arising in managing these systems depend on the way contextual factors interact with the kind of tool used. For instance, in the accreditation process the evaluation criteria are externally generated, generic criteria covering all diagnoses, while in the indicator project specific indicators were identified and crafted for each diagnosis. This takes us to the core of the problem of evidence and the evaluation criteria, which have to be established when the system is constructed. Who is responsible for it? This presents a formidable challenge: on the one side, an information system is organized through the negotiated interaction of managers, experts, politicians, and various institutions; on the other side, since issues of criteria setting arise that evaluators are often expected to help with, are evaluators expected to extend their role to such tasks?

Leeuw looks at the other end of the evaluation knowledge management: what kind of knowledge is better suited to feed policy decisions? His focus is on the relationship between the kinds of information collected, institutional location, and use of these data. He compares the record of an autonomous body, the audit system, with that of two government agencies, located inside the Ministry of Education (the "Report on the State of Education in the Netherlands," which is issued annually and in which information is given on developments in the country's state of education, and which, in turn, is intended to fulfill many needs: that is, help parents in the school choice, stimulate the autonomy of the school and its quest for quality, inform authorities) and the Ministry of Justice (the program for monitoring and evaluating the effectiveness of criminal justice interventions: monitoring recidivism). The audit system, which collects knowledge about organizational prerequisites and procedures, is unable to link it positively to a learning process; the two governmental agencies, which are more responsive to outside developments, focus more on substantive or explanatory knowledge—drawn from many kinds of databases, domain literature, and statistical reports about mechanisms within society that make policies work or not work and produce better learning. Leeuw is interested in the chains of knowledge that connect the framing of the policy issues to the way evaluations are conducted: to how they are supported by longitudinal M&E systems, and to how they are utilized. To do this, he reconstructs the program theory of the use that governmental agencies make of information systems.

Bastoe links the streams of knowledge to the new development paradigm encompassing results-based management (RBM). Development is a complex process; it builds on the recipients, own priorities and is coordinated among interested parties (ownership, coherence, partnership, results-orientation). Accordingly, evaluation should move "from a situation where tools for planning, monitoring, evaluation and feedback are separated, to a situation where the different tools are integrated in a structured RBM system." Bastoe presents the case of the African Development Bank (ADB), which overcame a crisis by boldly espousing RBM principles and shifting the focus of evaluation from operational issues to development effectiveness issues. The case of ADB is studied against similar cases of readjustment, and the possible lessons learned from them: the strategies for change, the timing and pacing of the reform, and the institutional context. Apparently, the field of development seems to be best acquainted with guides and synthesized lessons learned; and the case of ADB shows that turning to reviews of experience in similar organizations and identifying key lessons for setting a RBM has been the first step before proceeding. The case, however, also shows the other side of syntheses: key lessons have to be adapted to one's own "dance of change."

With Part 3, we enter the field of un-channelled streams and, therefore, we deal more with evaluators' abilities to bring together different kinds of information other than making sense of existing ones. The three chapters in this part deal with thematic evaluations that attempt to assess the outcomes of instrument mixes. All chapters consider situations characterized by a multiplicity of interventions and the need to understand what works better where, trying to fit the new knowledge with existing knowledge.

My own chapter deals with two cases of new policies that state broad goals without envisaging by what means they should be attained, hence leaving it to the implementers. The Millennium Development Goals (MDGs) is a case in which the policy is shaped by the fact that goals have been negotiated at the highest international level, and are fixed. Here the evaluators are engaged with tools that try to assess the progress toward those goals by comparative analyses that allow for making sense of ranking, and that focus on learning from one another. The Italian policy of regularization of the shadow economy states a new goal that can be achieved in different ways by different constituencies reacting to various mechanisms. This is a typical situation in which the evaluator has to reconstruct what constitutes a success, whether it was obtained by direct or indirect means and how it works for the different constituencies. It is also a case in which the evaluator cannot rely on single studies, but must put together pieces of information that allow a comparison among the different contexts in which the policy is implemented, the way tools are combined, etc. Of course, the strategies of evaluation will be different in the two cases: in the former, it will be a game of ranking and learning; in the latter, a game of looking at intended and unintended consequences.

Eliadis and Lemaire analyze how the federal government of Canada has sought to expand the evaluative knowledge framework for non-legislative instruments by providing formal encouragement as well as support for various research initiatives. To avoid knowledge silos, horizontal knowledge brokering initiatives had to be taken. "Networked government" requires interaction between government and non-governmental actors; therefore it fosters building capacity and knowledge creation across the different actors. Further, synthesis is needed in order to understand what instruments are better suited for capacity building of governmental and non-governmental actors. And how they are better combined; for example, "a combination of a public perception of the likelihood of getting caught, along with a legislative sanction, was more effective than the law acting alone." A synthesis of instruments across the public sector shows the need for taking into consideration the economic, ethical, and social dimensions alike; that instrument mixes are context-sensitive and that all instruments have important repercussions for the legitimacy and accountability of public action.

Furubo's chapter is most concerned with the limits of traditional evaluation (even if it comes in a continuous flow of single studies that are simply repetitive) and their irrelevance for important policy shifts. His chapter, however, also offers interesting openings onto situations in which evaluative knowledge has, indeed, favored such changes that he attributes to institutional factors. Quoting the case of the Swedish stabilization policy during the period 1975–1995 and of the agricultural policy at the end of the 1980s, he found that changes were introduced when the politicians had obtained relevant information from the economic profession, research centers, and international organizations that had been able to mediate the new knowledge coming from evaluations with a more general science production, and that, in turn, were able to communicate this back to the politicians. Using yet another metaphor, that of a knowledge bank, Furubo believes evaluators who produce knowledge should relate not only to the final decision makers, but also to the "officials of the bank" who are "able to rearrange the information and relate it to earlier knowledge in the field" in a triangular relationship, composed of evaluators, these knowledge structures, and the political system.

Part 4 is devoted to those cases where the government has mandated evaluation in all ministries, with a view to fully realizing the ideal of the "knowledge society." But the institutionalization of the continuous flow of evaluative knowledge has its limits. Not only is the ICT itself of no help if people are not trained to use it, but also a mandated stream of evaluation risks creating stagnant waters if the institutional culture remains bureaucratic and is unable to learn.

Lee's chapter deals with South Korea, a country with a diffuse information technology literacy, were it not for its higher policymakers. South Korea has passed a bold law on evaluation, mandating not only evaluation performance in all ministries, but also evaluation use. Lee's study shows that civil servants accede frequently to the ICT for evaluation uses, along all the different modes forecasted by his model (ICT as a promoter, demoter, onlooker). However, the knowledge society has its requirements: if evaluation use is mandated by law, there should also be an effective incentive system, complete with specific regulations about failure to use evaluative information, and ways of motivating policymakers to such a use. And if all public officers are not literate enough to take advantage of the ICT, it would be necessary to "regularly and periodically orient decision makers with knowledge of ICT, readjusting legal and institutional arrangements to new evaluation environments."

Waerness and Øvrelid's chapter analyzes in-depth the Norwegian situation in which recent regulations also have attempted to introduce systematic use of evaluation in the government budget process. The comparative study of three ministries, with related agencies, looks at how evaluations are conducted and utilized in three environments that differ in institutional arrangements, administrative culture, and relationship with the beneficiaries. Notwithstanding the great effort in producing evaluations, they continue to be conducted as single studies.[9] They are used more cognitively for policy formation—as with single studies—than instrumentally for budgeting (contrary to what might have been the initial rationale for the reform). Moreover, they have not strengthened cross-sector cooperation and institutional coordination. Since the explanation for such a situation is mainly provided in terms of the logic of the ministries, it seems as if the evaluation system were not aligned with the institutional changes that should necessarily go hand in hand with the public sector reforms.

This point is stressed by Ballart and Zapico in their chapter, which deals with the needs for evaluative criteria suited to strategic budgeting in the new public sector environment, namely an unstructured policy context demanding decentralization. The latter needs a qualitatively stronger (not weaker) role in accountability and evaluation. New criteria for evaluation have been envisioned. The old 3 Es (efficiency, effectiveness, economy) are no longer sufficient for situations where goals are continuously changing or outcomes cannot be anticipated. Instead, new criteria of success are sought in the 3 Ds: diagnosis (capacity for identification of new problems or redefinition of current problems), design (capacity for formulation of new solutions), and development (capacity for implementation of new solutions as a learning process). These new criteria can guide the evaluation function if suitable approaches are used that allow the budget to go "beyond the straightforward evaluation of programs by agencies, producing the kind of evaluative knowledge that deals with the complex interactions which exist between various types of interventions and effects." This may also help the center to "play a role in the diffusion of those experiences that appear to be successful from the perspective of stakeholders."

Part 5 approaches some of the predicaments seen in part 4, presenting cases in which the stream of knowledge has been composed of a mix of tacit and codified knowledge, and the evaluators have been able to make the evaluation process a participating one to which the stakeholders have brought their experience and understanding.

Marra analyzes four cases of how the results of evaluations were processed inside the World Bank. Beyond being single studies, the process through which the results of the four evaluations were discussed and compared with other knowledge, in different organizational settings, was in itself a way of creating a new stream of knowledge. Marra has explored how streams of evaluative knowledge can reinforce organizational knowledge, creating processes over time, especially when evaluation participatory processes help socialize streams of evaluative knowledge containing tacit as well as codified knowledge. This has implications for the organization's advancement strategy, since the organization needs to orient the process of knowledge creation across its levels. Organizational members are involved with a tangible form of knowledge, achieved by combining existing knowledge, products, procedures, and components with the new evaluative concepts. These participatory processes of evaluative knowledge generation and sharing pave the way to substantive innovation in public management.

Forrs and Rebien show that this process of organizational knowledge creation has to strike a balance between order ("management") and disorder ("learning"). They agree with Marra on the importance of participatory processes for organizational learning, but add a note of caution on the smoothness of such processes. In the two cases that they analyze (a complex social problem in Sweden and a case of international collaboration) learning takes place when a new situation creates a certain level of chaos and insecurity leads to "seeing things in a different light," in which humor needs to be accepted. But advancements exist, of an incremental, small-wins type.

Lastly, Rieper reminds us of where it all started. We were wondering about the uses of knowledge, and we came across the streams. And now Rieper goes back to the classics and locates an understanding of streams in their thinking.

## Notes

1. According to Furubo, the paradox is that what triggers policy shift is most often the effect of serious crises or accidents that are simply received by the news, without any mediation by an evaluative judgment. However, the nature of the political context in which evaluation takes place makes mediation of evaluation results, with other ideological, emotional, or simply opportunistic inputs, a natural occurrence.
2. We consider evaluative knowledge all the knowledge that allows making evaluative considerations; thus, not only what has already been framed as an evaluation, but also the knowledge that contains criteria for valuing. However, there may be different perceptions as to the latter task. See, for instance, Dahlen-Larsen's discussion about the setting of criteria in the hospital information system. See also Forss-Rebien: "We have too much information but not enough knowledge (knowledge = information transformed into learning, action, and change). Evaluations are part of the information industry, they do not necessarily produce knowledge. They will do, if they strike a careful balance between order (management) and disorder (knowledge, learning)."
3. Many chapters refer to the debate on evaluation use, and provide the main conceptual elements for moving into it. See Stame and Lee. The latter provides an analytical model that integrates types of evaluative use with types of ICT roles.
4. Suffice here a quotation from Weiss (2004): "I do not advocate cognitive, use, but it is what happens more frequently..."
5. Pawson (2002a).
6. Experimental designs have always suffered from the great difficulty of getting external validity, and the syntheses aim at filling this gap (see Perrin). See also Cook (2004).
7. This advancement has certainly benefited from the work of Carol Weiss on social programs and Ray Pawson (2002b) on realistic syntheses, which many authors take as their compass.

8. See, for example, Lipsey and Wilson (2001), and Weiss (2004: 160). It is noteworthy that in order to avoid the limitations of single studies, Lee Cronbach had already thought along a nautic metaphor when he praised the advantages of a "fleet of studies" (Greene, 2004).
9. Judging by the Furubo and Waerness and Øvrelid chapters, there seems to be a Scandinavian model of "streams of single studies"!

**References**

Cook, T. (2004). "Causal Generalization." In M. Alkin, ed., *Evaluation Roots*.

Greene, J. (2004). "The Educative Evaluator: An Interpretation of Lee J. Cronbach's Vision of Evaluation." In M. Alkin, ed., *Evaluation Roots*. Thousand Oaks, CA: Sage.

Lipsey, M. W., and D. B. Wilson. (2001). *Practical Meta-analysis*. Thousand Oaks, CA: Sage.

Kirkhart, K. (2000). "Reconceptualizing Evaluation Use: An Integrated Theory of Influence." Iin V. Caracelli and H. Preskill, eds., *The Expanding Scope of Evaluation Use*. New Directions for Evaluation, no. 88. San Francisco: Jossey-Bass.

Nutley, S., I. Waleter, and H.T.O. Davies. "From Knowing to Doing. A Framework for Understanding the Evidence-into-Practice Agenda." *Evaluation* 9(2) (2002).

Pawson, R. "Evidence-Based Policy: In Search of a Method." *Evaluation* 8(2) (2002a).

Pawson, R. "Evidence-Based Policy: The Promise of 'Realist Synthesis.'" *Evaluation* 8(3) (2002b).

Weiss, C. (2004). "Rooting for Evaluation: A Cliff Notes Version of My Work," in M. Alkin, ed., *Evaluation Roots*. Thousand Oaks, CA: Sage.

# Part 1

## Channelled Streams of Evaluative Knowledge

# 1

# The "E" in Monitoring and Evaluation—Using Evaluative Knowledge to Support a Results-Based Management System

*Ray C. Rist*

### Introduction

Over the past two decades, there has been a movement within governments across the globe to reform and reshape the ways in which they function.[1] Demands by citizens for their governments to be accountable for results, transparent, and to provide more efficient and effective services echo now from continent to continent. The paradox of citizens asking for more services and programs despite steady state or even fewer government resources, for more quality and availability like the private sector, for more responsiveness from fewer civil servants, and for accountability while pressing for decentralization have left governments experimenting with a multitude of strategies in response. These pressures are helping to drive a global public management revolution.

While this revolution has taken hold mostly in the OECD (Organization for Economic Cooperation and Development) countries (cf. OECD, 2000a), it has not stopped there. Indeed, in the developing world, a poorly functioning public sector has emerged as a key factor in the lack of progress towards sustainable economic growth (World Bank, 1997). Thus, public sector reforms are now also clearly emerging in developing countries as varied as, for example, Chile, the Philippines, Sri Lanka, India, Uganda, Malaysia, Mexico, and South Africa, which are likewise facing increasing pressures from their citizens, their private and civil society sectors, and the international community to improve both the structures and processes of governance.

One important lesson learned from reform initiatives is that when a government switches its focus from measuring whether a program is "on track" to whether the program is achieving its desired objectives or goals (results), its overall performance improves. (Performance is meant to assume a measurable level of program and policy effectiveness and efficiency.) Improvements can come in different forms—for example, emphasizing more productivity, more public reliance on private markets, more decentralization from national to sub-national units of government, clear lines of responsibility and accountability, more responsiveness to citizens as clients, and an increased capacity to monitor and evaluate the performance of the public sector (cf. Perrin, 2003).

Whatever the chosen means, these strategies emphasize that governments should focus their efforts to achieve the results they promise to their citizens. It also then follows that if governments are to achieve these promised results, they should (and politically need to) be able to provide to their citizens evidence of having done so. That evidence should be transparent, trustworthy, and readily available. A results-based monitoring and evaluation (M&E) system is an important tool that allows governments to acquire this evidence.

The challenge is how governments can begin to build results-based monitoring and evaluation systems so as to provide credible and trustworthy information for their own use and to share with their citizens. The reality is that putting in place even a rudimentary system of monitoring, evaluating, and reporting on government performance is not easy in the best of circumstances. But the obstacles for developing countries are greater and more formidable, even as they begin to construct more traditional M&E systems (Kusek and Rist, 2004).

It should also be acknowledged that it is not a new phenomenon that governments monitor and evaluate their own performance in attempting to achieve promised results. For this reason, a theoretical distinction needs to be drawn between traditional M&E and results-based M&E. Traditional M&E focuses on the monitoring and evaluation of inputs, activities, and outputs, that is, project or program implementation. Governments have over time tracked their expenditures and revenues, staffing levels and resources, program and project activities, numbers of participants, goods and services produced, etc. Indeed, traditional efforts at monitoring have been a function of many governments for many decades or longer. In fact, there is evidence that the ancient Egyptians (5000 BC) regularly tracked their government's outputs in grain and livestock production (Egyptian Museum, Cairo, Egypt).

Results-based M&E, however, combines the traditional approach of monitoring implementation with the assessment of results (Mayne and Zapico-Goni, 1999). This is why, for example, the 1994 Government Performance and Results Act (GPRA) in the United States used both words in the title of the legislation—"performance" and "results." These two concepts are not identical nor are they redundant. It is also why both need to be measured within the framework of the M&E system being discussed here. It is this linking of implementation progress (performance) with progress in achieving the desired objectives or goals (results) of government policies and programs that makes results-based M&E most useful as a tool for public management. Implementing this type of M&E system allows the organization to modify and make adjustments to the implementation processes in order to more directly support the achievement of desired objectives and outcomes.

A results-based M&E system can help policymakers answer the fundamental questions of whether promises are being kept and goals are being achieved. (Note the present tense.) Such a system can also become an early warning and response system for managers when the evidence suggests that a divergence is growing between promises made and performance achieved. Indeed, good M&E systems should be viewed as a means of surfacing problems in organizations in so far as their performance is concerned. If governments are promising improved performance, there needs to be some means of demonstrating that such improvements are or are occurring, that is, there is a need for measurement. But the issue goes well beyond measurement per se. A government needs to both document and demonstrate its own performance to its stakeholders as well as use the performance information to continuously improve itself. As Binnendijk (1999: 3) observed:

> One key use is for transparent reporting on performance and results achieved to external stakeholder audiences. In many cases, government-wide legislation or executive orders have recently mandated such reporting. Moreover, such reporting can be useful in competition for funds by convincing a skeptical public or legislature that the agency's programs produce significant results and provide "value for money." Annual performance reports are often directed to ministers, parliament, stakeholders, customers, and the general public.
>
> Performance information should also be used for internal purposes, such as for management decision-making and identifying areas of improvement. This requires that performance information be integrated into key management systems and processes of the organization, such as in policy formulation, in project/program planning and management, and in budget allocation processes.

Implicit in Binnendijk's analysis is that performance measurement is a management tool for both government officials and stakeholders. First, by using the performance information in policymaking and program management, governments are in a position to better assess their own levels of performance. Also, it is through the reporting on "how well" government is doing compared to real or desired criteria that numerous parties can participate in "the business of government" and make suggestions on how to improve performance in pursuit of desired results. This phenomenon is evident in many developed countries where performance and results information, and other official documents such as the budget, are regularly published by the media or made otherwise available to citizens. Citizens in the OECD countries, for example, regularly pressure their national and sub-national governments to be responsive to their needs as well as be accountable for the funds put into the trust of lawmakers and officials alike. Again, in many developing countries, the processes are less evident and less substantial—but they are not absent (Chile, Mexico, Uganda, South Africa, and Malaysia being five notable examples).

Meeting these objectives of credible reporting to citizens and using the information as a management tool means new perspectives are needed in thinking about how we monitor, how we evaluate, and how we use the information generated by such an M&E system. Indeed, it also calls for reconsideration away from our focus on evaluation information produced by evaluation studies to one on evaluative knowledge generated by streams of evaluative knowledge.

## Refocusing the Evaluation Craft to Support Performance-Based M&E Systems

It is the basic thesis of this chapter that the global emergence of a results-focus in the public sector will necessarily require an expanded, if not indeed, a different logic and approach to the undertaking of evaluation work. Succinctly, no longer can governments wait for indeterminate periods of time for individual process or impact evaluations to inform on the progress of government initiatives. What government managers need is information that helps them manage, helps them make decisions on resource allocation, and helps them report both inside and outside of the government on progress being made (or not) on achieving stated outcomes. In this context, evaluation becomes a means to improve, not to prove (Worthen and Schmitz, 1997).

Waiting for evaluation studies that come after a project, program, or policy is executed or waiting for evidence of implementation that comes late and slow is not helpful to contemporary managers. (It is necessary to note that, of course, these are not the only uses of evaluation, but looking to evidence on implementation or on outcome/impact studies to give definitive answers on performance remains a central focus of evaluative work.) Increasingly, time is of the essence in the public sector and information requirements are in real time. Decisions will be made when they have to be made. If evaluation findings are available when the decisions need to be made, all to the good. If they are not, the decisions still get taken. The realities of bureaucratic life have to be acknowledged (see Furubo, this volume.) There is no longer the luxury of waiting for individual evaluation studies (either formative or summative) to be designed, implemented, analyzed, results drafted, reviewed, re-drafted, etc. There is no time to wait for Godot.

*Reflecting the central theme of this book, what is now required is the real-time production of streams of evaluative knowledge, not the production of still more and more discrete and disconnected evaluation studies.* If evaluative knowledge is to be part of the tool kit of managers, then this information is needed in a timely and useful fashion. As will be developed here, the implications for applying evaluative knowledge within a results framework will reshape the traditional assumptions about the conduct, reporting, and use of evaluations. We will come to this discussion in a moment.

## If Performance Information is the Key, Then Where Does It Come From?

Performance information can come from multiple sources. For example, there can be media reports on fraud and corruption, citizen demonstrations against poor public services, tax revolts over public expenditures, academic research, turning to the private sector for goods and services, and elections that become referendums on the keeping of political promises. What we will focus on here, however, are two of the more systematic means of gathering and analyzing performance information—a monitoring system and an evaluation system. Both are needed, but they are not the same. The distinctions between monitoring and evaluation are made here for both conceptual and practical purposes. However, it is also important to note that in the actual construction of M&E systems, the distinctions are not so sharp—nor do they have to be. Some blurring of the boundaries between monitoring and evaluation is already occurring in many organizations. More can be expected.

*Performance monitoring* can be viewed as consistently measuring progress toward explicit short, intermediate, and long-term results. It also can provide feedback on the progress made (or not) to decision makers who can use the information in various ways to improve performance. The OECD (2002b: 30) definition of performance monitoring is succinct:

> Performance monitoring [is] a continuous process of collecting and analyzing data to compare how well a project, program, or policy is being implemented against expected results.

Monitoring involves measurement—and what is measured is the progress towards achieving an objective or outcome (result). However, it is generally the case that the outcome cannot be measured directly. It must first be translated into a set of indicators that, when regularly measured, will provide information as to whether or not progress is being made towards the achievement of this same outcome. For example: If a country selects the outcome of improving the health of its most poor children by reducing childhood morbidity by 30 percent over the next five years, it must now identify a set of indicators that translate childhood morbidity into more specific measurements for this target population. Indicators that can help assess the changes in childhood morbidity might include, for example: (1) the incidence and prevalence of infectious diseases, such as hepatitis; and (2) the incidence and prevalence of gastrointestinal diseases.

Measuring a disaggregated set of indicators provides important information as to the progress being made (or not) in achieving the intended results of government programs and policies. If, for example, the tracking of indicators over time documents that fewer and fewer poor children in a city or region have access to clean water, then the government can use this information to reform programs aimed to improve water quality, or strengthen those programs that provide information to parents about the need to sterilize water before providing it to their children.

Ensuring the utility of performance information for various stakeholders is a key reason for building an M&E system in the first place. Government managers are necessarily one key group of users. But they are not the only group who can benefit from and have information on government performance. Yet, unfortunately, in many societies some or all of these other groups are often left out of the information flow, including citizens, NGO groups, the media, and the private sector. (And this does not even address the perpetual problem of government agencies not sharing data among themselves! See Waerness and Øvrelid, this volume.) Monitoring data have both internal (governmental) and external (societal) users and uses that need to be recognized. The broad sharing of these data can increase transparency, accountability, and democratic involvement.

It is important to note here that performance information obtained from a monitoring system reveals the level of performance of what is being measured at that time—although it can be compared against both past performance and some planned level of present or anticipated performance. Monitoring data do not definitively reveal or provide independent attribution as to why that level of performance occurred or provide the likely causality to changes in performance from one reporting period to another.

Still, one is not left empty-handed in this regard with only monitoring information. John Mayne, among others, has written on the contributions that performance monitoring can make to our understandings of attribution. In an article on "Contribution Theory" (Mayne, 2001), he stresses that with a monitoring system working as it should, the system will be able to provide good information that at least suggests whether the theory of change is working as it should. While such data do not in the classical sense "prove" causation, the growing evidence from monitoring can trigger an evaluation to delve more deeply into the issue. (And again, the need for evaluative knowledge in a performance-based system is not so much to prove as to improve.)

*Performance evaluation* provides for a complementary study of organizational and managerial performance to that provided by monitoring. Building a system that provides evaluative knowledge on performance within an organization or government can bring in other data sources than just extant indicators (by using interviews, focus groups, or surveys, for example); can address factors that are too difficult or expensive to continuously monitor (e.g., client satisfaction or empowerment); and perhaps most important, can tackle the issue of trying to determine why and how the performance trends being tracked with monitoring data are moving in the directions they are. Such data on attribution (while almost inevitably incomplete and subject to all sorts of challenges) are not to be taken lightly and can play an important role in an organization making strategic resource allocations. As Binnendijk (1999: 17) notes:

> Because of timing as well as the need to use more rigorous methods and in-depth analysis, some performance issues, such as long-term impact, attribution, cost-effectiveness, and sustainability, can probably be better addressed by evaluation than by routine performance monitoring reports.

An evaluation system that focuses on providing evaluative knowledge to managers and policymakers is one that has several key attributes. First, it focuses on the timely production of relevant information regarding results being achieved. Second, it focuses on the analytic needs of the managers and how such analysis is incorporated into the decision-making processes of the organization. Third, it is consistently informed by the information being generated within the monitoring system. (There are no fire walls between the monitoring and the evaluation functions.) Fourth, it emphasizes synthesis and timeliness over uniqueness and precision. Fifth, and because of the need to incorporate the knowledge into the management processes, it emphasizes the production of evaluative knowledge from within the organization rather than from without. Internal evaluation efforts are given priority over those evaluations done outside the organization. And finally, in this system, the twin pivots of learning and accountability are given equal emphasis; they are two sides of the same coin.

*The complementarity of evaluation and monitoring within a results-based system should be reinforced.* Each supports the other—even as each asks different questions and will likely make different uses of information and analyses. The immediate implication is that to move to a results-based M&E system requires building an information and analysis system with two components—monitoring and evaluation. Either alone, in the end, is not sufficient.

The complementarities of monitoring and evaluation are of several types. First there is *sequential complementarity* where monitoring information can generate questions to be subsequently answered by evaluation—or the reverse where evaluation information gives rise to new areas or domains of monitoring to be initiated. An example of the first would be where projected trend lines do not materialize and the adoption of an innovation does not happen. The question, then, is why are the projections so different from reality? (The evaluative questions might include: Is it because the program logic is flawed, that the implementation process went astray, or that it is too soon to be able to measure outcomes?) An example of the second would be where evaluation information turns up new groups of unanticipated beneficiaries or change in an area not presently being monitored (e.g., strength of new NGO partnerships) that should now be monitored.

Second, there is *information complementarity* where both monitoring and evaluation can draw from the same data sources, but ask different questions and frame different analyses. This type of complementarity allows an organization (and a manager) to avoid the need to be supporting parallel monitoring and evaluation data systems. Longitudinal or time series data generated within an M&E system, for example, can be informative both for those tracking particular performance indicators as well as for those who would want the data to inform an evaluative information system.

Third, there is *organizational complementarity* where an organization continually shares both monitoring and evaluation information with managers and staff to enhance performance accountability and learning. This form of complementarity comes about in organizations that strive for transparency, an "information rich" decision-making environment, and one where continuous improvements are the norm. Both forms of information are used to help guide existing and planned initiatives. Further, the two functions are administratively together rather than separate.

An additional point to make in this regard is that an M&E system can be designed for and applicable to the project level, the program level, the sector level, and the country level. (For a global overview of the development of evaluation in this context, cf. Furubo, Rist, and Sandahl, 2002.) The specific indicators may necessarily be different (as the stakeholders' needs for information will also be different at each level), the complexity of collecting the data will be different, the political sensitivity on collecting the data may change, and the uses of the information may change from one level to another.

But in the end, it is the creation of a results-oriented system reporting on performance information aligned among all levels that is critical, that is, there is a "line of sight" between levels that is critical. The line of sight notion is important here. It emphasizes that at any level in an organization, the contribution of that particular level (and all the personnel at that level) to the overall strategic outcomes needs to be clear to themselves and to others at different levels as well—everyone needs to know how everyone else is contributing. There should be no ambiguity about the outcomes or how every level contributes to them.

The same can be emphasized about the line of sight alignment of projects to programs to policies. Projects are making contributions to program outcomes, which, in turn, are supporting the achievement of sector or national performance outcomes.

For such a system to be realized, information has to flow up and down the organizational chart rather than being collected at only one level or another, stored and used at that level, but never being shared between levels. Blocking the performance information from being shared ensures that the linkages between policies, programs, and projects stay disconnected and uncoordinated.

At each level, performance information is necessary and there should be means to collect it. And while different levels will have different requirements that need to be understood and respected, the creation of an M&E system requires interdependency, alignment, and coordination across levels (cf. Kusek and Rist, 2001, 2002, 2003, and 2004.) Further, when performance information is collected at one level, but there is no use of the information at that same level, the quality of the information starts to decay. Collecting data when one has no stake in those data (as they are only for use by others) is a sure-fire way of generating apathy and indifference as to the quality and timeliness of the information being collected.

Linked to this need for vertical interdependence is also the need for horizontal interdependence. Performance-based information needs to flow in all directions within an organization. Managing in public sector organizations is to manage in a web of relationships, shared responsibilities, and mutual accountabilities. Organizational effectiveness requires information on performance that is transparent. If that transparency is shrouded, then managers are isolated and less able to coordinate policies and programs.

This chapter places a strong and co-equal emphasis on both monitoring and evaluation as integral to constructing a viable measurement system for a results-based management approach. The monitoring function—the "M" in M&E—to track performance is emphasized here as an absolutely essential tool for managers. It is the monitoring system that gives information over time, via the selected outcome indicators, on the direction of change, the pace of change, and the magnitude of change. This system can also identify unanticipated changes. All are critical to know whether policies, programs, and projects are moving (or not) as intended. Likewise, it is the monitoring system that tracks the level of inputs, the range and number of activities, as well as outputs—all of which are necessary (but not sufficient) to also track performance outcomes.

But as noted earlier, monitoring data, however, will suggest (note John Mayne's position discussed above) but not necessarily prove or provide attribution of why changes in performance have or have not occurred. Monitoring data alone also do not provide causal evidence of how changes are coming about—only that they are or are not. Likewise, monitoring data of themselves can suggest the strengths and weaknesses in the design of the change model embedded in the policy, program, or project. But monitoring data are not definitive in this regard. The same can be said for assessing the quality and appropriateness of the implementation efforts. Consequently, to address these and other important questions regarding the generation of results within organizations, evaluative knowledge is necessary—the "E" in M&E.

## Building Up the Evaluative System

The emphasis here is that performance-based M&E systems are to be used as a management tool—much as a manager would use the budget system or the human resource system. (Only here the emphasis is on managing to performance outcomes, not to the distribution of financial inputs or staff!) The evaluation component in this context significantly expands and moves beyond that understood as the traditional implementation or impact approaches to evaluation.

Again, the evaluative system being described here also moves beyond the accumulation of discrete evaluation studies to the production of streams of evaluative knowledge. Evaluations restricted to assessing causes and changes after an intervention or initiative is over are a small part of this system. But to avoid being misunderstood that such evaluations are not needed, the point is that they are, but impact evaluations are not oriented to be a management tool. Rob van den Berg also notes that impact studies are difficult to use as a management tool because they are costly, have a long time horizon, often have crucial data sets missing, and not infrequently stretch beyond the activities and outputs to find evidence of impact (van den Berg, 2005 forthcoming). Thus, their relevance is generally marginal to the information needs of managers in the short and intermediate term. Still, and to be inclusive, multiple forms of evaluation information can over time contribute to a working M&E system. It is a matter of focus and application as to how to deploy evaluation within a management system.

Other means of evaluation are seen in this context to be more fruitful, more flexible, and more relevant to the kind of information system we are addressing here than are classic impact studies. The chapter in this volume by Perrin outlines a number of evaluation approaches that can come under the umbrella of high managerial utility. The ex-post or impact approach has characteristics that make it highly unlikely that its findings will find their way into the ongoing management of government organizations and units aimed at achieving public sector results.

The emphasis on ex-post evaluations as the means to strive for the definitive answers on attribution and causality (trying to "prove" something) necessarily then precludes that there can be "real-time" uses of evaluation by public sector managers—for expost evaluations by definition are just that—after the fact. And again, the evidence that policymakers circle back years later to take impact evaluation information into account as current management decisions are being made is not compelling. (The one exception might be in organizations with a long-standing internal evaluation unit. Here the institutional memory can work to the advantage of the unit and the accessibility of organizational data sets can make impact evaluations part of the ongoing work plan. Thus, both the timeliness and relevance of such work can be enhanced.)

And as a brief aside here to follow up on this point, the conventional, oft cited, "project or policy cycle" where evaluation information comes in the five-part cycle of "Planning, implementation, completion, evaluation, and feedback" is not compelling. This is where an outmoded and inaccurate understanding of management actually occurs. This model gives a false sense of rationality and predictability—of projects and policies being under control. The world is not this neat. Evaluation is appropriate at all operational phases (theory construction, planning, implementation, and completion) and it should not be restricted to after-the-fact. Further, the emphasis on conducting evaluations after the fact is misplaced. The evidence on the relevance and utility of longer-term impact evaluations as a management tool is not strong. Actually, there is a great deal of evidence on non-use, on information coming too late, of key decision makers having moved on, and on the original questions no longer being appropriate. The evidence of instrumental policy use of impact evaluations within results-focused organizations is hard to find.

It is continuously produced evaluative knowledge that can help create understandings in real time of what is actually happening to projects and policies, and not just the presumptions of what should be happening. The box below on the New York City Policy Department is instructive in this regard. (Note also the chapter in this volume by Spinatsch on the health observatories as another example of how continuously produced streams of evaluative information supports the program and policy needs of managers.)

The focus here is on an *evaluation system* that is relevant at all stages of a policy, program, or project. In the creation of results-based M&E systems, we stress that evaluation information is useful to the conceptualization and clarification of change models and intervention designs; to the implementation of these efforts by government and non-government partners; in assessing the contributions that the policies and programs did or did not make to the changes that were documented; and in generating lessons to assist policy and program managers in their ongoing direction of government actions.

The development of an evaluation capacity in government supports a results-based management approach and the uses managers can make of evaluation information. Good evaluative information can provide answers to a broad range of questions relevant to performance and the achievement of outcomes. We will identify a number of these questions as well as the evaluation strategies available to answer them.

### Uses of Evaluative Knowledge in a Results-based Framework

The emphasis here on building sources of ongoing evaluative knowledge in contrast to sporadic and individual evaluation studies spaced out over generally lengthy periods of time is deliberate. We stress that performance-based M&E systems need to be providing to government officials knowledge that is useful and timely in managing and guiding government resources and

> **Using Performance Data to Track and Reduce Crime in New York City**
>
> Over the past decade, the New York City Policy Department has used a special results-based M&E system to monitor the daily incident of violent crime. "CompStat is a sophisticated performance measurement system that reorders an organization's day-to-day operations, as well as its overall orientation toward its core mission and goals. CompStat is based upon the compilation, distribution, and utilization of 'real time' data in order to allow field managers to make better-informed and more efficient decisions." (O'Connell, 2001: 6)
>
> As former New York City mayor, Rudolph Giuliani noted, "We have 77 police precincts. Every single night they record all of the index crimes that have occurred in that precinct and a lot of other data. We record the number of civilian complaints. We record the number of arrests that are made for serious crimes and for less serious crimes. It is all part of CompStat, a computer-driven program that helps ensure executive accountability. And the purpose of it is to see if crime is up or down, not just citywide, but neighborhood by neighborhood. And if crime is going up, it lets you do something about it now—not a year and one half from now when the FBI puts out crime statistics ... Now we know about it today. And we can make strategic decisions accordingly." (O'Connell, 2001: 9)
>
> As a result, during a five-year period, "New York City experienced a precipitous drop in the burglary rate (53 percent), a 54 percent drop in reported robberies, and an incredible 67 percent drop in the murder rate ... These extraordinary achievements were realized in large part due to the department's innovative model of police management, known as CompStat." (O'Connell, 2001: 8)
>
> The NYC police department was able to combine performance data on such things as location, and locations of violent crimes, time of day of crime, etc. These data were collected for city precincts and projected onto mapping data. They were able to track trends in the data, and for the first time, the department was able to use performance information to actually reduce crime. The result has been that "New York City now holds the undisputed title as the safest big city in the nation ..." (Source: NYC.gov, 2003)

interventions. And because the value of an evaluation comes from its use (and not its cost), we can begin our discussion on evaluation with an emphasis on use.

While the evaluation literature is replete with long and technical discussions on different types and categories of use, we want to bypass that material and go to a pragmatic list of six uses that we have seen government managers make of results-based evaluative knowledge. (We are sure there are still more.) The conceptual level of the issues presented here tends not to be those that can be addressed by individual evaluation findings. The challenges faced by managers are the broader policy and program issues that continually surface in the upper echelons of their organizations. They are decisions where managers have to "steer" their organization and not try and "row" their way through problems. Information has to be analyzed and synthesized; it has to be appropriately focused; and it needs to be timely.

1. *Help make resource allocation decisions*—evaluative knowledge can inform managers on what policies or programs have been more or less successful in terms of their goals and thus what level of resources they might merit. Likewise, evaluative knowledge can help guide decisions on whether the results of pilot efforts suggest a going to scale or, alternatively, even dropping the initiative altogether. Here is also where evaluative knowledge can link the budget processes of governments and organizations to performance outcomes. Budget allocations based on performance information can be justified in ways quite different from when allocations are distributed without evidence of performance. Rewarding success based on performance evidence is not the same as giving all units a uniform increase of, for example, 2 percent. In the latter instance, there is no distinction between rewarding success and rewarding failure.
2. *Help to re-think the causes of and solutions to a problem*—frequently, policy and program interventions appear not to be having any notable consequences on an existing problem. While the absence of change in the condition of the problem may be attributable to either poor design or poor implementation (and more on this later...) it may also be that the intervention is of no consequence because the causes of the problem are different than originally presumed. Evaluative knowledge can raise the need for a re-examination of the presumed casual relation of why a problem exists—and what countermeasures might alternatively be needed from those now deployed. This use of evaluative knowledge is essentially to test the theory of what causes the problem to exist and what strategy of intervention can bring about a change in the severity or persistence of this problem.
3. *Identify emerging problems*—evaluative knowledge can highlight and help clarify issues that are not yet widespread, but will clearly (and eventually) require the attention of government officials, for example, growing drop-out rates in select groups of youth, the numbers of orphans where the parents have died from AIDS, or drug use among sub-teens. Here is an instance of where monitoring and evaluation information can be complementary. The monitoring data start to give evidence of an emerging situation, for example, school drop-out rates begin increasing. While the monitoring data are tracking this trend, the evaluative efforts can begin to look at presumed causes, outcomes of previous interventions, existing organizational capacities to address the situation, possible alterative responses, and others.
4. *Support decision-making on competing alternatives*—often governments will approach a problem situation by first piloting more than one strategy. For example, a government may try to address youth unemployment through in-school programs, special apprentice programs in the private sector, vouchers for employers who will hire youth, etc. But after each pilot has been operational for some period of time, which has the more compel-

ling evidence of success? Which merits more support and which less? Evaluative knowledge that synthesizes across pilots and across reports of findings can help inform the management decision—given a need for an understanding of resource demands, institutional capacity, access to target populations, implementation constraints, retention and completion rates, and so on.

5. *Support public sector reform*—evaluative knowledge can provide evidence to citizens on the pace and outcomes that reform efforts are (or are not) having. For example, evidence that school improvements are being made, that corruption is being diminished, or that more of the rural poor are receiving health care can give credibility to government efforts in these areas. Likewise, governments need to be honest with citizens and provide information when reforms are falling short of achieving anticipated outcomes. Candor about strengths and weaknesses is essential if the analysis from the evaluative system is to be trusted. A system that deliberately only provides positive (happy) news is one soon ignored.

6. *Building consensus on the causes of a problem and how to respond*—evaluative knowledge can contribute to the discussions among government officials and other groups of stakeholders on what is causing the conditions and how to create an appropriate response. Building agreement on the nature of the problem is not to be taken lightly and often involves real political pressures and alternative perspectives. Gaining a consensus on how the problem is to be understood should precede any deployment of countermeasures to try and solve or at least diminish the problem. (And when this is not possible, the calls for pilots will likely grow.) Evaluative knowledge can inform with summary evidence of alternative potential causes and also evidence on the relevance and impact of previous responses.

As we have stressed, evaluative knowledge is relevant and helpful to government managers at all phases of their management of policies, programs, and projects. So the question of timing is easily answered at one level—any time there are concerns for which evaluative knowledge can be useful is the time to gather evaluative information. The six examples above begin to suggest the breath of opportunities for evaluative knowledge. Further, in the building of these new evaluative systems of knowledge for results-based management systems, it is essential to recognize the need for continuous collection, analysis, and reporting of what is learned. Systems with large time gaps in information production are essentially back to the old model of intermittent evaluation reports as outputs—wait as you must for what you can, etc. The goal is, in contrast, continuous flows of analytic work—streams of knowledge. (See again the box on the New York City Police Department and the chapter by Spinatsch in this volume.)

To summarize this brief discussion on the uses of evaluative knowledge in an M&E system, government officials and their partners can use evaluative knowledge to focus on the broad strategy and design issues ("Are we doing the right things?"), on operational and implementation issues ("Are we doing things right?"), and on where there are better ways of doing it ("What are we learning?").

But to go deeper in addressing when to deploy resources to gather evaluation information, four instances that would warrant evaluation information are as follows. (Note—we recognize there are others beyond these four, but these are illustrative of when we think a system of evaluative information is essential).

1. *When regular measurements of key indicators suggest a sharp divergence between planned performance and actual performance.* Consider these two charts:

## When Is It Time to Make Use of Evaluation?

When regular results measurement suggests actual performance diverges sharply from planned performance

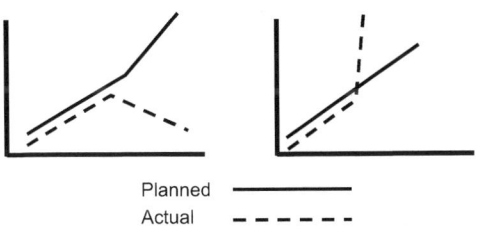

Planned ———
Actual  – – – – –

What is apparent here is that planned and actual performances are diverging. The question of the manager is "Why?" "What is going on here that either we are falling behind our planned performance so badly (left chart) or that we are doing so well that we are ahead of our own planning frame (right chart)?" Managers will recognize from their own experience that the relation of planned and actual performances is most often not identical and some variation is expected. But when that divergence is dramatic, sustained, and has real consequences for the policy, program, or project, then it is time to step back, evaluate the reasons why, and assess if new strategies are needed (in the case of poor performance) or learn how to take the accelerated performance and expand its applications elsewhere.

18     From Studies to Streams

2. *When performance indicators consistently suggest weak or no results from an initiative.*

Consider this graphic:

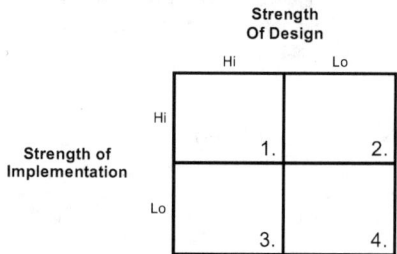

### When Is it Time to Make Use of Evaluation?

When you want to determine the roles of both design and implementation on project, program, or policy outcomes

Box 1 is the best place to be—the design (a causal model of how to bring about desired change in an existing problem) is strong and the implementation of actions to address the problem is also strong. This is where managers, planners, and implementers would all like to spend their time and efforts—making good things happen for which there is demonstrable evidence of positive change.

Box 2 generates considerable ambiguity in terms of performance on outcome indicators. Here is the situation of a weak design that is strongly implemented—but with weak to no evident results. The evidence suggests successful implementation, but few results. The evaluative ("why") questions would then turn to the strength and logic of the design. For example, was the causal model appropriate? Was it sufficiently robust, which if implemented well, would bring about desired change? Was the problem well understood and clearly defined? Did the proposed change strategy directly target the causes of the problem?

Box 3 also generates considerable ambiguity in terms of performance on outcome indicators. Here is the situation of a well-crafted design that is poorly implemented—and again, with weak to no evident results. This is the reverse situation of Box 2, but with the same essential outcome—no clear results. The evaluative questions here focus on the implementation processes and procedures—did what was suppose to take place actually take place, when, in what sequence, with what level of support, with what expertise among the staff, etc? The emphasis is on trying to learn what happened during implementation that brought down and rendered ineffective a potentially successful policy, program, or project.

Box 4 is not a good place to be—a weak design that is badly implemented leaves only the debris of good intentions. The evaluation information can document both the weak design and the poor implementation. The challenge for the manager is to figure out how to quickly close down this effort so as to not prolong its ineffectiveness and negative consequences for all involved.

3. *When resource allocations are being made across policies, programs, or projects.*

Evaluation information can help managers in this area with analysis on what is or is not working efficiently and effectively. The trade-offs in budget and personnel allocations are multiple. Competition among competing demands is real. Evaluation information can assist in the process, especially where the government is working to install a performance-based budget system. But it is also important and realistic to acknowledge that evaluation information cannot override and negate political, institutional, or personal agendas that are real and inevitably come into play.

4. *When similar projects, programs, or policies are reporting divergent evidence of outcomes.*

The situation of comparable initiatives with clearly divergent outcomes raises the questions of what is going on where. Among the questions that evaluation information can address: Are there strong variations in implementation that are leading the divergences? Or are the key individuals involved not understanding the intentions and rationale of the effort and thus providing different guidance on the ground leading to essentially different approaches? Or, as a third possibility, are the measures being used in the reporting so different that the comparisons are rendered invalid?

### In Sum

The emphasis in this chapter has been on the continuous role that evaluative information can and should play in the management of a results-based public sector. The development of an M&E system that provides information on performance and movement towards outcomes and goals is essential to the sustainability of such a system. Without such information, how is one to know the difference between success and failure, or between knowing if one is rewarding success or failure? Our intention here is to open up the discourse on how to move away from a model of evaluation where studies are done with more emphasis on their technical perfection than on their timely and relevant production of useful information; or with more emphasis on trying ex-post to ascertain causality and attribution than on giving program managers real time information on whether outcomes are being achieved; or in thinking that more and more studies, disconnected and discrete, are the appropriate future for how to build evaluative information into a management tool.

We are envisioning systems of evaluative information that are close to real time, approximately accurate in their measurement of indicators, focused on tracking performance against outcomes, and sought out by public sector managers as a credible tool—just as they look to their budget, human resource, and auditing systems for relevant management information.

We know such systems now exist across the globe and are used by managers as part of their management tool kit. The challenge in the coming years for the evaluation community is to expand and strengthen such systems; introduce them elsewhere; reward those who focus on system building and not grinding out more and more studies; get closer to public sector managers to understand what evaluative information needs they have; build expertise in indicator construction; and link evaluative information and resource allocation decisions more directly.

## Note

1. The views expressed here are those of the author and no endorsement by The World Bank Group is intended or should be inferred. Special thanks for a range of helpful comments to Jonathan Breul, Jody Zall Kusek, John Mayne, Linda Morra-Imas, Bert Perrin, and Nicoletta Stame.

## References

Binnendijk, Annette. (1999). "Results Based Management in the Development Cooperation Agencies: A Review of Experience." Paris: OECD.

Furubo, J. E., R. C. Rist, and R. Sandahl, eds. (2002). *International Atlas of Evaluation*. New Brunswick, NJ: Transaction Publishers.

Kusek, J. Z., and R. C. Rist. "Building a Performance-Based Monitoring and Evaluation System: The Challenges Facing Developing Countries." *Evaluation Journal of Australasia* 1(2) (2001).

_____. "Building Results-Based Monitoring and Evaluation Systems: Assessing Developing Countries Readiness." *Zeitschrift fuer Evaluation* 1 (2002).

_____. "Readiness Assessment: Towards Performance Monitoring and Evaluation in the Kyrgyz Republic." *Japanese Journal of Evaluation* 3(1) (2003).

_____. (2004). *Ten Steps to a Results-Based Monitoring and Evaluation System: A Handbook for Development Practitioners*. Washington, DC: The World Bank.

_____. (2002b). "Glossary of Key Terms in Evaluation and Results-Based Management." Paris: OECD.

Mayne, J. "Addressing Attribution through Contribution Analysis: Using Performance Measures Sensibly." *Canadian Journal of Program Evaluation* 16(1) (2001).

Mayne, J., and E. Zapico-Goni, eds. (1999). *Monitoring Performance in the Public Sector: Future Directions from International Experience*. New Brunswick, NJ: Transaction Publishers.

NYC.gov.2003. "New York City Continues to be the Nation's Safest Large City." http://www.nyc.gov/html/om/html/2003a/crime_falls.html.

O'Connell, Paul E. (2001). "Using Performance Data for Accountability: The New York City Policy Department's CompStat Model of Police Management." Arlington, VA: PricewaterhouseCoopers Endowment for the Business of Government.

OECD. (2000a). "Overview of Results-Focused Management and Budgeting in OECD Member Countries." Twenty-Third Annual Meeting of OECD Senior Budget Officials, Washington, DC, June 3-4.

Perrin, Burt. "Implementing the Vision: Addressing Challenges to Results-Focused Management and Budgeting." *OECD Journal on Budgeting* (2003).

van den Berg, Rob. "Results Evaluation and Impact Assessment in Development Cooperation." *Evaluation* (forthcoming, 2005).

World Bank. (1997). *World Development Report: The State in a Changing World.* New York: Oxford University Press.

Worthen, B., and C. C. Schmitz. "Conceptual Challenges Confronting Cluster Evaluations." *Evaluation* 3(3) (1997).

# 2

# How Evaluation Can Help Make Knowledge Management Real

*Burt Perrin*

## Introduction

We are said to live in the knowledge age. Information and knowledge are everywhere. The problem that organizations (and individuals) frequently face is not insufficient information, but rather information overload. Information does not necessarily translate into knowledge. And without some basis for dealing with the mounds of information instantly available, too often the result is inappropriate use or even misuse of selective bits of questionable information out of context.

Information—and knowledge—can come from many different sources. Learning from personal experience clearly represents one important source of knowledge. But it is increasingly obvious that this is insufficient, and by itself can lead to false knowledge and to distortions. For example, as Senge (1990) has indicated, we cannot observe the results of our actions because impacts occur temporally and spatially apart from what we are able to observe. It also is evident that one can learn as much from the experiences of others involved in similar (or even in quite different) activities from one's own. Clearly, knowledge based solely upon one's own direct experiences would be severely restricted.

Similarly, as all the contributors to this book indicate in one way or another, there is increasing recognition of the limitations of single evaluation studies, restricted to a particular intervention at a particular point in time. No one single study can be definitive. Planning, management, and policy development increasingly need to draw upon streams of both formal and informal types of information, where evaluations represent just one type of input.

But how does one deal with all these streams of information? As Forss and Rebien indicate in this volume, "organizational knowledge" is an oxymoron. The same applies to knowledge management (KM). Knowledge is inherently variable and frequently represents the unexpected. Yet management implies structure and control. KM also presents other challenges. For example, how do we know what strategies or approaches are *really* effective, under given circumstances and conditions? If proclaimed arbitrarily, so-called "knowledge" is useless—or worse. "Management" in the context of KM also can be problematic. If this somehow involves placing some order on the mess that would otherwise be information overload and enabling people to get the information they need, then the term seems benign enough. But management also represents control. Who decides what constitutes acceptable "facts," what information is worth knowing, what information is allowed to enter or not enter a KM system? As Cracknell (2001a), for example, discusses, it is more than mere paranoia to suspect that such decisions are made to control and to put forth certain philosophical positions.

Nevertheless, some form of knowledge management is critical. How else can one deal with ever-increasing amounts of disparate and seemingly contradictory information streaming in from numerous sources? But the primary challenge to KM is much greater than just dealing with a large *quantity* of information. How does one separate the wheat from the chaff, determine what information is potentially relevant and useful, and what is not? How does one decide what information is valid and trustworthy, and to what extent? More basically, how can one translate information into useful, practical knowledge that can be applied on a timely basis here and now in the real world?

Without some form of KM, we are certain to drown in information—yet, at the same time, cut ourselves off from potentially vital information that can help improve policies, programs, and activities at all levels. But unless there is some basis for deciding what information is and is not relevant and valid, the "knowledge" arising from KM runs the risk of being arbitrary and illusory. There can be a real danger of KM representing just another management "flavor of the month."

I feel that there is a major potential for evaluation to provide substance to the knowledge claims of KM, and to help it live up to its promise. This chapter discusses two approaches to making KM real. In the next section, I discuss various means of synthesis or cumulation of learnings[1] from across a range of studies and sources of information. This is followed by a discussion of how evaluation can assist in the identification, dissemination, and use of good practices across different settings—as opposed to "best" practices, "proven" models, or other similar-sounding approaches, as a basis of a KM system.

## Creating Knowledge through Synthesis

*Why Synthesis?*

As the theme of this book suggests, there is increasing recognition of the limitations of single evaluation studies to generate knowledge or to provide useful guidance for policy. Briefly, why is this?

For starters, any single evaluation study is likely to be limited in both internal and external validity and in the appearance of such. As Campbell (e.g., 1979; Cook and Campbell, 1979), for example, has indicated, any individual evaluation has inevitable limitations that often can call into question the validity of its findings. Without looking across a variety of different settings and contexts, it can be difficult to determine if an approach that works in one setting might do so in a different context—or even at a later point in time with the same program and with a similar target group.

Further, busy program managers, policymakers, and practitioners simply do not have the time to wade through a large number of evaluation and research reports in order to draw out common themes and to identify what might or might not be relevant for them. They are all too likely to dismiss all evaluations when they encounter the inevitable differences across studies, without digging to understand the reasons for these differences. Unexpected findings from individual studies or findings contrary to conventional wisdom built up over the years are likely to be rejected out of hand—and for good reason (e.g., Campbell, 1979). In addition, individual evaluation studies typically look backwards, at what has or has not happened in the past, rather than provide the type of guidance that policymakers require: what should be done in the future. It rarely is possible for a specific evaluation to provide appropriate guidance in a timely fashion for the policy process (e.g., Pawson, 2002a, 2002b).

As a result of these and other factors, there is a growing disillusionment about the ability of evaluation to contribute to policy development (e.g., Cracknell, 2001a). A number of commentators in a special issue of the *American Journal of Evaluation*, looking at the future of evaluation (Lipsey, 2001; Mark, 2001; Patton, 2001; and Pawson and Tilley, 2001) while coming from somewhat different perspectives, agree that we have developed little cumulative knowledge and tend to evaluate each program as if it is unique. They identify the need for more attempts at cumulation in order to be able to identify knowledge that can actually aid in program and policy development and in increasing our understanding of what works when, for whom, in what circumstances, and why. In Thomas Cook's (1997) keynote address regarding the status and future of evaluation to the 1995 international evaluation conference in Vancouver, he identified as one of his three key themes the recognition that knowledge claims will increasingly be based upon syntheses rather than on the results of individual studies.

Evaluation synthesis has the potential to overcome many of the limitations of individual evaluation studies. First and foremost, synthesis can represent a quick and inexpensive way of drawing from existing data. There sometimes is a tendency to move into new data collection and new evaluation studies without first considering if there may be better ways of making use of what already exists. Unlike specific evaluation studies, syntheses usually can be carried out quickly and on a timely basis, and thus feed into the planning and policy timetable. By considering a number of studies together, it is often possible to compensate for the inevitable methodological weaknesses of individual evaluations.

As the U.S. General Accounting Office (GAO, 1992) indicates, synthesis can answer questions that a single study cannot. In particular, looking at what takes place across a variety of different types of settings and situations can enable themes and patterns to emerge that would be impossible in an evaluation constrained to a single setting. The broader the range of what is included in a synthesis, for example, with different types of program approaches, and even looking at practices cutting across different content areas, the more confidence one can have in identifying the key themes and mechanisms at work, as well as the role of context. Syntheses can identify interactions and explanations for apparent "contradictions" across specific studies.

Syntheses, often more than individual evaluations, can be proactive rather than reactive, and can speak directly to policy implications arising across a body of study and of experience. Frequently, they can be used to "translate" technical findings into policy and layperson's terms, and can represent a useful communications approach. By concentrating on the identification of learnings and implications for future directions, they can take a positive focus and may be less threatening than individual evaluations. In this way, they often are received more positively. In turn, this can generate support for future evaluation. It is also more difficult for conclusions based upon consistent findings from across a number of different programs and studies to be dismissed, particularly in a changing policy context, than those from a single study.

Syntheses can have their limitations as well. Generally, they are limited by the relevance and quality of existing information. Weak documentation in some existing studies can make it difficult to assess their quality. Syntheses obviously are not a substitute for individual studies, as they depend upon these as the source of "data." Syntheses are no panacea, and sometimes can do no better than to identify what is *not* known. This, of course, can be valuable in its own right.

Given the above, the value of synthesis should be evident. Nevertheless, it still is done too infrequently, and too often as a throwaway, for example, a token literature review to set the stage for the "real" work (i.e., yet another single study that rarely relates to the body of information once the study is under way), or relegated to a junior staff to carry out. There is limited recognition of the various forms of synthesis, and too many syntheses are poorly done, adding to, rather than helping with, the problem of information overload. Most existing guides to synthesis have an academic rather than a practical policy focus. The key to effective policy-oriented synthesis is to identify the purpose of the study, how it can be used, and who specifically is expected to be able to use it. This determination should guide *all* aspects of the synthesis. It is important to identify or to anticipate policy questions and alternatives, and what types of information could inform the policy development process. Otherwise, the synthesis runs the risk of addressing the wrong questions and being irrelevant to policy. This advice, however, is contrary to much of the literature on synthesis and reviews, which tends to take more of an academic than practical policy perspective.

**Types of Syntheses**

I consider below three alternative approaches to synthesis:

- Cluster Evaluation (and thematic evaluation)
- Synthesis of Existing Studies
- Integrative Reviews

*Cluster Evaluation*

The concept of cluster evaluation was first developed by the W. K. Kellogg Foundation as a means of identifying learnings across a range of projects that share some similarities, as well as a number of differences (Kellogg Foundation, 1998). Kellogg developed this approach after realizing that project-level evaluations rarely identified implications going beyond the specific project, including contributing to systemic change, broad policies, and public policy debate, as well as contributing to grant making/funding.

As Sanders (1998) has indicated:

> Cluster evaluation is not a substitute for project-level evaluation, nor do cluster evaluators "evaluate" projects. Project-level evaluation is focused on project development and outcomes related to the project stake-holders. Cluster evaluation focuses on progress made toward achieving the broad goals of a programming initiative. In short, cluster evaluation looks across a group of projects to identify common threads and themes that, having cross-confirmation, take on greater significance. Cluster evaluators provide feedback on commonalties in program design, as well as innovative methodologies used by projects during the life of the initiative.

A cluster evaluation examines a "cluster" or range of projects that are similar to some extent, but not *identical*. In some cases, the projects can be quite different from one another. For example, consider the following examples:

- Six conferences all sponsored by the World Bank, but with different objectives, target audiences, size, budgets, and other characteristics (Perrin and Mackay, 1999).
- Four projects all dealing in some way with the literacy needs of out-of-work, out-of-school youth, but taking somewhat different approaches, e.g., a community college instructional program, a tutoring program sponsored by a community agency, an outreach program, and a college program essentially looking at how its services could be better coordinated and given a community development focus. Two of the projects were urban, the other two rural.
- Twenty-six projects funded by a Canadian foundation, involving very different objectives and target groups (broadly in the human services area), different types and sizes of sponsoring agencies, and grants of different sizes and funding periods and at varying stages of development.

This is quite different from a multi-site evaluation, which examines the same program that has been implemented in the same way, or as close to this as possible, in multiple settings. This has implications for methodology. For example, a multi-site evaluation can apply the same method in all settings, using the same instrumentation and closed-ended approaches, if desired. This is not possible with cluster evaluation, where the projects that constitute the cluster can have somewhat different objectives, addressing different client groups, and in different manners.

When common themes are found across a diverse range of projects, one can have greater confidence in their broad applicability. With a range of different types of projects in different types of settings, it is easier to identify the impact of context, and frequently to be able to identify the necessary conditions for given effects to occur. But if the cluster is overly broad (this might be the case with the twenty-six foundation grants in the third example above), the types of conclusions that are possible are most likely to be of a general nature (which may still be useful, e.g., regarding planning and leadership within non-profit organizations, use of volunteers, factors facilitating collaboration, and other factors that can transcend sectors and program areas).

Cluster evaluation, at least as defined by the Kellogg Foundation, can be prospective rather than retrospective in nature, taking place while the projects are in operation. Kellogg views cluster evaluation as a complement, rather than a substitute, for project-level evaluation. Cluster evaluations require at least some data collection from the projects in the cluster, and can be both formative and summative in nature.

Cluster evaluations also typically involve participation of the projects in the evaluation. For example, this can include bringing together representatives of the projects, together with the cluster evaluator, to participate in identifying, or at least validating, themes emerging from across the projects. This can have value going beyond the evaluation per se. For example, in the second example listed above, the four projects were forced into the cluster by the funder (a government agency) and required to work together. Initially most saw little point to this, seeing their own project as unique. By the end, however, they were able to see some commonalities despite their differences and how they could learn from one another, and identified the cluster evaluation process as one of the overall highlights of their projects.

Kellogg has indicated that the purpose of cluster evaluation is to be constructive, using aggregate information to identify common themes and to learn not just "what happened" but "why those things happened." Its major purpose is "to improve, not to prove," to identify learnings and implications for future initiatives (Worthen and Schmitz, 1997). Kellogg does not use cluster evaluations to rate or to compare projects. It only asks for aggregate information, in order to encourage projects to be open in identifying weaknesses as well as accomplishments of their project that can be useful in planning other undertakings.

A *thematic evaluation* can be similar in many respects to a cluster evaluation. Thematic evaluations are sometimes, but often are not, prospective in nature. They typically explore a common theme (e.g., employment of women) across usually a larger number of projects than are included in a cluster evaluation. Thus, thematic evaluations tend to have a somewhat narrower focus than do cluster evaluations, which can be wide open with respect to the types of themes that can emerge. Thematic evaluations rarely provide for participation of the projects in the evaluation process.

*Syntheses of Existing Studies*

This technique refers to collectively considering the findings and implications arising from a finite number of existing studies, such as recent evaluation and research studies that an agency or department has carried out or commissioned or otherwise has at its disposal. Surprisingly, there has been scant attention to this approach in the literature. This approach can represent a way of getting the best use of information that one already has and has paid for.

For a variety of reasons, evaluation reports often are not fully used or acted upon when they are first submitted, and quickly forgotten soon after. This can have little or nothing to do with the quality or potential value of the evaluation. For example, there may be competing priorities at the time. Or the policy context and/or the officials involved may have changed by the time the study has been completed. Often the value of an evaluation (or of any other kind of study) or the importance of the issues that it raises may not be readily apparent—sometimes not until much later. In a different policy context, there may be ways of pulling out implications for future directions that were not relevant at the time an evaluation study was initially carried out. An internal evaluator can play a major role in seeking the appropriate moment to bring forth one or more previously commissioned studies to place on the table once again, and at the very least, to get the maximum value out of already existing information.

And as indicated earlier, a synthesis often can go beyond what individual studies can say. For example, if findings are too challenging or unexpected, they are unlikely to be acted upon, at least initially. But if similar findings and implications arise from multiple sources, then this can be much harder to dismiss. Looking across multiple studies can make it possible to identify consistent themes and patterns, as well as the "whys"—key factors and characteristics most closely associated with effectiveness at various levels.

In addition to contributing to the policy development process, a synthesis potentially can represent a way of using simple, non-technical language to disseminate information to program constituents and to other stakeholders about evaluations and what they mean that have been carried out. For example, adult literacy practitioners may have little interest or ability to wade through the thousands of pages of technical documents that a government department is likely to have at its disposal. They may very well be interested, however, in a synthesis of the key findings and what these can mean to them in their own work.

Or consider the example of a Canadian provincial social services department that funded a number of innovative projects with the common objective of enabling social assistance recipients to obtain employment and to become self-sufficient. The department commissioned some fifteen different evaluation studies, collectively worth just under $1 million. These reports, however, were long and technical and not suitable for sharing with stakeholders, such as community agencies involved in delivering the projects and in serving the broad target group. As a result, the department commissioned me to prepare the "glossy," a short report summarizing the major findings and implications of these evaluations in language appropriate to practitioners and laymen. Surprisingly, this also was the first overall look at the range of projects and evaluations, and was able to identify some implications (e.g., the more costly programs tended to be most effective) not previously identified, despite all the resources devoted to evaluation.

*Integrative Reviews*

These reviews involve going beyond one's own sources of information, to identify what can be learned from a review of preexisting evaluations and other sources of information from a variety of sources and jurisdictions. A review potentially can draw upon a wide range of information from *anywhere*. As a review typically does not look specifically at an agency's own programs, it can be less threatening than other forms of evaluation, especially in a new policy context.

As with other forms of synthesis, a key to success is deciding, initially, upon the purpose of the review, such as the policies it can influence, and the key questions to be explored. Focus is of particular importance in an integrative review. It is all too easy to get completely distracted and overwhelmed. Reviews that attempt to identify every possible study, with minimum identification of implications, are rarely of value—but are all too common. As the GAO (1992) indicates, the synthesis should be designed backwards from the needs of the end user.

> The evaluation synthesis is driven, not by the quest to increase knowledge, but by a specific need—requested or anticipated—for certain information. This means that the work must always begin with a framework of questions which impart logical cohesion to the effort.

Key challenges in carrying out a literature review include deciding upon the scope of the review and what types of information to include, locating these documents, and assessing the applicability and quality of the studies and documentation that have been obtained. In general, reviews should include information from multiple sources, including: published and unpublished evaluation studies, other reviews, descriptive data and other documents regarding the subject matter, expert and lay opinions, and critiques. It is particularly important to locate complementary sources of data, for example, studies using different methodologies, from a variety of jurisdictions and across disciplines. For example, in assessing services for people with disabilities, one should look for documentation from advocates, as well as from government and academic sources. Use of multiple sources, independently triangulated, provides for greater confidence in the findings and conclusions that can be drawn from a review (e.g., Campbell, 1979; Pawson, 2002a; Patton, 2001).

While useful information can come from any source, unpublished documentation tends to be most current and most applicable for policy. As Cook (1997) has indicated, some of the most useful information can be found "hidden under rocks" in the fugitive or "grey" literature. The GAO (1992) and Pawson (2002a) have pointed out that information about what does *not* work can be just as useful as information about what does. Yet as they also observe, the published literature has a positive bias, and one could say the same with respect to most official government reports.

One need not confine oneself to formal evaluation studies as such, or even to what has been labeled as "research." Pawson and Tilley (2001) provide an ingenious demonstration of the potential value of drawing upon a variety of different types of inquiries, old and new and based upon data from around the globe, providing useful guidance regarding the strengths and limitations of different approaches, in varying contexts, to the collection of blood. Pawson (2002b) presents a beautiful example of the benefits of looking across sectors and policy domains, using a realist approach to identify what can be learned about the effectiveness of incentives drawing from studies in: health, safety, corrections, transport, housing, and education.

While electronic database searches represent one tool to identify existing information, one rarely should stop (or even start) there, as is too often the case. For a meaningful review, it is almost always essential to tap into networks, to contact key informants, to follow up on the leads of others, and to use a snowball approach to locate existing studies and documentation. Indeed, it frequently makes sense to combine a literature review with at least some degree of key informant interviewing. Use of Internet evaluation discussion lists can be an invaluable tool in obtaining information about key documents and individuals, as well as ideas about where to look for others.

When a large number of studies have been identified, there can be a danger of information overload. For policy purposes, it usually is most useful to pull out key findings and implications, rather than providing a listing and synopsis of the various studies that have been reviewed. (Pawson, 2002a, speaks to the lack of value of the latter approach, which he says is the most common approach to narrative reviews.) Indeed, one of the key objectives of a review usually should be to present, clearly and concisely, the key implications arising from a large number of sources, in order to eliminate information overload rather than to provide yet more of it. We also have a paradox. A focus on the purpose of the review and how it could be used is essential. Yet one needs to be open to what the data say, even if this means changing one's initial preconceptions or expectations.

Carrying out an effective review is more an art than a science, to be able to divine patterns arising among divergent sources of information. As Pawson (2002a, 2002b) emphasizes, the purpose of a review should not be to identify exemplary models or "best buys" ("approach 'x' or case 'y' seems to be the most successful") that can be applied in any context. Instead, the main focus should be, in his words, to develop "a tailored, transferable theory" that indicates that "this program works in these respects, for these subjects, in these kinds of situations" (Pawson, 2002b: 342).

Pawson (2002a: 176) further observes that: "The analysis and usage of data is a sense-making one and not a mechanical one." It requires someone with an open, inquiring mind who is able to pull out key findings, themes, and implications arising from across the available evidence. One needs to guard against the dangers of an overly reductionistic approach, such as with numerical meta analysis. This approach involves statistical manipulation of the data across studies looking at similar types of program interventions, in order to be able to compute mean effect sizes. The first limitation of this approach, used in and of itself, is that it is restricted to quantitative studies, in most cases to studies involving an experimental, or at least a quasi-experimental design. Pawson (2002a) critiques meta analysis in-depth, and identifies three major additional limitations:

- The melding of program mechanisms, where interventions are rather arbitrarily placed into program categories that can mask the potential of very different approaches to bring about personal and social change.
- The oversimplification of program outcomes, with the outcomes of complex programs reduced to a single quantitative measure of effectiveness.
- The concealment of program contexts, so that there is no information about *why* a given effect might have taken place, given that a program might work well for one class of subjects but not for others, or in certain contexts but not in others.

Perhaps Pawson's major criticism of meta analysis is its objective of identifying "best buys," those programs that are most effective, irrespective of context, and that are worthy of emulation. Pawson also makes the same criticism of "narrative reviews," which he claims examine a family of programs "in the hope of finding those particular approaches that are most successful" (pp. 170–171).

Who is best suited to carry out an integrative review? The ideal synthesizer needs at least some familiarity with the subject matter, in order to be able to pose the right questions, and to know where to look and whom to contact for information. A background in policy analysis is at least as important as one in research, although the latter is needed in order to be able to assess the quality of studies and what types of conclusions, if any, can be drawn given the available evidence.

Perhaps most importantly, the ideal synthesizer needs a broad, open mind, open to serendipity and to the unexpected, comfortable with complexity and who can avoid getting overwhelmed by detail in order to be able to see the forest for the trees. Rarely is a "clean desk" person, who prefers everything ordered and in its place, the best person to carry out an integrative review. Effective synthesis requires the ability to go beyond the data, with the ability to see (or in some cases, at least initially, to "feel") emerging patterns and potential explanations that might not be apparent to someone with too straight a mindset. An effective synthesizer should have the ability to assess different forms of information from a range of sources that cut across program sectors and jurisdictions. An ideal reviewer/synthesizer should be an experienced person, familiar with various policy domains, rather than a neophyte or junior. Unfortunately, too often reviews are approached in exactly the reverse way, resulting in reviews of questionable validity and of little use.

## Good Practices[2]

*Why Good Practices?*

Consider the situation of the International Labor Organization's International Program for the Elimination of Child Labor (ILO-IPEC). ILO-IPEC works in some seventy-five countries with a wide range of partners. Many other international, national, and local organizations are also actively involved in the fight against child labor and in particular its worse forms (e.g., trafficking, slavery or bonded labor, hazardous work). There are no simple answers to address the conditions that result in child labor. How can one share what is learned with others involved in similar activities, in order to be able to gain from the experiences of others and to avoid having to reinvent the wheel?

This is an increasingly recognized need and challenge, in both the public and the private sectors. As O'Dell and Grayson (2000) observe:

> Executives have long been frustrated by their inability to identify or transfer outstanding practices from one location to another. They know some facilities have superior practices and processes—and the results to prove it—yet executives continue to see operating units reinventing or ignoring solutions and repeating mistakes ... The process of identifying and transferring practices is trickier and more time-consuming than most people imagine.

As Cracknell (2001b: 137) indicates in a review of the use of feedback and knowledge specifically in development organizations: "Acquiring new knowledge is not too difficult: learning from it is far more challenging." Failure to learn from experience inevitably impedes the ability of any organization to improve, and ultimately to be effective at what it is supposed to be doing.

Thus, good practices (GPs) information provides a means of being able to learn from and to apply the experiences of others. It represents institutional memory, ensuring that important information is not lost or forgotten, and constitutes an important element of a learning organization. It is the essence of a KM system. Indeed, in many cases the terms GPs and KM frequently are used synonymously.

## What is a Good Practice? How Can It Be Used?

A GP can be defined as anything that works in some way, whether fully or in part, and that may have implications for practice at any level elsewhere. A good practice can represent *any* type of practice, small or large. It can represent a practice at any level, that is, ranging from broad policy-level activities to nitty-gritty grassroots practices in the field. It need not represent an overall project or program. Even if a project overall has not been successful, there still may be good practices that it has developed or applied. (Conversely, even if an overall project has worked well, this does not mean that everything it has done has been effective.) Furthermore, a GP could also represent something that only emerges after comparison across multiple settings, such as through some form of synthesis, which could be proactive (e.g., via a cluster or thematic evaluation) or retrospective (e.g., a review of existing reports and documentation) as discussed previously.

A key aspect is that a GP be something that *actually has been tried and shown to work*, with at least some evidence of effectiveness, that is, as distinct from what may be a potentially good idea but has not actually been tested. It could, however, be work in progress, representing preliminary or intermediate findings.

The overriding criteria should be the potential usefulness of a GP to others in providing new ideas or guidance or stimulating thought about how one could be more effective in one's work. It is rarely appropriate for GPs to be copied from one setting to another. As Pawson (e.g., 2002b) indicates, programs invariably "work" for some people in some situations, but not in other cases. The context invariably differs across settings, and thus even highly successful interventions may not "travel" well.

Patton (2001) indicates that principles (in contrast to highly prescriptive and specific courses of action) to guide practice can be very helpful. At the least, good practices can provide "food for thought" and ideas about possible adaptations. The more that a similar approach has been tried and shown to work in multiple and varied settings, the more likely that it might also apply in some respect elsewhere as well.

Note that this is quite different from concepts such as "best" practices,[3] "model" programs, "proven" practices, and the like that are put forth as exemplary approaches worthy of emulation. The first issue with best practices is how something comes to be anointed as "best." Too often, this is declared arbitrarily, with a given practice branded as "best" in the absence of any clear criteria or evidence. Patton (2001) indicates that calling something a "best" practice typically is more of a political assertion than an empirical conclusion. He adds that the "best practices" label has been applied to almost any kind of insight, empirically based or not, and thus it ceases to have any meaning.

Also, the very language of "best" practice implies that there is one "best" way of doing something, irrespective of context or circumstances. As Patton (2001: 330) notes: "Seldom do such statements [of "best practices"] identify for whom the practice is best, under what conditions it is best, or what values or assumptions undergird its *best*-ness." Attempting to copy an approach that may be effective in one context to another is a sure route to failure and to disillusionment. It represents a misuse of KM. But many KM systems propose just that, proclaiming "best" practices and models that others are urged to emulate.

How well should a potential practice be substantiated before it could be considered "good"? In my own research, I encountered two schools of thought. One perspective, perhaps stated most commonly by researchers and evaluators, is that it is not legitimate to endorse a practice as "good" unless it has been subject to rigorous evaluation and has been proven to work in multiple settings.

The other perspective, found most frequently among both managers and practitioners, is that one cannot wait years for the "perfect" answer or the definitive evaluation, that decisions and actions constantly must be made on the basis of imperfect information and that timely information and ideas based even on less than perfect data can be more useful than nothing. In particular, I have found that there is considerable interest in learning what others who are facing similar problems are doing *now* and what appears to be working for them, and that just because a practice has not been subject to formal evaluation does not mean that they cannot learn from it. Indeed, effective practitioners constantly seek out opportunities, formal and especially informal, of sharing experiences with their peers.

It is apparent that there is a trade-off between perfection on the one hand, and current information on the other. One also can speak of a continuum, ranging from well-developed and tested approaches at one end, to rough and unproven, but perhaps imaginative and creative ideas at the other end. I found a concern arising in my own research as well as in the literature (e.g., Cracknell, 2001b; O'Dell and Grayson, 2000) that too high a standard, with formal research or evaluation as a prerequisite, can act as a disincentive for practitioners to share their experiences with others as potential good practices, and can even inhibit innovation.

Which perspective is right? In fact both can be legitimate. Different levels of decisions require different types and confidence of information. For example, grassroots practitioners who are trying out new approaches to intractable problems often on a day-by-day basis (e.g., reducing poverty, teaching a child with learning disabilities to read) most frequently require "soft" information and ideas to consider, and perhaps to try on for size. Conversely, a much higher standard may be required if information is to be used for the implementation of a major new policy or program approach with major financial and political implications, and perhaps also by researchers, theorists, and academics for their own work.

Thus, an effective GP system needs to be open to multiple needs. At ILO-IPEC, we addressed this challenge by coming up with three levels of good practices as follows:

*Level 1 promising practices:* Practices at this level need not be substantiated by data or formal evaluation. But they have actually been tried and a strong logical case can be made about their effectiveness, in accordance with criteria that have been developed specific to programs and activities in the child labor area.

*Level 2 demonstrated practices:* Practices at this level have been evaluated in some way, at a single setting. Although this practice is localized, it has characteristics that may be applicable to other settings or situations.

*Level 3 replicated practices:* Practices at this level have been evaluated and shown to be effective at multiple settings. These could be different locations served by the same project, or could be similar activities across countries, projects, and/or sectors.

This is an approach that has been used in other organizations as well, for example, the American Red Cross. It enables users to refer to practices at alternative levels of confidence, depending upon their preference and requirements. It encourages people to make suggestions about what should be included, minimizing the risk of missing what could be exemplary practices. One should also bear in mind that the primary use of GPs is to put forth ideas to consider, rather than to serve as an approach that should be copied in its entirety.

Such an approach can be dynamic. For example, Good Practices may suggest ideas for evaluation, either of individual practices or some form of cluster evaluation, which could result in re-classification of practices from Level 1 to Level 2 or 3. If a similar number of Level 1 (or 2) practices have been identified independently, it may be appropriate to combine them into a Level 3 description. Conversely, if encouraging practices are not supported by further evaluation or evidence, it might be appropriate to drop them from the database.

Some form of review or adjudication procedure is needed to decide which potential practices should be included in the database, and at what level. This can be done simply by a designated coordinator, or even by an internal evaluator. But bearing in mind the concern about the gatekeeper role that Cracknell (2001a) has identified, it might be appropriate to engage other stakeholders in some way in the adjudication process. In general, one should err on the side of inclusion and on quick response with respect to Level 1 entries. A higher standard might be more appropriate for higher levels. In any case, criteria and standards for inclusion/rejection should be transparent.

### Key Elements of an Effective Good Practices "System"

As indicated earlier, identification of GPs is the easy part. But it is not enough. Some form of "system" is needed to provide for the sharing and understanding of GPs, and for their use. More challenging is addressing the barriers that inhibit understanding and transfer of these practices to other situations.

The American Productivity and Quality Center (O'Dell and Grayson, 2000) framework identifies four critical environmental enablers that are prerequisites to a GPs "system": technology, cultural factors facilitating sharing, strategy and leadership, and measurement/evaluation. These same factors are also mentioned in other documents and literature (e.g., Cracknell, 2001b; DFID, 2002). "System" is put in quotes because it refers not in a narrow sense to an information system, but to a multidimensional approach involving all four dimensions. As used here, a GP "system" is synonymous with KM.[4]

*Technology—Insufficient by Itself*

A key consideration is that while technology has a helpful role to play, it will not be the driver of sharing GPs. A database, by itself, does not constitute a GP "system," and by itself rarely will result in use. As O'Dell and Grayson (2000) explain:

> The first reaction to the desire to share practices is frequently to create a technical solution, usually an online database ... the theory being that if people only knew that the practice existed, they would adapt it ... What happened? Often nothing. Despite sometimes massive internal corporate program campaigns, few people entered information about their practices and few accessed it.

O'Dell and Grayson add that: "The really important and useful information for improvement is too complex to be put online, too much tacit knowledge is required to make a process work." As they say, effective databases are brief rather than comprehensive, and are designed to enhance and support, rather than to replace, existing sharing mechanisms. They can provide insights into what has been done rather than "the right answer." Indeed, many organizations have found that directory or "pointer" systems, assisting people in making contact with others, can be at least as useful as a listing of good practices.

As suggested above, databases rarely are used much just by themselves. As O'Dell and Grayson (2000) observe: "Busy managers and professionals will rarely take the time to enter a practice into a database unless it is part of their job." GPs databases work only when selected employees are assigned responsibility for finding and entering practices, as well as helping others use this information.

Nutley, Davies, and Walter (2004) distinguish between knowledge *push* and knowledge *pull* approaches. As they indicate, a database approach to KM represents a knowledge push approach (sometimes referred to as supply-driven), which assumes that "the fundamental problem for knowledge management is the limited flow of knowledge and information within an organization... Conversely, knowledge pull approaches (sometime referred to as demand-driven) are concerned with the problems of engaging employees in the process of sharing and searching for knowledge" (p. 10). They indicate that considerations of organizational culture and tacit as well as explicit knowledge, as discussed below, are also important to the effective sharing and use of knowledge and form part of knowledge pull approaches. From their review of the literature, Nutley et al. indicate that pull approaches to KM tend to be more effective in resulting in knowledge sharing than push systems that emphasize technology and the transfer of codified knowledge. Thus, while technology can represent a useful, even an essential, tool, by itself a technical solution such as a database is not sufficient for a GP or KM system.

*Cultural Factors Facilitating Sharing*

Cultural considerations, where people are motivated, supported, and rewarded for sharing information, is a basic prerequisite and is the most important factor related to sharing and transfer of knowledge, including good practices. This finding emerges strongly from the literature (e.g., Cracknell, 2001a, 2001b; DFID, 2002; O'Dell and Grayson, 2000; Nutley et al., 2004; Perrin, 2003).

Understanding the distinction between explicit knowledge and tacit knowledge is key to the development of a meaningful GPs "system." As Marra discusses in more detail in chapter 14, explicit knowledge can be recorded, codified, and written down. Tacit knowledge, in contrast, can only be shared and transferred to others through human interaction of some form. While this typically comes about through one-on-one personal contact, tacit knowledge also can be shared via formal and informal group discussions such as can take place in and around workshops and meetings, online discussions, and other similar venues.

O'Dell and Grayson (2000) indicate that tacit knowledge involves the know-how, judgment, intuition, and "little tricks" that are essential to the transfer of good practices. In this respect, tacit knowledge typically is seen as more relevant than explicit knowledge to application. Indeed, it has been estimated (e.g., DFID, 2002; O'Dell and Grayson, 2000) that 80 percent of knowledge that needs to be transferred is non-codifiable (i.e., tacit) in nature. Cracknell (2001b) adds that the research on how people learn indicates that there can be considerable "learning by involvement," whereas "learning by communication" (e.g., through receiving reports, attending seminars, etc.) is seldom as effective—or likely to be applied.

For the above reasons, leading organizations in the KM arena have facilitated and supported the development of informal networks of people working on common issues, most frequently referred to as "communities of practice." These networks typically communicate mainly through electronic exchanges, with the help of a facilitator, supplemented by the occasional face-to-face meeting. Networks can be active for every short periods of time, or indefinitely, depending upon the interest. For example, the World Bank now has more than 100 of what it refers to as Thematic Groups (TGs):

> [These] are groups of people who are passionate about a common subject. They are mostly front-line staff, working in the regions and networks. They consist of a core leadership/facilitation team of about 3-5 co-leaders drawn from both the regions and networks. Leadership and membership in TGs is voluntary and open to all staff in the Bank Group. TGs also have external partners, and knowledge sharing becomes seamless across the group through the email distribution lists and Websites.

Ironically, when opportunities are provided to share and to discuss tacit knowledge, particularly in a group context, this can result in the capturing of at least some of this knowledge in written form. This represents one example that Marra speaks of in her chapter of how tacit knowledge can be transformed into explicit knowledge. For example, the TGs in the World Bank frequently produce publications and newsletters arising out of their discussions, presenting good practices and other information.

DFID (2002) and Cracknell (2001b) have indicated that frequently there is interest among staff in "horizontal sharing," so that staff in far-flung locations can communicate directly with one another without having to go through headquarters. Ironically, this can be greatly supported by centralized approaches such as a good practices database, a pointer system or directory of expertise within (and sometimes outside of) the organization, and support for informal sharing such as through communities of practice.

The above considerations also have implications both for the effective *identification* of good practices, and for their *dissemination*. It suggests both the use of formal, as well as informal, approaches in both instances. For example, GPs can be solicited through formal submissions or nominations. But often they can be buried in regular progress reports and in other documentation, including evaluation reports. Evaluations can be carried out specifically for the purpose of identifying GPs. Cluster and thematic evaluations can be particularly useful for this purpose.

Most frequently, however, GPs will surface through formal and informal meetings, workshops, and other gatherings. The challenge is for someone designated to capture these insights, following up as necessary to acquire more information about potential good practices. This is consistent with the approach at the World Bank, where Cracknell (2001b) indicates that its "knowledge assets are seen as comprising three categories: people's experiences, bank documents (including evaluation reports), and embedded knowledge (e.g., knowledge incorporated into training manuals, legal agreements)."

Similarly, formal means such as technical reports, compendia, and database listings often are thought of as the main (or only) means of disseminating information about good practices. But as suggested above, most information that is put into action arises through other means, including through informal discussions, meetings and workshops, communities of practice, and the like. These can provide useful forums for presenting GPs. Also, "just-in-time" information can be provided on an individual basis by a good practices coordinator or equivalent. As well, publications in alternative forms, including fact sheets, newsletters, with the emphasis on brevity, can be more effective than longer, more technical reports in identifying and generating interest in alternative approaches.

*Leadership and Strategy*

Meaningful sharing of information, including the identification and use of good practices, cannot be mandated. A culture of learning and of sharing is essential, with genuine interest in learning about what can do differently or better (e.g., Cracknell, 2001b; Nutley et al., 2004). It should be noted that sharing is contrary to the vertical organizational structure and reward system of most large organizations. Typically, one is rewarded for doing one's own job, not for helping others to do theirs, even though this can have a negative impact on the performance and impact of the overall organization.

Senior management can set in place conditions that can facilitate and support sharing, such as have been discussed above, or conversely, inhibit it. In particular, it is important that senior management provide visible and tangible support, as well as provide opportunities and rewards for sharing.

*Measurement and Evaluation*

Clearly, evaluation is critical in order to be able to establish what in fact is a "good" practice. There is little to gain, and sometimes much to lose, by promoting practice as "good" that in fact may be deficient. But, as discussed earlier, this is not enough. Information about *why* the superior results were obtained, *how* this was done, and the circumstances in which this took place is essential in order to be able to act upon this information. Evaluation that provides *understanding* about what has happened and why is at least as important as the actual results.

The process of evaluation is critical to whether it can facilitate sharing and acting upon GPs information, or alternatively act as a barrier. Indeed, O'Dell and Grayson (2000) say that measurement and "paralysis by analysis" frequently gets in the way and acts as a hindering rather than a contributing factor to sharing and transfer of knowledge.

Traditional evaluation approaches put a premium on formality and on distance. But as we have seen, a focus on explicit knowledge transmitted through largely technical reports neglects how people really acquire and use information. It ignores the impact of process and involvement, which is critical to action. Evaluation approaches that tap into existing communication channels rather than acting outside of these, and that complement rather than attempt to replace other streams and sources of knowledge and that promote the sharing of tacit as well as explicit knowledge, are most likely to result in use.

Nevertheless, evaluation has a critical role to play in various respects regarding good practices. In addition to helping assess what is "good," and why, evaluators can help others in thinking evaluatively, and in using information appropriately. Evaluation studies can be a source of GPs, provided that these are pulled out and disseminated in simple language to practitioners and not left buried in technical reports. And perhaps most importantly, evaluation units and internal evaluators can play a major leadership and coordination role within their organizations in developing and managing a good practices system.

## Conclusion—Implications for Evaluation and for Evaluators

As this chapter has attempted to demonstrate, knowledge increasingly arises through the identification of themes and learnings arising from across multiple streams of information rather than from single evaluation studies carried out in a single setting at a single point in time. In order to be able to provide useful guidance for policy and for program improvement, evaluators—and evaluation commissioners—need to give greater emphasis to the various forms of synthesis such as outlined in this chapter.

With information increasingly coming in the form of streams, evaluation increasingly is being used as a process rather than as a product (e.g., Cracknell, 2001b). This, in turn, highlights the need for a learning approach to evaluation, where the emphasis is on understanding the reasons *why* something works or not, and on suggesting ideas and potential approaches to consider. As Cook (2000) has indicated, causal explanation without causal understanding is useless. Attempts at replication of even well-documented exemplary programs generally have resulted in disappointment. The objective of syntheses and good practices should be on identifying general guidelines (Patton, 2001) or theories underlying a given practice (Pawson, 2002a, 2002b), on providing ideas to consider and to adapt, rather than prescribing highly prescriptive and specific approaches, model programs or "best buys" that cannot possibly be appropriate in all contexts and with all possible target groups.

With a learning approach, the objective should be on creating a culture of evaluation, where managers and staff are constantly raising questions about what they are doing, and actively searching for ways of doing things differently or better. People also are more likely to use evaluative information when they are actively involved in the process. Knowledge management systems, databases, and formal reports should be viewed as supports rather than as ends in themselves.

When dealing with information from across different settings and evaluation studies, where potential users can be geographically dispersed, a somewhat different approach to involvement and communication may be needed than with single evaluation studies. One might consider tapping into existing informal and formal networks and existing sharing mechanisms, such as communities of practice where they exist (or can be created), other means of electronic communications (e.g., on-line discussion groups, chat sessions), or bringing people together such as through a cluster evaluation approach. As indicated earlier, good practices databases should provide brief rather than detailed information, with the objective of providing ideas and contact information, so that interested people can find out more on their own and adapt ideas to suit their own situation. In this way, less can be more.

Evaluators also need somewhat different skills in being able to deal with streams of information than in carrying out individual studies. In order to carry out meaningful reviews and syntheses of any form, one requires enough technical expertise to be able to assess the strengths and limitations of various sources of information. One needs at least enough content information in order to sense what information might be relevant or not. But as indicated earlier, skills in listening, in reading between the lines, and a comfort with going beyond the data, are required. Like a good detective, one needs an open-enough mind in order to be able to "sense" potentially emerging patterns, and to follow up on leads. In addition, strong interpersonal skills, particularly in areas such as active listening, facilitation, and communications, are as critical as the more traditional technical skills in research and methodology in order to assist managers and practitioners in understanding the implications for their own work of what has happened elsewhere (e.g., Zorzi et al., 2002, 2003).

As I have attempted to indicate, evaluation has the potential to provide substance to knowledge claims and in a manner that can promote a knowledge and learning culture that is critical to use. I have identified various forms of syntheses as well as a good practices approach as two overall strategies that can assist in learning from experiences in different settings and situations. In this way, evaluation can help make the promise of knowledge management real.

## Notes

1. "Learnings" is a relatively new word in the vocabulary. As a rule, I find it less pedantic and academic than the more common "lessons learned."
2. Much of the information in this section is adapted from work carried out with the International Labor Office—Program for the Elimination of Child Labor.
3. Just to muddy the waters, one can observe that terminology is frequently hazy in this area, without a high degree of consistency. In some cases, "best practices," when used in the plural, is intended to mean much the same thing as good practices as advocated here (e.g., this is how "best practices" is used by O'Dell and Jackson, 2000).
4. KM can be used to refer to the management and transfer of GPs. Technically, this would include—but goes beyond—GPs. But in practice, some organizations speak of KM and others of GPs (and sometimes even of best practices) while meaning the same thing. And as discussed below, there is little value in setting up a database of GPs in the absence of accompanying mechanisms to provide for sharing and use, i.e., without a KM system.

## References

Campbell, Donald T. (1979). "'Degrees of Freedom' and the Case Study." In Donald T. Cook and Charles S. Reichardt, eds., *Qualitative and Quantitative Methods in Evaluation Research*. Thousand Oaks, CA: Sage Publications. Reprinted in Donald T. Campbell. (1988). *Methodology and Epistemology for the Social Sciences: Selected Papers* (E. S. Overman, ed.). Chicago: University of Chicago Press.

Cook, Thomas D. (1997). "Lessons Learned in Evaluation over the Past 25 Years." In Eleanor Chelimsky and William R. Shadish, eds., *Evaluation for the 21st Century: A Handbook* (30-5). Thousand Oaks, CA: Sage Publications.

_____. (2000). "Towards a Practical Theory of External Validity." In Leonard Bickman, ed., *Validity and Social Experimentation: Donald Campbell's Legacy Vol. 1* (3-44). Thousand Oaks, CA: Sage Publications.

Cook, Thomas D., and Donald T. Campbell. (1979). *Quasi-Experimentation: Designs and Analysis Issues for Field Settings.* Chicago: Rand McNally.

Cracknell, Basil E. "Knowing Is All: Or Is It? Some Reflections on Why the Acquisition of Knowledge, Focusing Particularly on Evaluation Activities, Does Not Always Lead to Action." *Public Administration and Development* 31 (2001a): 371–379.

———. "The Role of Aid-Evaluation Feedback as an Input into the Learning Organization." *Evaluation* 7(1) (2001b): 132–145.

DFID (UK Department for International Development). (2002). "Doing the Knowledge: How DFID Compares with Best Practice in Knowledge Management." Internal draft paper.

GAO. (1992). *The Evaluation Synthesis.* GAO.PEMD-10.1.2. Washington, DC: United States General Accounting Office.

Kellogg Foundation. (1998). *Evaluation Handbook.* Battle Creek, MI: W. K. Kellogg Foundation. Also available online at: www.wkkf.org.

Lipsey, Mark W. "Re: Unsolved Problems and Unfinished Business." *American Journal of Evaluation* 22(3) (2001): 325–328.

Mark, Melvin M. "Evaluation's Future: Furor, Futile, or Fertile?" *American Journal of Evaluation* 22(3) (2001): 457–479.

Nutley S. M., H.T.O. Davies, and I. Walter. (2004). "Conceptual Synthesis 2: Learning from Knowledge Management." *Research Unit for Research Utilization*, University of St Andrews (downloadable from http://www.st-and.ac.uk/~ruru).

O'Dell, Carla, and C. Jackson Grayson. (2000). *Identifying and Transferring Internal Best Practices.* A White Paper. American Productivity and Quality Center. Available at: www.apqc.org/free/whitepapers.

Patton, Michael Quinn. "Evaluation, Knowledge Management, Best Practices, and High Quality Lessons Learned." *American Journal of Evaluation* 22(3) (2001): 329–336.

Pawson, Ray. "Evidence-Based Policy: In Search of a Method. *Evaluation* 8(2) (2002a): 157–181.

———. "Evidence-Based Policy: The Promise of 'Realist Synthesis.'" *Evaluation* 8(3) (2002b): 340-358.

Pawson, Ray, and Nick Tilley. "Realistic Evaluation Bloodlines." *American Journal of Evaluation* 22(3) (2001): 317–324.

Perrin, Burt. "Effective Use and Misuse of Performance Measurement. *American Journal of Evaluation* 19(3) (1998): 367–369.

———. (2002a)."Towards a New View of Accountability." Paper presented at the European Evaluation Society Annual Conference, Seville. Available online at: http://www.europeanevaluation.org.

———. "Implementing the Vision: Addressing Challenges to Results-Focused Management and Budgeting." *OECD Journal on Budgeting* (2003) (also available online at: http://www.oecd.org/EN/document/0,,EN-document-287-9-no-20-26305-287,00.html)/.

Perrin, Burt, and Keith Mackay. (1999). *What Makes for Successful Conferences? Lessons Learned from an Evaluation of Six Conferences Sponsored by the World Bank Institute.* WBI Evaluation Studies No. ES99-34. Washington, DC: World Bank Institute, The World Bank.

Senge, Peter M. (1990). *The Fifth Discipline: The Art and Practice of the Learning Organization.* New York/London: Doubleday.

Worthen, Blaine R., and Constance C. Schmitz. "Conceptual Challenges Confronting Cluster Evaluation." *Evaluation* 3(3) (1997): 300–319.

Zorzi, Rochelle, Martha McGuire, and Burt Perrin. (2002). *Evaluation Benefits, Outputs, and Knowledge Elements.* Canadian Evaluation Society. Report available at: http://consultation.evaluationcanada.ca/results.htm.

Zorzi, Rochelle, Burt Perrin, Martha McGuire, Bud Long, and Linda Lee. "Defining the Benefits, Outputs, and Knowledge Elements of Program Evaluation." *Canadian Journal of Program Evaluation* 17(3) (2003): 143–150.

# Part 2

# Information Systems at Work for Evaluation

# 3

# Management of Evaluative Knowledge in National Health: Some Comparative Observations

*Markus Spinatsch*

### Introduction

In the last twenty years, the making of public policies in highly developed countries has undergone a fundamental paradigmatic change. "New Public Management," global budgets, service contracting, and privatization have at least partially replaced traditional steering through conditional programs and financial inputs. Strategic and operational responsibilities were separated between different state actors who have to account for the resources they have been using and the effects that were achieved. This transition affected above all the state and its organizations, but it also deeply influenced the parastatal and non-governmental sectors, where semi-public or private organizations and actors accomplish public tasks. Concomitant to this paradigmatic shift, the relevance of facts in policymaking increased. Empirical evidence became one of the core principles for planning, steering, and accounting of policies, programs, and projects.

Health is one of the key policy fields affected by this shift towards evidence. Health policy, focusing on maintaining and promoting health, preventing disease, and offering care, is one of the core tasks of the state, one of the most costly as well as the most cost-increasing domains of public expenditure (OECD, 2003). Decreasing these expenditures, ensuring access to health services for everyone, and improving the quality of services are some of the big challenges of public health in the highly developed world. In an evidence-oriented culture, dealing with these challenges by increasing efficiency, quality, and effectiveness implies first of all a great demand for information and knowledge.

National Health includes a great variety of stakeholders such as politicians, policymakers, researchers, health care providers, professionals (physicians, pharmacists, nurses, etc.), and non-governmental organizations or private companies (e.g., the pharmaceutical industry or insurances). All these stakeholders use (and produce) a wide range of information and knowledge, about the health status of the population, health relevant behavior, biomedical or clinical research findings, accessibility and efficiency of health services, and the cost and financing of health care.

As Rist states in his chapter, managers and practitioners cannot search or wait for the best available knowledge, they just use what they can get immediately, what is easily available and simple to process. In many cases, these needs are covered by statistics or ready-made indicators rather than by complex knowledge of research or evaluations. Much of this needed information and knowledge exists at different places in national societies, but it does not always meet the needs of the potential users. In two studies about the needs of information or knowledge and problems of accessibility among national health stakeholders in Switzerland we identified several obstacles that prevent an optimal use of the existing empirical facts for informed decisions (Spinatsch and Hofer, 2002; Spinatsch and Weiss, 1999):

- There is a great lack of transparency and of overall view about where what kind of evaluative knowledge in what quality is available.
- Access to the existing and known knowledge is in many cases limited for reasons of data protection or ownership of knowledge. Particularly non-governmental or private owners of health-relevant knowledge, as for example, physicians associations, insurances or the pharmaceutical industry, often do not or only selectively open their knowledge bases.
- Much of existing and accessible information is not evaluatively usable, because it is of no interest for the demanders (this is often the case for academic research and sometimes for statistics).
- Accessible and usable information is often not prepared and presented in a form that suits the needs of potential users. The more the evidence-oriented culture is growing, the more differentiated are the needs, the more sophisticated are the demands for information, and the higher are the demanded standards of quality.

Whereas these obstacles hamper an optimal use of the existing information on the demand side, the supply side is mainly challenged by the problems of overflow: how can the existing data, information, and knowledge be sorted (for today and for the future) into important and non-important; how can it sustainably be saved and archived; and—most importantly—how can it enter in the organizational and transorganizational memory in a way that it is easily accessible for potential users today as well as in the future?

However, overflow of health-relevant information and knowledge is but one side of the medal. There still exist information gaps in many aspects of national health, especially in the domains of cost and financing, leaving many demands for information unanswered. Finally, one has also to consider the asymmetric relation between demand and supply of information. New realities or problems often create an immediate demand for new information and knowledge, whereas the production of valid and usable information on new subjects often needs a considerable amount of time.

Especially since the development of the Internet that started in the early 1990s, many initiatives are under way with the general objective to narrow down the gap that exists between the supply and the demand of evaluative knowledge in health. Following, some selected examples of such approaches are briefly presented and commented on from a perspective of potential users. All the approaches have in common the fact that they intend to collect, structure, and diffuse existing health information. They differ in the degree of complexity of the managed information, with relatively simple data and indicators on one side and rather complex research and evaluation knowledge on the other side. The first part is focused on statistical data and indicator-based monitoring systems that cover many aspects of public health such as the health status and health behavior of the population, the accessibility, performance, and costs of different health services etc. The second part is focused on supplies of more complex health-relevant knowledge, addressed to a great variety of potential users, mainly in health care and health services. The presentation is based on published self-declarations of the respective institutions in spring 2003; it does not imply any statement about the accuracy or quality of the provided information or knowledge.

## Management of Data and Indicators

Statistical data leave many information needs unanswered and monitoring systems are based on data that are produced by representative surveys covering a defined population at a particular time. This kind of knowledge production is highly standardized and therefore—from the perspective of the user—of low complexity. It is mainly used for the general observation of problems (identification of intervention needs) and of outcomes (results of interventions). It is independent of context, fits well for comparisons (across and over time), but it is rather superficial and leaves many information needs unanswered.

### *Health Statistics: From Data to Information*

For a long time, statistics were the only source of "objective" information that decision makers, stakeholders, and the great public could use to get orientation and inspiration for health-related decisions. For many years, the production and diffusion of statistical data was an exclusive task of the governmental statistical offices. The results were published in the form of frequencies and simple cross tables. With the growing complexity of the social conditions and with the increasing rationalization of the activities of the state, these simple forms of information became insufficient. There was a growing need for more insight into social and societal connotations of the reality, including causalities and other analytical relations.

Thus, since the 1970s, in many countries statistical publications became more sophisticated, containing—beyond the still indispensable tables with basic data—elaborated indicators, commented time series, and detailed analysis of selected policy fields or synthetic reports. The new information technologies multiplied not only the processing of data, but also the options of analysis, presentation, and diffusion of statistical information. Simultaneously, the governmental organizations lost their factual monopoly in producing statistical data. In the field of Public Health, interest groups, and private companies, that is, associations of physicians or hospitals, the pharmaceutical industry or insurances companies, established their own statistical databases using data from specifically commissioned surveys or from internal controlling and other administrative systems like hospitals (Spinatsch and Hofer, 2002).

Today, the national statistical offices are just one among many producers of health-related statistics. To state it with the self-understanding of the Statistical Office of the European Communities (Eurostat): "Statistics are the bedrock of democratic market societies...indispensable for decision-makers at all levels—for planning, implementing and monitoring policy."[1] Their products have the advantages of being credible and of good quality, guaranteeing continuity, national coverage, and international comparisons. Their main disadvantages are more or less substantial information gaps and the limited possibilities to satisfy specific needs of particular clients.

*Health Observatories: Monitoring Public Health*

In the interest of compensating some of these limits and bridging the gap between the growing needs of comprehensive and qualitatively good information and the lack of transparency, access, and usability to the existing information, some countries have established public health observatories. It is common to all these observatories that they do not produce any data themselves but that their mission is to bring together, prepare, and disseminate existing statistical data in order to monitor health and disease trends in an effort to improve the knowledge about the health status and other health-related issues of the population. Beyond this common objective, there exist remarkable differences in the specific tasks and organizational structures of health observatories in different countries.

Management of Evaluative Knowledge in National Health    53

In France, since the beginning of the 1980s there exist twenty-six regional observatories (ORS) covering the whole country including overseas departments, unified in the national federation of regional health observatories (Fnors).[2] Indicators on forty-five different health subjects, based on statistical data from thirty-three different sources, are published and made accessible on the Internet, aggregated at regional, departmental, and national levels. Beyond the basic tasks of collecting, validating, and diffusing existing data, the observatories also analyze and synthesize the existing data, conduct specific surveys and documentary research, perform evaluations, and offer consulting. The subjects their indicators cover include health status, health behavior, and the supply and demand of health care for the general population as well as for specific target groups.

Since 1994, the Canadian Institute for Health Information (CIHI)[3] has been monitoring national public health in Canada. It provides direct online access to statistics from various sources about health conditions, services, human resources, and spending. In 2002, Statistics Canada established a system of comparable health and health system performance indicators for Canada, the provinces, and the territories. It contains common indicators for fourteen areas of health status, health outcomes, and quality of health care services. Whereas these indicators can be accessed directly online at the Internet site of Statistics Canada,[4] CIHI provides a structured list of contents of these indicators and online links to the database. Beyond offering direct or indirect access to health data and indicators, CIHI is also working on the identification and promotion of health indicators and health information standards, conducting analysis and special studies, and publishing reports.

In Germany, the Federal Health Monitoring System[5] was established in 1999. It systematically collects scattered information from the multitude of institutions in the health sector. The data are harmonized in such a way that a comprehensive picture of the entire health sector is painted. Different products and forms of presentation meet the different needs of various user groups. The system provides comprehensive information on all relevant aspects of health (status, care, services, costs, financing, etc.), made accessible online as tables, diagrams, and texts. Simultaneously, the collected information is also analyzed and continuously published as the "Health Report for Germany" in book form. Additionally, the German observatory elaborates on and periodically publishes special reports on health-related information of special interest, for example, allergies or bone and joint disease.

As in France, health observatories in England are established at the regional level. In the year 2000, an observatory was established in each of the nine NHS regions.[6] The observatories are linked together and act collectively through the Association of Public Health Observatories (APHO). A database of public health national data sources with 210 defined datasets has been developed, which can be searched for a particular area of interest (e.g., cancer, hospital, ethnicity). The results provide details of information that is available on the topic selected and from what sources. The data are not (yet) directly accessible on the PHO-Internet site. In addition to the monitoring function, English observatories also intend to provide methodological advice and to perform evaluations and impact assessments, particularly on inequality aspects. Beyond the proper work of collecting and disseminating indicators, they also aim to identify gaps in health information, to give early warning of future public health problems, and to highlight areas for action.

The Swiss Health Observatory[7] was established in 2001. It provides online access to indicators about seven different domains, covering all relevant aspects of public health. Beginning in early 2005, information on 111 out of 123 listed and 160 planned indicators was accessible in the form of assembled and commented tables and graphs. In order to supply complete and comprehensive information about health in Switzerland, the observatory also evaluates data stored in databases of other institutions such as the federal office of statistics, health insurances, the Organization for Economic Cooperation and Development (OECD), or the World Health Organization (WHO). Apart from generally monitoring health and the health-care system in Switzerland, the observatory conducts studies in different fields of health, for example, old age, psychological health, or health-care systems. It also carries out specific analyses and advisory services on request and addresses important current issues in health policy in collaboration with a network of experts. Finally, the observatory also plans to collaborate with other Swiss health institutions to elaborate a national health report.

On the international level, the OECD[8] and the WHO[9] are collecting and publishing a great number of health-related statistics and indicators. Both organizations play a vital role in providing access to information and knowledge and in promoting transnational comparability of health indicators. In 1995, the European Commission set up the European Monitoring Centre for Drugs and Drug Addiction (EMCDDA)[10] with the objective to supply objective, reliable, and comparable information at the European level concerning drugs and drug addiction and their consequences. Beyond the functions of collecting, analyzing, and disseminating existing data, the center is particularly concerned with improving data-comparison methods.

*Two Strategic Options for Health Observatories*

The Internet is obviously an excellent opportunity to create transparency and to provide access to the available information. With regard to the presented health observatories, there are basically two different strategies to provide this access. The first approach, which might be called the *synthesizer* strategy, is to define a set of indicators (based on the needs of the users, on one side, and on the availability of data on the other side), to collect the relevant data, to get it quality checked, prepared, and harmonized in a way that at the end, all indicators are presented in the same form, broken down by the same independent variables (e.g., gender, age, region, etc.), and available for the same time spaces, thus allowing comparative time series between different indicators. This strategy not only allows users to get a quick overview of what exists and to follow always the same line of action to find the information they are looking for directly on the site of the observatory. In addition, it also creates new knowledge by analyzing, transforming, and synthesizing existing information. It is very user-friendly, but it implies a considerable validating and processing work for the observatories and is therefore rather expensive.

The second strategy is to make an inventory of the existing information, to present a technical description of the data, and to provide a hyperlink to the source where the data are available (deposited at the Health Observatory or elsewhere). This solution, which might be called the *broker* strategy, leaves it up to the user to collect the needed information from different sources, to check the quality of the data, and to harmonize it in a way that best fits his needs.

All the observatories presented above use both strategies with different products, but the German and the French observatories clearly prioritize the synthesizer model, whereas the Canadian and the English observatories favor the broker strategy. The Swiss observatory is also geared toward a synthesizer strategy. It does not directly publish single indicators but presents graphic illustrations with short descriptive reports to a particular subject. The values behind the presented graphs are accessible through a simple hyperlink.

The results of our client survey (Spinatsch and Hofer, 2002) show that practitioners who use monitoring data are interested in having simple and quick direct access to the information they need. If they are looking for common health information on the Internet, they wish to find with a few clicks exactly what fits their need. This expectation suggests that observatories that follow a synthesizer strategy are in a better position to serve the clients, at least if the information is presented in a form that really suits the needs of the users. In this respect, it appears that the German observatory with its harmonized and simple supply of information probably fits best the needs of the clients.

A reality test performed on the presented observatories[11] reveals the difficulties and the uncertainties a potential user is confronted with while searching for information on an observatory. Not all strategies lead to the searched data, an indication that the data exist does not yet mean that it is available, and if the searched data cannot be found, the user does not know if it is because he did not use the correct search strategy on the site, because the data do not exist at the observatory (but perhaps elsewhere), or because the data do not exist at all.

All observatories add value to the data they collect and provide. The more an observatory adds value to the data, the higher is its legitimation for existence. In this respect, too, the synthesizers, who not only collect, index, and hyperlink data that exist elsewhere but who also transform these data and place the data on their own site, are closer to the using practitioners. However, the transformation of existing data also changes its nature and narrows down the options of its use. In this sense, users who have the qualification and the time to gather original data and to transform the data themselves following their particular needs are probably better served with a broker strategy.

Finally, the presented health observatories also differ strategically concerning their political self-understanding and integration. The German and, to a lesser extent, also the French observatories are above all technically oriented. They concentrate on the presentation of valid, quickly accessible data for any kind of interested users. The German observatory produces a sophisticated health report; interested clients with further analytical needs are hyperlinked to other institutions that provide such services. The French observatory offers analysis and evaluations based on their data, but these activities are clearly a second priority. The other observatories have a greater variety of products, including not only general analysis or evaluations, but also in-depth studies on selected health fields like inequality or psychological health and other research activities. The intention of the English and the Swiss observatories to identify information gaps, to develop early warning systems, or to identify areas of action for public health shows their relative proximity to the political actors of public health.

## Management of Research and Evaluation Knowledge

Contrary to the standardized production and presentation of data and information presented before, the production of research and evaluation knowledge is generally based on various methodological approaches (and not standardized), context dependent and therefore of high complexity. It provides deep insights into selected aspects, and although it does not generally fit directly for comparisons or generalizations, it provides a major source for synthesis. It is used mainly for designing or shaping programs and for deep insights into the impacts and outcomes of interventions.

Following the work of Nonaka (1994), we can distinguish between *explicit* and *tacit* knowledge. Explicit knowledge is codified and draws on research results. It is documented on paper or electronic databases and is thus physically accessible in the form of books, papers, or data files, directly or through physical infrastructures such as libraries or databases. Tacit knowledge is undocumented, spread in the heads of individuals as well as organizations or networks. It implies facts, norms, values, and interpretations about professional as well as everyday subjects. It is only accessible through individuals and therefore vulnerable to subjective biases. Generally, it can be stated that the more complex a need for information is, the more important it is to have access to individuals who dispose of tacit knowledge (Hansen et al., 1999).

Informed individuals often have not only an overview of the existing explicit knowledge, they are also able to consider the relevant contextual factors and can provide ad hoc synthesis of explicit and tacit knowledge that suits the particular needs of the practitioners.

As we have shown above, knowledge management can be limited to provide access to knowledge that exists elsewhere (broker strategy) or it can imply not only the access to, but also the transformation of existing knowledge (synthesizer strategy). In relation to the perspective of making existing knowledge in health systems accessible and usable, there are two basic modes of, knowledge transformation: the *knowledge processing mode* brings together existing explicit knowledge to create new explicit knowledge, being documented and physically accessible. The *networking mode* mobilizes existing tacit knowledge to diffuse and possibly create new tacit knowledge by bringing together people as knowledge carriers. Referring to the work of Nonaka, as it is presented in the chapter by Marra in this volume, the first mode would represent the model of "combination," the second mode would represent the model of "socialization."

In the following, some examples of knowledge processing as well as of networking approaches are presented. The selection is illustrative rather than representative, leaving aside physical and electronic libraries, which provide possibly the widest, but the least specified access to explicit knowledge.

*Knowledge Processing*

The Cochrane Collaboration[12] is probably one of the best known approaches to manage existing knowledge in health with the aim of helping people make well-informed decisions about health care. The activities of this international organization are based on the work of Archie Cochrane, a British epidemiologist, who stated in the early 1970s that health care professionals, consumers, researchers, and policymakers are overwhelmed with unmanageable amounts of information and that at the same time there exists a great collective ignorance about the effects of health care. In response to his call for systematic up-to-date reviews of all relevant randomized controlled trials of health care, the "Cochrane Centre" was established in 1992 in Oxford (UK). One year later, people from eleven countries co-founded "The Cochrane Collaboration." The major task of the organization is to perform systematic reviews of randomized controlled trials in health care. These reviews are conducted by collaborative review groups composed of researchers, health care professionals, consumers, and others. They receive support from specific methods groups, from the Cochrane Field/Networks, and from the Cochrane Centers, which also coordinate the activities of the Collaboration. The output of the Cochrane Collaboration are published in the Cochrane Library,[13] an electronically accessible infrastructure composed of several databases, including the "Cochrane Database of Systematic Reviews."

The Agency for Healthcare Research and Quality (AHRQ),[14] created in 1989 by the U.S. Department of Health and Human Services, provides evidence-based information on the outcomes and quality of health care, patients' safety, and access to effective service. The evidence developed through AHRQ-sponsored research is aimed at helping decision makers in clinics, in the health care system, and in public policy to make informed decisions in all relevant aspects of health. Besides sponsoring classical research activities that contribute to the achievement of its mission, the Agency also funds activities of knowledge management like the Evidence-based Practice Centers (EPC).[15] The thirteen EPCs, located in the United States and in Canada, review relevant scientific literature on clinical, behavioral, organizational, and financial topics to produce evidence reports and technology assessments. They also conduct research on methodologies and the effectiveness of their implementation, and provide technical assistance in translating the reports and assessments into quality improvement tools and in helping to inform coverage policies. With its project "Translating Research into Practice," the AHRQ focuses on "closing the gap between what we know and what we do."[16] Intending to support the translation of knowledge and tools acquired into measurable improvements in health care, the agency promotes partnerships between researchers and representatives of health care systems and organizations to help accelerate and magnify the impact of practice-based, patient outcome research in applied settings.

The Evidence Base of the British Health Development Agency (HDA)[17] aims to provide its clients (practitioners and researchers engaged in public health work) with access to the best available information on what works to improve health and to reduce health inequalities via the Internet. Evidence Base is a searchable database of electronically available systematic reviews of effectiveness, literature reviews, meta-analyses, expert group reports, and other review-level information. It contains summaries of reviews and full reports commissioned or carried out by the HDA, as well as links to reviews, reports, databases, organizations, and institutions concerned with gathering and publishing evidence elsewhere on the Internet.

HealthInsite,[18] an initiative of the Australian government, is a single entry point to quality checked information from leading health information providers, including health organizations, government agencies, and educational and research institutions. It provides hyperlinked access to a wide variety of health information on all important issues and includes health-related statistics and reports from research, evaluations, policymaking, press releases, etc.

*Networking Organizations and People*

"Netting the Evidence"[19] is an Internet platform established and maintained by the School for Health and Related Research of the University of

Sheffield. It intends to facilitate evidence-based healthcare by providing support and access to helpful organizations and useful learning resources, such as an evidence-based virtual library, software, and journals. More than fifty organizations dealing with health evidence are presented with a short abstract (objectives and main activities) and a link to their homepage.

C.H.A.I.N. (Contacts, Help, Advice and Information Network for effective health care)[20] is a network designed to facilitate links between health care professionals, teachers, managers, librarians, specialists, researchers, and other professionals working in the British NHS family of organizations. It currently has about 2,800 members. The purpose of this network is to enable members from different organizations, professions, and levels of involvement to identify and make contact with each other. It has been established in response to a demand for information from people working in the NHS about "who is doing what" in evidence-based health care and research. C.H.A.I.N. is part of the NHS research and development program. It has at its core a multidisciplinary contact directory that captures key information about members' interests, background, and role as well as contact details.

*Different Strategies, Access, and Usability*

Among the four presented knowledge processing organizations, the British and the Australian examples are mainly (HDA) or exclusively (HealthInsite) bound to a broker strategy. The contribution of HealthInsite is on selection, quality checking, and structuring existing knowledge without adding value through knowledge transformation. HDA provides access to its own commissioned or carried out studies and reviews, thus it generates new and transforms existing knowledge. But its objective is much wider, providing access to "the best available information" on the Internet. The Cochrane Collaboration and AHRQ are both bound to a synthesizer strategy in the sense that they transform existing explicit knowledge. Whereas the major focus of AHRQ is to generate new knowledge to fill gaps of quality and outcome evidence by commissioning new research, its substructure, the EPCs, concentrate on transforming existing explicit knowledge through synthesis. As AHRQ is particularly concerned about utilization of its knowledge, it also generates and diffuses specific knowledge about how the known explicit knowledge can be used in practice.

Contrary to all other knowledge processing organizations that have a great variety of functions, strategies, and clients, the Cochrane Collaboration is very specific and methodologically narrow, as it only deals with randomized controlled trials of physician-to-patient care. Within such a setting, where context variables such as working context (hospital), professional training and identity, as well as technologies, are relatively homogeneous within as well as among highly developed countries, the Cochrane approach is a remarkable way to select the best available knowledge out of the always growing stream of knowledge, to transform this existing explicit knowledge into new, more valid, and, therefore, better knowledge for practitioners, at least as far as those working on the same methodological foundations. In this sense, the very transparent Cochrane approach probably corresponds in a high degree to the "professionally based intervention strategy" of Nutley et al. (2003), "typically available for use within a professionalized healthcare organization... disaggregated from their context for the purpose" (p. 140). However, the simple fact that the high degree of homogeneity among the medical professionals guarantees a low degree of complexity of the interventions also shows the limits for a replication of such an approach for other intervention areas, for example, prevention, where context variables are most relevant. In addition, this stated homogeneity among medical professionals might also be questioned as is done by Nutley et al. (2003), who state that health professionals do not simply apply abstract scientific knowledge, but collaborate in discussions and teams.

Under such collaborating conditions and even more so in other, more complex domains of health, terms like "best practice" or "body of evidence" become relative. Knowledge is rarely self-evident, always contested, and in constant change. Therefore, as Perrin develops in his chapter in this volume, knowledge-based practitioners are better off if they are looking for "what works" or for "good practice" rather that for "best practice." Such a more modest, but also more realistic conception tends to consider ideas rather than approaches to copy, and rather than "evidence based" it might be called "evidence informed" or even "evidence aware." This way of learning from existing knowledge—independent of its methodological foundations and of its analytically proven effectiveness—also allows for making use of important knowledge that does not necessarily correspond to high selection standards like the ones observed by the Cochrane Collaboration.

Whereas offers to share explicit knowledge through the Internet are abundant—the few examples have just illustrative character—it is much more difficult to find sites that provide access to tacit knowledge through networks. The two British examples presented can give an impression of the advantages and disadvantages of networking. The platform "Netting the Evidence" helps to identify and get in contact with other organizations oriented to health evidence. But for the practitioner, access to usable tacit knowledge, available from individual persons with particular experience, is quite far away, rather complicated, and eventually of questionable success. In this respect, the C.H.A.I.N. approach is more promising, as it leads all interested NHS members directly to the carrier of tacit knowledge.

## Conclusions

We are living in a time of exponential growth of knowledge production. A large part of this knowledge—at least in its documented, explicit form—is in one way or another made accessible on the Internet. With the fast spread of the

Internet, the transparency of the market of health-relevant information and knowledge has increased. It is the exponential production and high degree of transparency that create a situation of overflow of evaluative knowledge and information. Under these circumstances, the major challenge for the practitioner who is in search of evidence is to have and keep an overview and orientation in this fast-growing and changing market. The presented examples supply support to potential users in their search for the knowledge they need. Lean approaches like the German health observatory or the Cochrane Collaboration, based on a homogeneous methodology and concentrating on one or a few products, provide fast and precise access to information and knowledge, but what they offer is very selective and thus limited by content and quality. These approaches fit well for those particular users who know exactly what they are looking for. Wider ranging sites like AHRQ, HealthInsite, or the Swiss health observatory, which supply many different products, serve a greater variety of users with different and not always very precise needs and varying quality standards. Especially for such polyvalent sites, a well-structured overview, coherent guiding of the visitors, and simple and fast access to the desired information are essential to satisfy the needs of their users.

Despite the fact that there is a steadily increasing flow of evaluative knowledge, the Internet is far from being a place where all questions find a suitable answer. As the presented sites show, there still exist considerable gaps of information, and many of the presented sites are in one way or another involved in the production of additional knowledge to fill existing gaps, thus contributing to the always increasing stream of studies. On the other side, not all sites provide free access to their knowledge, as is the case with the database of the Cochrane Collaboration and certain hyperlinked sites of the British HDA or the C.H.A.I.N. network. Many Internet sites—claiming to be still under construction—promise much more than what is really available (in early 2003).

Concerning the usability of the provided evaluative knowledge and information on health on the presented sites, the structure of the supply appears to be biased in several aspects. Individual health care and health status of the population are more thoroughly covered than costs and the financing of health; hard empirical evidence in the form of statistics, indicators, and scientific research towers above soft knowledge like evaluations, expert reports, or grey literature. The strong dominance of supplied explicit knowledge over tacit knowledge contradicts the assumption that 80 percent of all knowledge is tacit (cf. the chapter of Marra) and that with the always increasing complexity of decisions to be taken, access to individuals as carriers of tacit knowledge becomes even more important.

All presented sites are concerned with the quality of information and knowledge they provide access to. The brokers concentrate their quality control basically on the selection process of the knowledge they give access to by using more or less rigid and transparent criteria, leaving it to the user to go more deeply into details of the information he is using. The synthesizers generally not only check the quality of the knowledge they use, they also transform it and concentrate their diffusion policy on the new knowledge they create rather than on the inputs they use. For many practitioners, who often are short of time and lack scientific qualification, this transformation of existing into new knowledge is very important, as they can leave the search, selection, assessment, and recodification of the basic knowledge to the synthesizers, having direct access to their synthesis. Perrin mentions in his chapter the high importance of producing synthesis not only to collect, reassemble, and interpret existing knowledge, but also its inherent function to make scientific language commonly understandable. This translation process is not only a technical one between different languages, but also and primarily a social one between different cultures with their own perceptions, norms, and values.

Knowledge that is made accessible for use must not only be understandable, it also must be credible. Credibility of knowledge is created through transparency and trust. Transparency concerns first of all the methods applied to produce the knowledge, but also the criteria for selection and quality control applied by the provider and, last but not least, the interests of those who commissioned and produced the knowledge. For providers following a broker strategy, transparency is possibly the key element to underline the credibility of the knowledge they provide. The more a knowledge provider is bound to a synthesizer strategy by transforming the knowledge he assembles through recodification, synthesis, and interpretation, the more difficult it becomes for the user to judge the credibility of the end product. Even if all transformation steps are made transparent, many users would not find enough time or would not feel themselves competent enough to reconstruct and judge the production process of the knowledge they use. Under these circumstances, trust becomes the key element to assure the credibility of the knowledge provided. At the beginning, trust can be assured by the status of a provider (e.g., academic or public); later it becomes mainly a question of good experiences.

Health-relevant knowledge and information are mainly decentrally produced and stored. The actors of the knowledge market—producers as well as users—are interlinked in a loose network under the umbrella of "national health." Such naturally grown networks have the advantage that knowledge can be produced in time and close to the needs of the users; they guarantee a great variety of information and innovativeness for new knowledge to be generated, and they are less vulnerable to global influences like budget cuts or changes in paradigms. However, natural networks are not transparent and the existing knowledge is not always available or usable. Where evaluative knowledge comes up in streams rather than in single studies, these networks with their lack of transparency and accessibility become suboptimal, as they can less and less serve the needs of decision takers at all levels of national health—

from individual care up to national public health policies. The presented internet sites are interesting and promising approaches to manage the steadily growing flow of knowledge and make it accessible for potential users and are eventually important milestones on the way from naturally grown networks towards national health information systems (Kendrick, 2001). Such national systems could assure that the production and diffusion of health-relevant knowledge and information are transparent, accessible, and efficiently managed so that these systems can be used at their best for further planning, implementation, and evaluation.

## Notes

1. Yves Franchet, key source of harmonized European statistics, http://europa.eu.int/comm/-eurostat/Public/datashop/print-catalogue/EN?catalogue=Eurostat&service=about_catalogue.
2. http://www.fnors.org/
3. http://secure.cihi.ca/cihiweb/dispPage.jsp?cw_page=home_e
4. http://www.statcan.ca/
5. http://www.gbe-bund.de/
6. http://www.pho.org.uk/
7. http://www.obsan.ch/d
8. http://www.oecd.org/EN/home/0,,EN-home-12-nodirectorate-no-no—12,00.html
9. http://www3.who.int/whosis/menu.cfm
10. http://www.emcdda.org/
11. In order to check the accessibility of the indicators of the presented observatories, a short exemplary test was performed. All five observatories were searched for the number of deaths due to liver cirrhosis in the year 2000 for the whole nation. This is a commonly used mortality indicator that exists for many countries and has been in use for a long time. The search was performed with three different strategies: (1) a content-oriented approach, starting at the home page and following hyperlinks with an inherent logic (i.e., monitoring > mortality > liver cirrhosis), (2) using the search function of the observatory, and (3) using the Google search function for the site, both with the keyword "cirrhosis" (in the national language of the observatory). Only in one case did this test lead to the result searched for: using the internal search function of the German observatory led with two more clicks to the data (6,511 cases). At the French observatory, the same strategy led to the respective figures for all regions in the years 1998 und 1999, but not aggregated for the Nation and not for 2000. Replying to the internal search function, the English observatory provided a correct data description of the indicator and a link to the source where it should be available, but the source was not accessible. Using the Google search strategy led to texts that contained rough estimations of the searched indicator at the French and Swiss observatories. The content-oriented strategy resulted in figures about alcohol-related deaths in 1995 for Germany; in the French observatory the search process ended on a page still under construction. For Canada, no results were found with either of the strategies.
12. http://www.cochrane.org/
13. http://www.update-software.com/Cochrane/
14. http://www.ahcpr.gov/
15. http://www.ahcpr.gov/clinic/epc/
16. http://www.ahcpr.gov/research/trip2fac.htm

17. http://194.83.94.80/hda/docs/evidence/eb2000/corehtml/intro.htm
18. http://www.healthinsite.gov.au/
19. http://www.shef.ac.uk/~scharr/ir/netting/
20. http://www.doh.gov.uk/ntrd/chain/chain.htm

## References

Hansen, M., S. Nohria, and T. Tierneys. "What's Your Strategy for Managing Knowledge?" *Harvard Business Review* (March-April 1999): 106–116.

Kendrick, S. "Using All the Evidence: Towards a Truly Intelligent NHS." *Scottish Executive Health Bulletin* 59(2) (2001).

Nonaka, I. "A Dynamic Theory of Organizational Knowledge Creation." *Organization Science* 5(1) (1994): 14-37.

Nutley, S., I. Walter, and H. Davies. "From Knowing to Doing: A Framework for Understanding the Evidence-into-Practice Agenda." *Evaluation* 9 (2 (2003): 125–148.

Organization of Economic Cooperation and Development (OECD). (2003). OECD Health Data 2003: A Comparative Analysis of 30 Countries; http://www.oecd.org/EN/document/0,,EN-document-12-nodirectorate-no-12-42365-12,00.html.

Spinatsch, M., and S. Hofer. (2002). Aufgabenüberprüfung der Schweizerischen Gesundheitsstatistik, Probleme und Perspektiven im Kontext eines nationalen Gesundheitsinformationssystems. Neuchâtel, Bundesamt für Statistik (unpublished). http://www.m-spinatsch.ch/d/DetailsPublikationen/BFS-GES.html.

Spinatsch, M., and W. Weiss. (1999). Gesundheitsobservatorium Schweiz. Ergebnisse von Informationsgesprächen mit Verwal-tungsvertretern von Bund und Kantonen. Neuchâtel, Bundesamt für Statistik.

# 4

# Organizing Knowledge: Evidence and the Construction of Evaluative Information Systems

*Peter Dahler-Larsen*

> *"Design like science is a tool for understanding as well as a tool for acting."*
> Herbert Simon

### Introduction

This chapter is concerned with the construction of information systems designed to produce evidence-based data.

By an information system I mean a continuous stream of information that plays an integrated role in the functioning of an organization or a field of organizations. As examples of information systems, I think of systems that describe how to use performance indicators, how to run annual audits, or how to combine several evaluation methods in support of organizational learning and/or policy decision making. Information systems are complex and large scale. They cover hundreds of practitioners and thousands of incidents in a diversity of settings such as all hospitals in a country, elementary schools in different countries, or some other evaluand of a similar scope. Recently, we have witnessed an immense increase in the focus on such evaluative systems in policymaking (Stame, this volume), in public management (Rist, this volume), and in specific policy areas such as health or education (Cave, Hanney, Henkel, and Kogan, 1997).

An information system is a recipe for the selection, organization, and retention of large amounts of information. The design of the information system provides a structure that regulates how organizations select, organize, and retain what counts as knowledge. Although the subsequent use of such systems is, of course, interesting in itself, the focus here is on the very construction and design of information systems. As Herbert Simon (1981: 188) suggests in the opening quote, the design of an information system is also at the same time an attempt to understand what is being described. By their very design, evaluative information systems help define the meanings of the evaluand, the criteria of evaluative judgment, and the underlying policy problem. It is therefore important to study how information systems are constructed.

It is an important belief today that the principle of *evidence* should be of key concern in the construction of information systems. In place of uncertainty, evidence-based practices promise rationality and predictability (McLaughlin, 2001). With systematic evidence in hand, we can do away with conventional, unreflected, and sometimes prejudiced practices. The ambition in the concept of evidence is to qualify the production of information at a level above trivial social, ideological controversy, and political logrolling. The ideal embedded in the concept of evidence is one of information beyond dispute.

However, *how to organize an information system that produces information beyond dispute is not beyond dispute.* It is basic wisdom in the sociology of knowledge (Berger and Luckmann, 1966) that all information is relative to time and space. No knowledge is produced independent of social circumstance. Information systems require organization, financial support, political support, stakeholder participation, infrastructure, and legitimacy. Some evidence-oriented forms of knowledge are organizationally very demanding in terms of logistics and in terms of collegial governance (e.g., peer review, clinically controlled trials, and large statistical systems). No form of knowledge production is independent of ordinary social, organizational, and political worlds. Information systems are a function of an interplay between technical advances and political interests and agendas (Cave, Hanney, Henkel, and Kogan, 1997: 1). Information systems are, like evaluations (Weiss, 1983), political phenomena. In this perspective, the road to evidence may be contested all the way.

Nevertheless, today it is an important managerial task to proceed with the practical construction of information systems that are regarded as valid, reliable, trustworthy, and useful. This is done in different ways, each striking a different balance between the promise of uncontested knowledge and the sometimes contested ways in which this promise is attended to in various organizational and political realities.

What are some of the factors that need to be in place for an evidence-based information system to emerge? What are the problems that must be overcome or at least negotiated?

The difficulties in constructing evidence-based information systems will be illustrated with reference to two case stories about an indicator system and an accreditation system used in the Danish hospital sector. Both systems comprise several hospitals, many diagnoses, and hundreds of doctors and nurses. Both have survived the initial phases of construction. Both are competing to become part of a full-scale national information system for the whole health sector.

In the next section, I present different conceptual approaches to the construction of information systems. Next, I offer a list of factors that must somehow be in place for an evaluation system to be constructed. These factors make up the analytical grid for the presentation of the two case stories. I then analyze the different approaches to evidence revealed in the two cases. Finally, I discuss what can be learned from the case stories.

## Perspectives on the Construction of Information Systems

Each of the following three perspectives offers a broad and general model of how schemes for social knowledge (such as information systems) come about, and they also pinpoint different problems that any specific knowledge system will have to come to terms with. The three perspectives are outlined under the headlines of

- the logic of appropriateness in organizational behavior
- the social construction of knowledge

### Bounded Rationality

In a rational perspective, the benefits connected to the use of an information system (such as increased efficiency) should be carefully compared to the costs of building the system plus its potential downsides, such as irrelevant initiatives to score well on the stipulated evaluation criteria as well as the direction of organizational energy away from the search for new goals (March, 1995: 37). However, the costs and benefits of each step in the design of an information system are uncertain, and the choices made are very process-dependent (Simon, 1981: 151).

The real bottleneck under such conditions may not even be the lack of information about the consequences of various design alternatives, but rather the time and attention of the human decision makers involved (Simon, 1981:166). The resulting decision should be understood not in terms of optimizing, but should merely be "satisficing" and "defensible" (Simon, 1981:169). Any given information system may not be the absolutely optimal one, it may be the satisfying one given a number of earlier steps taken at any given point in time in the construction process.

The bounded rationality perspective does not suggest how the design of an information system may be influenced by social norms and values within a given "bounded" rationality. Neither does it highlight the interplay between different actors who may take part in the construction process, each with his/her own bounded rationality.

## The Logic of Appropriateness in Organizational Behavior

In contradistinction to conventional assumptions about goal-oriented organizational behavior, March and Olsen (1989) suggest that organizational forms and practices are often chosen because they are seen as appropriate within a given social set of norms, values, and expectations. While such a normative environment may be termed an organizational field (DiMaggio and Powell, 1991), the neo-institutional organizational theory suggests that any given organization within the field tends to comply with these expectations whether or not a given organizational practice adopted by the organization is actually of instrumental value. Such compliance often leads to isomorphism in any given organizational field. Isomorphism may be coercive, normative, or mimetic. In coercive isomorphism, organizations adopt a particular form or practice because powerful external actors or authorities in the field impose sanctions. In normative isomorphism, practices are adopted because they are enforced by groups with strong norms, such as professions. In mimetic isomorphism, practices are adopted because organizations seek to gain legitimacy and reduce uncertainty by imitating other organizations that are seen as prestigious. Information systems may be constructed because fashionable or organizational norms require that this is what respectable and modern organizations do at the moment (Røvik, 1998).

Finally, information systems may be used to build up social prestige. While the focus in this perspective is not on the "content" or the instrumental use of the evaluation system, the design of an information system (and its components such as methods, criteria, and problem-definitions) may be better understood as ritualized reflections of recipes, norms, values, and expectations floating around in fashionable organizational fields around the focal organization (Meyer and Rowan, 1977). Only a few contributions describe how individual organizations edit, redesign, or reinvent elements in organizational fields to make them fit better with individual organizational identities (Sahlin-Anderson, 1996).

Omitted from the neo-institutional perspective of organizational behavior is the dynamic interplay between different stakeholders with different worldviews and interests in the micro-political game of constructing an organizational element such as an information system. What it does highlight, however, is how important it is for the constructor of an information system to be signaling accordance with broader norms, values, and symbols in the organizational environment.

## The Social Construction of Knowledge

The branches of the sociology of knowledge that focus on scientific findings and technological innovations have made interesting contributions during the last twenty-five years. Knorr-Cetina (1981) and Latour (1987) have shown that scientific results and technological innovations are delicate achievements that owe their specific form to a large number of socially contingent factors. Necessary factors are not only infrastructure, finance, and the like, but also crucial support of key actors in decisive moments to relatively loosely structured ideas that only later turn out to become winning ideas. Sometimes a breakthrough is in the pipeline for years because an important factor is missing. A critical factor is thus the ability of key entrepreneurs to maintain a sufficient level of belief in the result among key supporters especially at times when a project otherwise appears to be substantially in trouble.

Along the way, finances, organizations, relations of trust, commitments, equipment, and key ideas are negotiated and renegotiated. Various stakeholders and institutions may stay on board for different reasons. Others are excluded or leave voluntarily. Social support is a key factor, and cannot be taken for granted.

The sociology of knowledge perspective suggests that the production of knowledge is not deterministically controlled, and there is no underlying mechanism that secures its automatic progress. Instead, any production of knowledge is tightly embedded in particular social contexts and depends on a highly contingent alignment of a number of factors. The element of timing is important, because no success is secure if all the necessary factors are not in place at the same time.

If an evaluation system succeeds, its reforming effect may have as much to do with connecting the interpretations and commitments of participants and audiences as with affecting effectiveness and efficiency (Brunsson and Olsen, 1993: 21). The meanings that different stakeholders attach to the information system, its overall functioning as well as its components, may be critical.

What the sociology of knowledge perspective suggests is that the construction of an information system is a delicate, socially embedded accomplishment. However, the perspective itself does not always suggest which factors more specifically are relevant for the design of a given system. In the following section, I offer a hypothetical list of factors that need to be in place for an information system to be constructed.

## Factors in the Construction of an Information System

Although the following list of such factors is not exhaustive, I argue that well-functioning information systems cannot ignore any of the factors. I shall present them here in hypothetical form and later demonstrate the actual role of each factor in the cases presented.

### Table 4.1
### Factors in the Construction of an Information System

(a) an organizational structural unit working for the system
(b) evaluation criteria
(c) information technology to handle the collection and retention of data
(d) a self-representation that explains the justification for the evaluation system
(e) sufficient social support of the following kinds
- financial support
- political support
- support among implementators of the system
- support from actors involved in actual data collection

(a) *An organizational structural unit working for the system.* Large-scale projects in organizational settings need to be organizationally anchored either in existing structures or in new structures designed for the purpose. They need such affiliation not only for manpower, but also for managerial attention and legitimacy. It is not insignificant how an information system is organizationally anchored. Its vertical position influences the access to top managers, politicians, and the like. Its horizontal position describes the type of organizational function, sectoral affiliation, and professional mindset with which the evaluation system is likely to be imprinted. The organizational affiliation of the system also influences how various stakeholders take positions in relation to the system. The evaluation system is likely to be received in the light of existing intra- and inter-organizational patterns of cooperation or conflict. In other words, the organizational-structural location of an evaluation system affects the design and content of the information system, its chances for successful implementation, and its survival.

(b) *Every evaluation system is based on certain evaluation criteria.* If common quality criteria are defined across substantially different areas of intervention, the criteria tend to standardize the interventions in such a way that only those aspects of quality that can be abstracted from the substance of each activity tend to get measured. Criteria rest on a certain definition of an underlying problem or question to be answered. While an evaluation system produces data, it also produces a mental framework with reference to which the data are relevant. Criteria tend to have a defining or "framing" effect on the evaluand. In this sense, information systems with evaluative information do as much to "construct definitions" of quality and performance as to monitor them (Shore and Wright, 1999: 570).

Examples of such underlying problem definitions are: "Are practices consistent with evidence-based procedures?" "What is the relation between resources and outputs?" "Is our country lagging behind other countries?" "How can we explain the variation between organizations?" "Is the lowest performance below politically acceptable standards?"

In an optimal situation, criteria lead to data that have an obvious interpretation (Cuenin, 1986: 10) However, since the choice of criteria is sometimes socially controversial, information systems need to define and defend a set of criteria or stipulate a legitimate procedure that leads to the selection of criteria. This is often where the principle of *evidence* enters the scene. The idea is that ideological controversy, political games, prejudice, and bias are removed or starkly reduced when the selection of evaluation criteria is evidence-based. At the same time, methodologies and criteria need to be manageable within existing limits defined by resources and social acceptability.

(c) *Information technology to handle the collection and retention of data.* It is sometimes forgotten how much our way of life in the information society depends on information technology. Most evaluation systems rely on computers, networks, software, etc. More specifically, the technology needs to be aligned with the social organization of the information system. For instance, data in different parts of an organizational field (or an organization) need to be processed in compatible formats. The technology providing access at all relevant knots in the network supporting the system needs to be in place. Therefore, evaluation systems sometimes struggle with resources to build up information-technological infrastructure; in addition, potential struggles over turfs and rights to data often manifest themselves as "practical" problems with information-technological infrastructure. (See Lee, this volume.)

(d) *A self-representation.* Information systems need to present a sort of "business philosophy" or "service declaration" to justify their existence and to explain why they should be supported. Sometimes evaluation systems seek to justify themselves with reference to a broad "lack of evaluation information." Sometimes organizational recipes such as evaluations connect to fashions in organization theory as well as to broader values such as accountability, rationality, justice (Meyer, Boli, and Thomas, 1994), or, perhaps in the most contemporary versions, merely to performativity (Lyotard, 1982).

Evaluation systems may also specify exact types of intended use, but more so a broad, poetic description of many possible uses, all positive, may offer the best strategy for public support. High and unspecific hopes for an information system may under some circumstances be optimal as a first step, because different internal and external stakeholders may have different reasons to support the system. These reasons may be politically motivated, but also purely functional, since the functions of an information system may be different in different parts and on different levels of an organizational structure (March, 1995: 135). The construction of an information system is—like most other political innovations—thus more likely to be oversold than undersold. The justification for an information system therefore sometimes takes the form of a broad and general optimistic belief in the good uses of rational information (Feldman and March, 1981).

While such philosophy may function internally as a sort of organizational auto-communication, sharpening attention and energy in the organization, supporting morale, high spirits, and belief in the future as well as in an organizational mission and identity (Broms and Gahmberg, 1983), the self-representation of an evaluation system may also be crucial in establishing a critical level of external support.

(e) *Social support.* Information systems are not built in isolation. Their practical design and functioning depends on various kinds of support. Information systems require a sufficient level of support from *political authority*. This is not only because they can be costly, but also because they can illustrate a need for reform or directly prepare the ground for political action. Another type of support necessary for an evaluation system is found among *implementers* of the system. Especially in complex, network-based, and highly differentiated policy fields, as well as in highly professionalized organizational settings, a common information system requires a comprehensive cooperation that cannot be issued by order of a hierarchical, bureaucratic organization. In this situation, the survival of the evaluation system depends on the knowledge, attitudes, and capacities of key implementers. Last, but not least, the support of *people delivering the data* to the evaluation system—professionals, users, clients, etc.—is crucial. If the quality of the input to the system is affected by a lack of belief in the value of the overall system, the overall credibility of the evaluation system may be in jeopardy.

My assumption is that any evaluation system will have to find a way to bring most if not all of these factors into alignment with each other. This is not necessarily an easy task, since support from all relevant partners may not be easily compatible with certain other choices of design, resources, and methodology. How it can be done in practical micropolitics in real-life contexts, depending on the interaction between managers, professionals, specialists, politicians, etc., should be studied empirically.

The following sections offer two case stories based on interviews and documents. Each exemplifies an approach to the complex, complicated, and by no means smooth construction of an information system. Each exemplifies a particular strategy concerning the principle of evidence. Each illustrates various pros and cons of that strategy.

## Case Stories

### Case I: The Accreditation Project

The Political Board of the hospitals in a major city decided that the hospitals should go through an accreditation process. The U.S.-based Joint Commission was contractually engaged to carry out the accreditation. The Joint Commission operates with about 360 criteria, presumably evidence-based criteria that are generally used in accreditation processes in hospitals in many countries. Nevertheless, the criteria carry a trace of their origins in time and space. An important *raison d'etre* of the Joint Commission is that accreditation is required by insurance companies to reimburse American hospitals for the costs of treating patients. For these reasons, the criteria focus very much on issues of risk and safety.

These criteria are generic across diagnoses and types of treatment. For this reason, many of the criteria were process-oriented, for example, checking whether the hospitals provided manuals for operating staff describing how to handle a number of incidents such as emergencies, etc. These criteria were not always seen as relevant in the Danish context. For example, some felt that while the U.S.-based consultants checked the ability of each hospital to prevent patients from gunshots and rape while in hospital, these criteria were less important in Denmark, because these guarantees are so rarely jeopardized in any hospital in Denmark. There is no variation on this variable. What is not included in the accreditation is also a matter of debate. Doctors criticize the accreditation process for not looking at issues such as training of young doctors. It is generally argued, however, that the beauty of the whole accreditation process lies exactly in the fact that no hospital can negotiate its own special version of the overall criteria.

To prepare for the accreditation process, the quality office provides courses for more than 600 staff members. As many become aware of the centrality of procedures and manuals covering various incidents, a high number of rules and procedures are put in place a few weeks before the accreditation. Staff members later reported in interviews that many of the procedures described in manuals were not adhered to in practice, partly due to lack of training among staff and lack of access to computers carrying the information necessary to implement certain procedures, etc. To enhance a focus on the most important standards a simple color-coding in materials describing the standards was introduced.

Other staff members reported during interview that there was quite an intense traffic of information from accredited wards to not-yet-accredited wards during the very process of accreditation. By this means, the latter were given last-minute information about how to prepare oneself for the visit of the accreditation team.

At one time, a newspaper cited staff members, especially former staff members, who undermined the credibility of the whole accreditation process by claiming that in some instances "facts" had been fabricated with the sole purpose of presenting a certain image of the hospital to the accreditation team. Some staff also argued it was unwise to spend large sums of money on accreditation when they lacked modern equipment necessary for treatment of patients.

Hospital management insisted that the accreditation process had been fair and reliable. No present staff members continued to claim the contrary. A survey among staff was carried out which revealed that 71 percent of the staff agreed or partly agreed that they were satisfied with the process of accreditation. This fact was used by management to justify the overall process. After a while the accreditation process was completed, and the political board decided to proceed with an accreditation schedule in the future. As a consequence thereof, the hospital system expects to produce about 25,000 procedural guidelines to meet the demands of accreditation in the future.

*Case II. The Indicator Project*

The National Indicator Project (NIP) was established in 1999 in cooperation with the Ministry of Health, the counties and the Copenhagen Hospitals, and a large number of professional organizations representing doctors, nurses, physiotherapists, etc. (Mainz, 2001: 6401). A steering group with representatives of all of these is responsible for planning, implementation, and evaluation of NIP (Ibid.: 6406). All central stakeholders in the health sector are said to be represented in the project (Ibid.: 6406).

The overall aim of the project is to develop a set of evidence-based quality indicators that can ultimately be used to measure and compare all treatments by all hospitals in Denmark. In several sources of information such as a newsletter (NIP Newsletter 1, Sept. 2001), NIP emphasizes that indicators and standards are to be developed on the basis of available scientific evidence.

Among the goals for NIP are the opportunity to have a qualified comparison among hospital units and hospitals, a qualified set of references for a dialogue between politicians and professionals, and development of the quality of the services (Mainz, 2001: 6406). A comprehensive plan is developed for how criteria are to be selected, how data should be produced, how predictive variables should be collected and used to adjust for variations in case mix, how data are to be interpreted, how feedback is made available for each hospital ward, how the results go through an audit process, and how data are finally made publicly available (Ibid.: 6402).

A central part of NIP is the determination of criteria and standards for good practice. These standards "are determined on the basis of scientific literature to secure maximum evidence. If scientific evidence is not available...the standards will be set on the basis of consensus among competent clinicians" (Ibid.: 6401). For each disease (diagnosis), five to eight indicators are to be determined (Ibid.: 6401).

In the first phase of the project, six diagnoses and four counties for each diagnosis were selected for a pilot study.

The operational work with indicators took place in indicator groups. These were planned to consist of nine to fifteen representatives from all relevant health professions in relation to each diagnosis (NIP Manual, 2004: 5). The representatives were selected based on merits and competence. The selection took place in cooperation with the professional societies. Staff members were allotted to each group. The role of the staff was to secure the scientific evidence available for the group, to manage the group process, and to make sure that all decisions made by the group were documented (Ibid.: 7). The staff produces a first draft of indicators based on scientific literature. These are rated according to the quality of the evidence supporting each indicator. For example, grade A means that an indicator is supported by a randomized clinical trial. In a later phase, each member of the group rates the different criteria according to practical feasibility and importance (Ibid.: 14). This rating takes place anonymously by each member of the group (Ibid.: 15). The idea behind this is to make sure that "all members of the group participate with weight in the decision-making process" (Ibid.: 15).

The practical feasibility supposedly depends on whether existing data are available or whether new data can be produced within realistic limits (Ibid.: 14). The criteria for importance are to be "scientific evidence or indisputable professional consensus" (Ibid.: 14).

The group then discusses each indicator and the members again rank the indicators anonymously. In the subsequent determination of the criteria, the indicators and standards can be decided on the basis of group consensus provided that scientific evidence is not available and provided that the issue is rated "important."

The criteria are then sent to computer specialists, who prepare the systems for registration of data. While the long-term goal is a web-based on-line registration of all relevant data, the technological infrastructure for this process was not always in place during the pilot project. Since the Danish hospitals are owned by the counties, there is no formal requirement of a common registration system. As an interim solution, the relevant data for four of the six diagnoses are brought to NIP on paper.

## Analysis

The two cases will now be analyzed using the factors presented earlier as an analytical grid. First of all, the *organizational-structural location* of the unit responsible for the implementation of the information system is different. In the accreditation case, an internal office is given a clear political mandate to go forward with the acquisition of an accreditation. In the indicator case, the office is but one office in one county, and thus it cannot command hospitals in other counties to participate.

Although there was *political support* in both cases, only in the accreditation project was the office carrying the torch directly authorized by the same administrative and political structure in which the participating units were enclosed. The political and managerial determination to move forward on the issue is unquestioned. In the indicator project, the political support comes from a more remote association of counties, which means that the office carrying the related relates to the participating hospitals in a less hierarchical way.

These factors influence the *technological infrastructure* undergirding each of the systems. It is a clear strength of the accreditation process that once it is formally completed and the report from the accrediting agency is delivered, the data are also "in the box." In other words, when an accreditation was bought, the necessary structure of data collection was bought at the same time. Not so in the indicator project. Although the indicator groups were asked to take into account the feasibility of data collection based on the stipulated criteria, there were substantial problems in the subsequent data collection phases since there was no common and efficient computerized platform for the on-line registration of the necessary data. There is no central structure in the Danish public sector that authoritatively commands the individual counties to comply with specific standards in terms of, say, software platforms, etc. In other words, the office responsible for the indicator system was not in a position to authoritatively structure the information technology necessary for the implementation of the project. The fact that some data in the initial phases of the indicator projects have to be delivered on paper is thus not a good sign for the overall image of the project.

The two cases reveal distinctly different approaches to *criteria-setting*. In the accreditation project, the evaluation criteria are externally generated generic criteria covering all diagnoses. There is a focus on manuals, procedures, good practices for hospital management, and the like. The criteria have been developed by the accreditation agency, which takes responsibility for the evidence-based nature of the criteria.

In the indicator project, specific indicators were crafted for each diagnosis. This was a demanding process since each group of experts had to go through the total process of identifying, discussing, and selecting specific indicators. An elaborate set of rules was followed in order to come up with a limited number of indicators for each diagnosis. Although the international literature was consulted, it could be argued that the resulting set of indicators had a specific Danish flavor to them originating from this local process.

A critical difference in the delineation of evidence-based indicators is thus that in the accreditation case, evidence was imported into the scene from abroad, whereas in the indicator project, the evidence-based indicators were crafted in the national project itself.

The non-negotiable nature of the terms of the whole accreditation process, of course, provides it with an air of objectivity and neutrality, if not "evidence." However, it was exactly the unmodified import of indicators in the accreditation project that made many feel that many of the indicators were of limited relevance in the Danish context. In addition, the decision to commence the accreditation project was a top-down process and the terms of the accreditation projects were non-negotiable.

This was not so in the indicator project. This project was based on local identification of specific evaluation criteria. Elaborate rules were set up to protect minorities in the indicator groups from being "bullied" and to prevent particular interests from dominating the process (although organized interests representing the views of patients were not included). In the end, the principle of scientific evidence does not in all cases determine the full set of indicators; in addition, group consensus has a role to play, and sometimes the resulting set of criteria seems to be a good compromise showing what the indicator group is able to support in toto, rather than a strict set of highly ranking scientific evidence-based criteria. It should also be remembered that the consensus-oriented approach came up with criteria that could not be supported with existing technological infrastructure. In other words, the price for consensus was low practical feasibility.

These two strategies towards evidence-based criteria—import versus local consensus—probably led to varying degrees of *support from staff in the individual units where the systems became implemented.*

Some doctors spoke up against the accreditation project, and in a few extreme situations some staff even in newspapers questioned the "fabricated" nature of the procedures presented to the accreditation team. This shows the vulnerability of a top-down approach to the implementation of externally imported criteria in a complex organization, although, of course, the accreditation was completed in the end.

In the indicator project, support from doctors and nurses was ensured through their organizational representation in the indicator groups. In addition, hospital wards participated in the initial phases of the indicator project on a voluntary basis. The indicator project did not run into the types of opposition that were expressed so openly in the accreditation project.

However, the self-representation of each of the systems remained intact in both cases. The fact that there was an element of local negotiation, which did not always lead to optimal evidence, did not prevent the indicator project from emphasizing its rigorously evidence-based philosophy. Neither did the fact that some participating staff openly questioned the validity of the accreditation procedure have any impact on the alleged evidence-based approach to accreditation. Both projects continued to present themselves as "evidence-based" without further qualification.

## Conclusion and Implications

It is not evident how to arrive at evidence-based criteria. Managers involved in the construction of evaluative information systems make compromises between a number of factors that must be in place to secure the construction of an evaluative information system. The perspective on the construction of knowledge presented here—that all such construction is socially and organizationally embedded and requires the interaction of many factors to move forward—does not imply that the construction of evaluative information systems is "irrational" or illegitimate in any way, nor that the socially produced knowledge does not count as knowledge (Longino, 2002). It merely suggests that the construction of an evidence-based information system is not always taking place solely in the way suggested by its own self-understanding.

The two cases suggest that there are different organizational approaches to the delineation of evidence. The distinction between imported vs. locally produced "evidence-based" evaluation criteria is a central distinction. None of them are without problems. Even apparently untouchable imported criteria require the loyal compliance, if not commitment, of the local people who deliver the "raw data" describing their own practices vis-à-vis the external evaluators. The resistance towards the project—which expresses itself as a delegitimation of the project by some in the media—is probably partly due to the non-negotiable character of the accreditation process and the criteria. On the other hand, the locally produced criteria may have a less convincing aura of objectivity, but they score higher on local acceptability. This may be a strength not only for the implementation of the system, but also for its larger legitimacy, although technically speaking there remains a rhetorical distance between its focus on the principle of evidence and negotiable and consensus-based approach to the delineation of such evidence.

Each approach to evidence signifies different combinations of the factors necessary for the design of an information system. Evidence is a discursive product whose meaning is constructed with reference to particular frameworks, technologies, and social relationships (McLaughlin, 2001: 354). Evidence is more socially embedded, is more up to organizational support and resources, requires more practical skills and attention to social circumstances, and provides less certainty to its users than often believed (Beck, 1992: chap. 7).

A further implication is that the perspective on construction of information systems presented in this chapter encourages us to expand our focus on what we usually call "the evaluator." Conventionally, behind an evaluation is an evaluator whom we think of as responsible for the rationale that leads to the design of an evaluation. Also the wider normative and ethical ramifications of evaluation are believed to be anchored in the evaluator (as a legal and ethical person). However, evaluative information systems are anchored in complex organizational settings and extend so much in time and space that the responsibility for the system cannot necessarily be personalized, and there is no guarantee that "evaluators" have a major role to play in the design of information systems (in which, by the way, evaluative information may not be clearly distinct from other types of information). Instead, an information system is likely to be an abstractly organized and often negotiated function of the interaction between, say, managers, experts, professionals, consultants, politicians, and various organizational departments if not several institutions. At stake may be different worldviews, interests, and a complicated game of influence. What we conventionally expect in methodological and moral terms from a personal evaluator cannot automatically be extended to this larger anonymous social and organizational configuration. This is just one of the things we have to reconsider as we move our focus from singular evaluation studies to organized information systems.

## References

Beck, Ulrich. (1992): *Risk Society*. London: Sage.
Berger, Peter, and Thomas Luckmann. (1966). *The Social Construction of Reality*. New York: Anchor Books.
Broms, Henri, and Henrik Gahmberg. "Communication to Self in Organizations and Cultures." *Administrative Science Quarterly* 28 (1983): 482–495.
Brunsson, Nils, and Johan P. Olsen. (1993). *The Reforming Organization*. New York: Routledge.
Cave, Martin, Stephen Hanney, Mary Henkel, and Maurice Kogan. (1997). *The Use of Performance Indicators in Higher Education*, 3rd ed. London: Jessica Kingsley Publishers.
Cuenin, S. (1986). International Study of the Development of Performance Indicators in Higher Education. Paper given to OECD, IMHE project, Special Topic Workshop.
DiMaggio, Paul J. and Walter W. Powell. (1991). "The Iron Cage Revisited: Institutional Isomorphism and Collective Rationality in Organization Fields." In Walter W. Powell and Paul J. DiMaggio, eds., *The New Institutionalism in Organizational Analysis* (63–82). Chicago: The University of Chicago Press.
Feldman, Martha, and James G. March. "Information as Signal and Symbol." *Administrative Science Quarterly* 26 (1981): 171–184.
Goldenberg, Edie N. "The Three Faces of Evaluation." *Journal of Policy and Management* 2 (1983): 515–525.
Knorr-Cetina, Karin. (1981). *The Manufacture of Knowledge*. Oxford: Pergamon Press.
Latour, Bruno. (1987). *Science in Action: How to Follow Scientists and Engineers Through Society*. Cambridge, MA: Harvard University Press.
Longino, Helen E. (2002). *The Fate of Knowledge*. Princeton, NJ: Princeton University Press.
Lyotard, Jean-Francois. (1982). *Viden og Det Postmoderne Samfund* [La Condition Postmoderne]. Århus: Sjakalen.
Mainz J., P. Bartels, S. Laustsen, T. Jorgensen, A. M. Thulstrup, A. Linneberg, and T. Thomsen. "The National Indicator Project for Monitoring and Improvement of Core Health Care Services." *Weekly Journal for Doctors* 2001: 163: 6401-6406.
March, James G. (1995). *Fornuft og Forandring*. Copenhagen: Samfundslitteratur.
March, James G., and Johan P. Olsen. (1989). *Rediscovering Institutions*. New York: Free Press.
McLaughlin, Janice. "EBM and Risk. Rhetorical Resources in the Articulation of Professional Identity." *Journal of Management in Medicine* 15 (5) (2001): 352–363.
Meyer, John, John Boli, and George M. Thomas. (1994). "Ontology and Rationalization in the Western Cultural Account." In W. Richard Scott and John W. Meyer, eds., *Institutional Environments and Organizations* (9–27). Thousand Oaks, CA: Sage.
Meyer, John, and Brian Rowan. "Formal Structure as Myth and Ceremony." *American Journal of Sociology* 83 (1977): 340–363.

National Indicator Project (NIP) for Measurement and Improvement of Core Health Care Services: Manual for the Work Process in the Indicator Groups. The Coordinating Secretariat: 2004. Available at: www.nip.dk

Røvik, Kjell-Arne. (1998). *Moderne Organisasjoner*. Bergen-Sandviken: Fagbokforlaget.

Sahlin-Anderson, K. (1996). "Imitating by Editing Success: The Construction of Organizational Fields." In B. Czarniawska and G. Sevon, eds., *Translating Organizational Change* (313–326). Berlin: de Gruyter.

Shore, Cris, and Susan Wright. "Audit Culture and Anthropology: Neo-Liberalism in British Higher Education." *Journal of the Royal Anthropological Institute* 5 (1999): 557–575.

Simon, Herbert A. (1981). *The Sciences of the Artificial*. Cambridge, MA: The MIT Press.

Weiss, Carol H. (1983). "Evaluation Research in the Political Context." In Elmer L. Struering and Marilyn B. Brewer, eds., *Handbook of Evaluation Research* (31–45). Beverly Hills, CA: Sage.

# 5

# Managing Evaluations in the Netherlands and Types of Knowledge*

*Frans L. Leeuw*

### Not Much Organizational Learning Typical for the Dutch Central Government?

In March 2003, the Algemene Rekenkamer (Netherlands Audit Office) published the report: "Between Policy and Implementation; Lessons from Recent Evaluations." The report summarized some twenty-five studies done by the office between 1997 and 2002. It looked into the question of what the (central) government has learned from these studies, conclusions, and recommendations. The Audit Office analyzed the "gap" between policy formulation and implementation. Topics were amongst others juvenile delinquency, food safety, enculturation of immigrants, vulnerable pupils, and the reintegration into society of disabled workers.

The conclusions were as follows:

- implementation of policy programs is often not according to the intentions and goals of the programs;
- information within the ministries about the implementation is often lacking;
- information about the effectiveness of the policies is lacking too.

The National Audit Office explained these findings by pointing to four factors:

---

* Thanks to Frans Janssens, University of Twente/Inspectorate for Education and Edward Kleemans (WODC Den Haag) for earlier comments. Thanks also to Melanie Ehren Ma (Ph.D. candidate, University of Twente) for allowing me to make use of certain parts of her dissertation in progress.

- inadequate preparation of policy programs;
- too much focus on policymaking, and too little focus on implementation;
- insufficient attention for evaluation, accountability, and cost-benefit analysis;
- apparent incapability to learn from lessons from the recent past.

In the media the report was quoted as confirming the thesis that Dutch (central) government is a bad learner.

## Is It Really That Bad?

Is the situation in the Netherlands as bad as it looks? Not necessarily. Compared to the late 1970s, there has been a clear increase in audits, evaluations, inspections, policy analysis, and policy studies in the Netherlands. New inspectorates, regulators, and local audit offices have been established. More studies have been carried out ever since. Did not the Algemene Rekenkamer during the early 1990s annually count some 100 evaluation studies? Now over a thousand can easily be detected. This figure only refers to studies regarding central government and a number of quangos (Algemene Rekenkamer, 2000; 2002). Recently, an advisory committee of the government (RMO, 2003) referred to the "measurement industry" as a characteristic now typical of the Netherlands and pointed at unintended and negative side effects of this development. A Dutch political scientist described the increased number and intensity of evaluations, audits, and parliamentarian investigations in terms of the "inquisition democracy."[1] Civil servants and heads of quangos and agencies are more and more scrutinized by audits and evaluations.

Also, over the last decade increased attention has been paid to the organizational infrastructure for evaluations inside departments. This has been done largely following suggestions of the Algemene Rekenkamer.

Results from the Rekenkamer's government-wide audits on the effectiveness of subsidies, public information campaigns, the evaluation infrastructure, inspectorates, compliance with laws, quangos, and licenses have played a role in the design and development of the infrastructure for evaluation, accountability, and transparency of central government (Leeuw and Rozendal 1994; Leeuw 2000). Major changes in the Budget and Accounting Act, prescribing every policy program to be evaluated every five years, have been taken seriously partly due to recommendations by the Rekenkamer. The implementation of a government-wide accountability approach, similar to the Government Performance and Results Act,[2] has led to the articulation of some 400 goals of the central government. Annual reports summarize the progress made.

Longitudinal data about developments in domains like criminal justice, education, health, welfare, and well-being are collected and reported every two years by the Social & Cultural Planning Bureau, together with streams of data about among others the quality of schools and hospitals (Educational and Health Inspectorates). They play an important role in assessing current policies, developing new policies, and "checking" implementation.

Customizing statistical data by the Central Bureau for Statistics, including online facilities to make one's "own" tables, charts, and graphs, completes this picture. The increased attention of Parliament for (empirical) inquiries of social problems and policy "fiasco" should not be forgotten.

### Different Perspectives...How Come?

The characterization given by the national audit office therefore represents only *one point of view*. Others are more positive about the level of learning of the Dutch government vis-à-vis the stream of data and studies now available. In mid-2003, a conflict arose between the Ministry of Finance and the Algemene Rekenkamer related to this topic.[3] The Ministry of Finance accused the auditors of not having an eye for what was accomplished with regard to accountability, evaluation, and oversight. The minister also accused the auditors of producing negative energy; instead of stressing the cumulativeness of data-collection, analysis, and reporting the auditors continued to stress what had not been achieved. Others raise the point that the framework the auditors work with (focusing on accountability arrangements in particular) helps to produce a "measurement industry" that only in a restricted sense is directed towards explaining and solving social and policy problems. Audit work has become a world of its own, according to the Raad voor de Maatschappelijke Ontwikkeling (RMO, 2000; 2002). This characterization resembles Mike Power's concept of auditing as a "ritual of verification" (Power, 1999). Authors like Van der Knaap (2003), Van Hoesel (2003), and Leeuw and Rozendal (1994) stress the other line of reasoning. They make clear that the production of substantive knowledge about trends in society, impacts of policy programs and explanations, has clearly stimulated organizational learning in the public sector.

The hypothesis I want to explore here is that these divergent views largely stem from the different types of evaluative knowledge that are produced in the Netherlands.

### Types of Knowledge and Evaluation

Types of knowledge are getting more attention from the evaluation community. Nutley and Davies (2003) distinguish between five types of (evaluative) knowledge, varying between:

- knowledge about problems
- knowledge about what works
- knowledge how to put it into practice
- knowledge who to involve and
- knowledge why.

Barzelay (1996) in a survey of OECD countries identified seven different types of performance audits, including four main types: efficiency audits, effectiveness audits, performance management capacity audits and performance information audits. Schwartz and Mayne (2004) make a distinction between (program) evaluations produced by organizations, programs, and researchers; public performance reports produced by organizations; and performance audits produced by external audit offices, and reports by public inspectorates.

In line with earlier work ( Leeuw, 1998), I distinguish between two types of evaluative knowledge:

- Knowledge about organizational (pre)requisites, conditions, and procedures like "planning and control" devices and management information systems inside the public sector that are believed to be important if one wants to realize effective and efficient (public) policies;
- Substantive or explanatory knowledge about mechanisms within society that make policies work (or not) and that are assumed to be of relevance to realize effective and efficient (public) policies. This type of knowledge is focused on what makes policy programs and interventions work and in which contexts. Examples are knowledge about the effectiveness of public information campaigns, and why "naming, shaming and blaming" of criminals, low-quality schools, and hospitals (Pawson 2002) are effective (and when not); and how generic policy instruments like subsidies work.

Put (2005) recently has reconstructed the types of norms and knowledge implied in the work done by the U.K. National Audit Office and the Algemene Rekenkamer and found a similar result.

## Objectives of the Chapter

The chapter first describes the type of knowledge produced by the Algemene Rekenkamer when it carries out its performance audits and evaluations. Next, the underlying theory of these activities is articulated. Then, the type of knowledge produced by two other evaluation institutes is described and articulated in terms of the underlying theory. It regards the Inspectorate for Education and the Ministry of Justice's Research, Statistics & Information Center (WODC). Here also the underlying program theory of both organizations will be reconstructed. Finally, the question is addressed as to what the relationship is between types of evaluative knowledge and utilization and learning. In terms of methodology, this chapter presents theory-driven case studies of three knowledge institutes in the Netherlands.

## Type of Knowledge Produced by the National Audit Office

*Background*

The National Audit Office is several hundreds years old. Nowadays, some 325 people are employed by the organization. Besides an Annual Report, approximately thirty performance audits are published annually. They look into many different topics and organizations. An important instrument that stimulated performance audits and internal evaluations by ministries is the Office's government-wide investigations into policy instruments: subsidies, levies, information campaigns, laws, covenants/soft laws, licensees, and contracts. A government-wide study on the evaluation infrastructure was published in 1990. It described the ways in which evaluations were carried out by the departments; which results were used; how much public money was involved; who was responsible for the studies and the results; and what were the intended follow-ups. In this investigation (Mulder et al. 1991; Leeuw & Rozendal, 1994) it was concluded that the evaluation function inside government was underdeveloped. Immediately after this (devastating) report, central government declared its intention to issue legislation on evaluations and accountability. Many activities were implemented, which, among others have led to what is now called "a measurement industry" (RMO 2002:24).

### Type of knowledge produced

Three studies (Bemelmans-Videc 1998; Leeuw 1998; Leeuw & Crijns 2005) analyzed the type of evaluative knowledge produced by the National Audit office. Bemelmans-Videc analyzed some fifty studies carried out between the late 1980s and mid-1990s, this author analyzed a dozen between 1996 and 1998; and Leeuw & Crijns (2005) recently added several more.

These studies do reveal the underlying assumptions ('program theory') of the National Audit Office when analyzing the implementation and effectiveness of policy programs and instruments. Examples of this program theory follow (Leeuw, 1998; Leeuw & Crijns, 2004).[4]

The audit office gathers information about policy development, implementation, and effectiveness largely through analyzing documents, including interoffice material. It also interviews civil servants. Sometimes a more social science oriented type of data collection takes place, for example, when persons holding licenses are being interviewed.

The program theory of the organization focuses largely[5] on organizational mechanisms like:

- information systems,
- coordination,
- cost-benefit analysis,

**PROGRAM THEORY:**

When a governmental actor (i.e. Ministry, agency, or quango) complies with laws and rules when developing and implementing a policy (program, intervention, or tool)

**and**

when this actor takes care of the ministerial responsibility for these activities

**and**

when the policy this actor is implementing is underpinned, testable, planned, and is "optimal"

**and**

when this actor has carried out a cost-benefit analysis prior to implementing the policy

**and**

when this actor has installed independent procedural arrangements and processes to evaluate the effectiveness and efficiency of this policy

**and**

when this actor has installed management-information systems

**and**

when this actor has informed Parliament about the policy,

**and**

when this actor is a "learning agent,"

**and**

when this actor is communicating with the groups /peoples/ organizations that are the "object" of the policy with a focus on creating commitment,

**and**

when this policy is being coordinated,

**and**

when this policy is socially acceptable as well as accepted by stakeholders

**and**

when regional differences with regard to policy implementation are taken into account

**and**

when governmental ministries have some degree of freedom with regard to implementation,

--------------→ **then**, as a consequence, this policy will be effective and efficient.

- planning,
- documentary evidence, and
- audit trails.

Not much attention is paid to the contexts of policy-making processes in different policy domains or under different policy regimes. Neither is attention paid to assumptions underlying different programs, or to possible side-effects these organizational prerequisites can have. Given the literature on "effects pervers" of audit(-oriented) information (Power, 1999; Leeuw, 2000) and given the incentives at work when audit type information is high on the agenda, the possibility of a performance paradox occurring could have been addressed but isn't.

Increasingly, studies like Meyer & Gupta (1994), Smith (1995), Leeuw (1998), Ghoshal and Moran (1996), RMO (2000; 2002), Van Thiel & Leeuw (2003) and Behn (2003) show that focusing on knowledge about procedural and organizational aspects of policy making and implementation does not at all guarantee producing (explanatory) knowledge about the impact of policies within society. Being knowledgeable about management information systems, audit trails, and "planneability" of policies is no guarantee for an effective implementation of policies. Research has shown that other factors such as:

- the underlying program theory;
- leadership of public sector organizations;
- public choice type mechanisms (bureaucratic back scratching, sunk costs, etc.);
- attitudes and cultures inside bureaucracy; and
- trust and commitment

are at least as important as the administrative-procedural factors that form the focus of the National Audit Office.

## Type of Knowledge Produced When Evaluating the Quality of Education and the Effectiveness of Criminal Justice Programs

*Background*

Both education and criminal justice were among the topics the National Audit Office studied in its report "Between Policy and Implementation" (2003). With regard to crime prevention the auditors concluded that "information about personnel consequences of policy decisions in this field is lacking." Also, more information should become available regarding the processes and its consequences in the chain of actors within the administration of justice.

With regard to education the audit office looked into the implementation of policies regarding vulnerable pupils. It concluded that it would take until

2006 before (all) the information on these pupils could be collected. This information is believed to be necessary in order to assess the impact of the policy designed to improve the quality of primary and secondary schools and to reduce the number of school dropouts.

Within the executive branch of the Netherlands government, though at some arms' length, there are several organizations collecting and analyzing data about these and other topics. I now look into the type of evaluative knowledge two of these organizations produce. One organization is the Dutch Inspectorate for Education, which looks into the quality of Dutch primary and secondary schools, the vocational education institutes and—to some extent—universities and polytechnics. It is over 200 years old; it employs some 500 people.

The other is the Research, Statistics and Information Center of the Ministry of Justice (WODC). It is almost fifty years old.[6] It evaluates policy instruments, programs, and organizations of the Justice department and other judiciary actors (like prisons). But it also looks into the effectiveness of policies regarding immigrants, asylum seekers, and their social integration. Statistical analysis and forecasts are amongst the core activities of the institute. Some 100 people are employed by the center, which is semi-independent (which means that reports are published independently from the Ministry and under the sole responsibility of the Center). See for more information: www.onderwijsinspectie.nl; and www.wodc.nl.

I first look into the Education Inspectorate and at the knowledge produced there.

During the last decade, the Inspectorate had the following functions:

- The first function is to provide a public account of the quality of education in order to enable stakeholders to use valid, reliable, and independently produced information on quality. The criteria used are derived from (governmental) documents and from studies of educational scientists and experts in the field of quality assessment. Draft versions of the lists of criteria are discussed with stakeholders, including labor unions, employers' organizations, societies of teachers, and heads of schools, etc.
- The second function is to check compliance with the rules and regulations that have been set for schools.
- The third function is to provide a starting point for improvement and development. This so-called "stimulating supervision" requests that the inspectorate disseminate knowledge about quality, quality care, and good practices.
- The fourth function is to produce (macrolevel) benchmark reports.

According to Van Bruggen (2003), the objects of the Inspectorate are threefold:

- The level of the individual pupil, student, teacher;
- The level of the individual school; and
- The level of the educational system at the regional or provincial or national level.

For reasons of space I focus only on the second level, the individual school level. Here an important activity of the Inspectorate is to uncover important differences in quality among schools. This forms the background of the development of (self-) evaluations produced by schools. In the Netherlands the production of self-evaluations is either obliged or indicated by law. The Educational Inspectorate reviews these self-evaluations. But it also collects information directly by means of school and classroom visits at the level of operations and activities inside schools, e.g., on learning results; on the pedagogical climate in class; and on social relationships between schools, parents, and pupils.

Van Bruggen (2003) mentions three goals of the evaluations of the Inspectorate. One goal is "to help the parents (or students in senior secondary schools or further and higher education) in their decisions about school choice and in their involvement in parent committees, other groups around schools and in governing the schools." The second goal is "the stimulation of the autonomy of the individual school and its quality and quality care." A third goal is "to inform authorities—school boards, regional /local authorities, the Minister of Education and Parliament about the quality of the school(s) in order to enable these actors to take measures, in particular if the quality is below expected or prescribed standards."

Annually, in addition to (thousands of individual) school reports the Inspectorate publishes its (macrolevel) Report on the State of Education in the Netherlands, in which information is given on trends and developments regarding the country. It summarizes evaluations and studies done by this office and by others. Partly on behalf of this report, the Inspectorate is involved in many evaluations, ranging from assessing the impact of ICT in schools and personnel policies to questions dealing with the validity of examinations and the quality of assessments in higher education. The Inspectorate carries out its own data collection by analyzing (legal) documents, visiting schools, interviewing school heads and teachers, and, though to a lesser extent, through interviewing parents and pupils/students. It is also involved in observations of teaching quality in practice. Next to that large amounts of (administrative and behavioural science) data from other sources like the Central Bureau for Statistics, the student loans Bank, and many others[7] are used. For some years now, the Inspectorate has developed an infrastructure for this type of work, including data warehouse facilities.[8]

Though incomplete, central parts of the program theory underlying the Inspectorate's work comprise the following statements.[9]

**PROGRAM THEORY:**

The more the Inspectorate evaluates the compliance of schools with rules and legislation, the more these schools will guarantee a basic level of education, and the more they will live up to these standards;

and

the more the inspectorate evaluates the quality of education, the more schools will realize added value to the pupils;

and

*the more the inspectorate stresses self-evaluations of schools, discusses the norms & standards with stakeholder-inspectees and only collects data* on site *when and if self-evaluations do*

-not exist

-are of insufficient quality or

-reveal problems with regard to the quality of education,

the larger will be the likelihood that schools will realize added value to pupils;

and

the more the inspectorate uses the results of other M and E types of activity (like evaluating the impact ICT has on teachers, pupils, and curriculum or like assessing the personnel policies of school managers), the larger the impact of the Inspectorate;

and

when the inspectorate publishes the (annual) school quality review and quality cards to the public in a printed and in a digital version, the more parents, pupils, and stakeholders (incl. Government) will take notice of this information;

the more they do so, the more schools will pay attention to the quality of education and the more schools will take care that added value to parents, pupils, and others is realized;

and

the more parents have knowledge about the quality of education, the more they will use this information in discussions with the school;

the more parents do discuss this topic, the more schools will try to improve the quality of education;

and

the more the Inspectorate formulates recommendations how to improve the quality of education, the more schools will take notice of these recommendations and the more they will take care that added value is realized;

and

> *when the inspectorate also publishes its* macro level report on the state of the art of Dutch education *on line and in a printed version (both reader-friendly) in which topics of high societal relevance are discussed, the more the inspectorates will realize that parents, pupils, and others in society trust that Dutch education is of adequate quality;*
>
> **and**
>
> the more the inspectorate carries out
>
> -compliance studies/audits/inspections,
>
> -school quality evaluations,
>
> -other (ICT-type) evaluations, and
>
> - macrolevel state of the art studies,
>
> ---------→ **then**
>
> the more policy makers and politicians will take notice of the Inspectorate's report and will use the results; the same is true with regard to society itself, schools, school employers, etc.

This reconstruction makes clear that the primary focus of this organization is to produce substantive knowledge about educational quality and compliance with rules and regulations by schools. It does so by evaluating self-evaluation reports, but also through primary data collection at the level of schools. Also, use is made of existing databases.

### Type of Knowledge Produced at the Research, Evaluation and Information Center of the Ministry of Justice (WODC)

This center began in 1949 as a bureau for documentation and information diffusion. Since the early 1970s it has developed into a center for social science research, evaluation studies, policy analysis, and statistics. It looks not only into topics of criminal justice but also into administrative laws, immigration policies, social cohesion of minorities, quality of laws, and other institutional aspects of the Justice Ministry and its partners. Annually, some ninety studies are carried out. One-third are carried out by in-house researchers and evaluators, two-thirds by others (universities and not-for profit) institutions that are commissioned by the Center.

There are several focal programs of the institute. They are largely developed on the basis of needs and discussions with actors related to or being part of the Justice ministry and its partners. However, developments within the social and legal sciences are also input to the program.

One focal program is the monitoring and evaluation of organized crime, another is the monitoring and evaluation of the effectiveness of criminal justice interventions. A third concerns the effectiveness of aliens policies and policies on persons requesting asylum, including the integration of these persons into society. Developments regarding civil law, such as mediation and legal aid, are also topics of a focal program.

In addition to these focal programs, there is longitudinal and infrastructural research largely comprising large-scale datasets enabling the institute to produce quick scans when needed, but also more fundamental knowledge. All-sources analysis is crucial here. The goal of infrastructural research is to make information available to policy makers, and to other actors on the basis of large-scale, up-to-date databases. To give one example: the *monitor on recidivism* (also called the Offender's Index) is a crucial instrument for research. It came into existence in the mid-1990s. It contains complete criminal histories and is complete for all persons that were prosecuted since 1997. The database is updated every three months and is historical in nature: there are no removals. In addition to its contributions to answering descriptive questions (who are repeat players, who not, what are the characteristics?) this monitor is important for assessing the effectiveness of intervention programs.

The Center is involved in coordinating program evaluations specifically related to the Dutch version of the GPRA, called VBTB. The central element is the articulation of policy goals, instruments, operationalizations, and policy impacts. These are measured on an annual basis. One of the characteristics of VBTB is its focus on growth, allowing departments to annually improve on the quality and quantity of the information available and the impact realized. The Center assists in these activities, uses its data sources, and carries out some of the evaluations under its own guidance.

Although incomplete, central parts of the program theory underlying the Inspectorate's work, were comprised of the following statements.

The focus of the Justice Research Center is to produce largely *substantive knowledge*. Empirical studies, data-based analyses, forecasts, research reviews, and knowledge transfer activities are part and parcel of the institute, both ex post and ex ante. To combine the different knowledge bases into chains of knowledge (Leeuw, 2004) is one of the more recent activities.

## Conclusions: On the relationship between Types of Evaluative Knowledge and Utilization and Learning

We found that despite the many years of stressing the importance of procedural arrangements on evaluation, auditing, inspection, and supervision by the national audit office, and the compliance with these recommendations by the Dutch executive, the audit office is of the opinion that *the executive is not a good learner.* As an almost logical consequence, the auditors go for more procedural rules, more arrangements, more activities...and more procedural knowledge.

> **PROGRAM THEORY:**
>
> When during the selection process of topics to be evaluated by the center explicitly attention is paid to the ideas, desires, and needs of policy makers and partners of the Justice ministry,
>
> **and**
>
> when there are dialogues between policy makers, politicians, and evaluators about the topics (not including the methodology) that will be evaluated,
>
> **and**
>
> when evaluations are carried out on matters regarding questions of compliance with rules and regulations/policies as well as processes and societal impact of these policies and programs,
>
> **and**
>
> when these evaluations are done in a (semi-)independent context where external researchers/professors almost always chair the quality control committees of investigations,
>
> **and**
>
> when different (triangulated) methods and techniques are used when carrying out the evaluations, including a focus on program and policy theories,
>
> **and**
>
> when the publication ( printed and on line) of these studies is done in a professional way through press releases and similar activities,
>
> **and**
>
> when next to the evaluations of specific programs, policies, and instruments, also longitudinal infrastructural M and E takes place,
>
> **and**
>
> when the results from these infrastructural research activities are published in a more general way but also customized to specific needs,
>
> ----------→ **then** these evaluations will play a role in policy dialogues and in the implementation of policies and programs.

The two other organizations focus more on *substantive knowledge and evidence,* assuming that by sharing this knowledge with the inspectee or the evaluator, their attention will be focused to the evidence and, consequently, they will use the findings, studies, and streams of information and learn from them.

**94    From Studies to Streams**

In order to understand why this difference exists, it is important to note the rather different *institutional position* of the *National Audit Office* vis-à-vis *the two other institutions*. While the Rekenkamer is a supreme audit institution, independent from either the executive or the legislative branch of government, both the Inspectorate for Education and the Judiciary Research Center are *less autonomous*, and, hence, probably more responsive to outside developments. Autonomy has its price.

As Livingstone (2003) recently showed, even the location of research and knowledge activities in a *geographical* way partly determines what type of knowledge is produced. Then it is easily to be understood that *organizational and institutional locations and arrangements* can also have effects on knowledge production. However, what also might be concluded is that there is a danger of being a completely independent audit institution. Apart from more general side effects of being a monopoly, within the world of knowledge there might be the extra danger that those institutions do not explicitly search for *falsifications of one's theory*. However, Popper taught us that no one is infallible, not even a fully independent supreme audit institution.

## Notes

1. 't Hart (2001) uses the term "inquisition democracy."
2. Government Performance and Results Act.
3. See: the Dutch newspapers NRC Handelsblad Monday June 31, 2003; de Volkskrant, June 29th, 2003.
4. Leeuw (1998) analyzed 12 studies published between 1996 and 1998; Leeuw & Crijns (2004) some 15 more, published between 2000 and 2003.
5. When one compares studies carried out between 1996–1998 and between 2000–2003 one sees that the audit office in the more recent studies also pays attention to substantive criteria (i.e., criteria that are specifically related to the policy field under investigation). Examples are that "policies should also produce facilities for adolescents who run the risk of becoming a drop out," "sustainable reintegration policies should be developed in order to help disabled workers to return to a job," etc.
6. Between 1949 and the early 1970s as a Documentation Center only.
7. Examples are: oversight data resulting from periodic stocktaking of all Dutch schools; demographics of schools, universities, polytechnics; demographics of pupils, students; dropout data; data on teachers, etc.
8. This Ph.D project is part of the University of Twente's Educational Research Institute, the Netherlands. It is partly sponsored by the Inspectorate of Education, Utrecht.
9. Partly based on Ehren, Leeuw & Scheerens (2003), which follows from ongoing Ph.D-research by M. Ehren (University of Twente, the Netherlands). M. Ehren evaluates the program theory of the Inspectorate of Education in the Netherlands, next tests the theory, and finally addresses the question of the impact of this Inspectorate vis-à-vis its goals. She uses interview and document analysis techniques.

## References

Algemene Rekenkamer. (2000). Organisatie van Beleidsevaluatie. Tweede Kamer, Vergaderjaar 1999–2000, 27 065, nr. 2. Den Haag: Government Printing Service.

Algemene Rekenkamer. (2002). Staat van de beleidsevaluatie, Tweede Kamer, Vergaderjaar 2002-2003, 28 656, nr. 2. Den Haag: Government Printing Service.

Barzelay, Michael. (1996). "Performance auditing and the New Public Management: changing roles and strategies of central audit institutions", in: OECD-PUMA, Performance auditing and the modernisation of Government, PP. 15-57 Paris: OECD.

Behn, R.D. (2003). "Rethinking accountability in education: how should who hold whom accountable for what?" International Public Management Journal, 6 (1): 43-73.

Bemelmans-Videc, M.(1998). "De Algemene Rekenkamer: controlenormen en stijlen in een veranderende bestuurlijke context." M. Hertogh et al. (ed). Omgaan met onderhandelend bestuur. Amsterdam: University Press, Amsterdam.

Ehren, Melanie, Frans L. Leeuw and Jaap Scheerens. (2003). "On the impact of the Dutch Educational Supervision Act", American Journal of Evaluation, 26: 60-77.

Ghoshal, S. & Moran, P. (1996). "Bad for practices: a critique of the transaction cost theory." Academy of Management Review, 21,13-47.

Hart, Paul 't. (2001). Verbroken Verbindingen: De Politisering van het Verleden en de Dreiging van een Inquisitiedemocratie, Amsterdam: De Balie.

Hoesel, Peter van (2003). Beleidsonderzoek als professie. Inaugural address, Erasmus University Rotterdam: Erasmus University Press.

Knaap, Peter van der (2003). "Theory-Based Evaluation and Learning: Possibilities and Challenges." Evaluation, 10: 16-34

Leeuw, Frans L. (1998). "Doelmatigheidsonderzoek van de Rekenkamer als regelgeleide organisatiekunde met een rechtssociologisch tintje?" Recht der Werkelijkheid, 14:35-71

Leeuw, Frans L. (2000). "Unintended side effects of auditing: the relationship between per-for-mance auditing and performance improvement and the role of trust." In W. Raub and J. Weesie (eds.). The management of durable relations. Amsterdam: Thelathesis.

Leeuw, Frans L. (2004). Kennis voor ketens. Annual WODC-lecture. WODC, den Haag.

Leeuw, Frans L and M.Crijns (2005). "Normnaleving door organisaties. Sociologie toegepast op een actuele vraagstuk." Bestuurskunde, 14: 40-49.

Leeuw, Frans L. and Piet J. Rozendal. (1994). "Policy evaluation and the Netherlands's Government: scope, utilization and organizational learning." In: Frans L.Leeuw, Ray C.Rist and Richard C. Sonnichsen (eds). Can Governments Learn. Pp. 67-89. Transaction Publishers: New Brunswick.

Livingstone, David (2003). Putting science in its place: geographies of scientific knowledge. Princeton: Princeton University Press.

Meyer, M.W. and Gupta, V. (1994). "The performance paradox." Research in Organizational Behavior, 16, 309-369.

Mulder, H.P. et al.(1991). "Gebruik van beleidsevaluatie-onderzoek bij de rijksoverheid." Beleidswetenschap, 5:203-228

Nutley, S., I. Walter and H. Davies. 2003."From knowing to doing: a framework for understanding the evidence-into-practice agenda." Evaluation, 9: 125-149

Pawson, R. (2002)."Evidence-based policy: the promise of 'realist synthesis." Evaluation, 8: 340-358.

Power, M. (1999). The audit society. Oxford: Oxford University Press

Put, Vital (2005). Normen in performance audits van rekenkamers. Een casestudie bij de Algemene Rekenkamer en het National Audit Office. Ph.D, Katholieke Universiteit Leuven: Leuven.

RMO (Raad voor Maatschappelijke Ontwikkeling). (2000). Aansprekend burgerschap. De relatie tussen de organisatie van het publieke domein en de verantwoordelijkheid van burgers. Den Haag.

RMO (Raad voor Maatschappelijke Ontwikkeling).(2003). Bevrijdende kaders, sturen op verantwoordelijkheid, Den Haag.

Smith, P. (1995). "On the unintended consequences of publishing performance data in the public sector." International Journal of Public Administration, 18: 277-310.

Robert Schwartz and John Mayne (Eds.).(2004). Quality matters: seeking confidence in evaluation, auditing and performance reporting. New Brunswick: Transaction publishers.

Van Bruggen, J. (2003) The Netherlands—the School Sector. In: The Danish Evaluation Institute. Educational Evaluation around the world: An international anthology. Copenhagen: The Danish Evaluation Institute.

Van Thiel, Sandra and Frans L. Leeuw (2003). "The performance paradox in the public sector." Public Productivity and Management Review, 25: 267-281

# 6

# Implementing Results-Based Management

*Per Oyvind Bastoe*[1]

The implementation of "Results-Based Management" (RBM) is one way of moving from "studies to streams," a shift from a dependence on specific evaluation studies towards accessing broad evaluative knowledge. RBM puts evaluation and performance monitoring elements into a "system" that also includes planning elements and feedback elements.

This broad perspective is one of the reasons for governments and agencies to implement RBM. It helps managers understand how intentions and objectives are translated into actions and results. It moves the focus from input and output to outcome. Perrin (2003) argues that one of the major factors that has led to public management reform like RBM is a concern that too often governments are preoccupied with processes and rules. At the same time it is often not clear what benefits are actually arising from public service expenditure and activities in the long run. Moving to a focus on outcomes involves a shift in thinking, and requires managers to bear in mind that they are engaged in activities and in producing outputs not for their own sake but in order to achieve "big picture" outcomes in line with the mission of the program.

Another reason for implementing RBM is the growing disillusionment with conventional evaluation praxis. Many governments and organizations experience only limited use of evaluation findings. Evaluation findings do not automatically feed back into a receptive and responsive decision-making process (Bastoe, 1999). Evaluations are most useful when used strategically, focusing on key questions of particular interest. Institutional arrangements determine whether or not evaluations play a part in the policy cycle, are systematically linked with other functions, or are carried out on an ad hoc basis. This involves setting out the functions and their institutions in an interlocking structure of responsibilities and with networks of procedural interrelationships. Such an arrangement allows the processes to contribute to and draw on each other to produce synergy in management. This assumes both a deliberate strategy of organizational design and a link between administrative and political forms in the policy process. RBM is such an integrated system.

RBM differs substantially from Management by Objectives (MBO), the foundation of management systems in many companies and governments from the early 1970s to the early 1990s. Whereas MBO focuses on inputs and outputs, RBM concentrates on results—that is, on outcomes and impacts. While MBO originated in centrally managed administrations, RBM is designed to fit decentralized organizational structures. While MBO assumes full organizational control over outcomes and fixed relationships between inputs and outputs, RBM is adapted to volatile operating environments. It promotes nimble organizational responses and it is grounded in partnerships.

Although implementation modalities vary according to the nature of the organization (whether an agency or branch of government, a private enterprise, or a development assistance organization), all RBM systems are characterized by the following features (World Bank, 1998):

- Clear corporate goals and objectives;
- A performance measurement system focusing on results;
- A learning culture grounded in evaluation;
- Stakeholder participation at all stages of program design and implementation;
- Clear accountabilities in a decentralized framework;
- Links between results, planning, and resource allocation.

RBM is also a way of managing evaluative knowledge to increase learning and performance, consistent with the discussions in previous publications from the International Evaluation Research Group on different approaches for organizing monitoring and evaluation to increase performance improvement and learning.[2] *These studies clearly demonstrate that structural elements (how monitoring and evaluation is linked to other management processes), cultural elements (behavior, credibility, ownership, etc.), and capacity elements (demand and supply) need to be addressed to succeed.*

This chapter examines experience with implementing RBM, focusing in particular on the ongoing process of implementation in the African Development Bank (ADB). The chapter will explore how the process of implementing RBM is developing in the organization, and will also discuss some pitfalls and challenges facing the implementation process and attempt to give some constructive suggestions. The ADB provides a valuable case study of how to move from "studies to streams," from a situation where evaluations have a marginal role in the organization and are considered to have limited relevance to ongoing processes, to a situation where the whole organization is committed to results orientation.

ADB is a complex organization in terms of its tasks (development and poverty alleviation in Africa), its membership structure (77 regional and non-regional countries), and its environment (the headquarters has been temporarily moved from Abidjan to Tunis because of the civil war in Ivory Coast).

ADB is not the first development organization attempting to implement RBM. The U.S. Agency for International Development (USAID, the Canadian International Development Agency (CIDA), United Nations Development Programme (UNDP), and several other development agencies are undertaking similar reforms. This interest in RBM is supported by the emerging new development "paradigm" (Hanna and Picciotto, 2002). This paradigm—characterized by the terms ownership, coherence, partnership, and results-orientation—appeared through a number of lessons learned from a generation of development assistance, including the reality that concrete results emanating from traditional development assistance have not lived up to expectations. Achieving and measuring intended development results is a more complex process than previously thought, primarily because development assistance does not work unless it builds on the recipients' own priorities and is coordinated among interested parties.

Experiences from these and similar efforts to implement results-based management systems have been captured in different ways in the literature—in the form of guides (e.g., the United States General Accounting Office 1996 guide on "Effectively Implementing the Government Performance and Results Act"), in the form of case studies (e.g., the World Bank's 1998 internal assessment of results-based management in its own organization), and in the form of synthesized lessons learned from implementing results-based management in a variety of organizations.[3]

These reviews of experiences point to a number of possible pitfalls in designing and implementing results-based management systems. There is some agreement that the following are among the key challenges:

- *Too Complicated and Too Comprehensive*

There is always a danger in trying to do too much at one time. Experience indicates that a lasting RBM system is best developed in cooperation with different stakeholders from the bottom up, with gradual expansion into a major corporate system, rather than the other way around. Unless it gains operational legitimacy and relevance, RBM may not be sustainable. It is important to start with pilots and a gradual, simple implementation, and pay close attention to costs.

- *Over-Elaborate Techniques*

Measurement and indicators—no matter how numerous—only provide a partial contribution to the information managers' and decision makers' need.

RBM is more than techniques and measurement—it implies that result information be put into an organizational context and used in a conscious way through analysis, evaluation, and interpretation.

- *Too Many Indicators*

Any system that tries to cover all information needs—both operational and strategic—becomes overly complex. It is important to select the vital few indicators that test progress on strategic objectives—not individual activities.

- *Lack of Understanding of the Cultural Aspects*

RBM needs to include a systematic attempt to integrate learning in daily work. An "inner understanding" in the form of insight, values, attitudes, and personal development must be included to generate change and growth. There are constant pressures to make short-term results look good. Experience from change processes in "values-based, vision-driven" organizations shows that a long-term perspective is necessary for success.

- *Attribution and Participation*

At the aggregate level (outcome, and impact levels) it is difficult, if not impossible, to attribute changes and results to certain projects and programs. Shared vision, joint accountability, and collective use of indicators and data help avoid these pitfalls and make RBM a tool of partnership and participation.

- *Partnership*

Too heavy an emphasis on corporate reporting can be disempowering to local managers and partners. A balance between development effectiveness and corporate reporting can be reached if RBM is implemented in a collaborative way that acknowledges the differing needs of various stakeholders.

In general, the experience underlines that a customized results-based management regime is critical. As Mayne points out: "It is important that the system be developed according to the needs and situation of the users. No single system will be appropriate for every organisation" (Mayne, 2001).

Consequently, the starting point for understanding the case of RMB implementation at the African Development Bank is to examine the context and the particular situation the organization is in. It is also important to think about the future of the organization: explore different organizational development scenarios and think about risks and opportunities in the next decades.

## The Background for Implementing Results-Based Management in ADB

Consistent with the background of other organizations engaging in the same type of process, the key ingredients in the ADB context are external pressure to improve performance and an internal sense of crisis. Indeed, these conditions are perhaps even more clearly articulated in the case of the ADB.

In 1995, the ADB's new president initiated major financial and administrative reforms to address profoundly weak organizational performance. Multiple and shifting mandates, serious weaknesses in governance and financial management, and an inadequate human resource base burdened the organization. Difficult economic circumstances resulted in a lack of demand for the ADB's financial products. These challenges were compounded by the Bank's credit policy, which was inconsistent and incompatible with underlying economic conditions. The Bank also had too many poorly performing projects within its soft loan mechanism—the African Development Fund facility. Western donors had refused to replenish ADF funds due to allegations of corruption and fraud. These difficulties ultimately led to substantial arrears and default within the Bank's lending portfolios. In August 1995, Standard & Poor's downgraded the Bank's senior long-term debt, citing "increasing politicization" of the Bank's corporate governance and management. The respected publication *Euromoney* called the Bank an "international embarrassment ... hopelessly inefficient and shoddily managed." *The Economist* said the Bank was "an inefficient, corrupt and politicised shambles."[4]

Fundamental reforms were initiated to overcome this crisis, despite chronic funding constraints. Decision making was centralized at the senior management level; financial and management controls were put in place; staffing was reduced from 900 to 600 positions; transparent and competitive recruitment policies were established; the capital reserve and the pace of disbursement were improved; and 20 percent of total projects eliminated. As the confidence was gradually re-established, the ADB won an improved debt rating and the process of replenishing funds was put back on track.

Having achieved substantial progress in terms of stabilizing the organization's financial position, attention began to shift toward the development aspects of the Bank's mandate with a view to increasing the effectiveness of its projects and programs. The Bank initiated a process of broad-based consultations with major stakeholders in African development, and established its "Vision" to become "the leading development institution in Africa dedicated to reducing poverty and promoting sustainable economic growth on the Continent."

An organization study of the Bank was launched in 2000 with the objective of adapting the Bank's structure, operating principles, decision-making processes, and skills mix to the requirements deriving from its revised mandate and priorities, as well as from the obligation to improve the quality and efficiency of its operations.

With regard to improving the quality and efficiency of operations, the Board Committee on Development Effectiveness has placed an increasing emphasis on development effectiveness issues. A great deal of attention was devoted to the need for the Bank to move more aggressively toward adopting a results-based approach, defining clearer development objectives, achieving greater efficiency and tracking its effectiveness on the ground, and to shift the focus of evaluations accordingly (from operational issues to development effectiveness issues).

### Experiences from Implementing Results-Based Management Systems

External consultants were engaged to support this process.[5] The first exercise undertaken by the consultants was a review of experience in similar organizations. The review examined results-based management reforms in the Canadian International Development Agency, the Treasury Board of Canada, the Office of the Canadian Auditor General, the U.S. Agency for International Development, the United Nations Development Programme, the United Nations Children's Fund, the Inter-American Development Bank, and the International Bank for Reconstruction and Development. The purpose of the study tour was to gather information in order to assess the design and implementation of RBM systems in these organizations with a view to highlighting strategic lessons for ADB.

The eight organizations reviewed had significantly different experiences in implementing RBM systems—in terms of the approach they employed, the duration of the implementation, and the degree of success they achieved. The review identified the following "key lessons" relevant to the ADB's implementation of results-based management:

*RBM Requires a "Sense of Crisis" and a Strong Commitment by Senior Management*

The implementation of an RBM system should be driven by a "sense of crisis" appropriately nurtured by senior management. The aim should be to increase the Bank's credibility and strengthen donor support by improving and demonstrating, through the system, a greater aid effectiveness of Bank operations. Some observers consider that senior management should be prepared to devote up to 20 percent of its time to implementing the system.

*RBM Requires a Clear Vision of the Implementation as a Change Process*

It is quite clear that a fundamental requirement for a good RBM implementation strategy is a clear vision of the approach as a change process for the transformation of the Bank culture into a learning-based organization. This vision should make it clear that RBM is more than a reporting tool; it is a change process to improve the organization's performance in terms of aid effectiveness. It should also be clear that this change process will affect every aspect of the Bank's operations, including strategic planning and management, appraisal and incentive systems, resource allocation, and reporting on an empirical basis. The vision should foresee a transformation of the organizational culture into a learning organization whereby results will become the driving concern of daily operations and performance improvement will take place through the continual feedback of performance information into management decisions. The objectives of the vision will need to be defined clearly in a solid communication strategy to be communicated to the whole organization and to all partners and stakeholders.

## RBM Requires a Well-Articulated Strategy for the Change Process

Once the vision of RBM is defined, there is a need for a comprehensive strategy to guide the design and implementation of the system. The strategy should address the following elements:

- *A participatory learning process evolving over time.* Overarching the strategy is the whole approach to the operation, which should be conceived as a participatory learning process evolving over a considerable period of time and incorporating flexibility to make changes as experiences are gained.
- *An internally driven process that responds to specific needs.* The strategy for change should have a twin focus. First, to make sure that the operation is not a consultant-driven process but rather an in-house operation involving a large cross-section of professionals from field offices and headquarters so that the culture and the specific needs of the organization are fully taken into account—consultant assistance being sought only for quality assurance purposes. A second priority is to ensure that the system responds to operational managers' needs first, before serving the needs of top management.
- *Learning by doing.* To take account of the specific needs and culture of the organization, the process should build on existing systems and procedures, and should experiment gradually in a "learning by doing" approach. Experience in similar organizations suggests that one useful approach is to start out with a core group of interested and committed people and to generate results and success stories that can be shared throughout the organization.

## RBM Requires a Strategy for Building Strong Ownership

To build strong ownership, the process should be participatory and should be undertaken through a balanced top-down/bottom-up approach. On one hand, senior management should determine what information it needs for strategic management of the organization. On the other hand, an interactive and consultative process should be undertaken with operational managers, country partners, and other stakeholders to determine what information they need to manage their projects and programs. The system should be designed to generate this information and help task managers use it for their own purposes. The system should address the following elements:

- *Keeping the system simple.* The major driver of success is a solid buy-in on the results framework and its supporting system of technology. The first condition to facilitate such a buy-in is to keep the system as simple and as user-friendly as possible.
- *Providing adequate training and supporting guides and tools.* Practical reference tools and training are probably the most important ingredients for developing strong ownership of the system. It is, therefore, very important not to underestimate time for training and support. Better results are obtained from training when there is an interface with work, as this allows time for experimentation between training sessions.
- *Anticipating the risk of behavior distortions.* Moving from accountability for outputs to accountability for outcomes can have serious implications for the ownership of the system, and also runs the risk of introducing some distortions in managerial behavior. These could be in the form of strong resistance to the system or in dishonest reporting. With this type of approach to accountability, there can also be a tendency for managers to do more of what is easy to measure or to achieve, rather than what is more important. For example, there might be no strong correlation between a manager's personal performance and results obtained in the country because small results in difficult countries are not recognized. Everyone in the organization needs to have the opportunity to raise concerns about how these systems distort behavior.
- *Disaggregating long-term outcomes into intermediate outcomes.* Disaggregating outcomes into intermediate outcomes that are more manageable by task managers can go a long way in mitigating resistance. Concepts like "reach," and "enabling results," can be particularly useful in this regard.
- *Moving to an understanding of shared accountability.* An understanding of shared accountability is particularly useful in sector-wide programs and poverty-reduction programs where several partners are contributing to the same program and share their indicators. The objective is to develop a shared understanding of who is responsible for what.
- *Giving proper weight to results in the incentive system.* To avoid possible distortions in incentives and behaviors, the various criteria for promotion, panel clearance, budgetary allocations, etc., need to be

revised in order to give proper weight to results, taking into account the need to align staff incentives with corporate priorities.
- *Making sure that results information is integrated into management decision making.* The information generated is intended to inform assessments of the overall effectiveness of the system. The usefulness of the information generated and the extent to which it is used for management will be a strong indicator of strategy and vision ownership, as well as a strong factor for success. To facilitate this process, result information should be integrated into the management decision-making process, including supervision, portfolio review, completion reporting, etc.

### Readiness to Implement RBM

As we have seen from the lessons presented above, RBM implementation is far more than a technical and structural exercise. It also involves—and indeed requires—a process of behavioral and cultural change. The challenge for organizations committed to implementing RBM, like ADB, is to customize the RBM approach to the organization's situation and context.

An assessment of the current situation in ADB points to a number of strengths and opportunities in the organization. It also indicates that the major weaknesses and inadequacies in the Bank systems have less to do with the content of the instruments than with the mind-set with which they are approached and the way in which they are applied.

The reorganization and the execution of a new strategic plan has created a "window of opportunity" for the ADB to implement RBM. The RBM implementation process could be integrated to this change process by incorporating RBM values and concepts into the "mission exercise" through the communication strategy and the "change facilitator" network. Another opportunity for RBM is to take advantage of the enthusiasm and momentum associated with the strategic planning process by integrating the two processes so that the systems are developed hand in hand, in such a way that the RBM logic model serves as the foundation for the corporate scorecard. The recent and temporary relocation to Tunis also creates an opportunity to increase the vigor of the change processes and to speed up the implementation of RBM.

### Challenges and Opportunities

What then are the lessons from this example of RBM implementation? What are the critical elements in moving from a situation where tools for planning, monitoring, evaluation, and feedback are separated to a situation where the different tools are integrated in a structured RBM system? Is there an increased results-orientation in the organization? Is this a useful approach for moving from "studies to streams?"

Let us first turn to a similar discussion of public sector reforms in OECD countries. In a recent paper, Burt Perrin[6] discusses major challenges to a results-focused approach. Perrin's paper was written on the basis of an expert meeting in 2002 where representatives from twenty-seven countries exchanged experiences regarding public sector reforms to improve program effectiveness and efficiency and the quality of management and the budgeting processes, where an increased focus from inputs to the actual results and impacts of government activities is one of the key objectives of most reform activities.

Firstly, Perrin finds that a focus on outcomes is very important, but also very difficult. Many countries say that this has proved far more difficult than expected. In particular, they find it hard to see how one can connect what programs and managers do with distant and complex outcomes. Many of the countries acknowledged that outcomes receive only minimal attention. Instead, most efforts at performance monitoring thus far have focused mainly on inputs, activities, and outputs. Yet there are ways in which one can assess outcomes.

Secondly, the creation of a results-oriented culture throughout government is essential for actual implementation of a results-oriented approach. Unless managers and staff throughout government actually buy into a results focus, they most likely will just "go through the motions," and performance management risks remaining a paper exercise. While there is strong agreement about the importance of this issue, there is also recognition that it is not clear how to bring about the requisite changes in organizational culture.

Thirdly, the question of data quality also requires attention to ensure that the performance data that are obtained are meaningful and valid. Inaccurate or misleading data undermine effective decision making and can distort program activities. In order to ensure the meaningfulness of performance data, one needs to be sensitive to potential difficulties and how these can be alleviated or addressed.

Fourthly, leadership and support from the top levels of government is needed in order to bring about a results-focused approach. Leadership can take various forms, including: top-level support for a results-focused approach, capacity building, and effective communication. As well, proponents of results-focused management and budgeting need to lead by example, in particular by undertaking independent evaluation of reform initiatives. Audit also has an important role to play.

Fifthly, a strategic rather than a piecemeal approach is necessary. For effective performance management, an integrated approach involving both monitoring and evaluation is needed. It is important to develop an approach that recognizes the realities and complexities of working in the public milieu, with many interacting initiatives and factors. There are a variety of other important strategic considerations, such as: how a results-oriented approach can contribute to a whole-of-government approach; how it can be used when contracting externally for services; how performance information can be combined in a meaningful way with the budgeting process; and how it can be made relevant to Parliament.

Perrin's observations are clearly of interest and relevance to the process in ADB. ADB is facing similar challenges in its reform agenda. Perrin's comments regarding public reforms are also pertinent to the ADB process.

We would like to conclude this chapter by making some reflections based on the process in ADB so far. These reflections summarize some of the key lessons so far, and might be of relevance for other organizations engaging in similar processes of moving from studies to streams.

*The first reflection* relates to the need to be realistic about what an integrated system like RBM can accomplish. Organizations in crisis are often attracted to "grand solutions" that promise to solve all their problems. It is important to emphasize that previous work has underlined the fact that RBM should not be perceived as a panacea or remedy for all ills and difficulties. It is also important to keep in mind the limitations of a strong results-orientation. The common lesson: *"What gets measured, gets done"* remains valid (Thiel and Leeuw, 2002). This awareness is particularly applicable for organizations like ADB—which have both a political function and an active role in facilitating sustainable development.

*The second reflection* relates to timing. The experience with RBM at the ADB once again underlines the importance of appropriate timing and the need to exploit key "windows of opportunity." "Appropriate timing" implies attending to the internal and external factors that, in sum, give rise to opportunities to generate fundamental cultural and structural change. ADB currently has such an opportunity. The organization has been shaken by a number of internal and external events, but is eager to prove that it can be of enduring importance and relevance. This provides an ideal opportunity to implement a comprehensive approach like RBM.

Another aspect of timing has to do with the pace of reform. The rate of change is likely to have a significant impact on the results of the reform process. A change process can be too slow or too fast. In many organizations, political organizations in particular, there is a tendency to focus on short-term perspectives, priorities, and objectives. One of the reasons for this is the need to achieve visible results before an important decision. This creates pressure to achieve quick solutions to existing problems without taking the longer-term requirements into account. The trend of ad-hoc orientation is often apparent. The tendency to underestimate the time needed to create ownership is common. An often noted lesson is that a forced process often yields unanticipated and negative consequences at a later stage. A genuine change process takes "the time it takes," depending on aspects like confidence, degree of shared understanding, and openness among the participants. Some degree of shared perception of the need for reform has to be in place before genuine change can take place. Everyone involved has to get a chance to understand the reason for a change process, and a chance to alter their "mental models." A top-down approach needs to be combined with a bottom-up process. Mayne (2001) emphasizes the same point in his discussion of implementation of RBM in government organizations:

> ...organizations have to be patient and persistent. In this type of process, building consensus and maintaining momentum is crucial to success... Though it may be tempting to rush implementation, organizations have found that this only decreases the likelihood that the measurement system will be useful.

This is particularly important in highly politicized organizations, where the political timetable may present a formidable obstacle to implementation.

*The third reflection* relates to the breadth of the RBM approach. In many cases, the cultural aspects are only vaguely and tacitly acknowledged, with the structural and IT-systems aspects of the RBM receiving the most attention. Proposals to "flatten the organizational hierarchies," to "decentralize," and to "build capacity" need to be fully explored and specified if they are to succeed. As illustrated in the case of ADB, a new approach to performance management requires more than the adoption of new administrative and operational systems. An emphasis on outcomes requires first and foremost a performance-oriented management culture that will support and encourage the use of the new management approaches. Organizations like the ADB have traditionally had an administrative culture that has emphasized the measurement of inputs. In contrast, a performance management culture is focused on managing inputs and outputs to achieve outcomes. Cultural change is not an easy task and will take time. It is a long-term process that requires consistency and a commitment to refinement and improvement. Leadership in the form of a dedicated "champion" is often seen as essential. This "champion" can lead the process, motivate employees, partners, and stakeholders, and act as a pervasive spokesman for the process. A balanced approach will hardly ever give immediate results in a setting that involves a change of culture and work processes.

Is then implementation of RBM a worthwhile method for moving from studies to streams, of increasing the results-orientation in an organization? Both the ADB case and similar efforts from other agencies and government organizations are promising. It is too early to make a final judgment about the success or failure of these initiatives. The process of change will go on for many years to come. And it is important to keep in mind that a change process never is straightforward and linear with a predefined chain of events. Change processes are both complex and unpredictable. There are no simple recipes for how to meet all challenges. A pro-active approach can be a key to success. Senge et al. (1999) describe "pro-activity" as a new way of thinking, a balance between freedom and boundaries—a "dance of change." The ability to maintain flexibility and freedom while progressing towards agreed objectives is the central challenge in all change processes.

## Notes

1. I am thankful of the support from my colleague in ECON, Sam Bartlett, in writing this chapter.
2. See, for instance, Rist and Sonnichsen, 1994; Gray, Jenkins, and Segsworth Sec Refs., 1993; Mayne and Zapico-Goni, 1997; and Boyle and Lemaire, 1999.
3. Helgason's 1998 "Performance Management Practices in OECD Countries"; Binnendijk's review of experience in development cooperation agencies; Mayne's 2001 review of experience from Canadian and international jurisdictions.
4. Patricia Adams and Andrea Davis, "On the Rocks: The African Development Bank Struggles to Stay Afloat," *Multinational Monitor* 17 (7&8) (1996), http://multinationalmonitor.org/hyper/mm0796.09.html.
5. A consortium with the two Canadian consulting companies Universalia and Baastel in collaboration with the author of this chapter.
6. Burt Perrin, "Implementing the Vision: Addressing Challenges to Results-focused Management and Budgeting," OECD, 2003.

## References

Bastoe, P. O. (1999). "Linking Evaluation with Strategic Planning, Budgeting, Monitoring, and Auditing." In R. Boyle and D. Lamaire, eds., *Building Effective Evaluation Capacity. Lessons from Practice.* New Brunswick, NJ: Transaction Publishers.

Binnendijk, Annette. (1999). *Result Based Management in the Development Co-operation Agencies: A Review of Experience.* Background Document. Working Party on Aid Evaluation 32nd Meeting. OECD.

Boyle, R., and D. Lemaire, eds. (1999). *Building Effective Evaluation Capacity. Lessons from Practice.* New Brunswick, NJ: Transaction Publishers.

GAO. (1996). *Executive Guide. Effectively Implementing the Government Performance and Results Act.* Washington, DC: Comptroller General of the United States.

Gray, A., B. Jenkins, and B. Segsworth. (1993). *Budgeting, Auditing and Evaluation. Functions and Integrations in Seven Governments.* New Brunswick, NJ: Transaction Publishers.

Hanna, Nagy, and Robert Picciotto, eds. (2002). *Development Learning in a World of Poverty and Wealth.* World Bank Series on Evaluation and Development, vol. 4. New Brunswick, NJ: Transaction Publishers.

Helgason, S. (1998). "Performance Management Practices in OECD Countries." Paper. OECD-PUMA.

Mayne, J. (2001). *Implementing Results-Based Management: Lessons from the Literature.* Office of the Auditor General of Canada. March 2000.

Mayne, J., and E. Zapico-Goni, eds. (1997). *Monitoring Performance in the Public Sector: Future Directions from International Experience.* New Brunswick, NJ: Transaction Publishers.

Perrin, B. (2003). "Implementing the Vision: Addressing Challenges to Results-focused Management and Budgeting." Paper. Paris: OECD.

Rist, R.C., and Sonnichsen, R., eds. (1994). *Can Governments Learn?* New Brunswick, NJ: Transaction Publishers.

Senge, Peter, Charlotte Roberts, Rick Ross, Bryan Smith, George Roth, and Art Kleiner. (1999). *The Dance of Change. The Challenges to Sustaining Momentum in Learning Organizations.* New York: Doubleday. New York.

Thiel, S., and F. L. Leeuw. (2002). "The Performance Paradox in the Public Sector." *Public Performance and Management Review* 25(3) (March 2002): 267–281.

Universalia/Baastel. (2002a). *Study Tour Report.* Universalia Management Group. Ottawa.
_____. (2002b). *Readiness Assessment.* Universalia Management Group. Ottawa.
World Bank. (1998). *1998 Annual Report on Operations Evaluation.* Washington, DC.

# Part 3

**Thematic Evaluations and Their Uses**

# 7

# Complex Policies and Evaluative Streams of Knowledge

*Nicoletta Stame*

A debate on utilization has crossed the evaluation field for a large part of its existence. It was originated by a straightforward finding: for all the efforts spent at providing new evaluative studies there was a gap between the information collected for the evaluation of a project or program and what was utilized in decision making: some information was not utilized, what would have been useful was not collected. At the end, evaluators felt at the same time more modest and more curious about what was going on in adjacent fields. The situation we are in now has dramatically changed: a stream of evaluative knowledge, produced by the accumulation of studies and fostered by the new tools offered by the information technology, has a much greater chance of being utilized in the evaluation of new policy products, provided the evaluators have learned the previous lesson. To wit, evaluators must see their work as part of a system of greater evaluative knowledge production, and they need to be better acquainted with the working of their moving targets (systems of governance, and policy instruments).

## The Legacy of the Debate on Utilization

As soon as program evaluation was established—in the 1960s in the United States[1]—as an offspring of the first wave of social programs such as the War on Poverty, income maintenance, training programs, etc., problems about the uses of evaluation were raised. Commissioners were asking evaluators for nothing less than inputs for "rational" decisions to be taken about programs, in terms of "go/no go": Did the program work as expected? Did results match objectives? Was the program effective? And they complained if evaluations were not timely, the results not clear, recommendations not feasible, etc.: in other words, if evaluation did not comply with these requirements, those studies would have been considered a *waste*.

In their turn, evaluators noted that decision makers used that complaint as an alibi, since they preferred to listen to "political" inputs (their constituencies, the fad of the moment) rather than to "scientific" ones (evaluations). Clearly, "instrumental use" (intended use for intended users) was rare.

To cope with this disillusionment, evaluators have found that other uses were frequent:

a.  Cognitive use (Leviton and Hughes, 1981), enlightenment use (Weiss, 1998a): information collected for the evaluation of a program could be useful to another program or policy decision, or for reframing a policy problem;
b.  Process use (Patton, 1998): the main use of an evaluation could consist in its process, more than in its findings; and
c.  Influence (Kirkhart, 2000), which is a kind of eclectic synthesis of the previous ones: the findings of the evaluation of a program could influence the future of the program in an indirect way, according to three dimensions: process-results; time (before, during, after); intention (intended, unintended).

As is evident, each of these uses was favored by the kind of data collected, dealing alternatively with implementation, outcomes, process, etc. But they had something in common: the data were collected for a specific, *single study*, for the evaluation of a *given* project or program (be it a pilot, demonstration, prototype) that was supposed to work in a specific way: with its objectives, dedicated resources, stakeholders, results, time frame, etc. It might investigate only the program in question (as in instrumental use and process use) or it might want to move beyond it (as in enlightenment use and influence). In any case, it was the future of self-contained social programs that was the focus here.

At this stage, what was not discussed was the relation between use and the approach of the evaluator, that is, the theoretical framework within which data were collected. Initially, it was a programmatic oblivion, because the observation was that evaluations were not used as such, regardless of the approach employed.[2] In due time, the debate has entered this contested terrain, as is shown by the fact that process use is linked to the utilization-focused approach developed by Patton, as is the enlightenment use by Weiss, that is best suited to her theory-based evaluation approach. So Shadish et al. (1992) have considered a theory of use as a necessary component of any approach.

Eventually, the way out from the debate has led evaluators to what these authors (Shadish et al., 1992: 57) consider "increased humility about the use of their work." We can identify three instances of humility:

- As for instrumental use: the data may be useless because they are of bad quality. Hence the debate on quality, standards, etc., which is now widespread in all the national and supranational evaluation communities;
- As for process use: it is recognized that stakeholders may have lower expectations and be satisfied by learning through process; and
- As for enlightenment use and influence, Weiss suggests that in order to enhance the role of evaluation in decision making it would be better to inquire into the policy process in which evaluation takes place, which is "incremental" and not "rational."

This debate was mainly present in the United States, where programs had been introduced as a form of public intervention that might alleviate a situation where a real welfare state was lacking but most problems could no more be solved through the market exclusively. It would have been inconceivable in a continental European environment, where public intervention was dominant in social affairs, and ideological reasons for keeping public services and institutions in place were stronger than those offered by the test of research on their efficiency and effectiveness.

*The New World of Policy and Evaluation*

The situation has changed since the mid-1980s. In the United States and in the countries that had experienced the first wave of programs, it had become clear that single programs alone could not cope with complex problems. New kinds of more inclusive programs have had to be devised. In the continental European countries, where dealing with the inefficiency of older public systems could no longer be postponed, there was a shift toward a changing role of the state, becoming a regulator of what others (local authorities, private sector, NGOs) were called to do. This convergence is reflected in a better-informed dialogue among countries from distant parts of the world, and has produced a second wave of policies and programs. The latter can be of either of these two kinds:

a. programs that set general goals (social inclusion, socioeconomic re-equilibrium among territorial areas) and broad directions, and establish a budget at the central level, then leave it to the lower levels to finance whatever project they think fit: it is the model of EU Structural Funds, of many big programs for social inclusion, law 285/98 on infancy in Italy, social funds for development aid, etc. (Stame, 2004b).
b. thematic policies that aim at a cross-sectoral objective by the combination of many different programs and tools. Here there is no dedicated budget and the different interventions are financed out of many sources. These policies may fix goals in the form of concrete objectives and indicators, like the Millennium Development Goals (MDG), or of in-

termediate objectives, like the pillars of the EU strategy for employment (employability, flexibility, entrepreneurship, equal opportunity); or they can establish a new goal that encompasses previous interventions, like the surfacing of the shadow economy. A policy like this can use a mix of instruments: incentives, regulations, sanctions, persuasion, etc.[3]

The difference between how first wave (of the 1960s and 1970s) and second wave (from the 1980s onward) programs were designed is clear: whereas in the former the program detailed what course of events should have happened in order to attain a given result (this is also characterized as a "blueprint approach"), in the latter many different paths were expected to be taken as a result of the program, so that the results could be obtained in different ways. This had implications for the way evaluators approached them, and the debates that emerged among them.

In the former wave, the main evaluative questions referred to *effectiveness* and *attribution*: Did the program work as expected? Was the objective obtained? Did the main indicators of success positively change? And, is the result the effect of programmatic inputs and outputs (and should the merit be attributed to the program actors)? The implication was that if the answer was "yes, it worked as expected," the program would continue; if "no," it would be discontinued (or, at least, it should have been, according to a "rational" view that is hardly inspiring real life politics, but that had nonetheless elicited approaches to evaluation with a positivist flavor). At the same time, it was expected that the objectives of the program were clear, a point that has been subject to many criticisms: goals are usually vague, and they are continuously redefined. This problem has brought some authors to stress the need for submitting programs to the test of evaluability (Rossi and Freeman, 1989; Wholey, 1987), while others have opted for more radical alternatives, presenting different approaches, like goal-free evaluation (Scriven, 1993), a social reconstruction of goals (as in fourth generation evaluation, Guba and Lincoln, 1989), and so on.

In the latter wave, the main evaluative questions are:

*What is a good result? And how do we recognize it?* What has happened that has made for a change? How can we say that—all in all—health improved, employment rose, the environment is safer, etc.? Since the "good result" will be the combination of many elements, evaluators must resist the temptation to please those who fund the evaluation by providing the simple answer they want: reducing the evaluation of complex policies to the performance of just one or two overarching indicators, which are considered as the most important ones. Even worse, evaluators must be careful when indicators worked out for single programs evaluation are inappropriately used for the evaluation of a whole policy.

*What works better, where, when, and why?* Effectiveness and attribution have to be dealt with in a new way, since they do not refer to an expected course of events, but to the various instances of combination of the parts that compose the policy. Therefore, those questions can better be understood if complemented by questions about:

- Coherence: What is a good mix among programs, and among types of instruments? Are programs consistent with each other?
- Sequence: What is the sequence of interventions that makes for better results?[4]
- Subsidiarity: What should be done at what level?
- Flexibility: What works better where?

This makes for different evaluation methods and designs. In the former wave, the way programs were designed had initially oriented evaluators toward focusing on what constituted an expected success: a given level of employment, a given level of educational attainment, etc. The unit of analysis was a situation known to have been a target of the intervention, and the data would be collected with a view to test whether the results were obtained by the program or by other factors (hence the stress on experiments and counterfactual analysis, the logic of which—however—did not go uncontested owing to the difficulty of warranting external validity of the collected data).[5]

Those shortcomings are even more evident when we know—as with the latter wave—that many paths could be taken to implement a program, and that in any case the beneficiary would react to the mechanism inherent in the program from his/her standpoint. First, we have to look for various alternative options, observe the existing data, and inductively derive hypotheses from them, through comparative and longitudinal methods. Moreover, since in the latter we deal with a multilevel set of interventions (that also implies a partnership among different actors), the question of attribution will be different: no more a matter of whether we can attribute the result to the intended intervention, but what and who can be the cause of a result that has been obtained.

All this makes it impossible that such complex programs and policies be evaluated through data purposely collected in single studies and asks for evaluation designs that bring together different kind of studies and types of information. This task can be performed thanks to the abundance of data and information coming from many sources and made available by the information technology: databases on social indicators, on institutional performance, or from narratives and specialized literature accounts, which have been collected for other reasons but that already constitute a remarkable pool of knowledge. We may think of it as a stream of evaluative information that only asks to be put to use. In this case, the real problem of waste would be that of not utilizing what is available, and duplicating the efforts.

Two points of caution, however, should be raised in connection with the stream of knowledge. In the first place, when trying to take advantage of the advances in information technology, one should be careful not to fall prey to the temptation of utilizing pre-cooked data as can be found in databases, storages of lessons learned, or summaries of best practices; this stream of knowledge should not become a flood to be drowned in (see Perrin, this volume).

In the second place, and as a consequence, it is evaluators who can and should single the evaluative knowledge out of the stream of existing information by tailoring it for accountability and learning functions. This is not an obvious task, and needs appropriate evaluation approaches.

## Complex Policies and Evaluation Approaches

To my knowledge, there are two main families of evaluation approaches that have so far openly made use of the streams of knowledge: theory-based evaluations (TBE) and systematic reviews. They follow a different logic.

TBE approaches look at the mechanisms that can explain why a program works, and the differences among the ways it works in different contexts. Its intention is to open the "black box" of programs: the fact that programs do not spell out why something is expected to happen as a result of the input. To do that, the TBE approaches maintain that evaluation should find out what are the mechanisms supposed to be at work, then design an evaluation able to test the various passages. For Weiss (2000), it is a matter of discovering the many theories that the stakeholders can hold, and then deciding to test those that seem more promising (and for which better data are available). For Pawson and Tilley's "realistic evaluation" (1997), it is a matter of understanding how people in a given context may react to the mechanism that can be implied in a policy instrument, which can differ from one context to the next. For all these authors[6] an evaluation is not supposed to ascertain that a given program worked, regardless of why it should work, but it aims at finding out why in some conditions it might work better and in other ones worse. To work out appropriate evaluation designs, therefore, TBE cannot just submit a given target reality to the test of what happened with the implementation of the program, but it must play with theories, compare different situations, distant in time and place, different in status. This cannot be done unless one may utilize data of different nature (inquiries, administrative records, qualitative studies, indexes of quality standards, etc.) coming from different sources, depending—as Pawson and Tilley say—on "who may know it" and "where one can find it."[7] So these authors see a possible use of the new knowledge for the theory elaboration that it allows: finding out mechanisms, elaborating "middle-range theories" to open the "black box" and better understand the working of policies and how it can be improved.

An altogether different logic is that of "systematic reviews,"[8] which are supposed to inform an evidence-based policy. By definition, systematic reviews exist thanks to the availability of a stream of knowledge. The underlying idea is that instead of relying on a (new) single study policy decision making needs evaluations that draw conclusions from a larger body of knowledge, in a trial that will support the programs that offer better proof of their working. Single programs through which given problems have been tackled are analyzed and positive results are aggregated, in order to find out the best way that they could be generalized, along the traditional experimental method logic. Here the stream of knowledge is not used for the variety of information that it can offer, as with TBE, but for the multiplicity of similar single cases that can be collected, in order to provide the "best answer" to be proposed everywhere.

How can these approaches address the evaluation questions put by the new wave of programs/policies? As for TBE, it is certainly fitted for the second wave of programs, as it was elaborated as a consequence of them (Kubisch et al., 1995). And it may be adapted to enter into the working of policies, with their problems of coherence, sequence, etc. Indeed, Weiss notes that "much the same evaluative strategies are used in policy evaluation as in the evaluation of programs" (1998b: 7). The same cannot be said for systematic reviews whose aim is to single out which programs stand alone, and therefore seem little fit to an analysis that is based on complexity and multiplicity, as with the new kind of policies.

To sum up, evaluation of the new kind of complex policies needs multiple kinds of information, and it will benefit from existing streams of knowledge provided that the approach in using them will be one that appreciates variety and complexity, and does not aim at reducing a complex reality within restricted limits of a uniform kind of best practice.

## New Kinds of Policies and the Streams of Knowledge

In the following paragraphs we want to analyze two cases of thematic evaluations. The first one refers to a policy of fixed goals: the international strategy for development known as Millennium Development Goals (MDGs). The second refers to a policy that states a new goal in broad terms: Italian policy of regularization of the shadow underground economy.

For each of them I will look at how the main questions that I have listed above have been addressed so far:

1. What is a good result?: a matter of the relationship between goals, objectives and indicators;
2. How do we know it?: the problem of M&E systems, and how to use the stream of knowledge to feed them;
3. How was the result obtained, why? What shall we do with it?

First, we will briefly present the two cases, then we will draw some lessons from their comparison.

## Case 1: The Millennium Development Goals

This strategy for development has been formulated by no less than the community of states that compose the United Nations.[9] It stems from a pact by which the rich countries have promised to increase the amount of their aid and the poor countries have taken on the engagement of improving their governance.[10] They have agreed on eight goals, the MDGs, articulated in objectives, to be monitored through specific indicators. These goals should be reached by 2015 through the combined effort of all the involved parties. This policy has been conceived inside the framework of the new development approach (its cornerstones are: partnership, multidimensionality, ownership, and autonomy);[11] it is a result of negotiations between the parties that could come to agreement on these specific goals to the detriment of other goals that did not get a sufficient consensus.

The MDGs can be divided into the following aspects: poverty reduction (1), human development (2 to 7: education, gender equality, health), and global partnership (8). Indicators follow: for example, goal 2 states "eliminate gender disparity in primary and secondary school preferably by 2005, and to all levels of education no later than by 2015"; hence, the proposed indicators are: ratio of girls to boys in primary, secondary, and tertiary education; ratio of literate females to males of fourteen to twenty-five years old; share of women in wage employment in the non-agricultural sector; proportion of seats held by women in national parliament. The first seven goals refer to something that should change in developing countries. Goal 8, "develop a global partnership for development," refers to something that should change in the relationship between rich and poor countries.

What is new on this policy vis-à-vis previous cases of goals setting is that here goals are mainly stated as outcomes, and that they should be attained through a global partnership. However, as for the latter point there is a difference among the goals. For all of them it is clear that the outcome is the result of how the countries react to international aid, how they pool their resources and energies with those of the donors, and how they take ownership of the policies that have been enacted. But goal 8 says something else: the donors are considered not only for their aid policies, but for the coherence among their different sector policies; trade policies or barriers may contrast what aid policies would do for helping exports from developing countries versus current circumstances; immigration laws can obstruct a free movement of people that otherwise could favor the developing country, etc. This aspect is actually at the center of the interest of research groups such as the Center for Global Development, or the Global Policy Group, that have started inquiring into aspects of the existing policies that should become relevant for the evaluation of the attainment of goal 8.[12]

If we now turn to our first question (what is a success?) we will see that the answer is already in place: a good result is the one that approaches the goals. The logic of the program lies in the rigidity of the goal: once negotiations have taken place and all the parties have consented that a certain result is feasible and could be accepted, then this becomes the benchmark, nothing less. This point has, of course, its drawbacks. Apart from the well-known problem of goal displacement, the 2002 Annual Review of Development Effectiveness (ARDE) of the World Bank (OED) cites previous cases in which goals were stated but not attained,[13] which adds to skepticism: Will it be the same again? In that case, this policy would be doomed to failure.

Then comes the second question: How do we know that goals are attained? This aspect has received great attention; performance-based M&E systems have been envisaged (Rist, in this volume). These systems should not limit themselves to register the inputs (money received and spent) and the output (activity done), but they should concentrate on results, on change. It is true that the policy already states the changes to monitor through the indicators, and presumably it has singled them out because they are already available. But much needs to be done to collect all the data that are relevant to success; not only all the involved parties (governments, NGOs, etc.) should collect their data according to what is relevant to them, but it would be necessary to develop strategies for the harmonization of data collection among different agencies.

All true. But if M&E systems are a tool for results management, it should be clear what is the place of these systems inside the strategy for development. And this is the more delicate point, if in the literature on international aid we can read conclusions such as this: what is lacking is "systematically (collecting) evidence on what works in reducing poverty, what does not, and why" (Evans, 2000; in Hanna, 2002: 292), then what have we been learning thus far? M&E systems should be integrated into the fine-tuning of development strategies.

There are two models for this relationship, "ranking" and the "learning organization." The fixed goals are supposed to be attainable, as an average; then it is possible to rank the various countries according to their level of attainment of the goal. But how does this impact on results management and evaluation? How does it work? One possibility is that an incentive mechanism of "pride" and "shame" is in place. The good ones should be proud of their achievement and continue in their good practice, the bad ones should be ashamed, and supposedly do something to correct themselves. This might be an effective policy: shame is a strong push to learning for those who found themselves in the low positions, although it is marginally informative for the rest of us. In any case, as Pawson (2002) suggests, there are cases in which shame is effective and other ones in which it is not. In development strategies, shaming could be effective if there were a perfect consensus on the goals, and the parties really honored the principle of "reciprocal accountability,"[14] which seems foremost in the new development approach (World Bank, 2002: 7).

Otherwise, ranking may become a means for selecting some and leaving others behind, as it happens where instead of a partnership we have a game played by a stronger party that allots resources according to its own criteria, as in the U.S. strategy of development of the Millennium Challenge Account (Radelet, 2003). As a counterpart, those who do not score high may contest the criteria for ranking, or the accuracy of the data collected. With ranking, however, we do not understand why the actors did or did not attain the goal: the hypothesis is that all could have attained it, and if they did not it is a kind of self-fulfilling prophecy: they were inadequate; hence they did not attain the goals.

The logic of the "learning organization"—suggested by the 2002 World Bank's ARDE report as well as by Hanna—means that the M&E systems should be built in such a way as to be able to keep up with what is understood of the working of development policies. As Hanna (2002: 296) puts it, "strategies emerge from continuous interactions of top-down and bottom-up learning processes," This means that M&E systems, both of the donor agencies and of the countries, should be able to reflect the continuous understanding of what goes on, the expected and the unexpected, the good results of the first ranked, but also the surprising reversal of old verdicts about the last ranked. This approach would imply adapting actions to goals, better understanding the margins within which goals can be attained, investigating such lessons learned as "draw attention to the multisectoral dominants that contribute to outcomes" (World Bank, 2002: 35) or "improve the investment climate in order to extend the reach of markets, thereby providing greater job and income opportunities for poor people, and use markets or market type mechanisms to provide better basic services to the poor" (World Bank, 2002: 25).

It is noteworthy that this course of thought has been lagging behind for the more traditional goals of poverty reduction and social development (goals 1 to 7), while fresh new thinking has been worked out for goal 8 (partnership). Perhaps this is due to the fact that goals 1 to 7 deal with "intractable" problems that have so far been resistant to real improvements. But goal 8 is not an easy task either. Perhaps it is even more formidable. However, it has been possible to look at the topic of partnership through what we know from the data on trade, migration, etc., available in many databases. And this has spurred the search for new tools for the evaluation of the attainment of that goal.

*Case 2: The Regularization of the Italian Shadow Economy*

This policy has been recently promoted by the Italian government, after a succession of local and sector-wide interventions had been tried. This is a case of incremental policy that grows out of different interventions, some of which have a specific budgetary appropriation, while others come from longer, more broadly framed initiatives.

The Italian shadow economy is intertwined with the regular one in many ways, and it has many different causes, from high taxation, heavy bureaucratic rules, malfunctioning of the control system, to a sheer exploitation of the mismatch between labor and welfare policies. However, it is detrimental both to the worker, who may even receive a fair salary but is not protected from other risks, and to the employer, who cannot get the kind of financial and service support that public authorities would otherwise grant. The shadow economy has lived under very uncertain skies. Being considered either a marginal phenomenon or a way of maintaining consensus within the political system, it has been tolerated for a long time. Public controls have been scant; but when controls have been indeed enacted, then the result has been the sweeping away of productive activities and jobs.

The change in attitude toward the shadow economy has come in the second half of the 1990s, through converging trends: on the one side, research has shown the potentialities present in the Italian shadow economy: skills are formed, activities are created, and these support the production of the "made in Italy" that is quite visible. A wiser policy would have been that of regularizing these activities, thus offering them the chance of expanding and upgrading instead of being suppressed. On the other side, some trade unions, especially those active in the sectors more exposed to irregularity, which are the less protected (construction, textile, agriculture), have understood that if they wanted to do away with it, instead of a denunciation that would have brought unemployment to these workers, it would have been better for both parties to agree to gradual steps toward regularization.

These first trends have given rise to new labor policy tools, "contratti di riallineamento" (realignment contracts), and a new attention toward providing services in order to help firms understand that regularization is in their interests (CUORE: Centers for the Rehabilitation of Urban Economics).

National legislation was passed (art. 78 of law 448/98) and new institutions have been created for the coordination of the efforts at creating new occasions for regularization: a national Committee for Labor Regularization, local commissions, and a new figure of "tutor of regularization." An additional national law (law 383/01) was passed that offered a tax cut for those who would come out and declare their irregularity. The law was presented as a national effort, and hopes gathered for a sweeping movement that would have changed the situation.

Whereas in the past it had not been clear how the state should deal with the shadow economy (fight it or tolerate it), the new law has offered a clear-cut position: a great shift toward regularization is expected, for the benefits of the state finances and of the economy. The implication of all this—stated in the preparatory documents for the law—is that it would now be possible to monitor such progress by counting how many people have submitted their declaration of regularization. In other words, there emerged a consensus on what would be a "good result."

As it has turned out, things went in a different direction. The number of declarations has been low, and the press of any persuasion, politicians, and even trade-unionists have denounced the policy of regularization as a failure.

This conclusion is, however, questionable. What has not been positive has been the score obtained by a single indicator for a single instrument based on the assumption of a single main causing factor (an incentive to emerge as a way of reducing the fiscal burden). However, what does this indicator mean? Simply, the policy tool has been effective. But could the whole policy of regularization be reduced to that instrument or, worse, its evaluation of that indicator? Indeed, the policy of regularization had many tools at its disposal: carrots (incentives for regularization), sticks (control and fines), and sermons (the campaign "surfacing is convenient," the availability of services for regularization). Were there not data about the working of all these tools as offering alternative ways of understanding a general trend?

This is the way followed by evaluations conducted for and by the Committee,[15] who started questioning the mainstream answer offered to the question "how do we know it?" First, they tried to look into other possible data that could offer other insights: and this was done by utilizing the stream of statistical and administrative data that are collected for labor contributions (INPS), for labor insurance (INAIL), for understanding the labor market trends (Unioncamere), etc. All these data showed an unpredictable increase in regular jobs and in new firms. Then they looked at evaluations that had been conducted for other policy instruments: incentives like "credito di imposta" (tax credit); "prestito d'onore" (a loan to young entrepreneurs); and regulations like DNA (for labor accidents). All these sources showed regularization as their indirect effect (a kind of "joint production"). So evaluations had to make sense of contrasting results: there was regularization, but not due to the expected tools. What could be the explanation? Fearing the consequences of an open declaration, and listening to their consultants who were mostly skeptical about it,[16] few entrepreneurs submitted a declaration (the indicator was low). At the same time, however, part of the message had arrived. Many people have decided to regularize their own way.

What could then be said from an evaluative point of view? Those who declared surfacing a failure judged from the value of an indicator of success of a single program, which does not represent the complex policy, even if at some point it was politically at center stage (also due to the popularity of the Minister of Finance, thus creating the false perspective that regularization was just a matter of not wanting to pay high taxes). However, once one enters into the analysis of the panoply of possible ways of regularizing, it is necessary to bring together many data of different kinds, to be compared, cross-checked, from which to develop an hypothesis of how the different parts of society interested by the phenomenon might react.

At this point, it was possible to make sense of data collected in different territorial areas and productive sectors, and to start establishing some regularities. Perhaps people did not feel compelled in a country that has not a good record in paying taxes, and where social protection is itself assured by a strange combination of fragmentary interventions (Ferrera, 1997). But they know that in the European environment regularization is necessary if one wants to take advantage of services and facilities.

Moreover, it was possible to identify some weaknesses, and how to deal with them, from the point of view of the logic of such a policy. In fact, the question of coherence of policies is foremost even here. Regularization is a policy of local development. It is based on the idea that underground firms and workers could better utilize their resources for development if they were helped to surface. This, however, contrasts with the way agencies of work control, and also some trade unions, have traditionally dealt with the shadow economy, treating it as something negative to be eliminated. So, it was not simply a matter of having both parts do their job better, but of coordinating their activities under a common objective: local development. In the course of the evaluation, some examples of good integration among different policy tools have been found, like the protocol for the coordination between labor control and incentives for small firms in Bari, or the accreditation system for personal care services linked to a system of bonus for acquiring the services, as started in Modena.

## Are There Lessons to be Drawn?

We have analyzed some problems evident in the evaluation of two policies: a global one, the MDGs, and a national one, the Italian policy of regularization of the shadow economy. They are defined by goals that meet the needs of various constituencies, and that can be attained only through the combination of many interventions, touching upon different sectors. With such policies, however different they may be, it would be irrelevant to design an evaluation based on a single study, as it would have been done with projects designed according to a blueprint approach, and at the same time it would be irrelevant to look for a solution that satisfied all constituencies.

In both cases, a new trend of evaluative research is inspired by approaches that exploit the availability of existing data for the design of their evaluation. Here we are reminded that the "modesty" with which the previous evaluators took stock from the old debate on utilization meant pooling their knowledge with that of other knowledge producers, and being better acquainted with the policy process that they were up to judge.

In policies like the ones we have examined, goals represent the main central orientation, while the way of attaining them is open to the local or sectoral implementers' decisions. A first evaluative problem is therefore that of creating a link between objectives and results, of understanding what mechanisms can be utilized by what actors in what context, and hence help improve the policy. If goals are fixed, as with MDGs, the spontaneous tendency is toward ranking the various outcomes; and yet we have seen the risks of not integrating ranking with a learning organization approach. If goals are stated in a more general way, as in regularization of the shadow economy, the spontaneous tendency toward finding surrogate fixed goals should be resisted, and evaluation should be able to look at the sequence and combination of direct and indirect effects of those sector policies that might be relevant.

It may seem that addressing big problems and sector-wide policies is an ambitious task to be avoided. But our examples show that with appropriate approaches it is possible to manage the kind of information that can guide the incremental implementation of the new policies.

## Notes

1. This conventional view does not intend to diminish the evaluation researches that had been conducted prior to this age, especially in the field of education, social programs, and mass persuasion campaigns.
2. In the Evaluation Standards (Joint Committee on Evaluation, 1994), of which utility is the first one, it is explicitly stated that evaluations should be accurate whatever the approach developed.
3. Here I refer to the elaboration on carrots, sticks, and sermons (Bemelmans-Videc, Rist, Vedung, 1998)
4. One is reminded of Hirschman's idea of the need for understanding "how one thing brings to another"; and in development strategies it was evident that there could be "inverted sequences" (Hirschman, 1958).
5. It is not possible to mention here the debates in evaluation theory as regards the logic of experimentation, various kinds of causality, and validity. For illuminating works, see Shadish, Cook, and Leviton (1992) and Alkin (2004). See also Stame (1998).
6. I have discussed different versions of TBE in Stame, 2004a.
7. Example from Pawson and Tilley, 1997.
8. The Campbell collaboration, other similar movements.
9. See World Bank (2002, annex I and II).
10. The United Nations Conference on financing for development, held in Monterrey, Mexico, in March 2002.
11. For a good survey on the main related topics, see Hanna and Picciotto, 2002.
12. For an elaboration on the coherence of policies, see the website of the Center for Global Development (www.cgdev.org) and that of OECD (www.oecd.org/puma/strat/coherenc.htm).
13. World Bank, 2002: 5: a chronological chart, 1977 through 1996, of "targets...often set, but seldom met..."
14. The principle implies that "managers and staff, central planners and line ministers, headquarters and field units, are all responsible for success and failure." (World Bank, 2002: 7). Note, however, that this principle is referred to the spirit of the learning organization, hence to the model opposite of that which we are considering here.
15. See Meldolesi (2003) and Stame (2004c).
16. See Bàculo (2004).

## References

Alkin, M., ed. (2004). *Evaluation Roots. Tracing Theorists' Views and Influences.* Thousand Oaks, CA: Sage.
Bàculo, L., (2004). "La valutazione delle politiche di emersione nei sistemi locali meridionali." In N. Stame, *Per la valutazione delle politiche di emersione.* Milano: Angeli.
Bemelmans-Videc, M. L., R. C. Rist, and E. Vedung. (1998). *Carrots, Sticks and Sermons: Policy Instruments and their Evaluation.* New Brunswick, NJ: Transaction Publishers.
Evans, A. (2000). *Poverty Reduction in the 1990s: An Evaluation of Strategy and Performance.* Washington, DC: World Bank.
Ferrera, M. (1997). *Le trappole del welfare.* Bologna: Il Mulino.
Guba E., and Y. Lincoln. (1989). *Fourth Generation Evaluation.* Newbury Park, CA: Sage.
Hanna, N. (2002). "Promising Approaches and Development Challenges." In N. Hanna and R. Picciotto, *Making Development Work: Development Learning in a World of Poverty and Wealth.* New Brunswick, NJ: Transaction Publishers.
Hanna, N., and R. Picciotto. (2002). *Making Development Work: Development Learning in a World of Poverty and Wealth.* New Brunswick, NJ: Transaction Publishers.
Hirschman, A. O. 1958, *The Strategy of Economic Development.* New Haven, CT: Yale University Press.
Joint Committee on Standards for Educational Evaluation. (1994). *The Program Evaluation Standards*, II ed. Thousand Oaks, CA: Sage.
Kirkhart, K. (2000). "Reconceptualizing Evaluation Use: An Integrated Theory of Influence." In V. Caracelli and H. Preskill, eds., *The Expanding Scope of Evaluation Use. New Directions in Evaluation,* n. —, San Francisco: Jossey Bass.
Kubisch, A. et al., eds. (1995). *New Approaches to Evaluating Community Initiatives,* 2 vols. Washington, DC: The Aspen Institute.
Leviton, L., and E. F. X. Hughes. "Research on the Utilization of Evaluations." *Evaluation Review* 5(4) (1981): 525-548.
Meldolesi, L. (2003) "Policy for the Regularization of the Underground Economy and Employment," in *Review of Economic Coniditions in Italy*, n. 1.
Patton, M. "Discovering Process Use." *Evaluation* 4(2) (1998).
Pawson, R. "Evidence-based Policy: The Promise of 'Realist Synthesis.'" *Evaluation* 8(3) (2002).
Pawson, R., and N. Tilley. (1997). *Realistic Evaluation.* London: Sage.
Radelet, S. (2003). *Challenging Foreign Aid: A Policymaker's Guide to the Millennium Challenge Account.* Washington, DC: Center for Global Development.
Rossi P., and H. Freeman. (1989). *Evaluation, a Systematic Approach.* Thousand Oaks, CA: Sage.
Scriven, M. "Hard Won Lessons in Program Evaluation." *New Directions in Program Evaluation* 58 (1993). San Francisco: Jossey Bass.
Shadish, W., T. Cook, and L. Leviton. (1992). *Foundations of Program Evaluation.* Thousand Oaks, CA: Sage.
Stame, N. (1998). *L'esperienza della valutazione.* Roma: Seam.
\_\_\_\_\_. "Theory-based Evaluation and Varieties of Complexity." *Evaluation* 10(1) (2004a).
\_\_\_\_\_. "Evaluation and the Policy Context: The European Experience." *Australasian Journal of Evaluation* (2004b).
\_\_\_\_\_. (2004c). "La valutazione della politica di emersione: problemi e primi risultati." In N. Stame, ed., *Per la valutazione delle politiche di emersione.* Milano: Angeli.

Weiss, C. "Have We Learned Anything about the Use of Evaluation?" *American Journal of Evaluation* 19(1) (1998a).
\_\_\_\_\_. (1998b). *Evaluation*, 2nd ed. Upper Saddle River, NJ: Prentice Hall.
\_\_\_\_\_. (2000). "Which Links in Which Theories Shall We Evaluate?" In P. J. Rogers et al., eds., *Program Theory in Evaluation: Challenges and Opportunities, New Directions for Evaluation*, n. 87. San Francisco: Jossey-Bass.
Wholey, J. (1987). "Evaluability Assessment: Developing Agreement on Goals, Objectives and Strategies for Improving Performance." In J. Wholey, ed., *Organizational Excellence*. Lexington, MA: Lexington Books.
World Bank-OED. (2002). *Annual Review of Development Effectiveness.* Washington, DC: World Bank.

# 8

# Evaluating Knowledge about the Instruments of Government: The Canadian Federal Experience

*Pearl Eliadis and Donald Lemaire*

### Introduction

The proposition that "some forms of public action are more likely to address successfully certain public problems or social issues than others" lies at the heart of how governments approach choices about instruments, and governments have struggled for years to evaluate which instruments are best.[1] Through the evaluation of instruments—laws, spending, taxation, information campaigns, etc.—policymakers look at instruments, as distinct from policies and programs themselves, to capture predictive information about how particular instruments perform or at least how they are likely to perform.[2]

Like many OECD countries, Canada's interest in evaluating instruments is relatively recent. There has been a flurry of work, especially in the last decade, to improve the evaluative knowledge framework and to provide better knowledge about how instruments contribute to government performance and innovation. Nonetheless, evaluative knowledge about how instruments perform —especially relative to each other—is still weak. (OECD, 2002; Eliadis and Hill, 2002). Public servants complain that they are ill equipped to assess the relative merits of instruments and that more information is needed, especially with respect to the effectiveness of "innovative" instruments, including voluntary codes, international standards, and co-regulatory instruments. Basic research questions remain unanswered, including how policy goals are really achieved, which instruments are most likely to work, and how they interact.[3]

The purpose of this chapter is to look at some of the principal factors related to the development of evaluative knowledge frameworks on instruments at an institutional level in the federal government of Canada, as well as on progress in recent years.

## Evolution of Evaluative Knowledge about Instruments in Canada

Over the years, regulations and deregulations have been the main drivers of increased evaluative knowledge about instruments in Canada. In the 1970s and early 1980s, growing inflation and a reduced capacity for sustained growth generated concern about whether laws, and regulations in particular, were capable of addressing these phenomena, or whether they instead had led to a web of counterproductive hyper-regulation. There was skepticism about the value of these regulations and increasing interest in the search for alternative instruments.

It was believed that "command and control" instruments alone made it difficult to achieve compliance or to keep track of the different programs that government created.[4] But there was very little evaluative knowledge about how other instruments performed, alone or in relation to each other. Although command and control instruments were understood to be necessary in some contexts, other instruments, in mixes or alone, became a subject of growing interest to government, business, and civil society.

In the mid-1970s, the Economic Council of Canada commissioned several studies to assess the impact of the regulatory environment. One of them, The Choice of Governing Instrument, sparked interest in how governments choose various forms of public action in Canada (Trebilcock et al., 1982). The study was primarily concerned with testing the "axiomatic principle" that instruments are chosen as a function of technical or instrumental efficiency and with developing alternatives to that principle. The authors rejected efficiency and, in its place, proposed an alternative hypothesis of "politically rational instrument choice." The Choice of Governing Instrument was the first major study of its kind in Canada to identify critically the various considerations and tools that enter into the calculus of policy development and government action. While some of the forecasts made by the authors have not been borne out by experience, The Choice of Governing Instrument nonetheless had an important historical impact by explicitly locating the exercise of choice outside technical efficiency and in rational choice (Trebilcock, 2001). At the same time, there was an increasing focus on understanding the broad drivers of instrument choices as distinct from the features of individual instruments.

By the 1980s, several significant reforms encouraged deregulation and encouraged the identification and increased use of other instruments[5] However, as late as 1991-1992, Canada's Sub-Committee on Regulation and Competitiveness of the Standing Committee on Finance affirmed that there was still a clear preference for regulations as tools of government.[6] Since then, there have been attempts to rectify the "clear preference" for "command and control" instruments and to expand the range and use of alternative instruments.[7] The intent was to force policymakers to think in a more inclusive way about how governments choose instruments.[8]

Several initiatives took place during the 1990s that are too numerous to set out in detail here, but are well described in the recent OECD Report on Regulatory Reform in Canada (OECD, 2002). Two outcomes are worth noting, however: first, there were initiatives that resulted in attempts to divert instrument choices perspectives from legislative or regulation-based instruments to other kinds of instruments. Second, because most of the federal initiatives remained on a policy path that was created and developed through law-based instruments, the result was an oppositional, "either-or" relationship between law-based instruments and others. The impact of setting up choices in this binary way was a bifurcation of knowledge streams. A great deal of evaluative information was conducted with regard to law-based instruments, but little was being done from the perspective of managing or documenting knowledge outside of narrow project-based exercises. Naturally, policymakers responded by seeking evaluative information about what these other instruments are, how well they work, and how risky they are likely to be.

Most recently, this focus on regulation and deregulation re-emerged as a force for reform through a "smart regulation" initiative. In 2002, the head of Public Policy Forum, a leading Canadian policy think tank, called for a

> Smart Regulation initiative that would rescind hundreds, and perhaps thousands, of regulations[.] Smart regulation would open the door to the possible use of voluntary codes of conduct and self-regulation.[9]

This recommendation is characteristic of the Canadian either-or approach to instruments (regulations vs. new or voluntary instruments), and is coupled with a near-messianic belief that the elimination of the regulations (presumably meaning legislative instruments) will lead to an improved regulatory environment populated by the new instruments that emerge from business or other elements of society. The statement also appears to assume that alternatives such as voluntary codes of conduct and self-regulation are not already an important part of the Canadian "regulatory" environment and that the government can easily replace legislative schemes with other instruments.[10]

Shortly afterwards, the OECD released a study on Canada's regulatory reform and governance processes and recommended, among other things, the creation of a "Smart Regulation" project. The project was duly announced in the 2002 Speech from the Throne, and an external advisory committee was struck in 2003 "to recommend areas where government needs to redesign its regulatory approach to create and maintain a Canadian advantage."[11]

The external advisory committee's work was heavily focused on the formal regulatory structure, despite the calls in studies such as the 2002 OECD report for a broader use of other instruments. Although the deregulation and "smart regulation" initiatives promoted awareness of the need to generate knowledge about instruments, they have not actually led to an evaluative knowledge framework of other instruments and, indeed, arguably reinforced the traditional government focus on regulations.[12] More successful have been attempts to develop evaluative knowledge about instruments in the nested contexts of their institutions and policy styles. This will be discussed in the following section.

## Institutions, Policy Styles, and Evaluative Knowledge

Despite some of the sporadic attempts noted above, the structure and policy style of the federal public service have not been conducive to knowledge sharing about instruments. Indeed, until the late 1990s, there were few incentives to collaborate outside the vertical structures of the government hierarchy. The result was that knowledge tended to remain in silos.

There have been some improvements, for example, with the creation of horizontal knowledge brokering initiatives, such as the Policy Research Initiative in the late 1990s.[13] On the other hand, the few initiatives that have been undertaken in the federal public service to study instruments had few resources and could not reasonably have been expected to generate the kind of massive empirical research across broad categories of instruments that would be required for research along the lines of what has recently been achieved in the United States (Salamon, 2002).

Knowledge silos diminish the government's own capacity to assess and synthesize what it is doing. Each part of the public service tends to have good knowledge about the instruments used in its own bailiwick, and data are developed in sequential, project-specific, and results-based management frameworks. They are not distributed widely across the public service (or outside it) unless problems turn up in reports such as those of the Auditor General of Canada.[14] When this happens, of course, the reports become fodder for the press as examples of projects gone awry, a perception that is not conducive to information sharing. In short, barriers between departments and agencies have not become sufficiently porous to permit meaningful evaluative knowledge to be disseminated and absorbed.

Another structural impediment is linked to the fact that Canadian law-based instruments (especially regulations) are put through well-defined and relatively rigorous processes that allow for evaluation and some consideration of alternatives to regulation. But most other instruments are not subject to this kind of clear process or control, or at least not consistently, and have tended to evolve in an organic, ad hoc way across the federal government.[15] There is no standard for accountability to Parliament or otherwise across all instruments. Because of this decentralized and largely undocumented evolution, no one really knows the extent and number of instruments being used across the federal government. As well, no single institution has responsibility for all aspects of "instrument choice" (although in fairness, if instruments include every conceivable kind of government action and/or planned inaction, this would not be a very sensible exercise).

Finally, the tendency in the federal government in recent years has been to see instruments in terms of their effectiveness in isolation. In fact, choices are far more likely to be dependent on the perceived cause of the policy problem, the institutional context, or even familiarity of use as opposed to data on the effectiveness of a given instrument (Peters and Hornbeenck, 2005). Evaluative knowledge about instruments has also been hampered by the fact that there does not appear to be a clear way to map particular problems to particular tools (Eliadis and Hill, 2002). Data may not be readily transferable out of their context, and even if they are, their application is limited because of the "problem of comparing incommensurables and because the pros and cons are unlikely to be spread evenly across all interest groups (EEA, 2001: 168). The European experience is that identical policy problems are sometimes treated quite differently in different jurisdictions, and again, that this is largely a function of institutional and governance environments rather than the perceived effectiveness of particular instruments (Ringeling, 2005).

In short, if it is true that institutional context and complexity are as fundamental to good choices as the characteristics of a given instrument, then one might expect that instruments may fail for reasons that have more to do with the institution or environment than with any problem with the instrument itself.

There have been efforts to overcome both the structural and historical impediments, which have resulted in better knowledge flows about instruments and how to choose them. The efforts seem to have been most effective when the information about how instruments perform is pushed out of individual departments into the broader stream of government policy and linked to considerations of institutional style and context.

One example has been the work of the Auditor General of Canada, when studies have focused on reviews of broad classes of instruments and strategies to manage them rather than individual projects. For example, in 1999, the Auditor General audited several collaborative and delegated arrangements (funds and foundations, for example), in order to evaluate whether these "alternative arrangements" were accountable and effective. The Auditor General expressed concern that there was "no evidence that before entering into an arrangement the federal government had conducted any systematic assessment of its prospective partners' ability to discharge their responsibilities." None of the arrangements provided mechanisms for dealing with non-performance.[16] Other issues were raised about reporting and accountability to Parliament.

Since then, the Treasury Board Secretariat issued a Policy for Alternative Service Delivery, released in April 2002.[17] The policy recognizes the importance of the public interest and of accountability mechanisms, in addition to technical requirements of efficiency and cost-benefit analysis. Although the policy is limited to alternative service delivery and is heavily input-focused, the auditor general has in subsequent reports noted these efforts and improvements.

A second impetus for transcending institutional barriers to knowledge is linked to fundamental changes in the notion of governance itself. "Networked government" requires interaction between government and non-governmental actors, and understands government not as a top-down exercise but as a collaborative endeavor between state, citizen, and intermediaries: governance is not self-executing and government often works best by indirection (Macdonald, 2003). This shift in the government's institutional context means that there is not only a need to build capacity in government, but also a need to do so for other actors, both in Canada and beyond its borders.

## Capacity Building

Policymakers are under increasing pressure to develop instruments that allow both governmental and non-governmental actors to play a greater role. Capacity building is thus recognized as a central feature of instrument choice in Canadian federal guidelines, because of its strategic ability to build knowledge for and among networks of actors.[18] Where governments delivered most public services in the past, networks of organizations have begun to assume that role, sometimes bypassing government altogether.[19] In other instances, the expertise required in government in order to manage the new governance arrangements has changed dramatically.

*(a) Internal Governance and Capacity Building*

As the push to look at alternatives to formal regulation grew in the early and mid-1990s, several initiatives were undertaken to improve capacity within the federal government and to increase the knowledge base. Some criteria were developed by a group of departments in 1994 to guide decision makers in the federal guide entitled Assessing Regulatory Alternatives.[20] Although the guide was written from the standpoint of a person considering a legislative tool, it provided considerations for the use of other kinds of instruments. In 1996, the Deputy Ministers' Challenge Team (DMCT) on Law-making and Governance, a group of senior public servants, was created to improve "regulatory governance" and encourage more work on instrument choice.[21] At the same time, several initiatives were launched to improve information about performance in government through reporting mechanisms at the Treasury Board of Canada Secretariat (TBS).[22] These reports examined policy objectives and the effectiveness of various instruments through the lens of performance measures and result-based management.

In 1998, the Privy Council Office assumed responsibility for directives and guidelines on regulatory matters in an effort to centralize criteria and guidance across the public service. As part of this process, in March 1999, the Cabinet approved a guide on the law-making process for federal acts and regulations. The guide, which was updated in 2002, set out expectations for policymakers and despite its name, the directive dealt at some length with non-legal instruments.[23] It streamlined definitions and created new, broad categories of instruments from a functional perspective, demonstrating a more sophisticated approach to the relationship between good governance, instrument choice, and the public interest, including a reference to international obligations. The guide marks an important change in the attempt to move from individual "bits" of knowledge about individual instruments to broader categories, namely, information; capacity building; economic instruments (including taxes, fees, and public expenditure); rules, and organizational structure.

There have been some attempts to look at individual case studies and glean evaluative information about instruments. In 2000, Justice Canada released an interesting study, the Impaired Driving Case Study, which showed the effectiveness of bundling laws with other instruments (especially information instruments). The principal findings included a conclusion that a combination of a public perception of the likelihood of getting caught, along with a legislative sanction, was more effective than the law acting alone.[24]

Justice Canada went on to evaluate instruments from a legal risk perspective as the government led on instrument choice issues, but no research was issued outside of Justice Canada on this topic, apparently because of the difficulties inherent in removing individual instruments from their context and trying to evaluate their risk. This focus was underpinned by the assumption that crosscutting information about instruments and risk could transcend their context.[25]

This disconnected, "unplugged" approach to knowledge about instruments is certainly flawed. First, instruments rarely operate in isolation. Many, if not most, policy objectives are implemented through multidimensional combinations or "suites" of instruments (Salamon, 2002; Hood, 1986). The forms and interactions of these instruments—whether hybrids or mixes—shift, merge, and re-emerge with the result that many traditional instruments can become difficult to recognize or even name. Second, the role of context (both form and policy and an institutional perspective) is probably as important as the instruments themselves. As a result of an interdepartmental initiative in 2002 to build capacity in this area, several leading scholars and policymakers from Canada, the United States, and Europe were brought together to examine emerging issues related to instrument choice, including the problems of evaluative knowledge and reasons for the difficulties in making progress. Several general insights and principles were developed that, while not original at an individual level, were brought together for the first time in a single interdepartmental study in the federal public service:

1. Solely economic perspectives are inadequate to inform instrument choices, which should be primarily a function of governance criteria and not only (or even primarily) about cost, technical effectiveness, or economic efficiency.
2. The legitimacy of particular choices is bound up with political, legal, ethical, programmatic, social, and economic factors that operate across both domestic and global dimensions.
3. The debate must move from the individual instrument choice to instrument mixes, thus recognizing that instruments are context sensitive and rarely, if ever, designed or implemented in isolation.
4. All instruments, and particularly those that are designed and implemented at arm's length from the legislative process, have important repercussions for the legitimacy and accountability of public action.
5. Governance strategies and frameworks are needed to ensure both legitimacy and optimality in instrument design and implementation (Eliadis and Hill, 2002).

In short, the conclusion was that knowledge about instrument choices had to start with the right "inputs" before the right "outputs" could even be identified let alone evaluated. Efficiency and effectiveness had evolved beyond technical efficiencies and rational choice to a knowledge framework grounded in good governance and networked governance.

*(b) Capacity Building outside Government*

A more "networked" style of government has multiple sites of governance and political engagement (Howlett, 1991). Of particular interest in recent years are instruments such as codes, standards, and self-regulation that shift the cost and burden of policy development and enforcement from government to others. Business perceives such instruments as more collaborative, allowing industry to develop their own standards, for example, and lowering the cost of dispute resolution. Governments benefit in turn from industry expertise and involvement in the development of rules to control industry practices.

Most of these "innovative" instruments exist on a continuum of voluntariness. Many function through collaborative arrangements that rely on public sector involvement to a greater or lesser degree. From sponsorship to standard-setting, from publicizing best practices to "enforced self-regulation" and negotiated regulatory relief, governments can fine-tune their degrees of involvement.

Historically, evaluative knowledge about such instruments in Canada has been limited. There is little analytical work in Canada on how these instruments function or whether they are even in the public interest. There is a view, for example, that voluntary standards and other self-regulatory measures are used by pro-active industry associations and companies that avoid regulation. This is achieved in part by a focus on highly technical requirements with levels of detail that make it difficult to engage the public. One Canadian writer has observed that the development of technical standards in environmental management usurps public accountability and even the public interest by ousting broader policy debate:

> [T]he technologies of contemporary state environmental regulation embody, to a significant extent, the same managerialist tendencies to obscure the stakes, struggles and repressions of environmental politics, relying heavily on technical expertise, detailed, mundane, repetitive techniques of measurement, monitoring, calculation, assessment, inspection, etc., and relying increasingly on private market dynamics. While EMS [environmental management systems] are a particularly clear example of these tendencies, state environmental regulation shares the same characteristics to a significant degree.
>
> Viewed as governmental technologies, then, EMSs and standardization render environmental management a matter of technical expertise, organizational routine and market preference, contributing to the expulsion of a set of environmental and economic issues from the political domain.[26]

What is becoming clear is that voluntary standards and codes are capable of developing "command and control status" while bypassing Parliament because the courts use accepted standards as evidence of reasonableness or lack of negligence.[27] As one author has observed, once these standards become industry benchmarks, they can be endorsed by the courts and develop legal effects that may set lower standards than those that might otherwise be in the public interest.[28]

In recent years, the potential for evaluative knowledge about how such instruments function has been greatly improved: rapid movement of data, research sharing, and linked discussions are possible. Information sharing among scientists, NGOs, and public servants challenges traditional instruments and government choices at a faster rate and with greater effect than ever before possible. A great deal of this knowledge actually comes from beyond our borders.

*(c) Beyond Our Borders*

Globalization—whether defined as the end of geography or the increasingly rapid trans-border integration of institutions and networks—influences instrument choice in a number of ways. It has intensified the interaction of domestic and international spheres on instrument choices, and it has fundamentally changed the knowledge framework about how instruments should function. At a practical level, this means that international norms, transnational research, and best practices are shaping instrument choices outside the formal structures of government policies, studies, or directives.

In addition, international instruments such as covenants and protocols, trade agreements, bilateral and multilateral agreements, all are capable of creating obligations, norms, and principles that transcend state boundaries and form new normative bases for evaluative knowledge about how instruments should be chosen. The multiplicity of knowledge streams forces States to balance competing interests and to integrate or "weave" rules in order to achieve policy coherence.[29] Very little of this information is making its way into interdepartmental learning about policy development in Canada, outside of the efforts of certain individual departments. In fact, many obligations that are contained in ratified and signed instruments treaties are not expressly incorporated in the domestic sphere in Canada, with the result that they are not automatically incorporated into law. Legislation is generally needed to give full force and effect to an obligation that is contained in a treaty or covenant.[30] It is therefore not surprising that policymakers have not, historically, paid a great deal of attention to the standards in such instruments, except in departments whose job it is to worry about such matters such as Justice Canada or the Department of Foreign Affairs and International Trade.

There is, as a result, a "disconnect" between international instruments and policy approaches in several areas. For example, Parliament has not expressly incorporated most international human rights instruments into Canadian legislation. This may be surprising for non-Canadian readers, especially since Canada is seen as a leader in international human rights. It is true that Canada already has several human rights protections of its own, but the result of the "disconnect" is that in cases where there is a gap between international commitments and domestic law, the latter will prevail.[31]

As a result, it has been argued that Canada's understanding or knowledge of its own legal system has not yet adjusted to the changes in global governance that are affecting the evolution of Canadian law and policy: developing this understanding requires improved policy coherence and integration between government departments (Toope and Rehaag, 2005). This has obvious substantive impacts on evaluative knowledge about instruments that are designed to achieve good governance.

This disconnect is evident in policy guidelines published by the Privy Council Office, which direct policymakers to ensure "conformity" with international obligations in the law-making process, but as regards other instruments, policymakers are simply encouraged to consider the "effects" of international obligations.[32] One simple solution is the creation of an "international law filter," which would require policymakers to run selected policy instruments through a process that would assess compliance with international law (Toope and Rehaag, 2005). Extending this to knowledge frameworks about how instruments should be chosen, policymakers could use this idea in the systematic design and implementation of proposed instruments and improve the capacity to evaluate whether they are consistent with international norms, regardless of the type of instrument involved. For the purposes of this chapter, such a filter would be used as rigorously in the realm of alternative instruments as in law-based ones.

**Conclusion**

Evaluative knowledge about how instruments perform is a relatively new area of study in Canada and remains relatively weak. This is in part a result of historical factors, such as the emphasis on deregulation, as well as policy styles and structural impediments that have kept evaluative information in silos of departments.

As a result of deregulation efforts, the federal government has sought to expand the evaluative knowledge framework for non-legislative instruments by providing formal encouragement as well as support for various research initiatives. These efforts accelerated in the 1990s in order to rectify a perceived bias in favor of legislative instruments by encouraging policymakers to think about different, alternative instruments. Some of the efforts were of limited success, but there have been improvements in evaluative knowledge framework across a broader range of knowledge related to categories of instruments.

In particular, the implicit assumption that instruments are inert, and can be measured and assessed as such, has evolved to a better understanding of instruments in relation to different institutions and policy environments. Thus, policymakers have understood that instrument choice considerations are part of a complex web of social, economic, programmatic, legal, risk, and ethical considerations.

In Canada, Pierre Issalys has expressed the view that in choosing between various forms of public action, effectiveness and efficiency should only be considered after fundamental factors such as legitimacy, transparency, and equity have been weighed (Issalys, 2005). Again, while these observations may not appear revolutionary for experts in this area, the insistence on linking knowledge about good governance with instrument choices—and the fundamental role of choice and context in the equation—are welcome developments in the knowledge base of the federal public service.

Several initiatives have begun to address the knowledge gaps, most recently, the "Smart Regulation" committee, which will review and reconsider the regulatory framework in Canada. It remains to be seen whether the cycle of law-based regulatory intervention will continue to be the focus of reform efforts, or whether this latest round will advance the efforts of the last few years to promote an evaluative knowledge framework that both promotes innovation and retains accountability in the broader context of networked governance today.

## Notes

1. Thanks to Professor Roderick Macdonald of McGill University for this formulation of these assumptions guiding instrument choice.
2. See, generally, H. Lasswell, "Key Symbols, Signs and Icons," in L. Bryson, L. Finkelstein, R. M. MacIver, and Richard McKean, eds., *Symbols and Values: An Initial Study*, 77–94 (New York: Harper Brothers, 1954); M. Edelman, *The Symbolic Uses of Politics* (Chicago: University of Illinois Press, 1964); T. J. Lowi, "Four Systems of Policy, Politics and Choice," *Public Administration Review* 32(4) (1972): 298–310; L. M. Salamon, "Rethinking Public Management: Third-Party Government and the Changing Forms of Government Action," *Public Policy* 29(3) (1981): 255–75; Bemelmans-Videc et al., 1998; for Canadian perspectives, see Howlett, 1991; Eliadis and Hill, 2002; Eliadis et al., 2005; for a comprehensive U.S. perspective, see Salamon, 2002.
3. There are relatively few studies on how instruments actually function or interact in combination (*cf.* Gunningham and Grabosky, 1998). In the Canadian context, similar observations have been made about systematic study of voluntary standards, especially in the area of environmental management. See also S. Wood, "Green Revolution or Greenwash? Voluntary Environmental Standards, Public Law, and Private Authority in Canada," in Law Commission of Canada, ed., *New Perspectives on the Public-Private Divide* (123-65 at 144) (Vancouver: University of British Columbia Press, 2003). See also J. Freeman, "Collaborative Governance in the Administrative State," *UCLA Law Review* 45 (1) (1997): 1–98.
4. See, for example, in the Canadian context, Report of the Auditor General, 1999; Report of the Auditor General, 2001.
5. For an excellent overview of the evolution of regulatory reform and the emergence of regulatory governance in Canada, see OECD, 2002.
6. See the discussion of these developments and of the Committee's work in Lemaire, 1998: 63.
7. This preference remained in place until the 1990s as a preferred substantive instrument. See G. B. Doern et al., 1999: 389 ff. It is interesting to compare this with research from the 1970s on preferences of politicians: "politicians (especially collective cabinet) have a strong tendency to respond to policy issues (any issue) by moving successively from the least coercive of government instruments to the *most coercive*." G. B. Doern and V. S. Wilson, 1974: 337.
8. The authors acknowledge Dr. Margaret M. Hill, Infrastructure Canada, for this insight.
9. D. Zussman, "Let's Protect Canadians without Strangling Them," *Ottawa Citizen* (August 26, 2002): A13.
10. Alternatives to law-based instruments do exist, are widely used, and are effective in "regulating" behavior. ISO standards are a good example of the extensive use of industry-led standard development by a non-governmental source. Non-government regulatory instruments such as the Toronto Stock Exchange Guidelines are not "regulations," but they are highly complex, imposing a significant "regulatory" burden on reporting issuers. See Toronto Stock Exchange Joint Committee on Corporate Governance, 2001, *Beyond Compliance: Building a Governance Culture*, Final Report, November; Toronto Stock Exchange, "Request for Comments, Corporate Governance Policy—Proposed New Disclosure Requirement and Amended Guidelines" (March 26, 2002) http://www.tse.com. As well, many professions in Canada are already self-regulating, using internal codes of conduct and handling disciplinary matters internally, even though the standards are usually backed up by legislation.

## Evaluating Knowledge about the Instruments of Government    141

11. The project was announced in the 2002 Speech from the Throne and was intended to streamline the regulatory process in a number of areas such as pharmaceutical approvals and intellectual property. See Press Release, "Prime Minister Names Members of External Advisory Committee on Smart Regulation," www.smartregulation.gc.ca/en/04/pr-02.asp.
12. The Committee's final report was released in 2004 and is available at www.smartregulation.gc.ca/en/04/pr-02.asp. The report emphasizes that it is not focused on deregulation, and it refers to broad ranges of instruments as part of the regulatory framework. Nonetheless, the substantive recommendations focus primarily on regulations in the formal sense, and on technical recommendations for improving and streamlining the regulatory process.
13. The PRI was created in 1997 in order to address the need to bring together policy-relevant research from across government in order to better anticipate and manage medium-term policy needs in the federal government.
14. For example, a well-publicized audit of the transitional jobs fund managed by Human Resources and Development Canada revealed poor accountability and project management, leading to accusations of mismanagement. See, generally, Pal, 2001: 157.
15. An overview of the general categories of instruments that are available can be found in the federal government's *Guide to Making Federal Acts and Regulations* (2nd ed.) http://www.pco-bcp.gc.ca/default.asp?page=publications&Language=E&doc=legislation/lmgcatalog_e.htm. See chapter 1.1. Several federal departments have made very good efforts to develop criteria, standards, and evaluative frameworks around instruments:

- *1999 Cabinet Directive on Environmental Assessment of Policy, Plan and Program Proposals*: http://www.ceaa-acee.gc.ca/0012/0006/sea_e.htm
- *Standards Systems: A Guide for Canadian Regulators*, Regulatory Affairs and Strategic Policy Branch, Industry Canada: http://www.innovationstrategy.gc.ca/gol/innovation/site.nsf/en/in04936.html
- *Evaluative Framework for Voluntary Codes*, Office of Consumer Affairs, Industry Canada, March 2000. http://strategis.ic.gc.ca/epic/internet/inoca-bc.nsf/en/h_ca01227e.html
- *Developing and Implementing Voluntary Codes: Processes for Developing Effective Codes*, Industry Canada, 2005. http://strategis.ic.gc.ca/epic/internet/inoca-bc.nsf/vwGeneratedInterE/ca00964e.html.

16. See Auditor General of Canada (1999): 23.57 and 23.68.
17. Canada, Treasury Board Secretariat, 2002. The application of the policy extends to service agencies, crown corporations, administrative tribunals, shared governance arrangements, partnerships and collaboration with other levels of government, and contracting out.
18. Privy Council Office, *Guide to Making Federal Acts and Regulations* (2nd ed.) http://www.pco-bcp.gc.cadefault.asp?page=publications&Language=E&doc=legislation/lmgcatalog_e.htm
19. For a good survey of the literature in this area, with a particular focus on the evolution of Canadian implementation style in environmental policy, see M. Howlett, 2001.
20. The Guide was released by Treasury Board Secretariat, the Department of Agriculture and Agri-Food, the Solicitor-General of Canada and Transport Canada http://www.pco-bcp.gc.ca/raoics-srdc/docs/publications/assessing_reg_alternatives_e.pdf.

It was followed by the 1995 Department of Justice's Guide to the Making of Federal Acts and Regulations. This document did make reference to alternative instruments, as well as to the importance of looking at alternatives to law-based instruments, but—as its name indicates—the 1995 Guide was focused on law-based instruments.

21. DMCT is supported by the Regulatory Affairs and Orders in Council (RAOIC) Secretariat in the Privy Council Office, a Secretariat that was created in 1998 to work on horizontal regulatory issues in federal and international spheres, with a view to improving the quality in the regulatory process.
22. E.g., the annual Treasury Board of Canada Secretariat reports: *Getting Government Right* (1996); *Accounting for Results* (1997); *Managing for Results* (1998).
23. *Guide to Making Federal Acts and Regulations* (2nd ed.) http://www.pco-bcp.gc.ca/default.asp?page=publications&Language=E&doc=legislation/lmgcatalog_e.htm. See chapter 1.1.
24. Department of Justice, *Impaired Driving Case Study* (Policy Sector and Legislative Services Branch: Ottawa, September 7, 2000).
25. See Fact Sheet "Instrument Choice" in Department of Justice, Conference Materials, *Instrument Choice: A Toolkit for Effective Government Action* (Ottawa, March 26-27, 2002). Copy on file with authors.
26. Wood argues that this expulsion is reflected in the fact that, despite their major implications for environmental quality, public health, international competitiveness, and regulatory autonomy, voluntary EMS initiatives have received little attention from academics, almost none from news media and grassroots organizations, and have only recently begun to attract serious attention from public authorities. Wood, 2003: 144.
27. See, e.g., *Visp Construction v. Scepter Mfg.* (1991), 45 Constr. L. Rep. 170 (Ont. Gen. Div.). In that case, the defendant in product liability action was found not negligent because it had taken care to conform to voluntary standards of the Canadian Standards Association.
28. See *Privest Properties Ltd. v. Foundation Co. of Canada Ltd. et al.* (1998), 37 C.P.C. (4th) 126 (B.C.S.C.). In *Privest Properties*, the plaintiff brought action against the defendant for supplying fireproofing material containing asbestos. The plaintiff's claim against the manufacturer failed. Citing the decision in *Visp Construction Inc.*, *ibid.*, the Court concluded that the defendant had complied with the standards prescribed by the Canadian Standards Association. (Although the court also found no substantial evidence to establish that the product was dangerous or the removal of the material was necessary.) For a good general overview of some of the drawbacks of voluntary codes, see the Industry Canada website.
29. The term "weaving the rules" refers here to the interaction of international rules and norms related to human rights, trade law, environmental law, and labor law. Centre for International Sustainable Development Law, *Weaving the Rules*, McGill University, Faculty of Law (2002). www.cisdl.org.
30. With respect to international human rights obligations, see Report of the Standing Senate Committee on Human Rights, Promises to Keep: Implementing Canada's Human Rights Obligations (2001). http://www.parl.gc.ca/37/1/parlbus/commbus/senate/com-E/huma-e/rep-e/rep02dec01-e.htm
31. The Supreme Court of Canada has held that this is the rule, unless the international obligation can be used as an interpretative aid in relation to an existing Canadian law, in which case the international instrument can be used to support an interpretation of the Canadian law that is consistent with the international instrument, or unless there is an identifiable international value stemming from a ratified instrument that can be

used to inform the application of Canadian law. See e.g., *Slaight Communications* [1989] 1 S.C.R. 1038; *Baker v. Canada (Minister of Citizenship and Immigration)* [1999] 2 S.C.R. 817.
32. *Guide to Making Federal Acts and Regulations* (2nd ed.) http://Www.Pco-bcp.gc.ca/default.asp?page=publications&Language=E&doc=legislation/lmgcatalog_e.htm. Chapter 1.1- Choosing the Right Tools to Accomplish Policy Objectives.

## References

Auditor General of Canada. (1999). "Involving Others in Governing: Accountability at Risk." (Chap. 23) http://www.oag-bvg.gc.ca/domino/reports.nsf/741ca4e24fee97c985256e660055557b? Open Document.

Bemelmans-Videc, M., R. C. Rist, and E. Vedung, eds. (1998). *Carrots, Sticks and Sermons: Policy Instruments and Their Evaluation.* New Brunswick and London: Transaction Publishers.

Canada. External Advisory Committee on Smart Regulation. (2004). "Smart Regulation: A Regulatory Policy for Canada." http://www.pco-bcp.gc.ca/smartreg-regint/en/08/part_1.html#a01.

\_\_\_\_\_. Department of Justice. (2000). *Impaired Driving Case Study* (Policy Sector and Legislative Services Branch: Ottawa, September 7). Copy on file with authors.

\_\_\_\_\_. Industry Canada. *Standards Systems: A Guide for Canadian Regulators*, Regulatory Affairs and Strategic Policy Branch: http://www.innovationstrategy.gc.ca/gol/innovation/site.nsf/en/in04936.html.

\_\_\_\_\_. Industry Canada. (2000). *Evaluative Framework for Voluntary Codes.* Office of Consumer Affairs: March. http://strategis.ic.gc.ca/epic/internet/inoca-bc.nsf/en/h_ca01227e.html.

\_\_\_\_\_. Industry Canada. (2005). *Developing and Implementing Voluntary Codes: Processes for Developing Effective Codes.* http://strategis.ic.gc.ca/epic/internet/inoca-bc.nsf/vwGeneratedInterE/ca00964e.html.

\_\_\_\_\_. Privy Council Office. (1999). *Cabinet Directive on Environmental Assessment of Policy, Plan and Program Proposals*: http://www.ceaa-acee.gc.ca/0012/0006/sea_e.htm.

\_\_\_\_\_. Senate of Canada. (2001). Report of the Standing Senate Committee on Human Rights, "Promises to Keep: Implementing Canada's Human Rights Obligations." Senate of Canada 2001. http://www.parl.gc.ca/37/1/parlbus/commbus/senate/com-E/huma-e/rep-e/rep02dec01-e.htm.

\_\_\_\_\_. Treasury Board of Canada Secretariat. (2002). New Policy on Alternative Service Delivery. http://www.tbs-sct.gc.ca/pubs_pol/opepubs/TB_B4/information_e.asp.

Centre for International Sustainable Development Law. (2002). *Weaving the Rules.* McGill University, Faculty of Law. http://www.cisdl.org.

Doern, G. B., et al. (1999). *Changing the Rules: Canadian Regulatory Regimes and Institutions.* Toronto: University of Toronto Press.

Doern, G. B., and V. S. Wilson, eds. (1974). *Issues in Canadian Public Policy.* Toronto: Macmillan.

Eliadis, P., and M. H. Hill. (2002). *Conference Highlights: Instrument Choice in Global Democracies. Horizons* 6 (Policy Research Initiative, Ottawa). http://policyresearch.gc.ca/page.asp?pagenm=v6n1_art_15.

Eliadis, P., M. H. Hill, and M. Howlett, eds. (2005). *Designing Government: From Instruments to Governance.* Montreal: McGill-Queen's University Press.

European Environment Agency (EEA). (2001). *Late Lessons from Early Warnings: The Precautionary Principle 1896–2000.* Environmental issue report no. 22. Copenhagen. http://reports.eea.eu.int/environmental_issue_report_2001_22/en.

Gunningham, Neil, and Peter Grabosky. (1998). *Smart Regulation: Designing Environmental Policy.* Oxford: Clarendon Press.

Hood, C. (1986). *The Tools of Government.* New York: Chatham House Publishers.

Howlett, M. "Policy Instruments, Policy Styles, and Policy Implementation: National Approaches to Theories of Instrument Choice." *Policy Studies Journal* 19(1) (1991).

_____. (2001). "Implementation Styles in Canadian Environmental Policy: The Evolution of Instrument Choice." Paper presented to the Biennial Meeting of the Association of Canadian Studies in the United States: San Antonio, Texas, November 16. On file with authors.

Issalys, P. (2005). "Choosing among Forms of Public Action: A Question of Legitimacy." In P. Eliadis, M. H. Hill, and M. Howlett, eds., *Designing Government: From Instruments to Governance.* Montreal: McGill-Queen's University Press.

Lemaire, D. (1998). "The Stick: Regulation as a Tool of Government." In M. Bemelmans-Videc, R. C. Rist, and E. Vedung, eds., *Carrots, Sticks and Sermons: Policy Instruments and Their Evaluation.* (New Brunswick and London: Transaction Publishers.

Macdonald, R. (2003). Book Review, "The Tools of Government: A Guide to the New Governance." *Horizons* 6 (Policy Research Initiative: Ottawa).

OECD. (2002). *Government Capacity to Produce High Quality Regulation in Canada.* http://www.oecd.org/pdf/M00034000/M00034775.pdf.

Pal, Leslie. (2001). *Beyond Policy Analysis: Public Issue Management in Turbulent Times,* 2nd ed. Scarborough, ON: Nelson Thomson Learning.

Peters, G., and J. Hoornbeenck. (2005). "The Problem of Policy Problems." In P. Eliadis, M. H. Hill, and M. Howlett, eds., *Designing Government: From Instruments to Governance.* Montreal: McGill-Queen's University Press.

Ringeling, A. (2005). "Instruments in Four: The Elements of Policy Design." In P. Eliadis, M. H. Hill, and M. Howlett, eds., *Designing Government: From Instruments to Governance.* Montreal: McGill-Queen's University Press.

Salamon, Lester M., ed. (2002). *The Tools of Government: A Guide to the New Governance.* New York: Oxford University Press.

Toope, S., and S. Rehaag. (2005). "Globalization and Instrument Choice: The Role of International Law." In P. Eliadis, M. H. Hill, and M. Howlett, eds., *Designing Government: From Instruments to Governance.* Montreal: McGill-Queen's University Press.

Toronto Stock Exchange, Joint Committee on Corporate Governance. (2001). *Beyond Compliance: Building a Governance Culture.* Final Report, November. "Request for Comments, Corporate Governance Policy—Proposed New Disclosure Requirement and Amended Guidelines" (March 26, 2002) http://www.tse.com.

Trebilcock, M. J. (2001). "Journeys across the Divides" (lecture presented as part of the George Mason University Distinguished Visiting Lecturers Series, Arlington, VA, February 5). On file with authors.

Trebilcock, M. J., et al. (1982). *The Choice of Governing Instrument.* Ottawa: Minister of Supply and Services Canada.

Wood, S. (2003). "Green Revolution or Greenwash? Voluntary Environmental Standards, Public Law, and Private Authority in Canada." In Law Commission of Canada, ed., *New Perspectives on the Public-Private Divide* (123-165). Vancouver: University of British Columbia Press.

Zussman, D. "Let's Protect Canadians without Strangling Them" *Ottawa Citizen* (August 26, 2002): A13.

# 9

# Why Evaluations Sometimes Can't be Used— and Why They Shouldn't

*Jan-Eric Furubo*

### Introduction

Today evaluation is everything. The thirteen-year-old boy with football[1] as one of his main interests is involved in different forms of evaluation once or twice every week. Not only after the football games but also in school after he and his classmates have finished different projects. So this teenager has a fairly good idea about what evaluation is all about: exactly like many civil servants, politicians, or writers of books about evaluation. However, a description of purpose and methods would probably look very dissimilar in these different contexts.

It is not easy to find a common denominator among all those involved in what we today call evaluation, but if we try to find such a denominator, a common value, it will most likely have something to do with words such as use, learning, influence, and benefits. Evaluation is done with a purpose; it aims to have an impact on decisions, help us to avoid mistakes and to develop praxis, and so on. Evaluation is therefore very far from ideas about the search for knowledge for its own sake or as an activity aimed to satisfy our human curiosity about social behavior and causal relations in the development of society. Evaluations have to be useful.

If we can regard this usefulness as the raison d'être of evaluations we can easily understand the role that questions about use, utilization, learning, etc., have played in the evaluation discourse more or less from the beginning. These questions were also addressed in an earlier book published by this Research Group, namely, *Can Governments Learn?* (Leeuw et al., 1994). However, this discussion is even more relevant today. *The International Atlas of*

*Evaluation*, published in 2002, and one of the very few studies about the international development of evaluation, highlights the relevance of this question (Furubo et al., 2002). One of the main conclusions in the *Atlas* partly contradicts earlier discussions in this field. The earlier perception was that the evaluative praxis on a national level spread to more and more countries, starting in a handful of pioneer countries that adopted such praxis as early as the 1960s; in other words, more and more countries adopted an evaluative praxis in each period of time, to paraphrase Rogers (1995: 23).

The *Atlas* shows that quite a different development seems to be more likely. For a rather long time—perhaps a couple of decades—no evaluative culture or praxis had developed beyond more than a handful of Western countries. Then in the 1990s, a sizeable group of countries entered the evaluation era. The main difference between these two groups of countries, if we simplify things a bit, has something to do with internal and external forces. The first group, the handful of early adopters so to say, brought about an evaluative praxis due to internal forces that created a pressure and a need for conducting and using evaluations. Those countries that adopted evaluation praxis in the 1990s had been forced to do so as a result of external pressure from such institutions as the European Union, the World Bank, and the Organization for Economic Cooperation and Development (OECD).

The rationale for this pressure has, of course, been that evaluation leads to improvement. So the question of the actual use of evaluations and pre-conditions for political and administrative learning is certainly even more relevant today than it was ten years ago.

However, let us for a moment diverge in our discussion. We have so far talked about learning and use in a way that probably indicates that we regard them as synonyms. Of course this is not the case. We can make use of something without learning, and we can also learn without using. Let us illustrate this with a couple of examples.

In a study of a political program it is said that the program has been well implemented and has been extremely successful in reaching its goals. The probability that the responsible minister will use this evaluation is very high! The audience will probably have to listen to the politician when he or she boasts about the success of the program. So the evaluation will certainly be used. We can't exclude the possibility that the minister is also learning, but it doesn't follow from the form of utilization we have just hinted at. That's another story!

We can also imagine the opposite case. The minister happens to belong to that category of people who really follow the stream of evaluations in his or her ministerial field. And after a careful study of several evaluations of an important program the minister will conclude that a certain intervention is a failure, the program theory is wrong from the beginning and practically everything else as well. So our minister, as well as many of his civil servants, has obviously learned something. But will they act on the basis of this knowledge? Yes, this is again another story. The minister's final conclusion is perhaps that even if the program is a failure in every possible respect it has to go on: It is for example too risky to challenge some of the important pressure groups that have a vested interest in the continuation of the policy.

However, if we regard the raison d'être of evaluation as improvement we have to focus on whether the evaluative information leads to changes in decisions, praxis, and so on, both in a more immediate and instrumental way and in what can be regarded as a more conceptual way.[2] Thus, given these remarks we can see that questions on the use of evaluations and political and administrative learning have certainly become more urgent today than before.

For a discussion of these questions Sweden can be regarded as a very good case. In all comparative studies of the growth and development of evaluations Sweden has had an exclusive position. Hans-Ulrich Derlien describes Sweden as one of the five countries in the first wave of evaluation (Rist, 1990). Sweden's position is similar in the *International Atlas of Evaluation* twelve years after the publication of Derlien's article. Several of the different articles about Sweden as a flourishing country of evaluations (Sandahl, 1993; Furubo, 1994; Vedung et al., 2000; Furubo and Sandahl, 2002b) also emphasize the very early Swedish tradition, which easily can be traced back to the beginning of the last century.

These earlier descriptions demonstrate the magnitude of the evaluation activities in the Swedish political and administrative systems. There also exists a very elaborate structure for the commissioning and production of evaluative information in relation to different kinds of decisions. Internal evaluations are to some extent the task of all agencies. They have to report back on an ongoing basis about their activities, and it creates a stream of evaluative information.

Some agencies also contribute to this stream with special evaluations. Several bodies, research institutes, governmental commissions, and so on produce evaluations of an ad hoc character. This structure of producers of evaluative information generates, of course, a good amount of varied information.[3]

If we also take into account what is often pointed out, namely, an underlying rationalistic and instrumental attitude to the political decision making, it really becomes interesting to ask:

Do evaluations lead to learning among

- Politicians?
- Administrators?

and under what circumstances?

These questions can be discussed in different intellectual contexts. A great deal of effort has been put into studies and discussion about different forms of utilization, and the influence of evaluations. At the same time and partly in other intellectual circles, we find discussions about organizational learning and, more specifically, about learning in political environments, and governmental or political learning.

But when we discuss these questions we soon find that we cannot do it on a general level. The political and administrative systems at the national level produce many different forms of decisions, and we can guess that the discussion of our questions is not quite the same when it comes to a decision about a fundamental change in policy or a minor fine-tuning policy maneuvre or technical decisions related to the implementation.

It is therefore possible to distinguish between different kinds of decisions. We can, for example, talk about

- Fundamental policy decisions
- Middle-range decisions regarding fine-tuning of policies or "maintenance decisions"
- Operative decisions in the ongoing implementation.

It is, of course, always a bit arbitrary how we place different decisions in such a categorization and what is placed in one category one day can certainly be put into another category next week or next year. It is perhaps therefore more realistic to talk about a scale at which you at one end point have more fundamental policy decisions on a rather *aggregated policy level*, decisions that can question the mere *existence* of a governmental policy, its basic *goals* and its principal *means*. At the opposite end of the scale, we will find what we without further discussion may regard as pure and simple technique, for example, operative decisions that are part of the ongoing implementation of an intervention or a program. Between these points we find numerous decisions, which perhaps can be labeled as a sort of fine-tuning or policy maintenance. These decisions are related to more disaggregated goals and the use of instruments on a lower level in the end-means hierarchy.

**Figure 9.1**
**A Scale of Decisions**

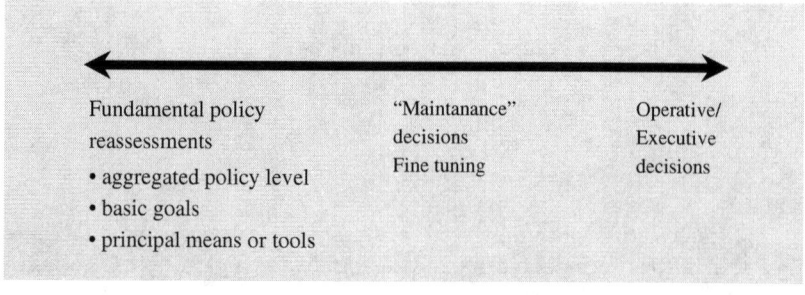

One more thing can be added about these kinds of categorizations—which may be relevant in our discussion about use, non-use, and perhaps the misuse of evaluations: we often meet different players involved in the decision-making process, depending upon which category the decision belongs. In a country like Sweden it can even be said, at least on a textbook level, that the division between the ministerial structure and the different agencies, numbering about 300, reflects these categorizations. Somewhere, a borderline has been drawn between politics and implementation. On one side of the borderline, we have what is regarded as implementation—the task of the agencies, and, on the other side, is what is regarded as policy or politics.

However, even if this kind of categorization confronts us with some difficulties, the real problems will of course present themselves when we continue to the more empirical questions about what we actually know about the role of evaluations in different kinds of decisions.

### Few Empirical Studies

The reason that the empirical questions are difficult is, of course, that we have very few empirical studies in Sweden about the use of evaluations and governmental learning in relation to evaluations. So, to a great extent, what can actually be said in this field has a hypothetical character.

This is certainly the situation at the endpoint of our scale, with which we are going to start, namely, fundamental policy reassessments. Studies about how different forms of evaluations have influenced decisions and changes in the central goals, their relative weight, and the choice of policy instruments are rare; what is indicated in this material is that evaluations have influenced fundamental reassessments of policies in just a few, exceptional situations.

### Evaluations Do Not Lead to Fundamental Changes of Policy...

In the chapter about the Swedish Experience in *Can Governments Learn?* the discussion in this respect is based on a couple of different sources.[4] The conclusion in *Can Governments Learn?* is that evaluations do not lead to a questioning of the basic assumptions underlying a certain policy—if we consider central policymaking processes at the level of the government and Parliament (Furubo, 1994: 59).[5] It says further that "A conclusion that may be drawn from our examination of the extent to which evaluations lead to learning is that only in exceptional cases do evaluations appear to play a part in significant changes in orientation of policy."

We cannot find more than a couple of later Swedish studies that address the question of use in such terms that they are relevant in this context and give us the same picture. In a report of September 2002, based on interviews from a special investigation group within the Ministry of Finance, the situation in relation to what I have called fundamental reassessments is summarized in the following way: "Experience demonstrates that reassessments have often been caused by events usually depending on the disclosure of a special and unsatisfactory state of affairs" (Finansdepartementet 2002: 56). So the limited sources at our disposal indicate that the conclusion from 1994 is valid. It is also important to note that the conclusion is not contradicted by studies of policy formation and policy shifts in different areas. In studies related to areas such as housing policy, energy policy, crime prevention, and so on information from evaluations is not very often referred to as a major explanation for changes of any significance. The information acquired from evaluations does not seem to be a major explanation for significant policy changes.

### ...But They Are Used in Fine-Tuning and for Operative Decisions

Moving in the direction of the other end of the scale, to fine-tuning and more operative decisions within the implementation process the situation seems different. When looking at this, we find the following conclusion in *Can Governments Learn?* where it is stated there that on "a more technical level the situation is quite different. In such a context evaluations are able to play an appreciable role—and much evidence would indeed seem to indicate that they do."

As indicated in the quotation, it was possible ten years ago to find evidence that supported the statement about the use of evaluations in these more administrative processes. However, today we have more material at our disposal, considerably updated.

It is obvious that the amount of evaluative information relating to more ongoing decision making has increased. In a study from 1998 (RRV, 1998) the appearance of result information in the budget bill in fourteen different areas was compared at two points in time. The result was a marked increase in the evaluative information. Another study about the dialogue between the ministries and the agencies also indicated that the information the agencies delivered was used in the ministries' discussions about the agencies' future activities (ESV, 1999).

A study from 2002 (Statskontoret, 2002) indicates a further increase in relation to the extent to which evaluations are mentioned in the annual budget bill, and the same picture is given in other reports and studies. It is therefore safe to say that we have had an increase in the evaluative information that has reached decision makers over the last ten years. This is evaluative information related to what has been accomplished by the agencies, its quality, its cost, and the internal administrative efficiency of these agencies. It is an orientation towards output and performance rather than towards effects and preconditions for effects.

The study from 2002 shows that about one-third of the evaluations that were mentioned in the budget bill in 2002 were used as justification for present policies. About 15 percent of the evaluations are used as an argument for change and in 17 percent of the cases the government indicates that they will look further into the matter and then return with proposals to Parliament. So, if we regard the cases in which the evaluations are used to justify or legitimate present programs, more than two-thirds of the evaluations have been used.

In another study from 2002 (Lejdhamre, 2002), about the use of performance audit reports from parliamentarian auditors and the National Audit Office, the author gives the same picture. The report seems to have been used in what we have talked about as fine-tuning or operative decisions.

Thus, it appears that evaluations do play different roles in different parts of our scale. How can this be explained? Can this picture actually represent the truth? Can we find reasonable explanations for this lack of utilization of evaluative findings in relation to more fundamental reassessments, that we so seldom use evaluations in relation to significant changes in policies? And can we explain the different degree of utilization in relation to decisions about the more detailed construction of a policy or its implementation? Yes, it is possible to find at least some explanations that make this picture plausible.

### Explanation 1: The Role of Values versus Evaluative Information

The first explanation is that the very nature of some decisions makes the evaluative information highly irrelevant. A policy or intervention can be discussed and questioned both for a value perspective and for more instrumental reasons. The value component can be expected to be more salient when we move towards the fundamental reassessments endpoint in our scale, and the role of empirical information increases when we move in the other direction.

Therefore, it is easy to point out that the existence or basic orientation of a program can sometimes be regarded purely as a question of values. We can on one level imagine that all politicians agree—which is certainly not always the case—about the actual situation in some area, for example, the standard of housing, the social distribution of education, and so on. However, there can be quite different opinions about how a given situation should be judged. Some politicians may regard the situation as unsatisfactory, justifying a political intervention. Other politicians may regard the same situation as quite satisfactory (Sandahl, 1986).

And even in those cases in which all politicians agree that a given situation is unsatisfactory, there can still be divergent opinions concerning whether or not it is a political issue at all, that is, if the situation justifies political intervention. A politician arguing against an existing governmental intervention or program from such a value perspective has little use of information in evaluations. If the evaluations show that the existing program has been successful, and perhaps indicate that some changes could make it even more successful, it is still irrelevant information for the politicians who are against the intervention as such. The same can be said if the evaluations show the opposite: the intervention was a failure and that perhaps quite different instru-

**Figure 9.2**
**The Role of Values and Empirical Information in Relation to Different Decisions**

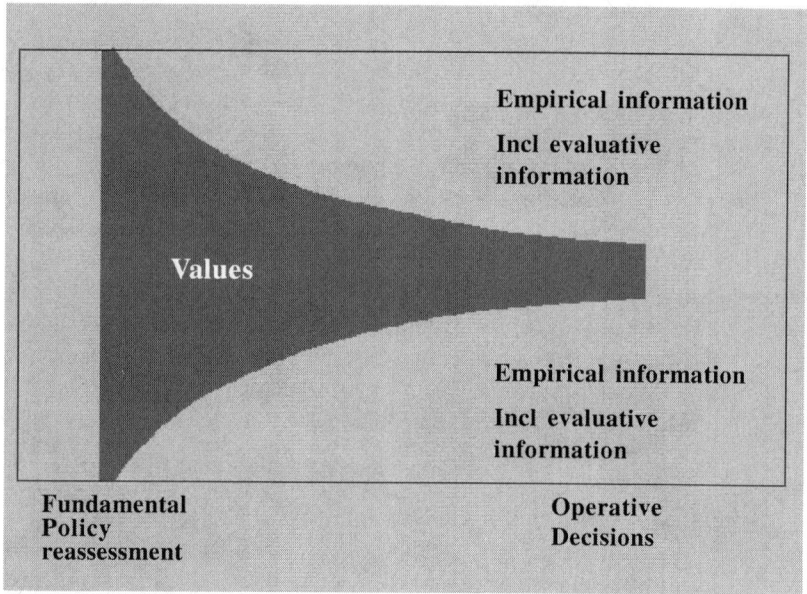

ments are needed to make the intervention successful. Even this information is, of course, quite irrelevant if one is against the intervention as such.[6]

In these situations, information from evaluations lacks relevance; the political position regarding the intervention or program is based on values about what is good and bad, better and worse, and about the role of government. A position does not depend on information concerning whether or not a certain intervention was a suitable means of reaching a certain goal or solving a certain problem in society.

But a very brief moment of reflection will probably also lead to the conclusion that decisions that concern the basic orientation of policies are value-based to a much higher extent than decisions on lower policy levels. In other words, the relative weight of values and empirical information is quite different in more fundamental policy decisions compared to more technical and instrumental decisions concerning the more detailed construction of a given policy or its implementation.

### Explanation 2: The Actual Produced Information Has a Shifting Degree of Relevance for Different Kinds of Decisions

But even if we, so to say, sort out these situations when a policy or an intervention, questioned from the perspective of values and evaluations, therefore lacks relevance, the politicians can still question the basic orientation of a policy or a program for more instrumental reasons. Decisions about the future fate of the intervention could be based on an assessment of how effective the intervention is in the fulfillment of certain goals. We are then faced with the question of whether or not the tools that government and Parliament have at their disposal can influence a certain development in society. And we can question which policy instruments are the most suitable, and also their basic construction in the specific situation.

We can certainly imagine that evaluations could contribute information in this kind of reassessment. Yet we are still confronted with the question of why evaluations do not seem to influence fundamental reassessments of existing policies to a greater extent.

One part of this discussion concerns the actual character of the evaluations that are produced in Sweden and probably in many other countries. Most of the studies, which are labeled evaluations in Sweden, do not provide information at the fundamental means–goals oriented level. For example, governmental agencies, governmental commissions, and different research institutions in Sweden have produced literally hundreds of evaluations about the use of information as a policy instrument in areas such as energy consumption, health, and so on. These evaluations provide information about the dissemination of the information, how efficient different channels are compared with each other, the changes in knowledge and attitudes in different target groups that can be attributed to the information, and so on. In other words the evaluations provide much knowledge about the implementation of, in this case, a certain policy instrument. However, they do not provide answers to questions concerning in what situations information is a suitable policy instrument in relation to other policy instruments, in what situations information should be used instead of other policy instruments, and in what situations information could lead to effects the opposite of what was intended.

There is even a tendency to produce fewer evaluations, which deal with the basic assumptions about how a certain intervention can influence different causal relationships and the circumstances for governmental interventions. There has been a tendency over the past ten years to produce evaluations in a much shorter time and to provide more easily accessible information.[7] More and more of the evaluations are oriented toward implementation, output, and performance and are parts of the system of agency reporting to the government. The information in the evaluations is therefore more relevant in decisions that are part of what I have called the maintenance of policies or operative decisions.

This explanation is empirical in character. It says that to some extent we produce the "wrong" evaluations if the intention is for them to be used in policy reassessments, and that we to some extent, produce the "right" evaluations if the intention is that they be used in more operative decisions. And this is certainly not a new answer in the Swedish discussion. In more than a few governmental documents produced during the last few decades—literally—it has been a complaint that the existing evaluations do not help in questioning policies and in deciding what resources should be allocated for different interventions, and which interventions have been the most successful.

## Explanation 3: Quality of Evaluations and the Knowledge Frontier

A third explanation is that many evaluations are of poor quality, even from a more technical point of view (ESO, 1996; Statskontoret, 1999), and this is, of course, a problem in relation to all kinds of decisions. The 1996 report is most harsh in its assessment of the quality of evaluations from twenty-two governmental agencies; these evaluations were conducted in relation to the agencies' own activities.

But a more fundamental quality problem has to do with the fact that many evaluations are repeated without any clear link to earlier evaluations. This can be illustrated with an example from the field of energy conservation, in which more than 100 evaluations were produced in the 1980s. Similar evaluations were then carried out in the 1990s. These evaluations have raised the same evaluative questions, in relation to the same policy instruments and with the same research design without any discussion of earlier results. The same picture is evident in the earlier example concerning the use of information as a policy instrument.

Thus, according to the above, the evaluation process itself enjoys only a very limited degree of learning. If you look at the enormous number of "day-to-day" evaluations that are made within the various administrations and research institutions, you can see how little use is made of previous evaluations. The same evaluations are repeated. Very much the same questions are asked and receive the same answers in a sort of evaluative ritual (cloning of evaluations).

This kind of evaluative amnesia makes the movement of the knowledge or evaluative frontier very slow. One aspect of this amnesia is also that many evaluations do not make use of more general knowledge and seldom relate to a more general body of knowledge, which may be highly relevant. Perhaps the reader can guess that at least experienced politicians and bureaucrats have understood an important rule: Do not trust the evaluators too much!

## Explanation 4: Difficult to Use, Inexact, and Unreliable Statements for Reassessment of Policies

These latter explanations have to do with the actual character of the evaluations. If we could find the main explanations following these lines, we could certainly reduce this to a question of how we could change the character of the evaluations produced.

But besides this empirically oriented answer, we also have to discuss our basic ideas about how evaluations can contribute to reassessments of policies and political or governmental learning.

# Why Evaluations Sometimes Can't be Used—and Why They Shouldn't 157

The role of evaluative information varies depending on where we are on our scale (Fig. 9.1) and it is also obvious that we need different forms of evaluative information depending on what kind of decisions we are talking about. When we are talking about how we can improve the technical construction of a given policy instrument we need a certain type of information, but when we are discussing whether or not it is a good idea to use this policy instrument at all, we need, of course, a quite different type of information. It is obvious that these different forms of information have many different characteristics. The first type of information is often of a character that makes it suitable for the ongoing production of information, which, perhaps, is not the case when we talk about the latter type of information.

In this context, it is relevant to make a distinction between how exact and reliable different evaluative statements are. This is illustrated in Figure 9.3. On the Y axis we can imagine, nearest the origin of coordinates, a limited measure, for example, an information brochure on influencing household's use of energy. A little further up we find the "package of information efforts" required to have an effect on energy consumption, and still higher up the total measures needed to influence energy use in society. On the X axis, we can imagine some kind of chain of effects where, in the example given, we see the reception of the information nearest the zero, and farthest to the right the influence on the environment, and the national economy that reduced energy consumption would have.

It is easily seen that we are talking about completely different kinds of information in "a" and "b" and without crossing over the line to a discussion about theories of knowledge we—and certainly the decision makers—can expect information in "a" to be very exact and, at the same time, reliable. Evaluative statements on the effects of complex interventions in still more complex social processes and courses of events are of a quite different nature.

**Figure 9.3**
**Different Evaluative Statements**

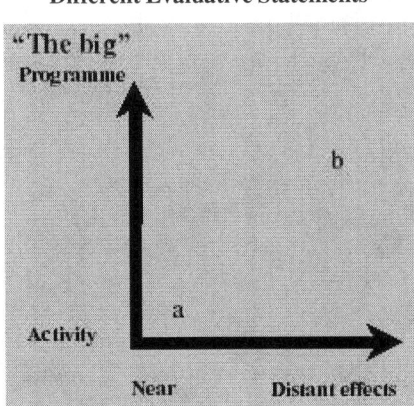

An evaluation that draws conclusions about the extent to which a reform of the school system, aiming to influence equality between men and women, has actually changed vocational choice, relationships in the home, etc., can hardly do so particularly well, and not with any high degree of reliability. The nearer to "b," the more improbable it is that different evaluations will come to the same conclusions.

The problem is, of course, that the "b" information is more relevant than "a" information, when it comes to decisions about the basic orientation of a policy. It is therefore difficult to imagine that this kind of often uncertain evaluative information should be transferred in a more immediate way to the political decision-making system. The lack of use in relation to fundamental policy reassessments can therefore seem very rational from the politicians' point of view. But, on the other hand, we can also expect that the decision makers make more use of the evaluative information in relation to the maintenance of policies and operative decisions. The information they need in these processes is more of the "a" character and therefore also more reliable. The difference when it comes to the use of evaluative information in different kinds of decision-making processes seems therefore reasonable even from this perspective.

### Explanation 5: Relation between Evaluators and Political Decision Makers

This brings us to the question of the relationship between what we can call the evaluative camp and the political camp. Discussions, even the more recent ones, about the use or influence of evaluations have used the evaluation and perhaps the evaluation process as starting points. The information in the evaluation has to be disseminated for the purpose of leading to different forms of use. On this point, it can be added that the discussion about the different forms of use has long since passed the stage at which the perception of use was an immediate response among decision makers to a specific evaluation.

But even if we are all aware of the sophistication of this discussion about use and utilization, the underlying idea is still very much based on a model that starts with the evaluation, which—hopefully—will be disseminated to the decision makers, who will react to the findings, in one way or another—directly or indirectly. [8]

This model or notion of the utilization process is perhaps a realistic one when it comes to implementation on a more administrative or operative level. But in reference to the relationship between evaluative information and political decision making this notion is perhaps too simplified.

To what extent the knowledge in different evaluations can influence policy reassessments has probably also something—and perhaps a lot—to do with the existence and the character of intellectual structures that are feeding the political system with knowledge. This factor is discussed in a study about the Swedish Stabilization Policy 1975-1995 (Joung, 1999). The author Lars Jonung tries to "explain the sequence of policy switches that characterize Swedish stabilization policy during the period 1975-95." The author highlights the importance of intellectual structures from which the political decision makers may possibly receive information. He points out the existence of a profession in close contact with the political system by saying, "politicians responsible for policy also obtained information, inspiration and arguments from the economic profession, that is, from economists active at universities and research institutes." Further, he points out the role of international organizations as another source of information.

If we relate the results in this study to our discussion, it would give rise to the question of the need for such intermediate structures between the evaluation side and the political side, intellectual structures, which digest the results of evaluations of—usually—rather limited programs or activities and relate them to a more general body of knowledge.

In the case of the Swedish stabilization policy, it was easy for the author to point out a well-defined academic discipline or profession with channels to the political elites. Perhaps we can imagine that the role of evaluations in political decision making varies depending on the existence of such intellectual or professional structures.

Thus, instead of the notion of a model in which evaluations are regarded as knowledge channeled directly to the political decision makers, an alternative way of looking at things is to use the analogy of a "knowledge bank." Different evaluations can contribute to this knowledge bank with information deposits. The officials of the bank, to continue the metaphor, interpret the information delivered in these different studies, rearrange the information, and relate it to earlier knowledge in the field. They finally communicate the knowledge of which they are in possession to the political elites.

That is to say: the immediate users of evaluations are not the decision makers, but the officials of our metaphorical bank. So the extent to which the information, which we have gained in connection with our earlier governmental interventions, actually will be channelled into the political and administrative system very much depends on the character of these intermediate knowledge structures.

Of course, the existence of such knowledge structures is very different in different areas. Sometimes you can talk about well-defined knowledge structures coinciding with academic disciplines. However, this is often not the case, and this makes things a bit more difficult. Further, the lack of such structures can, perhaps, to some extent explain why evaluations are used as little as they are.

But what I want to point out is that discussion about how evaluations can contribute to more fundamental policy reassessments perhaps should not focus on the relationship between evaluations/evaluators, on the one hand, and the political system on the other. Another perspective focuses on a more triangular relationship, and asks questions about the relation between the evaluation community and other knowledge structures, on one hand, and these structures and the political system on the other hand. It includes questions about the existence of different channels between these more general knowledge bodies and the political system, and also to what extent evaluations can contribute to this more general knowledge.

### Explanation 6: Crises Trigger Policy Shifts—Not Information

Finally, we will touch upon one more possible explanation. When it comes to more technical and administrative decisions, the right-hand side of the scale in Figure 9.1, it is possible to create systems that more or less force the decision makers to act on the stream of evaluative information.

The last ten or fifteen years have, under the umbrella of New Public Management (NPM), seen a lot of different organizational solutions aimed at forcing superior levels to react to information produced by subordinate levels. They may have been in the form of different contractual arrangements with negotiations about content of the contract and procedures for how the subordinate level has to report about how different goals have been reached, and also some sort of the statement from the superior level about how the tasks have been fulfilled. In Denmark, this latter phase has also included economic incentives for the directors (PUMA, 1999; ESV, 2001). The Swedish system, too, includes a negotiation phase before the government decides about the letter of appropriation, which includes goals on different levels. The government also has to react through statements in the budget bill on the information they have received from the agencies and give a judgment on how well the agencies have fulfilled their tasks.

Similar and other arrangements within agencies and other executive bodies have aimed at improving management, including systems in which information regarding cost, output, quality, etc., is channelled to the decision makers on an ongoing basis.[9]

However, very much the same ideas have been adopted when it comes to making decisions at the other end of the scale as in Figure 9.1. Much effort has been put into the construction of different systems aimed at guaranteeing an ongoing examination of different policies. On several occasions since the 1960s Sweden has tried to incorporate fundamental reassessments of the basic commitments of the state and the basic tools that should be used to achieve different goals, in more bureaucratic systems. These systems are intended to guarantee that such reassessments are conducted regularly, every third or fifth year or thereabouts. In short, and with some brutality, it can be said that these efforts have failed.

Behind these systems lies the notion that it is possible to force the decision makers to act on information even when it comes to more fundamental questions such as the existence of different interventions and their direction and principal means. This notion corresponds with the idea of social engineering and a rationalistic interpretation of how the political systems work. In other words, the underlying assumption is that decision making looks very much the same in the different parts of the scale in Figure 9.1. And this implies that information can be a driving force in the re-examination of a policy.

However, this assumption about information as a driving force behind fundamental policy shifts is probably too naïve and too rationalistic. Is it realistic to expect the political level to start to question a policy, in a more fundamental way, simply because one or two or even five or six evaluations point out different problems, for example, the lack of goal fulfillment and questions about the underlying rationale for the policy?

As we have seen earlier, it is very difficult to find Swedish examples of policy shifts based on information from evaluations. However, one Swedish example is sometimes mentioned in this context. This is the shift in agricultural policy at the end of the 1980s.[10] This shift took place in an area where numerous studies existed demonstrating the weakness and side effects of the policy. This policy shift, therefore, can possibly be explained in the terms of accumulation of evaluation knowledge; the accumulation of knowledge causes a shift in the balance point of the seesaw and leads to a reassessment of the policy.

However, it can also be added that this knowledge, accumulated over a long period, was part of a well-defined economic discipline with channels to the political elite. Exactly as in our earlier case about the stabilization policy it was therefore easy for the political decision makers to know where they could ask for knowledge, and to whom they could put the questions when the "time was right."

Moreover, in the discussion about policy shifts and political learning, it is stressed by many authors that questions about alternative courses of action are posed by the decision makers when they are facing crises or extreme situations. It is crises that force the decision makers to act, and instead of "more of the same," a deep crisis makes it possible to change policy in a more fundamental way; the crisis creates a window of opportunity.[11] To some degree, the perception or awareness that the politicians are facing a crisis can, of course, be based on "scientific" information; national statistics can demonstrate that central economic variables are developing in a very problematic direction or that the crime rate has reached an unacceptable level. However, the process and the interpretation of the situation as a crisis can also be caused by mass media and "scandals."

And if we follow this thought about the role of crises as an explanatory factor for policy shifts it leads us to several questions about how and in which situations it is fruitful to bring in information from evaluations in different decision-making processes; and it also provides a background for a discussion about the role of different knowledge bodies that can provide the answers when the politicians really want them. It also implies that we have to question the role evaluations can play in fundamental reassessments of policies.

## Finally

I have, in this chapter, tried to moderate the expectations of the role of evaluations and, in doing so, I have found it important to bring to light a couple of distinctions. They can seem too simple, but they are important.

We often talk about evaluations in a more general way thereby hiding the fact that the information provided in evaluations varies in a number of respects. And at the same time the decisions within the political and administrative systems are of many different kinds.

These points of departure have consequences with regard to what role we can expect evaluations and evaluative information to play. They also have consequences for the discussion about how frequently different forms of information should be produced and affect questions about responsibilities and the organization of the commissioning and conducting of evaluations as well as for the relationship between evaluation and other forms of knowledge production.

We can also probably imagine several different developments in this field. On the one hand, we have a tendency towards a more ongoing, continuous stream of evaluative information, which will be channelled more or less directly to the administrative decision makers from different systems. This kind of information is generated in more or less direct relation to the implementation of different activities. It gives the agencies, or, more generally speaking, the organizations responsible for the implementation of policies, a key role in the production of such information.

On the other hand, we have the development of other forms of evaluation, which has to be done on an ad hoc basis, and which needs to interact much more strongly than today with a more general science production.

## Notes

1. For American readers: Soccer.
2. However, it should be noted that this line of reasoning doesn't exclude symbolic and/or legitimating use.
3. In this context, the terms evaluation and evaluative information are used with great openness. However, even with such elasticity, I do not include all kinds of descriptive information. We can assume that some notion of reality lies behind every policy or every governmental program. The foundation of an intervention is the perception that you need to do something, in other words that you are facing a problem or, perhaps, will be facing a problem in the future. The purpose of an intervention is to reduce the magnitude of this problem or to avoid it, and an important kind of information therefore relates to the fulfillment of political goals. Securing such information is not always a simple task, but basically our national statistics, as in many other countries, can tell us to what extent the "big goals" have been fulfilled. Thus, a stream of such descriptive information is produced (Sjöström, 2002). To

what extent this stream reaches the political decision makers and in what way this kind of information is used in the political decision making is a question that I will not include in my discussion.

However, when I speak about evaluations that can be used in the reassessment of policies, I am oriented toward the idea that evaluations will give us some information about how a certain action, on a micro or macro level, can be judged; to what extent the action has caused a certain development.

This perspective lies very near the definition by Evert Vedung (1997: 3). "Evaluation = df. careful retrospective assessment of the merit, worth, and value of administration, output, and outcome of government interventions, which is intended to play a role in future, practical action situations."

4. The main sources are a study published by the Swedish National Audit Office 1991 (Riksrevisionsverket, 1991) in which 100 evaluations were examined and a dissertation about the Swedish commission system. In the latter, the author studied, among other things, the effect of accumulation and knowledge within the framework of the various governmental commissions on political positions, as well as other issues (Johansson, 1992).

5. One of the key concepts of the book is single-loop versus double-loop learning. Simplified, it can be said that the effects of double loop learning on decision making means that you question the basic assumptions underlying what you are doing. Both single-loop and double-loop learning can take place on different levels. When double-loop learning in *Can Governments Learn?* is discussed in relation to Parliament and government it implies what here is discussed as fundamental Policy Reassessments. This is illustrated with the following example (p. 61): "The Swedish Customs and Excise Department combats the illegal supply of narcotics in order to control the consumption of narcotics. These questions are raised at government and Parliament levels as if limiting the physical supply of narcotics is a good way of reducing the consumption of narcotics. If the government and Parliament were to alter the activities of the customs service on the basis of studies demonstrating that changes in the system of legal sanctions would provide a better way of affecting the supply of illegal drugs, then this would be an instance of double-loop learning. But we might also speak of double learning if the Swedish Customs Agency had, for instance, chosen to employ dogs as a central aspect of border control in the area of narcotics, only to change this policy, if it were to be shown that the use of dogs was predicated on the quite erroneous assumption with regard to the behaviour of smugglers (or dogs)."

6. A similar situation is when it is agreed that something is a problem, and also that this problem is one that the government has to deal with, but some politicians do not think they can afford it given other needs. You can, of course, say, "Yes, this is a very unsatisfactory situation and in my opinion this is something which should be resolved by governmental intervention, but we cannot afford it in the light of other needs." And the conclusion may be that a governmental program is abolished or a decision is made not to start a new program on grounds that at least limit the relevance of information in evaluations.

7. Indications of this are discussed in Furubo and Sandahl, 2002: 126, and in several reports from the National Financial Management Authority (ESV, 1999), and also in the discussion about the system with Governmental Commissions (ESO, 1998).

8. Vedung (1997: 265 ff.) discusses several forms of use with reference to, among others, Weiss, 1972, in terms of Response Steps in a Communication Theory based on McGuire, 1989. Weiss (1998: 305 ff) discusses use and dissemination in relation to decision makers and other stakeholders. Owen and Rogers (1990: 105 ff.) are strongly

oriented toward dissemination to the decision makers. For an overview about public administration, see Pollitt and Bouchaert, 2000; Wollmann, 2002.
9. For an overview about public administration, see Pollitt and Bouckaert, 2000.
10. This was also the example a former high-ranking governmental official mentioned in a debate about use of evaluations in Stockholm in April 2003. The example is interesting in several ways. It is a fact that Sweden changed its agricultural policy in a very fundamental way at the end of the 1980s. However, Sweden has more or less reversed the new policy and change it back to the old one, since Sweden became a member of the European Union in 1994.
11. Much discussion has taken place about Crises/Learning/Decision making. See, for example, Stern 1997; Hood 1994; Jonung, 1999.

## References

ESO (expertgruppen för studier i offentlig ekonomi, the expert group on Public Finance). (1998). *Kommittéerna och bofinken. Kan en kommitté se ut hur som helst?* (only in Swedish) DS 1998:57.
_____. (1996). *Kan myndigheter utvärdera sig själva?* (only in Swedish).
ESV (Ekonomistyrningsverket, The Swedish Financial Management Authority). (1999). *Informella kontakter i samband med regleringsbrev och årsredovisningar* (only in Swedish) 1999:19.
_____. (2001). *Resultatkontrakt* (only in Swedish) 2001:19.
Finansdepartementet (Ministry of Finance). (2002). *Regeringskansliets kontroll och styrning av statlig verksamhet* (only in Swedish).
Furubo, J. E. (1994). "Learning from Evaluations: The Swedish Experience." In F. Leeuw, R. Rist, and R. Sonnichsen, eds., *Can Governments Learn? Comparative Perspectives on Evaluation and Organizational Learning.* New Brunswick, NJ: Transaction Publishers.
Furubo, J. E., R. Rist, and R. Sandahl, eds. (2002). *International Atlas of Evaluation.* New Brunswick, NJ: Transaction Publishers.
Furubo, J. E., and R. Sandahl. (2002a). "Introduction—A Diffusion Perspective on Global Developments in Evaluation." In J. E. Furubo, R. Rist, and R. Sandahl, eds., *International Atlas of Evaluation.* New Brunswick, NJ: Transaction Publishers.
_____. (2002b). "Coordinated Pluralism—The Swedish Case." In J.E. Furubo, R. Rist, and R. Sandahl, eds., *International Atlas of Evaluation.* New Brunswick, NJ: Transaction Publishers.
Johansson, J. (1992). *Det statliga Kommittéväsendet—Kunskap, Kontroll, Konsensus* (only in Swedish—English summary). Edsbruk, Sweden: Akademitryck AB.
Jonung, L. (1999). *Med backspegeln som kompass—om stabiliseringspolitik som läroprocess.* Published by ESO (expertgruppen för studie i offentlig ekonomi, the expert group for Public Finance; only in Swedish—English summary) DS 1999: 9.
Leeuw, F., R. Rist, and R. Sonnichsen, eds. (1994). *Can Governments Learn? Comparative Perspectives on Evaluation and Organizational Learning.* New Brunswick, NJ: Transaction Publishers.
Lejdhamre, O. (2002). *Den statliga revisionen och de lokala investeringsprogrammen.* Uppsala universitet, statsvetenskapliga institutionen.
McGuire, W. J. (1989). "Theoretical Foundations of Campaigns." In R. E. Rice and C. K. Atkin, eds., *Public Communication Campaigns.* Newbury Park, CA: Sage.
Owen, J. M., and P. J. Rogers. (1990). *Program Evaluation—Forms and Approaches.* London: Sage Publications.

Pollitt, C., and G. Bouchaert. (2000). *Public Management Reform—A Comparative Analysis*. Oxford: Oxford University Press.
PUMA. (1999). *Performance Contracting, Lesson from Performance Contracting Case Studies, A Framework for Public Sector Performance Contracting 1999*. OECD/PUMA/PAC (99)2.
Rist, R., ed. (1990). *Program Evaluation and the Management of Government. Patterns and Prospects across Eight Nations*. New Brunswick, NJ: Transaction Publishers.
Rogers, E. M. (1995). *Diffusion of Innovations*, 4th ed. New York: Free Press.
RRV (Riksrevisionsverket, The Swedish National Audit Office). (1991). *Att mäta resultatanalysen—Vem analyserar vad, hur mycket och på vilket sätt* (only in Swedish).
_____. (1998). *Resultatinformationen I budgetprocessen—före och efter budgetlagen* (only in Swedish).
Sandahl, R. (1986). *Offentlig styrning—en fråga om alternativ* (only in Swedish). Stockholm: Riksrevisionsverket (The Swedish National Audit Office).
_____. (1993). "Connected or Separated? Budgeting, Auditing, and Evaluation in Sweden." In A. Gray, B. Jenkins, and B. Segsworth, eds., *Budgeting, Auditing and Evaluation. Functions and Integration in Seven Governments*. New Brunswick, NJ: Transaction Publishers.
Sjöström, O. (2002). *Svensk statistikhistoria* (only in Swedish). Södertälje: Gidlunds förlag.
Statskontoret (Agency for Administrative Development). (1999). *Mittutvärderingar av strukturfonderna—en övergripande utvärdering*, 1999: 53.
_____. (2002). *Utvärderingar—Av vem och till vad* (only in Swedish), 2002: 21.
Stern, Eric. "Crisis and Learning: A Conceptual Balance Sheet." *Crises and Learning* 5(2) (June 1997). Oxford: Blackwell Publishers.
Vedung, E. (1997). *Public Policy and Program Evaluation*. New Brunswick, NJ: Transaction Publishers.
Vedung, E., J. E. Furubo, and R. Sandahl. "Utvärdering i det svenska politiska systemet." *Nordisk Administrativ Tidskrift*. (2000): 2.
Weiss, C. H. (1972). *Evaluation Research: Methods for Assessing Program Effectiveness*. Upper Saddle River, NJ: Prentice Hall.
_____. (1998). *Evaluation*, 2nd ed. Upper Saddle River, NJ: Prentice Hall.

# Part 4

# Strategic Budgeting and Streams of Knowledge

# 10

# Evaluation Use and Information Communication Technology: What is the Real Issue?

*Yoon-Shik Lee*

### Introduction

Since the late 1960s when a study was done by Weiss (1967) of evaluation use, there have been a number of studies in this area, including those done by Cook et al. (1977), Patton et al. (1977), Alkin et al. (1979), Kennedy et al. (1980), Leviton and Hughes (1981), Patton (1997), Johnson (1998), Christie and Alkin (1999), Kirkhart (2000), and Atwood et al. (2002). These studies can be largely classified into several categories, such as studies of the concept of evaluation use, studies of the extent of use, studies of factors influencing evaluation use, studies of use model, studies of misuse, and the like. Those studies, however, fail to note the new evaluation environment, such as the knowledge-based society and digital economy, in which new approaches to evaluation, especially to evaluation use, are required because evaluation use is influenced considerably by the context surrounding the evaluation (King and Pechmans, 1984).

Evaluation in the knowledge-based society, which is due to ICT (information and communication technology) and values knowledge as "intellectual capital" (Patton, 2001: 329), appears to be affected by ICT including computer and communication network systems. That is because effective evaluation, an important source of information on policy/program performance, depends upon how efficiently the pertinent data can be collected, processed, and transmitted to the decision makers.

Furthermore, decision makers' policy making is affected by how efficiently the decision makers can get access to evaluative information,[1] which is produced for helping policymakers to improve existing policies/programs or to develop new policies/programs through various analytical activities including evaluation. ICT appears to play some roles in having them utilize the evaluative information (Davenport et al., 1998) as far as an evaluative knowledge management system (EKMS) based upon ICT is established because the EKMS makes it easy to get access to, share, and expand the evaluative information. However, it may be hard to say that establishment of EKMS necessarily leads to an increase in evaluation use. It is because such use of evaluative information has something to do with decision makers' interpretation of evaluative information (Oh, 1998).

Currently, a few studies tend to focus on the relationship between evaluation and ICT and found that ICT has a great deal of impact on evaluation (Hullett and Mitra, 1997). Nevertheless, few studies have been made of the role of ICT in evaluation use.

While evaluation produces information on policies and/or programs that may be valuable for decision makers, it is unclear whether decision makers actually use evaluation results and if they do, to what extent. On the other hand, when decision makers do not use evaluative information it is not certain what causes such non-use of evaluation in the knowledge-based society. Therefore, it becomes a serious problem as to how such evaluation use can be promoted or facilitated in the knowledge-based society.

This study attempts to tackle the issue. To that end this chapter will examine the following questions in order. What types of relationships exists between knowledge management and evaluation use? What is the role of ICT in evaluation use? What makes evaluation use valuable (or not) for decision makers in the government sector? To conduct this research, a case study approach will be adopted. For the case study, together with use of empirical data on legal and institutional arrangements of evaluation and on evaluation use in the ministries under consideration, public officials of the central government in Korea were interviewed. In addition, a brainstorming strategy was used for searching out evaluation practices in those governmental agencies.

In this chapter, ICT (information and communication technology) is the means by which evaluative information is collected, processed, stored, retrieved and utilized, and transmitted (Lee, 2002). The concept of evaluation use will follow the book's conceptualization, which is discussed in the introduction chapter; evaluation use will be conceptualized in a broad sense. Furthermore, evaluation use and evaluation utilization will be used interchangeably, as noted by Hofstetter and Alkin (2002). Thus, evaluation use means the utilization of findings or recommendations of evaluation, ideas and generalizations, and the design of the evaluation study, etc., as Weiss (1998) has suggested.

## Knowledge Management and Evaluation Use

In the knowledge-based society, knowledge management (KM)[2] is increasingly important and required for organizational development in so far as knowledge (as intellectual capital) becomes a major source of value-added and contributes to the competitive edge of a nation (Patton, 2001; Bailey and Clarke, 2000). Knowledge management refers to "a process that harvests and shares an organization's collective knowledge to achieve breakthrough results in productivity and innovation" (Patton, 2001: 329), while knowledge means "usable ideas" (Bailey and Clarke, 2000). The main objectives of KM[3] are (1) to make an organization as intelligent as possible to secure its viability and overall success, and (2) to otherwise realize the best value of its knowledge assets (Wiig, 1997: 1). KM is composed of knowledge acquisition, knowledge distribution, knowledge interpretation, and organizational memory (Huber, 1991). ICT here helps establish a system of knowledge distribution and makes access to and reference to organizational memory within the system at any time relatively easy (see Forss and Rebien, this volume). That is, ICT serves as an important tool for use of knowledge or of evaluative information. Therefore, KM depends to a considerable extent upon ICT.

Evaluation as one piece of information feeds into a slow, evolutionary process of program development (Patton et al, 1977: 148). Program development is a process of muddling through and evaluation is a part of the muddling activities (Hofstetter and Alkin, 2002:15). This suggests that evaluation may have an impact on decision makers' attitudes and/or behaviors in so far as it draws their attention to the use of evaluative information.

As the knowledge-based society emerges, evaluation has added knowledge generation as an additional purpose, moving from just generating findings about specific programs to generating knowledge (Patton, 2001: 332). Evaluation produces information on and, consequently, generates knowledge about policy/program development, which is valuable for the decision makers. This implies that evaluative knowledge tends to provide decision makers with more valuable information about policy/program development and/or improvement than single evaluative studies in that the former evaluative knowledge consists of a number of sources of evaluative information, that is, it creates streams.

It is further implied that decision makers' use of evaluative knowledge depends on evaluation quality, which includes technical sophistication, methodological approach, report readability, relevance, and information processing such as information presentation (Hofstetter and Alkin, 2002: 34), which is enhanced by ICT-based information management. At the same time, decision makers' use of evaluative knowledge may be affected by how efficiently evaluative knowledge is managed in order to meet their expectations. Therefore, it becomes obvious that evaluation use and knowledge management have a mutually reinforcing or empowering relationship.

## An Analytical Model of ICT Role in Evaluation Use

As ICT has been rapidly developed, e-government and e-commerce prevail in both the public and the private sectors. Government functions can almost not be done without using ICT. The same situation occurs with evaluation; evaluation as a means of evaluative knowledge management needs analytical tools, which are provided by ICT. ICT in evaluation activities facilitates efficient communication between evaluators or between the evaluator and the evaluated. ICT is also used for retrieving or sharing data necessary for evaluation, for a statistical analysis of evaluative data, or for distribution of evaluation results. Furthermore, ICT is more frequently employed to utilize new information on and/or knowledge about policy problems, which are increasingly complicated.

Roles of ICT in evaluation use can be categorized as follows (Gore, 1993; Bellamy and Taylor, 1998):

1. ICT as a promoter: In this case, ICT plays a role of facilitating evaluation use and helps decision makers to make use of evaluative information for their own sake.
2. ICT as a demoter: This role means that ICT becomes an impediment to evaluation use by decision makers because of their misuse of ICT or their lack of in-depth knowledge of ICT.
3. ICT as an onlooker: Decision makers' ignorance of ICT causes them to be indifferent about the benefits of ICT in utilizing evaluation results.

These roles are determined by who the users are, that is, whether decision makers are equipped with ICT knowledge, and by the condition of the ICT (that is, speed of access, form of information, evaluative knowledge management, etc.). Therefore, ICT can play multiple roles, depending upon the level of ICT knowledge and its condition throughout phases of the evaluation utilization process. In particular, how well the ICT-based evaluative knowledge management system is established and operated may determine the level of utilization of the evaluation results. As an example, at an early stage of the evaluation utilization process where decision makers do not know how to use ICT, and/or where the ICT condition is bad, ICT may serve as a deflator or onlooker. But at a more mature stage of the evaluation utilization process where decision makers are well trained with ICT skills and/or where they are well equipped with ICT infrastructure, ICT may serve as a promoter in using evaluative information. As a result, in so far as the two contingencies are not conciliatory, ICT is likely to produce a canceling-out effect in utilizing evaluative information.

From the mode of knowledge use constructed by Pelz (1978) and the typology of evaluation use formulated by previous studies (King and Thompson, 1983; Johnson, 1998), evaluation use can be classified into several types as follows:

1. *Instrumental/engineering use*: This refers to utilizing evaluation information as a basis of action, which indicates concrete use, behavior, or action, or "making direct decisions about changing programs based on evaluation results" (Shadish et al., 1991). This is to use evaluation information for action (Rich, 1977). Weiss (1998) contends that instrumental use is common under three conditions: (1) if the evaluation findings are relatively non-controversial, (2) if the changes that are suggested are within the program's existing repertoire and are relatively small scale, and (3) if the environment of the program is relatively stable, without big changes in leadership, budget, types of clients served, or public support.
2. *Conceptual/enlightening use*: This type of evaluation utilization occurs when an evaluation influences decision makers' and stakeholders' cognitive processing or thinking about present or future programs (Owen, 1992). Conceptual use is to use evaluative information for understanding (Rich, 1977). This has to do with Weiss' (1981) suggestion that over time "decision accretion"occurs, where experiences with and thinking about past evaluations influence and/or bring forth current decision making. Evaluative information enables decision makers to have a broader and deeper program understanding, which results in changing their understanding of what the program is and does (Hofstetter and Alkin, 2002; Weiss, 1998). This type of evaluation use is also called "enlightenment" use (Weiss, 1998).
3. *Process use*: This refers to evaluation use, which occurred when behavioral and cognitive changes took place in persons who participated in evaluations (Patton, 1997). It involves learning to think like an evaluator as a result of fulfilling in person "the act of conducting evaluations" (Hofstetter and Alkin, 2002: 24). It may have long-term payoffs through improved skills and communication and through increased use of evaluation procedures. In this regard, process use partially overlaps with instrumental and conceptual use.
4. *Symbolic/legitimate use:* This is the type of evaluation use in which decision makers use evaluative information for political purposes, such as enhancement of prestige and visibility for the program (Hofstetter and Alkin, 2002: 22). In other words, this type is also called legitimate use, which means use of evaluation to justify decisions already made on the program (Owen, 1992), and persuasive use, which means individual use of evaluation as part of the political process to advocate issues and to persuade people to act (Patton, 1997). This mode is also called "conspiratorial use" (Huberman, 1987)

To integrate both the types of ICT roles and the types of evaluation use, an analytical model of evaluation use under the ICT impact can be drawn as shown in Table 10.1. This model of evaluation use by ICT role helps understand how ICT has an impact on decision makers in each type of evaluation use. In other words, the analytical model gives some insights into what sort of role ICT plays in decision makers' use of evaluative information, which represents each cell of the model.

**Table 10.1**
**Evaluation Use by ICT Role**

|  |  | Types of Evaluation Use | | | |
| --- | --- | --- | --- | --- | --- |
|  |  | Instrumental | Conceptual | Process | Symbolic |
| Types of ICT Roles | Promoter |  |  |  |  |
|  | Demoter |  |  |  |  |
|  | Onlooker |  |  |  |  |

When analyzing each cell of the model, it is worth examining what makes decision makers take such a position on evaluation use. To this end, this study will use Hofstetter and Alkin's (2002: 34) classification of factors influencing evaluation use, which, in fact, comes from comprehensive review of previous studies of such factors. According to them, the major factors affecting decision makers' use of evaluative information can be broadly classified into three categories: (1) *personal factors*, which refers to the evaluator's credibility, professionality, communication with stakeholders, (2) *the context surrounding the evaluation*, which includes fiscal constraints, political considerations, and how the program fits into a broader organizational area, and (3) *evaluation quality*, which involves not only technical sophistication, but also methodological approach, report readability, relevance, and information processing such as information presentation.

The type of decision makers' evaluation use, which varies with the above three major factors, is affected by the type of ICT role. But ICT can play a certain role only when the decision makers have ICT literacy and ICT infrastructure that is well established is available to them. This implies that if ICT-based evaluative knowledge management systems are not available, the ICT fails to serve decision makers' use of evaluation results. Thus, it may be hypothesized that the ICT role according to decision makers' utilization mode of evaluation results varies with the frequency of using evaluative information because ICT helps decision makers who hope to relatively use evaluation results more often for developing new policies/programs or for improving existing policies/programs have easy access to the evaluative knowledge management system. In this case, it becomes obvious that ICT plays the role of promoter or accelerator in utilizing evaluative information.

## Evaluation Use and ICT in Korea

*A Case Study of Some Principal Evaluation Agencies in the Government*

The current status of evaluation use based upon ICT in Korea, analyzed here, focuses on evaluation practices of the principal governmental organizations that are in charge of policy/program evaluation services in the government. The government institutions under consideration include the Office for Policy Coordination (OPC), which is the highest organization coordinating overall evaluation services of the administrative agencies according to the Law on Evaluation of Governmental Affairs (hereafter, Law on Evaluation), and the Ministry of Planning and Budget (MPB), which is responsible for the performance management of financing programs of all administrative agencies in the governmental budget-making process. Finally, the Board of Audit and Inspection (BAI) is an independent, constitutional organization that is directly accountable to the president, and is responsible for performance audit and inspection.

### The Office for Policy Coordination and Central Administrative Offices

Evaluation of government affairs, which is stipulated by the Law on Evaluation in Korea, does not exactly mean policy/program evaluation as found in other countries. It is a rather comprehensive concept of evaluation, which includes not only policy/program evaluation but also evaluation of other administrative services. In addition, the evaluation method is not limited to the conventional program/policy evaluation methods; it also covers, for example, a citizens' satisfaction survey of government services at large. The Law on Evaluation was enacted to increase efficiency of and to secure responsibility for performing government duties by having the evaluation results reflect upon the implementation process and/or upon future administrative service plans.

Current status of ICT use in evaluation, which is shown in the Reports of Government Affairs Evaluation Results and of Major Policy Issues Evaluation Results of the First Half of Year 2003, is as follows:

To begin with, OPC open evaluation results, which are drawn from its evaluation together with PEC, are on the Internet homepage (http://www.pec.go.kr/) so that the evaluation agenda of PEC can be confirmed by administrative agencies and at the same time so that the general public can make any suggestions about policy evaluation tasks. Presidential directions are operated and managed through the "Presidential Direction Management System," which arranges presidential directions and sends them to pertinent central government ministries so that they can input into the system their own plans for and actual results of accomplishing the presidential directions; they also can make a progress report to the president though the information and communication system in every quarter of the year.

For instance, use of ICT in self-evaluation, evaluation of affiliated institutions, evaluation of local governments including a joint evaluation of local governments, which are conducted by Ministry of Government Administration and Home Affairs (MOGAHA), remains at the level of communicating and sharing information on evaluation process among members of the evaluation committee. In addition, evaluation results are often used for improving existing programs by correcting problems that are indicated, or for developing new programs, which indicates that evaluative information or knowledge tends to be used mainly for an instrumental/engineering purpose. Here, ICT helps merely retrieve and get access to evaluative information, which suggests that ICT plays a promoting role in policymakers' use of evaluation results; however, it is significant that the so-called evaluative knowledge management system was not established and available to the decision makers (PEC, 2003).

By the same token, in the Ministry of Information and Communication (MIC) ICT also serves as a means of irregular information exchange between MIC and civil members of the self-evaluation committee; the evaluation members exchange information on what is going on in major tasks of MIC and in evaluation-relating tasks by way of the Internet email system. Since February 2004, Government Policy Life Cycle System as a policy information management system has been introduced into MIC and operated there for the purpose of efficiently managing follow-up activities of the evaluation projects. It is, however, found that in MIC as in MOGAHA evaluation results are used for improving existing policies/programs or for developing new programs, which is not often the case. Thus, in MIC, evaluative information is utilized mainly for the sake of instrumental purposes where ICT also serves as a promoter by helping policymakers retrieve and get access to evaluative information.

In sum, it is suggested from the examination of evaluation practices, especially the use of evaluation results, in OPC, MOGAHA, and MIC, that although there is a limitation in fully using ICT because of the absence of an evaluative knowledge management system, it contributes to easy retrieval of and access to existing data necessary for policy activities and serves as a means of communicating and sharing evaluative information among evaluators, so that evaluation results can be constantly used for understanding existing policies/programs. Nevertheless, it is apparent that evaluation results are very rarely used for developing totally new programs and/or policy measures. Rather, evaluative information is frequently used for reviewing existing programs, because it is mandatory for the administrative offices by the Law on Evaluation. Therefore, although the use of ICT is limited, ICT plays a promoting role in policymakers' use of evaluative information, which contributes especially to instrumental use of evaluation results (PEC, 2003).

*Ministry of Planning and Budget*

Evaluation tasks of the Ministry of Planning and Budget (MPB) are largely categorized into evaluation of financial soundness recovery, evaluation of budget management efficiency, evaluation of fund/allotment management efficiency, evaluation of efficiency/transparency of budget systems, and evaluation of public sector reforms (Ministry of Planning and Budget, 2003b).

Currently, in relation to ICT use of performance evaluation results, MPB has a plan to develop an integrated Digital Budget and Fiscal Account Management System (DBFMS) (MPB, 2004). This system covers the whole process of budgeting and fiscal accounting of the overall public sector, including central and local governments and public enterprises from imposition of revenue to performance evaluation of fiscal management. The DBFMS helps collect and analyze both macro- and micro-information on public finance in a real-time fashion. To develop the fiscal information management system, a DBFMS Promotion Planning Team was established within MPB, together with related central government ministries, including the Ministry of Finance and Economy, MOGAHA, and the Board of Audit and Inspection. The team is composed of government officials of the related ministries, Certified Public Accountants, IT experts, and the like. The DBFMS is scheduled to be developed by the end of year 2005 and operated from year 2007 after amendment of relevant laws, such as the Budget and Account Act.

In sum, the above analysis of current practices of evaluation results that use performance evaluation results suggests that ICT in the MPB is in an early phase, although since 2003 it has maintained the Finance Operation System, which feeds performance evaluation results of financial programs back to financial operation. It is because the ICT-based DBFMS, which manages and operates financial information in the dimension of knowledge management, has been under construction since 2004. Nevertheless, such changes in financial management come from emphasis on knowledge management and performance evaluation so that performance evaluation results can be constantly managed and operated for performance-oriented financial operation.

MPB's efforts to fix performance management turn out to contribute to increases in efficiency and transparency of financial operation not only by connecting its compilation of the government budget with results of the external evaluation of policies and/or budgeting programs, but also by expanding external participation in the budgeting process. From a perspective of evaluative information use, this implies that budget making can be improved when a variety of evaluation results are taken into consideration and thus that such use of evaluative information for drafting the budget can be facilitated by ICT.

## The Board of Audit and Inspection

According to the Board of Audit and Inspection Act, BAI examines the final accounts of revenue and expenditure of the state, audits the accounts of the state (central government agencies), provincial governments, and other local autonomous bodies, and government-invested organizations in order to ensure proper and fair accounting. It also inspects the works performed by government agencies and the duties of their employees in order to improve the operation and quality of government services. According to the results of audit and inspection, BAI can take expost facto measures including request for correction, request for disposition action, and request for improvement and accusation about the institution that was audited and inspected.

According to the Year 2003 Report of Major Pending Issues facing BAI (BAI, 2003b), BAI attempted to conduct "e-audits" through "the State Affairs Evaluation Information System," which was established for managing overall evaluation tasks and evaluative information. Thus, BAI intends to gradually reduce field audits focusing on on-the-spot inspection. In addition, in case evaluation audits require much time or are not efficiently implemented, BAI will conduct follow-up audits periodically and report to the General Assembly as well as to the president on the results of its evaluation audits. If necessary, BAI also can transmit its evaluation audit results to the Ministry of Planning and Budget in order to have MPB reflect it in the budget of the following year.

In sum, so far there has been no specific discussion on evaluation knowledge management and use of ICT to facilitate utilization of audits, especially performance audit results. However, as discussion is made about building a national evaluation infrastructure where BAI plays a pivotal role in evaluation, BAI is attempting to shift the focus of its audit from conventional audit, such as regularity/legality audit and duty inspection, to performance audit together with an emphasis on electronic audit rather than on field audit. In addition, it promotes sharing of audit-related information with stakeholders through production and management of audit knowledge. As a result, through establishment of an ICT-based e-audit system, audit results are about to be used as evaluative information, with which the effectiveness, efficiency, and economy of a particular policy/program are tested and an alternative policy/program is developed, rather than merely as ground for securing regularity/legality of audit. This suggests that ICT helps facilitate activities of performance audit by increasing effectiveness of performance audit. Yet, it is necessary for facilitation of ICT-based audit that the existing BAI Law should be amended and that such problems as the overlapping of evaluation with other evaluations of the government, absence of appropriate performance audit methods, and lack of performance auditors' expertise should be solved in advance.

## Analysis of Survey Data on Evaluation Practices in the Major Government Ministries

A theoretical model for analyzing the roles and functions of ICT in facilitating use of evaluation results consists of two parts: The first part concerns an analysis of the interrelations betweens the factors affecting utilization of evaluation results, such as utilization necessity, and utilization objectives. The second part involves a search of the roles and functions of ICT in using evaluation results by analyzing the mutual relations betweens types of ICT roles, promoting factors, and impeding factors.

For this study, two types of data were collected: (1) the data obtained from interviews with thirty-five public servants of the twelve central government agencies from September 26, 2002, to October 2, 2002; (2) the data collected from a survey of 108 civil servants, including twenty government employees sampled from ten central government agencies, forty policymakers sampled from seven wide-area cities including Seoul Special City, and forty-eight civil servants sampled from forty-eight general cities in nine Do provinces from November 26, 2002, to December 2, 2002. Because of the peculiar features and essence of this research, the collected data are analyzed mainly with descriptive statistics, such as frequency and percentage analysis, although ANOVA and cross tabs are used for analyzing differences among groups of sampled respondents. The results of analyzing use of evaluation results in the Korean government are summarized as follows (Lee, 2002).

Firstly, government officials' use of evaluation results is not minimal, although their evaluation use concentrates on major governmental policy issues evaluation results, as many previous studies have pointed out. It found that 93.9 percent of the total interviewees use institutional evaluation results, while 42.4 percent use results of major policy issues evaluation. It also found that 85.15 percent of total respondents in the survey use institutional evaluation results, while 42.6 percent use only results of major policy issues evaluation. That may be because use of evaluation results is required by the Law on Evaluation; otherwise, the institution may be subject to disadvantage in the following year's budget making, while the government agencies, which are assessed to be the best practices, are awarded some incentives.

Secondly, it uncovered that in so far as ICT is used for utilizing evaluation results, government officials are able to get easy access to different types of evaluation results. In the interview with central government officials, 93.8 percent of the total interviewees relied upon ICT for use of evaluation results, while 81.8 percent responded that ICT works as a promoter in using evaluation results. As to evaluation use, it was also uncovered that 72.7 percent of the total interviewees used evaluative information for instrumental purposes, such as improvement of existing policies/programs or development of new policies/programs. In addition, 90.5 percent of central and local government officials responded that they used ICT in accessing evaluation results, and 81.2 percent responded that ICT serves as promoter of evaluative information use, while 88.1 percent noted that they used evaluation results for the purpose of instrumental utilization.

These findings imply that as previous studies have already pointed out, ICT helps facilitate evaluation use as long as officials are not kept from using ICT. Therefore, in so far as ICT infrastructure, including evaluative information management systems, are available to them, officials more frequently use ICT for purposes other than the instrumental needs.

Thirdly, according to the results of interviews with the central government policymakers, 27.3 percent of the interviewees responded that one of the most serious obstacles to their use of evaluative information involves personal factors, which include lack of vigorous communication among the stakeholders and policymakers' motivation for utilization, and an organizational context unfavorable to the use of evaluation results. Additionally, 18.2 percent of the respondents considered the poor quality of evaluation results and the nonexistence of a management system facilitating evaluation use as serious obstacles.

In the survey of civil servants in the central and local governments, 22.8 percent of the respondents revealed that organizational context unfavorable to the use of evaluation results and nonexistence of the management system facilitating evaluation use are the most serious problems blocking the use of evaluation results, while 21.8 percent indicated that lack of vigorous communication among the stakeholders and policymakers' motivation for utilization also stand against the use of evaluative information. In addition, it was revealed from the result of a cross-tabulation analysis that the effect of such factors hindering use of evaluation results varies significantly with organizations ($p = .001$).

The results suggest that organizational context is a major factor influencing the use of evaluation results. The organizational environment should be user-friendly, with the management system facilitating evaluation use. At the same time, to facilitate evaluation use, every effort needs to be made for increasing evaluation quality and for increasing the relevancy of evaluation results.

Fourthly, despite the importance of organizational constraints as impediments to the use of evaluation results, personal factors, including communication between stakeholders and motivation of policymakers for using evaluative knowledge, work as more serious negative impact agents. In addition, the quality of evaluation results appears to be the most significant, direct factor to affect actual use of evaluation results. This is paradoxical in view of the fact that the current Law on Evaluation requires administrative agencies to use evaluation results. However, the findings that most administrative agencies use evaluation results for policy activities show that government officials use evaluative information in spite of such an organizational constraint. In addition, in the situation where policymakers are controlled by even personal factors, such as communication and/or motivation of policymakers to make use of evaluation results, organizational constraints on their use of evaluative information appear to make policymakers' use of evaluative knowledge rather restricted.

## Issues in Enhancing Evaluation Use through ICT

The results of this study suggest that there are issues in relation to the use of evaluative information by ICT and these issues need to be appropriately resolved in advance in order to facilitate the decision makers' evaluation use through ICT.

First, use of evaluative information via ICT appears to depend upon both substantial factors and instrumental factors; it is affected by quality of evaluation results and also by the mechanism through which such evaluative information is easily and conveniently available to policymakers. The results of analyzing actual practices and the data collected from interviews and surveys of civil servants in Korea reveal that to facilitate ICT-based use of evaluation, the quality of evaluation itself and of evaluation results should be improved so that evaluative information is well taken by policymakers when they revise the existing policies/programs or when they develop new policies/programs. On the other hand, the latter instrumental factors concern legal and institutional rearrangement, let alone upgrading the technological conditions (ICT infrastructure, ICT-based knowledge management, etc.) so that decision makers can get easy access to the evaluative knowledge.

In view of the fact that Korea globally ranked sixteenth in the level of e-government in 2001, which was assessed by the UN and the American Society of Public Administration, that Korea ranked seventh in the mobile/Internet index of the International Telecommunications Union, along with 55.1 Internet users per 100 people, and that Korea's advanced IT industry occupies about 14.9 percent of GNP (MIC, 2003), it has enough technological capability to construct ICT-based infrastructure for evaluation use within the government. But still the overall organizational culture does not seem to fit with ICT-based evaluation use. Moreover, the quality of the evaluative knowledge base is also yet to be secured.

Second, an effective incentive system is not fully operative for facilitating use of evaluative knowledge in Korea; although the Law on Evaluation stipulates the use of evaluation results, there is no specific regulation about failure to use evaluative information. Furthermore, even though evaluation results are sent to the budgeting agency so that the results are considered when setting the budget for the following year, it has not happened at all so far. In that regard, a strong incentive system needs to be set up to encourage decision makers to use evaluative knowledge for purposes other than instrumental, so that they actually can change their decision behavior about programs/policies.

Third, ICT literacy of policymakers matters much in promoting the use of evaluation results. According to results of the above empirical study, personal factors, such as communication among stakeholders, affect policymakers' use of evaluation results. This indicates that evaluation use may depend much on how effectively communication is implemented among policymakers and other stakeholders. Thus, without being aware of how to use ICT, the ICT infrastructure does not make a difference for them in communication and, in the long run, in evaluation use. As a result, it could be desirable to make it compulsory for decision makers to undertake special educational training of ICT, particularly evaluation use relating to ICT, on a regular basis. This should help make interpretation and use of evaluative information for the developing of policies more feasible.

Fourth, measures need to be taken to secure the evaluators' qualifications in evaluation not only in local governments but also in the central government. There is also a need to exclude any political intervention in evaluation use especially in the central government, such as organizational prevention of sharing of evaluation results for political purposes. For instance, results of a major policy issue evaluation, which are very sensitive to the public or to stakeholders, tend not to be open to the public and thus other policymakers. As a consequence, competent officials are then apt to be kept from using these results.

In addition, evaluators, who are selected from internal and external experts in the areas, are generally expected to be equipped with expertise in evaluation as well as evaluation use. Those who assume evaluation duties are not necessarily experts in evaluation. Rather, scholars, research scientists, practitioners, and civil servants in the targeted areas of the policies/programs to be evaluated tend to be invited to take on the evaluation. Therefore, to improve the quality of evaluation results and consequently help policymakers have confidence in evaluative information, which ultimately contributes to creation of evaluative knowledge and to promote use of evaluative knowledge, it is necessary to secure high-quality evaluation expertise.

Finally, policymakers' motivation for using evaluative information, which acts as another personal factor, becomes a critical issue in facilitating the use of evaluation results. This indicates that unless policymakers have a special interest in evaluative knowledge, their use of evaluation results is not to be anticipated. This further implies that the organization context and/or technological infrastructure, let alone ICT literacy, fails to affect use of evaluative information. Therefore, it is necessary for policymakers themselves to be more interested in evaluative information, which has something to do with their responsibility and accountability for the programs/policies under their control.

In addition, as far as policymakers, to whom evaluative information is provided, are interested in the results, they hope to get access to and use valuable knowledge at any time, at any place, in any way, and in real time. To this end, ICT appears to be able to serve as a promoter of such evaluative information use.

## Conclusion

Evaluation use in the knowledge-based society appears to be affected considerably by ICT through strategies of knowledge management. Different from the case in the industrial society, evaluation use by means of drawing learning lessons from evaluation, which generates knowledge, requires effective knowledge management in the knowledge-intensive society. ICT, however, plays various roles from promoter to demoter, depending upon the level of the decision makers' ICT knowledge and upon ICT conditions. Therefore, to promote effective use of evaluative information by policymakers, it is inevitable to regularly and periodically orient decision makers with knowledge of ICT, as well as readjusting legal and institutional arrangements to new evaluation environments. Above all, an effective incentive system needs to be established for motivating policymakers to be interested in evaluative knowledge.

## Notes

1. This means information on evaluation results as well as on evaluation itself in this study. By the same token, evaluative knowledge indicates knowledge not only about evaluation itself but also about evaluation results, that is, evaluative information with a great deal of internal and external validity.
2. KM is distinguished from information management, which refers to a process that merely collects, processes, and condenses information (Patton, 2001: 329).
3. Systematic KM comprises four areas of emphasis from a managerial perspective, as follows (Wiig, 1997: 2):
   (1) Top-down monitoring and facilitation of knowledge-related activities;
   (2) Creation and maintenance of knowledge infrastructure;
   (3) Renewing, organizing, and transferring knowledge assets; and
   (4) Leveraging or using knowledge assets to realize their value.

## References

Alkin, M. C., R. Daillak, and P. White. (1979). *Using Evaluations: Does Evaluation Make a Difference?* Beverly Hills, CA: Sage Publications.

Atwood, R., Tori Egherman, and D. Russ-Eft. "Use and Non-use of Evaluation Results: Case Study of Environmental Influences in the Private Sector." *American Journal of Evaluation* 23(1) (2002): 19–31.

Bailey, Catherine, and Martin Clarke. "How Do Managers Use Knowledge about Knowledge Management?" *Journal of Knowledge Management* 4(3) (2000): 235–243.

Bellamy, C., and John A. Taylor. (1998). *Governing in the Information Age.* Philadelphia: Open University Press.

Board of Audit and Inspection. (1998). *50 Years of Audit and Inspection in Korea.* Seoul: BAI.

_____. (2003a). *Annual Reports.* Seoul: BAI.
_____. (2003b). *Major Current Issue Report.*
Christie, C. A., and M. C. Alkin. "Further Reflections on Evaluation Misutilization," *Studies in Educational Evaluation* 25 (1999): 1–10.
Cook, T. D., Judith Levinson-Rose, and W. E. Pollard. "Misutilization of Evaluation Research Some Pitfalls of Definition." *Evaluation Studies Review Annual* 6 (1977): 727-748.
Davenport, T. H., D. W. De Long, and M. C. Beers. "Successful Knowledge Management Projects. *Sloan Management Review* 39(2) (1998): 43–57.
Gore, Al. "From Red Tape to Results: Creating a Government That Works Better and Costs Less." *Report of Educational Research* 56(3) (1993): 331–364.
Hofstetter, C. H., and M. C. Alkin. (2002). "Evaluation Use Revisited." In D. Stufflebeam and T. Kellaghan (Eds.), *International Handbook of Educational Evaluation.* Boston: Klunner Academia Press.
Huber, G. P. "Organisational Learning: The Contributing Processes and the Literatures." *Organisation Science* 2(1) (1991).
Huberman, M. "Steps toward an Integrated Model of Research Utilization." *Knowledge: Creation, Diffusion, Utilization* 8 (1987): 546–561.
Hullett, C. R., and Ananda Mitra. "Toward Evaluating Computer Aided Instruction: Attitudes, Demographics, Context." *Evaluation and Program Planning* 20(4) (1997): 379–391.
Johnson, R. B. "Toward a Theoretical Model of Evaluation Use." *Evaluation and Program Planning* 21 (1998): 93–110.
Kennedy, M., W. Neumann, and R. Apling. (1980). *The Role of Evaluation and Testing Programs in Title I Programs.* Cambridge, MA: The Huron Institute.
King, J. A., and E. M. Pechman. "Pinning a Wave to the Shore: Conceptualizing Evaluation Use in School Systems." *Educational Evaluation and Policy Analysis.* 6(3) (1984): 241–251.
King, J. A., and B. Thompson. "Research on School Use of Program Evaluation: A Literature Review and Research Agenda." *Studies in Educational Evaluation* 9 (1983): 5–21.
Kirkhart, K. E. (2000). "Reconceptualizing Evaluation Use: An Integrated Theory of Influence." In V. J. Caracelli and H. Preskill, eds., *New Directions for Evaluation: The Expanding Scope of Evaluation Use*, no. 88. San Francisco: Jossey-Bass.
Lee, Yoon-Shik. (2002). *The Role and Tasks of IT in Accelerating the Utilization of Policy Evaluation Outputs in the Knowledge-Based Society.* Academic Research Report to Ministry of Information and Communication.
Lee, Yoon-Shik, et al. (1987). *Policy Evaluation: Theories and Applications.* Seoul: Bupyoung Publishing Co.
Leviton, L. C., and E. F. Hughes. "Research on the Use of Evaluations: A Review and Synthesis." *Evaluation Review* 5(5) (1981): 497–519.
Ministry of Information and Communication. (2003). *IT Policy Performances and Subject.* Seoul: MIC.
Ministry of Planning and Budget. (2003a). MPB Press Report.12.30.
_____. (2003b). *Self-Evaluation Results of the Second Half of the Year.*
_____. (2004). MPB Press Report. 5.3.
Oh, Cheol-Ho. "Rationality and Use of Information in Policy Making: An Empirical Analysis." *Korean Policy Studies Review* 7(2) (1998): 195–228.
Owen, J. M. (1992). "Towards a Meta-model of Evaluation Use." Paper presented at the Annual Meeting of the American Evaluation Association, Seattle, WA.

Patton, M. Q. (1997). *Utilization-focused Evaluation*, 3rd ed. Beverly Hills, CA: Sage.

―――. "Evaluation, Knowledge Management, Best Practices, and High Quality Lessons Learned." *American Journal of Evaluation* 22(2) (2001): 329–336.

Patton, M. Q., P. S. Grimes, and K. M. Guthrie. "In Search of Impact: An Analysis of the Use of Federal Health Evaluation Research" *Evaluation Studies Review Annual* 3 (1977): 59–81.

Pelz, D. C. (1978). "Some Expanded Perspectives on Use of Social Science in Public Policy." In J. M. Yinger and S. J. Cutler, eds., *Major Social Issues: A Multidisciplinary View*. New York: Macmillan.

Policy Evaluation Committee. (2003). Policy Evaluation Results of the Second Half of the Year.

Rich, R. F. (1977). "Uses of Social Science Information by Federal Bureaucrats: Knowledge for Action Versus Knowledge for Understanding." In C. H. Weiss, ed., *Using Social Research in Public Policy Making* (199–211). Lexington, MA: Lexington Books.

Shadish, W. R., T. D. Cook, and L. C. Leviton. (1991). *Foundations of Program Evaluation: Theories of Practice*. Newbury Park, CA: Sage.

Weiss, C. H. (1967). "Utilization of Evaluation: Toward Comparative Study." In *House of Representatives Committee on Government Operations, The Use of Social Research in Federal Domestic Programs*, Part III (426–432). Washington, DC: Government Printing Office.

―――. (1981). "Measuring the Use of Evaluation." In J. A. Ciarlo, ed., *Utilizing Evaluation, Concepts and Measurement Techniques*. Beverly Hills, CA: Sage.

―――. "Have We Learned Anything about the Use of Evaluation?" *American Journal of Evaluation* 19(1) (1998): 21–33.

Wiig, K. M. "Knowledge Management: Where Did It Come from and Where Will It Go?" *Expert Systems with Applications* 13(1) (1997): 1–14.

# 11

# Evaluative Information in the Norwegian Ministries

*Marit Stadler Waerness and Ragnhild Øvrelid*

### Introduction

This chapter focuses on the use of evaluations in three Norwegian ministries. First, we give a short description of the general institutional context, including the request for conducting evaluations. Thereafter, we examine three different policy areas in three ministries, describing them in more detail as three different areas for evaluation. We describe different aspects of the evaluation practices, especially how the information from the evaluations is being taken care of, followed up, or utilized in the ministries.[1]

Based on our understanding of these practices we focus on different aspects of use.[2] We relate the aspects of use to both the general conditions and contexts and to the special characteristics of each policy area, including its expected need for evaluations. We also discuss some of the challenges concerning the use of evaluation facing the three ministries. Finally, we highlight some recent changes in the ministries' evaluation practice that we find interesting and which gradually may come to alter the picture we have described.

### The Ministries: Some Characteristics

Ministries are both political secretariats and government bodies responsible for the overall sector policy development and management. Evaluations may be conducted and used in both functions. But when we discuss evaluation here, we focus mainly on the ministries as sector managers and on evaluations being conducted and used in that context.

Each of the seventeen ministries (2003) has responsibility for a number of state agencies and subordinate bodies, varying from one or two up to more than forty. The state agencies vary in both size and function, and so does the relationship between the ministry and the agency. The agency can be more or less a part of the ministry or have its autonomy and freedom from political instruction guaranteed by law. The management style of the ministry will depend on this relationship as well as on the nature of the goals and kinds of policy measures that are relevant to the sector.

The Norwegian government principle implies that each single minister holds an individual judicial and political responsibility for all actions and decisions being taken (or not taken) within his or her respective sphere—that is, within the ministry and its underlying bodies. In practice, each ministry specifies goals and performance requirements for the whole ministerial area and makes a report back to the parliament on the results achieved.

This form of ministerial rule increases the sector responsibility and smooths the vertical lines. But it follows a risk of fragmentation, less coordination, and horizontal cooperation among policy areas. The principle is therefore balanced by several coordinating mechanisms, the most important one being the function of the Cabinet where all the ministers are members. Another coordinating mechanism is the creation of ministries with a special cross-sector responsibility. For example, the Ministry of Finance and the Ministry of Labour and Government Administration have a general, crosscutting responsibility for—respectively—the state budget and the modernization of the public administration. Special regulations[3] have also been adopted to prevent sector-initiated reform from being realized without first considering the consequences for other sectors. The procedures whereby ministries (or directorates) circulate matters to other interested parties for comment are well established in the Norwegian government system.

But the coordinating effect of these mechanisms depends of course—among other things—on the actual capacity of the different institutions to deal with policy questions from each others' areas. Especially in the Cabinet the capacity is limited. All in all, ministerial rule is the dominating principle. We expect this principle to have an influence on the evaluation practice of the ministries.

## What Theory Says and What to Expect

Useful information can be defined simply as an adequate response to questions based on a felt need. Our hypothesis can be formulated as a positive relationship between question and answer—usefulness of evaluative information will depend on the genuineness of the question (given that the evaluation work is properly done).[4] The more the answer is an adequate response to specific questions asked by someone responsible, the more likely it is that the answer will have an impact. A negative version of the hypothesis will be—if evaluation is a response to a general requirement—that the usefulness will be arbitrary. We will use the *questions asked* as an explanatory dimension and the dichotomy *internal-external* to distinguish between different qualities of the demand of evaluation. The underlying assumption is that if the demanders and receivers of evaluations are different persons/units, there is less reason to expect use.

We expect to find both types of situations concerning the ministries' evaluations, on a scale from pure lip service at the one end to a conscious and dedicated need for knowledge at the other. Some evaluations are conducted only to satisfy formal demands; others arise solely from questions related to the ministries' work with policies and devices. In between we can construe a third situation where the evaluation is initiated and dealt with by a coordinating or external unit, separated from the one in charge of the matter.[5] How then will these situations manifest themselves when one looks at the evaluation work in the ministries?

We hypothesize here that suppose that a very strong regularity (in procedures and products) can be an indication of lip service evaluations, while diversity can indicate evaluations based on specific needs for information to solve specific problems.

For the last type of evaluations, we have some historical evidence. Norway, along with other welfare-state countries, has a tradition and belief in governmental intervention as a way of solving fundamental societal social problems (Furubo and Sandahl, 2002: 15). It is related to the breakthrough of what Evert Vedung calls "radical rationalism" (Vedung, 1991) and the first wave of evaluation in the 1960s and 1970s. This motivation still plays a part; we are probably more prepared to adopt evaluation as a tool for the development of different policies than countries with other traditions.[6]

The first type can be the product of external pressure from the international society and/or the constitutional framework of each country. The adaptation in several countries of an evaluation praxis in the 1990s can be explained as a result of external pressure from the European Union, the World Bank, and the OECD. In other countries the external and internal demands have merged, "...evaluation is now embodied in what can be called the "public management package" (Furubo and Sandahl, 2002: 20).

This is the case also for Norway. From 1980 onwards, Norway has gradually implemented radical public sector reforms of a kind that are internationally known as "New Public Management."

As in other countries, these reforms have made the ministry of finance a prime mover for evaluation (Furubo and Sandahl, 2002: 20). But the regulations are not encouraging a formal compliance. The rules state that evaluations should be done when needed, not at regular intervals and not without regard to costs and benefits. The ministries are expected to assess their own need for evaluations and decide what, when, and how. We will expect the consequences to be more evaluations and more focus on economical aspects.

The pressure from international society is in important ways weaker on Norway, so far being a wealthy non-member of the European Union. We suppose this strengthens the opportunities for having an evaluation practice based on internal demands.

An alternative diffusion hypothesis (Rogers, 1995) could be that Norwegian abundance has allowed for a fashion-like adaptation to evaluation-regimes that have been enforced in other countries. With today's access to information on the variation in questions and challenges that are addressed on the evaluation arena, this seems unlikely. Rather than looking for the impact of external models, we will discuss the implications of the access to information.

**External Trends and the Ministries' Evaluation Practice**

Among several development trends that may affect the ministries' evaluation practice, we have chosen two, which both seem substantial enough to be of importance:

1. The first relates to the fact that ministries, besides being special government bodies, can be understood as typical knowledge organizations in a modern society. We will see the ministries as part of the knowledge society and focus on their evaluation practice from this perspective.
2. The second deals with the changing institutional setting concerning the ministries' evaluation work. We will discuss how the Financial Management Regulations from 1997 with its result-based management perspective may have affected the ministries' evaluation practice.

**The Knowledge Society and Evaluation**

Modern Western societies are often described as information or knowledge societies. If we agree that there is something to be called a knowledge society and that there has been a transition going on in Norway from a rural/industrial society to a knowledge society,[7] we should ask how this trend might affect the role of evaluations. Some main elements in the knowledge society are the following:

1. Knowledge is the most important production resource. The ability to use knowledge is the key to success—for individuals, for organizations, and in society as a whole.
2. Many so-called knowledge organizations grow up. These organizations cannot be reflected in traditional models of organizations like industrial firms or bureaucracies. Instead of the typical hierarchical form and functional specialization, they will have an organization form that gives knowledge good conditions for growth and offers employees exciting and challenging duties, flexible work forms, and colleagues with a multiprofessional competence. In the knowledge society, these new organizations will gradually become more important, at the expense of more traditional forms of organizations.
3. The complexity and pace in modern society are growing and new challenges constantly developing. Governing has become more difficult. There

is no single knowledge base directly suited for dealing with the new society, and there is no single profession that can be said to be expert in dealing with it. The understandings of problems are disputed. People are disputing facts and descriptions of reality.

Some possible implications of this for the ministries' use of evaluations may be outlined.[8]

Related to the first element, the use of knowledge: Like all other organizations the ministries collect and utilize knowledge. Today there is probably more focus than earlier on how the ministries order, interpret, analyze, and bring information to the decision makers. Evaluations may play an important role in these processes, giving the information and knowledge needed. But there is a huge amount and variety of information available in the knowledge society beyond that which comes from evaluation. There is even talk of information overload. Too much information—evaluations included—may be a problem in modern society. The role of evaluations as a basis for producing knowledge is obviously an empirical question.

Related to the creation of knowledge organizations: The ministries, like other organizations, direct energy towards becoming knowledge organizations. This may have consequences for their daily work, internal organization, recruitment, and human relation policy. Evaluations are often multidisciplinary, long-term, and strategic projects. The work with evaluations in the ministries represents an opportunity for trying out new work forms, new types of recruitment, and developing the knowledge organization within the ministry. But at the same time there are clear limits to a ministry's flexibility, related to its political and constitutional responsibility.

Related to the increasing complexity: When governing becomes more and more difficult, the ministries meet the challenges of formulating a policy for this new complexity and at the same time, explaining this policy in such a way that politicians will be able to do their jobs in the governing of society. The steadily increasing complexity will also make it hard—and relatively meaningless—to maintain the traditional boundaries between the different sectors. Each ministry will have to secure its interests by taking part in various processes in other ministries and establish new forms of cooperation. The focus will have to change from administration of single cases to policy development, and from typical hierarchical decision-making processes to knowledge-producing processes. Evaluations may—by offering both theoretical and empirical knowledge and a multidisciplinary perspective—help the ministries in this new role. There are signs of an increasing interest in the Norwegian Parliament and in the ministries for evaluative analyses and studies of different kinds. But, on the other hand, seen from the perspective of information overload and disputes about descriptions of reality, not even the best evaluations can meet all the expectations. Evaluations can only play a modest role, and be one of the voices in the dispute. There are some quite pessimistic descriptions of the modern society such as The Postmodern Society or The Risk Society. In these descriptions, the value of empirically based knowledge is questioned on a fundamental base. Such knowledge will always be particularistic and relative, and therefore only valid in the situation in which it is produced. Political decisions have to be taken, and they are taken, but it is unclear on which ground. Evaluations may have a role to play, or they may not. This will be an empirical question.

The knowledge society seems, on the one hand, to *support and strengthen* the evaluation practice and the use of evaluations in the ministries. The ministries may use evaluations to fulfill their role as a knowledge producer, to become interesting work places, and to help govern the new complexities of the modern state. On the other hand, evaluations *compete* with many other types of information and knowledge, and the ministries' work with evaluations competes with other duties, like dealing with the day-to-day politics, serving the media, the running of the sector, and the need for sudden action. One may also question the role of evaluations in a complex society on a more *fundamental base*. In the knowledge society, evaluations can only play a modest role in government decision-making processes. We will come back to these hypotheses in the discussion of our findings.

### The Financial Management Regulations of 1997 and Evaluation

In 1997, a new set of rules for the Norwegian central government administration entered into force.[9] The regulations cover the financial and performance management processes in the ministries, such as planning, budgeting, following-up and reporting of results, and the management of subordinate agencies. They contain a few paragraphs on evaluations. The message is that each ministry should—with intervals, and as a part of its sector management responsibility—conduct evaluations.

The regulations focus on single, ex-post, and outcome evaluation studies. Implicitly, they take for granted that evaluations are used instrumentally as a part of the decision-making and managing process in the ministries. The conduction of evaluations is seen as a part of the result-based management process of the ministries. The information from evaluations is seen as a necessary supplement to the information received from the regular reporting of results.

The regulations represent the first attempt in Norway to introduce systematic use of evaluation in the government budget process. It represents a new impetus as well as a new institutional frame for the evaluation work otherwise done by the ministries. However, the ministries are given little specific advice on how to understand the role of evaluations in the management process and if it differs from the already established evaluation practice in the ministry. The evaluation concept is not defined, the evaluation object is not described, and it is not said at what intervals, in what situations, or based on which need or problem evaluations should be conducted. This openness in the regulations seems to be well in accordance with the ministries' sector responsibility and the philosophy of result-based management in general.

Studies in the ministries[10] show that evaluations are used in the dialogue between ministry and agency. But they were not used in the budget process and for allocating resources. About 40 percent of the leaders even saw evaluations as irrelevant for this purpose. Evaluations function as a common ground for orientation, discussion, and enlightenment in the management dialogue. But—in the short run—they do not guide management decisions (see Furubo in this volume).

### The Knowledge Society, the Regulations, and Evaluations

Bringing together what we have said about the development of the knowledge society and the evaluation practices in the ministries, we expect that the Financial Management Regulations will represent a challenge for the ministries.

- To conduct evaluations in the knowledge society represents a push towards broad, cross-sector studies, with an open and a long-term perspective, trying to describe complex phenomena and inventing new understandings. In the regulations and with the result-based management perspective there is a push towards the one-year perspective and single evaluation studies of organizations, activities, and budget allocations, making conclusions and being related to definite decision-making processes.
- Evaluations within the ministerial sphere traditionally comprise different kinds of information coming in different forms and medias, from different levels of government and at various stages of the decision-making processes. In the financial management regulations and with the result-based management perspective, the ideal is that evaluation is a well-defined activity and a definite part of each ministry's management and controlling strategy.

Our presumption is that the ministries have developed different practices concerning the use of evaluations, not being in perfect line with any of the perspectives described here. We will describe some of the practices and try to understand them from the perspective both of the knowledge society and of the Financial Management Regulations. We will also, where possible, try to relate the practices to some of the more theoretical discussions about the managing of evaluative information.

### Three Different Ministerial Areas

We have chosen three policy areas that are relatively easy to identify as specific policy areas and in which a substantial amount of evaluation is done.

## The Ministry of Foreign Affairs and Evaluation of International Development Cooperation

*The Policy Area—Some Characteristics*

Some important features of the international development cooperation area making it different from other policy areas are: (1) The total amount of the country's spending as percent of GNP is an end in itself. (2) The implementation and the effects of the policy are far away from the policymaking bodies, and key actors, institutional levels, and processes involved. (3) Much responsibility is put on the receiver, and the priorities of the government in the receiving country are always considered. Aid should imply empowerment.

These features create a complex and difficult policy area, with many risks involved. Everyone involved knows that projects and programs may fail, and the need for feasibility studies, assessments, reviews, controlling and following-up of activities is commonly understood. Monitoring and evaluation of results has also for a very long time been a part of the policy cycle. Even if implementation and effects are hard to measure and to evaluate, there is a tradition for doing it. The ministry is concerned about the following-up and evaluation of both the Norwegian aid money and its effects, and the total and long-term development effects in the receiving countries. Today's focus on empowerment is thought to increase the effectiveness and duration of the development cooperation. It is interesting to ask if the empowerment policy also has some consequences for the ministry's evaluation work.

*Tasks, Role, and Organization*

The Norwegian Parliament determines the objectives of development cooperation, decides which countries and regions are to be prioritized, and how much money is to be involved. The world's poorest peoples are the most important target group for Norwegian development cooperation, and this is reflected in the choice of countries.

International development cooperation belongs to the Ministry of Foreign Affairs. This ministry is the only ministry with two ministers—one for foreign affairs and one for international development cooperation. They work on a complementary basis, having divided the ministry's responsibilities between them.

One of the ministry's twelve departments is the Department for International Development Cooperation, which has a general function and coordination role including the management dialogue with NORAD (The Norwegian Agency for Development Cooperation). The department consists of two sections—an International Development Section and an Evaluation Section. Up until the year 2000, the Evaluation Section belonged to an especially constructed Planning and Evaluation Department for the ministry as a whole. But this construction never worked very well, and evaluation was brought back to the international development cooperation area.

NORAD is the only directorate under the Norwegian Ministry of Foreign Affairs. Its activities are based on the five main goals of Norwegian development cooperation.[11] The Norwegian development funds are not transferred to the target group directly, but are mostly channelled through the state government in the receiving country. A smaller part is channelled through other types of institutions and organizations—local administration, NGOs, private enterprises, or other parts of the civil society.

The aid budget is part of the allocation for the Ministry as a whole and covers all Norwegian development cooperation, including the part administered by NORAD. NORAD's use of funds is reported each year in the annual report. NORAD cooperates to a greater or lesser degree with local professional consultants with respect to evaluations and follow-up of development work in individual developing countries. Professional and technical communities also provide valuable assistance as advisers and development partners in Norway's partner countries. Recipients of development assistance have administrative responsibility for Norwegian development funds. NORAD emphasizes that developing countries themselves have the chief responsibility for development of their own countries.

In all the countries involved and for each stage of the development process, there is a growing claim for audit—both financial audit and performance audit. The audits being done may be understood as a supplement to other types of evaluations, or as something that may replace other types of evaluations.

*The Evaluation Work and Types of Evaluation*

The Evaluation Section is responsible for initiating and administrating the implementation of evaluations of both Norwegian development aid and Norwegian foreign policy. In 1998, a special instruction concerning the work with evaluations was issued. The instruction gives a definition of evaluation, explains the purpose, and regulates the process. The purpose of evaluation is to "produce knowledge which can be used in the formulation and implementation of the political goals," and to "make foreign policy better and more effective." The instruction also stresses the ministry's role in the following up of the evaluations. Interestingly enough, the ministry—when describing the use and utilization of evaluations—does not mention the budget process.

All areas within the responsibility of the ministry may be evaluated. But the tradition since the 1970s has been to evaluate international development cooperation, and still most of the ministry's evaluations deal with development aid programs and projects. Most of the evaluations are ex-post evaluations concerning impacts and outcomes of projects or programs. The evaluation research is undertaken by external consultants, about half of them being Norwegian firms. All evaluations are concluded with a published report. In the year 2000, the ministry spent all together $17 million Norwegian Krone (NOK) on evaluations, and five persons were working full time in this section.

The ministry's evaluations deviate from the project studies being conducted by NORAD, which run during the implementation processes, and where the affected groups are often taking part in the evaluation process. Here learning for adjustment is the main purpose. The ministry's evaluations are always done by an independent group of researchers or consultants, and at a late stage. The mandate is dealt with through a long process both inside and outside the ministry. According to the ministry's own definition of evaluation, the evaluations have three parallel purposes: control, management, and learning.

*The Evaluation Process*

The Evaluation Section produces an annual evaluation plan, which is accepted by the minister. This plan is based on suggestions from the different departments within the ministry, by NORAD, and the embassies.

All evaluations end up as a printed report. The report is sent for orientation and comments to all departments within the ministry, the embassies, NORAD, the local authorities, etc. Thereafter, a memorandum is produced by the Evaluation Section, following a certain format. It contains a short summary of the evaluation, conclusions and recommendations, and the different comments. The minister finally decides upon the memorandum. On the basis of the memorandum, the top civil servant in the ministry instructs the relevant departments or sections on the following-up of the evaluation and reactions to be done. Six months later, he will get a report telling what has been done.

The ministry is very concerned about the quality of the evaluation product. The Evaluation Section has recently written a handbook, which describes in detail the routines, the process, the methodological requirements, the quality assurance mechanisms, and so on. All interested parties will be informed that the evaluation is taking place and several are invited to comment on the evaluation mandate or suggest names of consultants. As soon as the mandate is ready and the consultant team chosen, the ministry will send out a memorandum to inform about the evaluation. After the evaluation report is finished, there will be another round of information to everyone. After a certain amount of time, each section and department within the ministry will present a response to the evaluation report from its area of responsibility. There is a relatively heavy focus on bringing the different parties into the evaluation management process. This may be a result of the organization of a special evaluation section outside the departments dealing with the subject matter that is evaluated. But it may also be understood as a response to a broad cooperation strategy and the focus on empowerment.

*In Sum*

In the international development cooperation area evaluations have long been an established component in the policy cycle. This could make a good case for evaluations being used and well integrated in the decision-making processes on all levels.

The Norwegian Foreign Ministry has also developed a well-tuned evaluation regime. There is a defined concept of evaluation and a special evaluation instruction recommending a certain approach, organization of the evaluation process, type of product and following-up processes within in the ministry. The evaluation work is organized in a special section of persons having the role as evaluation experts and only dealing with this. This probably leads to a professionalization of the evaluation processes within the ministry and to a general knowledge of evaluation within the ministry.

But there are also challenges and risks related to this type of regime.

- Single-study focus. The evaluation reports are well-defined and developed products. There is a risk that they get the status of results and ends in themselves. The challenge facing the ministry will be to strike the balance between the evaluation process, the product, and the knowledge and learning to be generated from it.
- The relevance for management. Each single evaluation takes a long time to conduct. When the report is finished, it is well taken care of within the ministry, with a number of formal procedures and special routines. But the important question is whether the information and knowledge to be generated from the evaluation is taken good care of and brought into the decision-making, management, and budget processes in the area. Our impression is that the Ministry of Foreign Affairs still has a way to go, both concerning the result-based management as defined in the Financial Management Regulations and concerning the knowledge society ideal.

## The Ministry of Education and Research and Evaluation of Universities and University Colleges

*The Policy Area—Some Characteristics*

One main goal defined for the higher education and research area is to be a driving force in the development of society. To realize this goal the ministry works, among others, through several institutions for higher education and research. With the exception of some private university colleges, all are state-run, but have considerable academic and administrative autonomy.

Much of the focus today is on the question of the quality. The ministry has newly initiated a reform of the quality of higher education.[12] Some elements of this reform are: (1) The higher education institutions should be spearheads for competence in the knowledge society; (2) Students shall succeed. There will be a new degree structure, more in harmony with the international system of higher education, and a new student finance system; (3) The institutions will get a more autonomous position. A new financing model is being introduced that is partly performance oriented, partly building on basic financing of the institutions; (4) New control regimes are made to assure that the institutions develop and follow up quality development strategies and make efficient use of their resources. The reform began implementation in 2003, and will be evaluated in 2006. For us it is interesting to see if we can find that the focus on quality has implications for the evaluation practice of the ministry.

*Tasks, Role, and Organization*

The Norwegian Parliament and the government define the goals and decide the budgetary frameworks for higher education. The work of the ministry is aimed at ensuring that Norway has a sound and well-functioning educational system as well as a productive and creative research environment.

The ministry is divided into six departments, one of these being the Department for Universities and University Colleges. This department is divided into three sections; one for the disciplines, one for rules and regulation, and one for budget and economy. The three sections work together in the management of the institutions. There are four universities and thirty-two university colleges in Norway, plus two arts university colleges and twenty-one private university colleges with state grants. Besides these institutions the ministry is administratively responsible for the Norway Network Council and the Norwegian Council for Higher Education working with common questions and cross-cutting issues on the higher education side. The ministry has also newly established a special independent institution for the assessment and evaluation of higher education, called NOKUT.[13]

*The Evaluation Work and Types of Evaluation*

There is no special department or section within the ministry responsible for evaluations. Evaluations are done as a part of the normal work of the different departments and the ministry as a whole. The ministry has not made any special definition of the word "evaluation," and there is no general instruction or formal set of procedures how to perform evaluations.

But there is a long tradition for performing evaluation in this area and a great number of evaluation bodies and evaluations being done, both within the education and research system itself and outside. The formulated purpose of the evaluation varies—it may be to increase knowledge, follow up reforms, support policy formulation or policy adjustment, help allocate resources, improve management, or assess quality. The evaluation object varies from huge reforms to single schools, universities, research programs, subjects or levels of education, and from ongoing activities and processes to time-bounded projects or programs. Various approaches and methods are used, and the evaluation product varies.

The ministry itself uses the following distinctions when talking about evaluations:

- There are evaluations being related to and initiated by the regulations for financial management: (1) The ministry is systematically working with evaluation of grants. This work is organized as projects with representatives from all the departments in the ministry. The top administration decides every year on a plan for which grants should be evaluated, based on suggestions from the departments. Normally, three types of grants will be evaluated each year. The evaluations follow a certain scheme, mandate, process, etc. The results from these evaluations will be used in the budget process, as a common ground for discussions about size, target groups, and priority. In the long run, the ministry also has a clear ambition to reduce the number of grants. (2) The ministry has established a regime for doing site visits at the higher education institutions. The purpose is to evaluate the institutions, financial management, budget control, and routines, and the visiting group from the ministry produces a report after the visit. These evaluation reports are mainly used within the department itself, partly to assure that the normal reports from the institutions may be trusted, and partly as a starting point for discussions about resources, systems, and organization of the financial management of the institutions.
- There are evaluations of education, disciplines, or institutions. These evaluations are typically done by the Norway Network Council, and focus on the substance and the quality of the education. The ministry is working on how to take a more systematic follow-up to these types of evaluations.
- There are evaluations of higher education reforms. The ministry has a tradition of systematically evaluating all large reforms. These evaluations will often be a part of the reform and used in the ministry's policymaking process.
- There are international benchmarking studies. The ministry has become quite eager to take part in international comparisons concerning all types of education, for example, the so called PISA-project within the OECD or in European comparisons about life-long learning. These comparisons are seen to represent a new and increasingly important instrument for the politicians in the ministry.
- There is the new type of evaluation for assessment and certification of higher education. A new institution for evaluation and accreditation of higher education (NOKUT, see earlier note) has been established for this purpose, to assure that the higher education institutions have good

quality assurance systems and perform well. NOKUT also has the possibility of removing certifications and allowances from individual institutions if the institution does not live up to certain standards.

According to the ministry, benchmarking studies, and the evaluations for quality assessment and certifications are increasingly important. This may be understood as a result of the increasing focus on quality.

*The Evaluation Process*

The ministry is concerned about how to further develop its planning and following-up of evaluations, to increase the utility and the effectiveness of the evaluation work. As a first step, the ministry has developed a common checklist to be used when starting up an evaluation process, noting things such as making clear from the very beginning the purpose of the evaluation and how it will be used, and to dimension the size and costs of the evaluation in relation to the purpose of the evaluation.

The ministry is also concerned about keeping the necessary distance between the ministry and the evaluator, to ensure objectivity and legitimacy. This is related to the fact that earlier the ministry had been criticized on this point on evaluations being done. Lack of neutrality has been an explanation for lack of quality of some of the big evaluations.

*The Ministry's Experience and Reflections[14]*

Evaluations in the field of higher education are said to have several positive implications for the relation between the ministry and the institutions:

- They tend to increase the ministry's authority and legitimacy;
- They tend to move the attention to the important aspects;
- They tend to become common platforms for discussion; and
- They tend to direct the ministry's work towards more strategic questions.

But there are also several challenges related to the evaluation work. The ministry admits that there is a common misunderstanding that evaluations can solve the problem of allocation of resources. There is also a risk of focusing the management process on what has been newly evaluated, and thereby neglecting other more important aspects concerning the institutions and their work. The ministry also points at the challenges concerning the handling and use of information, and the risk for information overload. The evaluations add to a huge amount of information in the higher education system. Evaluations may increase expectations of management above what is realistic. For example, the ministry will always be dependent on the actual willingness of the institutions to take the results of the evaluations seriously.

The ministry expects that the establishing of NOKUT will lead to a more systematic framework for some of the evaluation activities within the higher education system. This will also help the ministry in finding a more systematic role and responsibility for itself concerning evaluations.

*In Sum*

In the higher education area many different activities and types of processes are being included under the headline of "evaluation." The evaluation process, the method, the product, the use, and the follow-up to the evaluation vary from case to case. The evaluation work is organized as an integrated part of the department's normal work. In contrast to the Ministry of Foreign Affairs, there is no special group of evaluation experts. The ministry's role varies from evaluation to evaluation—and the ministry has become quite concerned about its role and responsibility for the planning and follow-up of the evaluations being done.

Traditionally, evaluations have been guided by national political needs. But during the last ten to fifteen years it has become quite obvious that evaluation is also a part of the internationalization process in the higher education system. Evaluation goes right to the question of competition between and quality ranking of institutions. The number of quite similar higher education institutions also allows for some of these new types of evaluations.

One of the strengths of the evaluation practice in this area is the integration of evaluation activities into the daily work of the ministry and the ministry's consciousness about what are the potential uses and risks of evaluation. The ministry is constantly working to establish better feedback procedures from evaluations to increase learning on different levels, but also to be more realistic concerning the expectations of evaluation. Given the huge variety of evaluations and evaluation activities the ministry probably also faces a challenge related to the question of professionalism and cost-effectiveness of evaluation.

## The Ministry of Social Affairs and Evaluation of the National Insurance Service

*The Policy Area*

The National Insurance Scheme was established in 1967 and is the very core of the Norwegian welfare system. The vital principle in the scheme is to secure a minimum standard for everybody, independent of earlier income, and an income level corresponding to earlier income. The scheme provides support through unemployment benefits, sickness and disability benefits, maternity benefits, housing support, and old age pensions. The allocations also cover the costs of medical rehabilitation and refunds for medical consultations and medicine.

Considerable changes have taken place both in society and in the overall pension system since the National Insurance Scheme was established.[15] People live longer and are pensioners for a greater number of years; women have entered the labor force; and the labor market is constantly changing.

- Many changes have made the rules difficult to understand and to practice.
- Norway, like most OECD countries, is experiencing a significant ageing of its population. Combined with higher average benefits this will soon result in a sharp increase in pension expenditure.

Throughout most of the 1990s, there also has been a growing trend in the number of people claiming sickness leave and those qualifying for invalid pensions.

The government's main strategy is to promote self-help, so that as many adults as possible can care for themselves through their own work, in line with the so-called "benefits-to-work" policy.[16] A tripartite agreement has been negotiated between representatives of the government (the ministers responsible for national insurance and the labor market, respectively) and the organizations of workers and employers (business and trade union actors) about a more inclusive labor market. The measures include voluntary company-level agreements between employers and the National Insurance Authority. A pilot project, which includes wage subsidies to employers that hire persons with varying work capacity, aims at transferring more people from the population on disability pension to the labor force. A new organizational body is established in all the counties—"centers for inclusive enterprises"—to assist employers and employees.

The government, in 2003, published a White Paper on merging the social welfare, labor market, and social security agencies into a single body in order to improve the coordination of public services. The government will evaluate an expansion of measures in the light of experience gained.

*Tasks, Role, and Organization*

The Norwegian Parliament is more involved in the decisions made in this field than usual. That makes the field an important one also for the Office of the Auditor General.

Cooperation between the Ministry of Social Affairs and the Ministry of Finance has a long tradition related to the area's importance for welfare and national economy. In the early 1990s, the ministry established a permanent committee—including a member from the Ministry of Finance—to assist with various calculations and assessments.

The Ministry of Social Affairs makes the budget and law proposals to the Parliament. Within the ministry, the social insurance department has the overall responsibility for implementing policy, adjustment of rules, and management of the National Insurance Administration.

The insurance service comprises the National Insurance Administration, offices at the county level and at the municipal level in which individual applications for social insurance benefits are handled. The service's main task is to handle social insurance benefits according to rules and budget decisions. That means a great number of cases—social insurance represents the main source of income for approximately one-quarter of the population, and one-half are receiving payments on a regular base.

The local offices' management lies with the National Insurance Administration, which is the senior professional and administrative body within the service. It is responsible for implementation of the regulations in force and also has a role in development. The agency is expected to contribute to formulating policies and strategies as well as updating of rules and regulations. It reports to the ministry on the services experiences and supplies the ministry with statistics and analysis to describe the development.

Until 1999, the agency had an internal audit department with 200 persons responsible for auditing the service. This department has been replaced by an integrated system to secure administrative quality. It has become a part of the managers' responsibility at all levels to formulate goals and demands, identify quality risks, find remedies, and follow up the development.

*The Evaluation Work and Types of Evaluation*

The different levels of the social insurance government administration have a corresponding responsibility for reporting and evaluation. The Social Insurance Department is responsible for research and evaluation concerning welfare and social service matters. The ministry engages in research through programs administered by the Norwegian Research Council.[17] The Ministry of Social Affairs funds positions at the universities as well.

The permanent committee where the Ministry of Finance is represented ("the calculation group") asks for evaluations with the intention of using them in the short- as well as a long-term budgetary context. The National Insurance Administration conducts the evaluations, scrutinizing how the different elements of the rules and remedies are working out, and goes in-depth on selected topics, as, for example, the inflow into disability pensions schemes. Statistics Norway produces much of the statistical material. A highlighted summary of the evaluation report is presented to the minister of social affairs for political consideration at the government's first conference on the budget frames for the next year.

The National Insurance Administration—on a yearly basis—delivers the regular information on results and development. It also initiates evaluations done by others.

The Office of the Auditor General conducts evaluations in connection with following up on parliamentary decisions.[18] Typical for this ministerial area is that management means management by rules, and managing is mainly about distribution of economic resources. This implies that heavy administrative tasks are related to control—to ensure that the decisions made are in accordance with the rules and that the system produces correct decisions in an effective way. Because of that, necessary knowledge in this area will be based on calculations and ex-ante assessments.[19]

The National Insurance Administration conducts evaluations related to the service and studies of the effects of devices and experiments—at their own initiative and their own administration as well as on the ministry's demand. One of the agency's departments analyzes the goal efficiency of different measures and different parts of the social insurance field. Both at the central level and regionally, different kinds of user studies and comparative analysis related to variations in payment and proceedings are conducted. Universities and freestanding institutes evaluate development and devices. The ministry also asks researchers to present the status of knowledge on different topics—for instance, at a conference in autumn 2002 on employment, sick leave, and disability pensions.

*In Sum*

Projections and studies of social development are important sources of knowledge in the area of national insurance service. The Ministry of Social Affairs in addition uses evaluations systematically—in its agency management, in its following-up on specific devices and trial arrangements within the ministry's area of responsibility, in cooperation with other ministries on common policies, and—when more comprehensive programs are concerned—on behalf of the government.

The ministry, the calculation group, and the agency initiate evaluations. Several institutions are involved in doing such work, including the ministry's own agency. Statistics Norway delivers statistics while the National Insurance Administration and others—institutes, universities, and university colleges—conduct evaluations and studies related to social welfare and living conditions. The ministry considers the economical aspects well attended to through the evaluating practice. It is not so confident with the ministry's follow-up of social aspects, which are not scrutinized to the same extent. Cross-sector collaboration also comes up short in relation to intentions.

In this area, the ministry counters one of the great challenges related to the use of evaluations, that is, to make the information instrumentally useful in the ministry's work with framing future politics and in making decisions on specific devices. Politics rests on several kinds of considerations, and in a service where results are determined by rules implicating individual rights to the citizens, development to a large extent follows automatically. It is not easy to see how information on consequences of existing rules and regulations can be transformed into knowledge that can be used to change politics, types of benefits, and in the long run, the growth in expenses.

In an increasingly complex society with changing values, attitudes, and choices at the individual level, it will also be increasingly difficult to predict the consequences of changes in policies. Some of the challenges in the national insurance field have to do with the working out of traditional benefits operating in a changed landscape. More extensive use of trial arrangements with new measures and ways of working may become a solution.

## Comparison and Discussion

*Different Division of Labor and Responsibility for Evaluation*

In all the three policy areas we have described, governmental authority is centralized (located at the state level), but at the same time important tasks are delegated to lower levels and subordinate bodies. In such delegated systems, evaluation may be an important instrument for controlling and following up the ministries' areas of responsibility. We do find that all three ministries use evaluations for the purpose of following up and controlling subordinate bodies and most important policy issues in the area.

The role of the subordinate bodies when it comes to the question of conducting the evaluations, on the other hand, varies between the three areas. Concerning international development cooperation, NORAD has the role of an external partner in relation to the evaluation process in the ministry. It produces itself many types of evaluate information, but it is the ministry alone that conducts the classical evaluation studies in the area. Speaking of higher education, the picture is far more complex. The ministry conducts evaluations of various kinds, and so do the different agencies and institutions in the area. A relatively new procedure is that the universities and university colleges conduct self-evaluations. There are also a growing number of internationally conducted evaluations of the education system being presented to the ministry. In the social security area, there has been a clear delegation of both development and management tasks to the central agency, including the responsibility for conducting evaluations.

The degree of involvement in the evaluation process from the ministry as a whole varies between the three areas. The Ministry of Foreign Affairs has developed a standard internal procedure for all evaluations, from the initiative to the implementation of conclusions. The Ministry of Social Affairs is to various degrees involved in studies and single evaluations, but the more systematic evaluation regime lies with the central agency. The Ministry of Education and Research has become more and more concerned with refining its role as stakeholder and manager, and therefore keeps a certain distance between the ministry and the evaluation process. The actual conducting of the evaluations also varies.

We have also seen different routines concerning the follow-up and utilization of the evaluations in the ministries. In the higher education area, the question of follow-up is not routinized, but a theme for discussion and a part of the process each time. The Ministry of Social Affairs follows different routines concerning different kinds of evaluations. For example, the prognostic studies are related to preparing of the budget, and the evaluation of pilot projects provides a base for decisions about continuation or not. In the international development cooperation area, all evaluation processes follow a standard operation procedure within the ministry, including the following up of conclusions.

The time horizon of the evaluation varies, from relatively short (evaluation of pilot projects in the social security area) to many years (large higher education reforms and long-term international development programs). In all ministerial areas we find both formative evaluations and summative evaluations, even if very few evaluations in the international development area are of a formative kind, and few in the social security area are of a summative kind. One possible tendency is that all three areas now strive for a better mix of short- and long-term, formative and summative types of evaluations. This may be a result of their becoming gradually more aware of their own evaluation practice as an *evaluation* practice, and thereby relating the work with evaluations to general evaluation norms and standards or to other practices.

We see that the ministries have different expectations concerning the immediate relevance of the different types of evaluations. But—generally speaking—their expectations concerning the utility of single evaluations are still quite high.

*Various Indications and Kinds of Use*

For some of the evaluations being conducted in our three areas there are clear indications that the ministries use the information instrumentally and directly. In the social security area, the forecasts of the social security expenditures are used as a base for calculating the size of next year's budget. In the Ministry of Foreign Affairs, each single evaluation study works as a starting point for an internal procedure including the summing up and spread of evaluative information. On the higher education area, the ranking of institutions and the accreditation of educational degrees on the basis of evaluations are clear expressions.

We have also identified other kinds of use, more indirect processes, and some situations where information from evaluations is used by the ministry but without recognizing it as a source of information or inspiration:

- Evaluations are used for control, by the ministry in question, the central agency, the Office of the Auditor General, or the political opposition. We find this in all three areas.
- Evaluations are used for learning and producing new knowledge related to adjustments of devices or getting new ideas. We find this in all three areas.
- Evaluations are used for communication, either between ministry and agency (this goes for all three areas), or between ministry and others (especially in the international development cooperation area).
- Evaluations are used as a means of quality assurance. We find this in two of the three areas, namely, higher education and social security.
- Evaluations are used as part of a quality assessment and accreditation system in the higher education area.
- Evaluations are used as a basis for prediction, planning, and budgeting in the social security area.
- Evaluations are used as a basis for deciding to stop or to continue pilot projects or to choose between devices. We find this clearly in the social security area.

These findings follow quite well the conclusions of earlier studies. As was found earlier, we also do not find that evaluations are used directly in the budget process or as a basis for the management of subordinate agencies. Instead the ministries tend to use evaluations for control and management of the sector area as a whole, and as one source of information among others to give common ground for discussing new ideas and learning.

We do not find that evaluations so far have strengthened the cross-sector cooperation and coordination. Most of the evaluations we have discussed with the ministries are related to the sector area in question. We have not seen any example of evaluations focusing on consequences of the policy for other policy areas or parts of society. The only exception is the evaluations following the tripartite agreement on a more inclusive labor market.

The classical literature on the use of evaluation talks about instrumental, intellectual, and political or symbolic use of evaluations. So far we have not been very much concerned with the symbolic use of evaluations in the ministries. We asked the ministries about evaluations being rooted in their daily work and related to their expected need for knowledge. In this situation, probably the symbolic aspects of use were under-communicated. But still we can apply this understanding also to our material.

- Some evaluations can be understood as negotiation elements necessary to produce consensus on whether to realize an initiative. The agreement of intention on devices to reduce sick-leave (administered by the Ministry of Social Research) may rest on a premise of evaluation.
- The use may change through the process. The actors may have changed, the situation may have changed, the evaluation results may arouse

other parties than expected at the start, or knowledge of a different kind than was asked for may be produced. (Valovirta, 2002) The large reforms in higher education may be understood from this perspective.
- Evaluations may have a consolatory function. Even if the evaluation results cannot be applied to new situations, it can be important to check if things were properly done. The ministries have a responsibility towards their past as well as their present and their future. All are needed to sustain the ministries' credibility. The Ministry of Foreign Affairs' evaluation regime on international development cooperation may be understood this way.
- An expanding market of evaluation suppliers is conducive to more use of evaluation and advocates for evaluation activity as meaningful in itself. This phenomenon will be known in the three policy areas.

## Understanding the Differences

We have described the three evaluation regimes as quite different from each other. The motives for conducting evaluation vary, the evaluation cultures are different, and the procedures for initiating, organizing the process, presenting the product, and following up the recommendations are not alike.

These differences may be related to different underlying rationalities in policies in the three areas. International development through state-to-state cooperation and empowerment is intended to create positive and long-lasting processes that can be continued by the recipients themselves, so that the stakeholder can withdraw. This poses other kinds of challenges than in the management of higher education institutions. This, in turn, poses other challenges to the ministry in question than to have the overall responsibility for developing and maintaining a benefit system for the population's economical security in a constantly changing society. The different rationalities may to some degree explain the different use of evaluation. The ministries will pose different questions and have different needs of information in their role as political actors. The evaluations will represent sources of information with different status in the general information market on the area in question.

The different organization structures in the three areas can also contribute to the different evaluation practices. Within higher education there are several institutions of the same kind, making systematic comparisons, benchmarking studies, and ranking possible. In the area of international development cooperation the systematic evaluation procedures involving different actors within and outside the ministry represent a strong force towards formalizing the follow-up of evaluations. In the social security area the fact that there is a central, national administration that regulates a locally implemented system may explain the interest for evaluating small-scale reforms and pilot projects before launching general changes.

## Ministerial Challenges

We will identify some of the challenges concerning the ministries' evaluation practice. The challenges differ between the three different governmental areas we have studied. In the international development area, the Ministry of Foreign Affairs faces several challenges related to the actual use of the information from conducted evaluations in the decision-making processes, including the management of NORAD, and as a basis for learning and development. We assume that the strict, formal evaluation regime with its long series of single studies and reports in itself may represent a contribution to these challenges.

In the social insurance area, it was pointed out that economic aspects were better understood and attended to in the evaluation activities than were the social aspects. It seems likely that this has something to do with the institutionalized cooperation with the Ministry of Finance and the strong link between ex-ante evaluations and the budget process. The ministry also searches for new evaluation themes, topics, and approaches to better cover its area of responsibility. We assume that this may represent a challenge for the ministry in relation to developing its evaluation practice.

In the higher education area, the ministry considers it a general challenge to absorb and make use of the multiplicity of evaluations and the huge quantity of information in its follow-up activities and sector management tasks. The ministry seems to be increasingly concerned with discussing and trying to develop its role in relation to evaluations. We assume this may be related to the great number of actors and types of evaluations with which this ministry is dealing.

In all three areas, evaluations are used for control purposes. External control on behalf of the Parliament and the Office of the Auditor General seems to be practiced most in the social insurance area, secondly in the international development area, and third, in the area of higher education. The ministries' own controlling activities have different foci. The Ministry of Foreign Affairs focuses its control activities on the transfers of money and the spending objectives. It is closely related to the activities of the auditing bodies at home and in the recipient country and of the bodies controlling the participating nongovernmental organizations. It is definitely something different from the evaluation studies focusing on the effects of programs and devices. The Ministry of Social Affairs relies partly on external auditing from the Office of the Audit General and partly on the internal control regime of the Ministry itself. In the higher education area, the internal administrative units within the ministry have both control and evaluation as part of their portfolio.

In all the areas there is a general principle that evaluations should both focus on specific objectives and results and have a cross-sector perspective going across administrative borders. All individual bodies as well as different devices shall be evaluated from time to time, and the effects for other sectors and society in general are to be considered. It is also a responsibility for the ministries to look forward, and they have coordination tasks between themselves. All these demands concerning information seeking and use of knowledge in the decision process have to be balanced against each other. All three ministries seem to be most concerned with evaluations closely connected to their own specific area of responsibility.

The government's so-called "modernization program" for the public sector[20] signals and prepares for more delegation, simplification, and user orientation. These objectives may put a new perspective to the evaluation practices we have identified. For example, it may be that the Ministry of Foreign Affairs is even more focused on outcomes in the future, and giving more weight to the recipients' point of view. Efforts have also been made to involve the recipients in the process of evaluation, which may be said to be in line with the objectives. Within higher education both the evaluation of institutions and evaluations for assessment and certification can be said to be in accordance with the user-orientation objective. But we should ask how far the user orientation goes, for example, when it comes to including the role and participation of the students in the evaluations. In the social insurance area, more evaluations focus on qualitative dimensions and on matters relevant for actual policy users in a direct sense. All this can be conceived of as being in accordance with the user-orientation philosophy. But it is also a tool for the ministry to better understand the mechanisms in society, and thereby enable the development of new devices and means. In all three areas it challenges evaluations to pay adequate attention to the users and to take seriously the differences between different categories of users.

### Some New Tendencies

Finally we will point to some of the changes and new tendencies we have observed in the ministries' evaluation practice.

- In the international development area, more attention is paid to communication and cooperation with stakeholders throughout the evaluation process.
- In the higher education and research area, more attention is paid to international comparisons, information about quality levels, and standards at the institutions.
- In the social insurance area, more attention is paid to prevention, new devices, and cross-sector cooperation, and the initiatives are followed up with evaluations.

The first possible explanation for these changes in the evaluation practice relates to the *changes in three policy areas themselves*. The focus on evaluation as communication and as a device to increase cooperation and mutual understanding between the stakeholders in the Ministry of Foreign Affairs is closely connected with the empowerment philosophy. Evaluations can help attain empowerment by sharing the same information and developing a common understanding of how programs are working for all stakeholders. Within higher education there is a tendency in the ministry for transform the evaluations into management tools related to the management of the higher education institutions. This seems to be a natural adaptation to the policy of decentralization of the higher education institutions of the last ten years. The social insurance area faces quite a precarious situation with rising expenditure and pessimistic financial prognoses. The ministry's engagement in evaluations concerning new policy approaches and policy tools can easily be understood from that perspective.

The *knowledge society* perspective may also help us understand the observed changes. In the social insurance area, for example, it seems reasonable to suppose that the request for evaluation as the basis for policymaking will increase in "the new complexity"—given the uncertainty connected to the effectiveness of different devices as well as to the consequences for the target groups. In the higher education area, the ministry seems to require more knowledge about the institutions and their results, to be able to establish a sufficient basis for a good dialogue and a management that will be conceived of as legitimate and just. Evaluations have a relatively high status in a knowledge-oriented system.

The ministries are still facing challenges related to development of their evaluation practice and use of evaluative knowledge. Our general conclusion is that the ministries should not try to find the final answers or solutions in general regulations or principles. We conceive a more promising road for the ministries to open up for discussions and exchanges of evaluation experiences, and to learn more from each other. And not least, they should learn from each other to become more modest about what to expect from evaluations and more ambitious concerning their own role as managers of evaluative information.

## Notes

1. Earlier a line was often drawn between prospective and retrospective analyses, with the term evaluation reserved for retrospective analysis (Rist, 1990). Use of the term has gradually become more elastic and the conclusion, for instance in the discussion in *International Atlas of Evaluation,* is that the important thing is to specify how the term evaluation is used (Furubo and Sandahl, 2002: 2–3). By evaluations we mean here all different kinds of studies, reports, etc., containing evaluative information that the ministries themselves refer to when talking about "evaluations."
2. Also our definition of *use* is inductive; we let the ministries themselves contribute to our way of defining and describing use.
3. The most important ones being the Public Administration Act (1967) and the Instructions for Official Studies and Reports (2000).

4. For this study, we take as a premise that evaluations have no other raison d'être than to be useful (cf. Furubo, in this volume).
5. In this third situation, the question of use turns into a far more complex (and controversial) question. There will be reasons to ask—why should I use it? And there will be many more reasons for not using it.
6. Cf. Stame (here) about differences between the United States and the European countries.
7. In 2000, Norway was ranked number two among 150 countries registered on twenty-three variables concerning four types of infrastructure: PC, Internet, information and social infrastructure. http:/worldpaper.com/2001/jan01/ISI). Norway was not represented among the countries registered in 2001.
8. This reasoning builds on some of the points being made in two reports from Statskonsult. *Framtidens departement. Utfordringer og muligheter for departementene* (A ministry for the future challenges and possibilities for the ministries), Statskonsult Notat 2000:4, and *Å styre det komplekse ... En komparativ studie av intern styring ved Rikshospitalet og noen andre kunnskapsorganisasjoner* (To manage complexity ... A comparative study of internal management at The Norwegian State University Hospital and some other knowledge organizations). Statskonsult Rapport 2000:7.
9. The Regulations for Financial Management in the Central Government Administration and Functional Requirements.
10. Erfaringsprosjektet—Rapport 4: *Styring i staten*. Finansdepartementet 2000. (The experience project—Report number 4: State management. The Norwegian Ministry of Finance.) Another survey study is referred to by Øvrelid and Bastøe (2002: 214).
11. These five goals are: (1) To combat poverty, giving priority to employment, health, and education. (2) To contribute towards promoting peace, democracy, and human rights. (3) To promote responsible management and utilization of the global environment and biological diversity. (4) To contribute towards preventing hardship and alleviating distress arising from conflicts and natural disasters. (5) To contribute towards promoting equal rights and opportunities for women and men in all areas of society.
12. The Report to the Storting on higher education submitted by the Government on March 9, 2001: Do your duty—Demand your rights [Report No. 27 to the Storting (2000–2001)].
13. Norwegian Agency of Quality Assurance in Education (NOKUT), established 01.01.03
14. This section builds on a speech by Vidar Horsfjord from the Ministry of Education and Research, titled *Evaluations in the Management of Higher Education Institutions*, in a seminar for the ministries arranged by the Ministry of Finance, 28.11.02.
15. Against this background, the government has appointed a pension commission that shall clarify the main objectives and principles of a sustainable national pension system. The commission's report is to be presented.
16. 2003 *The Long-Term Programme 2002-2005* Report No. 30 to the Storting (2000-2001).
17. An ongoing program on welfare research extends over six years (January 1, 1999—December 31, 2004). The Ministry of Children and Family Affairs, the Ministry of Labour and Government Administration, and the Research Council of Norway are also financing this program. Research funds are partly earmarked on the basis of the ministries' sector responsibilities for welfare issues and partly unrestricted—that is, financed by the Research Council.

18. For example—a decision made in 1998, that vocational training should be tried before applications for disability pensions are granted. The objective of the investigation was to assess the efficiency and effectiveness of the work performed by the National Insurance Service and the Labour Market Administration. Document no. 3:3 (2001–2002), *The Office of the Auditor General's investigation of disability pension and vocational rehabilitation.*
19. Ex-ante evaluations are important tools in the field of research as well and mentioned as such in the *Norwegian Research Council's Evaluation Handbook* (1996); cf. also note 15.
20. Statement to the Parliament on Public Administration Policy, 2001

## References

Dabelstein, N., and C. C. Rieben. (2002). "Evaluation of Development Assistance: Its Start, Progress, and Current Challenges." In J.-E. Furubo, R. C. Rist, and R. Sandahl, eds., *International Atlas of Evaluation*. New Brunswick, NJ: Transaction Publishers.

Furubo, J.-E., and R. Sandahl. (2002). "Introduction. A Diffusion Perspective on Global Developments in Evaluation." In J.-E. Furubo, R. C. Rist, and R. Sandahl, eds., *International Atlas of Evaluation*. New Brunswick, NJ: Transaction Publishers.

Rist, R.C., ed. (1990). *Program Evaluation and the Management of Government: Patterns and Prospects across Eight Nations*. New Brunswick, NJ: Transaction Publishers.

Rogers, E. M. (1995). *Diffusion of Innovations*, 4th ed. New York: Free Press.

Statskonsult Notat 2000:4. Framtidens department. Utfordringer og Muligheter for departementene

Statskonsult Rapport 2000:7. A styre det komplekse ... En komparativ studie av intern styring ved Rikshosp italet 09 neon andre kunnskapsorganisasjoner.

Valovirta, V. 2002. "Evaluation Utilization as Argumentation." *Evaluation* 8(1): 60–80.

Vedung, E. (1991). Utvardering I politik och forvaltning Studentlitteratur, Lund Øvrelid, R., and P. O. Bastoe, 2002. Norway: Toward a Results-Oriented Government Administration. In J.-E. Furubo, R. C. Rist, and R. Sandahl, eds., *International Atlas of Evaluation*. New Brunswick, NJ: Transaction Publishers.

# 12

# Evaluation Knowledge for Strategic Budgeting

*Xavier Ballart and Eduardo Zapico*

### Introduction

Rational budget reform has traditionally claimed the instrumental linkage between resource allocation and evaluation. Despite limited advances, this is still one of the aims of many current budget reform initiatives. This chapter deals with a number of issues related to the links between budgeting and new approaches to evaluation, taking into account the complexity of the public management context. Adapting budgeting to respond to the growing uncertainty and interdependence requires new criteria of success and evaluation as the basic framework of reference for management performance assessment. New approaches to accountability can also work as an incentive to encourage interactive learning.

Much of the recent thinking and research in the area of trust has been informed by work that emphasizes the role of human capital and social capital (OECD, 2001). Human capital focuses on the importance of a wide range of individual capacities, including informal learning, while social capital is a property of groups, communities, and organizations that emphasizes the role of shared norms and values as well as social behavior. Very close to this notion is the role of trust as a crucial factor for social cooperation.

In particular, we would like to explore the new roles of the central budget office (BO) in strategic resource allocation and the opportunities offered by new approaches to performance measurement for evaluative knowledge to become part of the budget process. We have reviewed potential opportunities for strategic leadership under uncertainty along the following lines:

- Developing new criteria of success to assess performance
- Applying alternative approaches to evaluation
- Building trust for evaluative knowledge to be effectively used
- Redesigning positive-oriented accountability systems

Our main concern is to identify and assess new arrangements that facilitate strategic budgeting using evaluative knowledge. The creation of formal structures and institutions to facilitate technical evaluation studies in the framework of the budget procedure will not suffice, neither will any simple formula based on well-identified evaluation models. Many conditions and factors are required to foster an environment conducive to the production of useful information, mutual exchange, and widespread organizational engagement. We envision evaluation as a space of knowledge creation (not necessarily by evaluators or budgeters) and BO as having a role in gathering information, managing knowledge, integrating it into existing knowledge, and promoting social learning by sharing applied knowledge to create value for stakeholders and society at large.

## Strategic Budgeting and Evaluation under Uncertainty

*Strategic Leadership from Central Budget Office*

The interest of public managers in using evaluation and public expenditure management tools may be quite different from the interest of BO. Any agency or manager should develop its own budget management and evaluation system without the center necessarily playing a role, beyond legal compliance and aggregate spending discipline. However, if evaluation and budget reform is to be part of an overall initiative for shifting from a traditional direct type of control to a more flexible type of spending management control, the need for central leadership seems to be clear.

The specific role of a central budget unit and the way it exercises its leadership for decentralization under a context of uncertainty need to be discussed. The relevant question is: what does central steering mean under a decentralized and uncertain policy context? This question suggests the need to change and adapt performance management, evaluation, and other related functions such as contract management and accountability (Office of Management and Budget, 1995).

With decentralization, changes in the responsibilities of the central unit are not just quantitative but also, and more importantly, qualitative. Current public sector reforms such as contract management, budgeting for results, and decentralization in general demand improvement in the management capabilities in both decentralized agencies and in central units. The former needs to undertake better evaluation and reporting. The latter needs not only to understand evaluation but also be able to provide leadership for the introduction, development, and coordination of a governmentwide decentralized management system among interdependent organizations, including evaluation. If, during the process of decentralization, agencies resist improving their evaluation, the center must actively play a leadership role in promoting evaluation, so that the government as a whole can learn from its experiences and each organization does not have to begin from scratch.

Some might argue that after decentralization the new role of the center is more limited as it would be circumscribed to coordination and postevaluation (Shick, 1990, 33). In this study we argue the opposite, that is, that the center needs to play a qualitatively "stronger" role after decentralization. We suggest that after decentralization the performance of the governmentwide management system, in a context of complexity, heavily depends on adequate strategic leadership from the center. The central budget unit has to pay special attention to increasing pressures towards fragmentation in a system struggling to work under a new type of accountability based on strategic direction and demonstrating performance (Mayne and Zapico, 1997).

Independent budget behavior and competition for resources might follow decentralization if there is no special effort from central units to improve coordination (Mayne and Zapico, 1997). Central budget's evaluation role is essential for the effective performance and management of the whole system. Furthermore, budgeting and evaluation are not just technical exercises. After decentralization in an unstructured or complex environment, it is necessary to increase the capacity of the center for budget flexibility and strategic leadership. This implies, among other factors: overall priority resetting; negotiating and designing new rules for the budget game; building proper channels of communication and developing institutional capacity for coordination and conflict resolution. It also means applying new criteria in evaluation and accountability in order to ensure the integrated functioning of the decentralized parts of the government.

Interest and support for performance budget reform from senior officials and central departments may appear and develop if the performance measures chosen for evaluation are considered relevant and credible. This suggests the need for redesigning the performance criteria. New types of performance measurement (the three Ds: capacity for Diagnosis, Design, and Development), which are discussed later, can help to define further the strategic evaluation role of BO under conditions of uncertainty.

Furthermore, new approaches to evaluation and some of its implementation requirements are also needed and suggested to deal with the obstacles blocking strategic leadership capacity from BO.

As shown in table 12.1, the more the public management context is unstructured—that is, characterized by the factors of uncertainty, instability, diversity, and interdependence—the more the need for new criteria of success and evaluation paradigm to be developed. Related problems for resource alloca-

## Table 12.1
### Strategic Budgeting and Evaluation under Uncertainty

| Unstructured Policy Context | Related Problems for Resource Allocation | New Responses and Approaches To Evaluation |
|---|---|---|
| **Uncertainty**: unknown cause-effect relationships; difficult measurement or data collection | Limited scope of traditional budget and performance indicators | **Strategic Leadership from Central Budget Office** |
| | Unintended costs and benefits | 1. New Criteria of Success: From 3Es to 3Ds |
| **Interdependence**: interaction among units, organizations, policies and constituents | Ambiguity of goal definition | 2. Approaches to evaluation under uncertainty |
| | Inability to control external factors | |
| **Diversity**: multiple and conflicting values and interests | Lack of coordination among interdependent actors and budget programs | 3. Building trust for evaluation knowledge utilization |
| | | 4. Positive-Oriented Accountability Systems |
| | Resistance to control and evaluation | |
| **Instability**: changing goals, policies and environment | Irrelevance of goals and spending policies | |

tion have been identified, such as limited scope of performance indicators, unintended effects, ambiguous goal definition, controlling external factors, lack of coordination and resistance to control.

Therefore, a core condition for active and strategic budget leadership in an unstructured context from a central budget unit is having capacity to confront diversity, interdependence, uncertainty, and instability. This context demands new responses to public budgeting and evaluation, including new performance criteria and evaluation approaches.

### New Criteria of Success: From Three Es to Three Ds

Major obstacles for proper budgeting, such as contextual and policy instability, participants, interdependence, diversity of interests, and, in general, unknown program effects, can often best be addressed by rethinking the nature, scope, and approach of evaluation. We need to reinvent evaluation and redefine the criteria of successful performance to match today's organizational realities (unstructured policy context demanding decentralization). Success with both evaluation and budget reforms requires responding to several sources of uncertainty.

The definition of "sound" performance used for evaluation should reflect the adapting responses to uncertainty. According to Mayne, "a well performing public program or service is one that is providing, in the most cost effective manner, intended results and benefits that continue to be relevant, without causing undue unintended effects" (Mayne and Zapico, 1997). This definition and the need for *continued relevance* has important implications for the evaluation of policy performance and the models chosen to improve public management and budgeting.

In this respect, it is important to firstly clarify how uncertainty affects and influences public managers' performance. In a context of uncertainty about outcomes of programs and/or policy instability, the ability to properly *redefine* goals and intervention modes is a precondition of success for public managers. The capacity and skills of managers to be economic, efficient, and effective (the Three Es) in achieving goals may be insufficient if the goals are changing or outcomes cannot be readily anticipated. In fact, the greater the organizational uncertainty, the more distorted will be the performance measurement system in use (Carter, 1991) and the less relevant is the use of the Three Es model for evaluation and assessment. This is because the model assumes the availability of precisely pre-defined and stable objectives and a well-known (or at least widely accepted) cause-effect relationship between organizational activities and outcomes.

It is widely believed that some policies are not susceptible to evaluation under a traditional Three E approach. This is, for instance, the case of community development initiatives. Community development practitioners (Hugues and Traynor, 2000) frequently point out that their work cannot be evaluated fully, because the evaluators do not fully understand the process of community development. In this respect, the principal issues that tend to be raised are:

1. Time scale (how long does it take to bring about social change in a community)?
2. Causality (how can change or growth be clearly attributed to the social intervention)?
3. Diverse views on success (how will a credible data set be assembled whereby to appraise outcomes when community members, community development staff, and planners each have a different concept of what constitutes success)?
4. Focus on process (sometimes seen as an end product in its own right).
5. Tendency to list activities on the assumption that such processes are likely to contribute to the well-being of the community. In other words, the setting up of structures (women's centers, health centers, crèche facilities) and processes (education, training, new culture) is often considered as more important than achieving a measurable outcome performance such as reduction in poverty (see Hugues and Traynor, 2000).

It is widely recognized that today public managers work under a context of change and uncertainty. Consequently, managers must have a capacity for readjustment and adaptation. This situation does not allow us to assess realistically organizational performance only on the basis of traditional performance measurements. There is a need for new measures that capture the capacity of managers to identify, respond to, and cope with unanticipated problems.

In any case, the Three Es and Three Ds approaches for evaluation are not incompatible alternatives. Using the traditional Three Es at least as 'tinopeners' signals for further study (Carter 1989) improves performance monitoring, which could be complemented with traditional program evaluation. But new measures or criteria of success are needed for assessing the management capacity for *Diagnosis* of new problems, for *Designing* new solutions, and for *Developing* or getting support for their implementation. According to Metcalfe, the Three Ds approach should allow the assessment of:

*Diagnosis* capacity for the identification of new problems or the redefinition of current problems, taking into account changes in the environment and the interests of stakeholders, and building a common perception of the problem.

*Design* capacity for the formulation of new solutions (policies and institutions), including the incentives to solve new identified problems and the adaptation of organizational and interorganizational structures and strategies.

*Development* capacity for the actual implementation of new solutions as a learning process, coping with resistance to change, redefining problems and solutions during implementation, and learning from experience (Metcalfe, 1991).

The Three Ds model looks at innovative and adaptive performance and demands questioning the definition of objectives, the cause-effect relationship, and the values underlining the public sector intervention. A parallel must be drawn here between, on the one hand, the Three Es vs. Three Ds distinction and, on the other hand, the single vs. double loop organizational learning discussed in an earlier book in this series by Leeuw, Rist, and Sonnichsen (1994) and the inter-organizational learning discussed by Metcalfe (1993).

The Three Ds approach is more relevant for assessing performance under uncertainty. Rather than examining how well performance criteria based on the Three Es have been met in cases where these criteria become obsolete or irrelevant, assessing performance from a Three Ds perspective looks at how well organizations and their managers confront unstructured contexts (see table 12.1), that is:

- respond to multiple pressures and unexpected challenges (diversity);
- exhibit flexibility in the face of changing circumstances (instability);
- work cooperatively within networks of organizations when delivering new programs (interdependence); and
- adapt to an unpredictable environment (uncertainty).

## Evaluation Knowledge for Strategic Budgeting 221

In an unstructured context, we suggest that the central budget office should assess public managers' performances with regard to their capacity for adapting to new problems beyond the traditional concerns of cost reduction, productivity, and quality improvement of current services. In such a context, maximizing adaptability rather than maximizing short-term utility is a different and more relevant criterion of success.

A pragmatic decision rule for both budgeters and managers might be to build a balanced mix of both evaluation based on the Three Es and a set of evaluations based on the more relevant Three Ds. The choice of appropriate mix would depend on the degree of uncertainty under which managers work. It would, thus, become important to distinguish between various situations. On the one hand, and to the extent that agencies have straightforward and undisputed objectives and deal with well-defined, homogeneous tasks and predictable outcomes, the Three Es approach and traditional evaluation will probably cover most of the management information needs. On the other hand, for organizations working in complex environments (with objectives subject to different views and interpretations, networks of organizations under policy change, central units dealing with administrative reform) the need for a Three Ds evaluation approach would become higher.

### Approaches to Evaluation under Uncertainty

The need for a more strategic leadership from central budget units leads us to look for new types of evaluation approaches that can stimulate and reward innovation and experimentation in a complex public policy environment.

In budgeting, there is a need for explanatory material allowing interpretation and adatation of the logical background of budget program performance. In this respect, evaluation often appears to be the necessary tool that can provide the needed interpretation to try and sort out the various contributing factors to program performance.

Measuring the Three Ds type of performance requires alternative evaluation approaches. In this sense, through decentralized evaluations focusing on participation, adaptability, and collective strategy building, some weaknesses of the traditional centralized budget process can be corrected. The following points present an overview of some types of evaluation approaches that facilitate assessments under the Three Ds model and provide some hints on BO new roles. Other chapters in the book treat these evaluation approaches in more detail.

*Pragmatic Approaches: Short, Timely Information*

The basic idea of providing usable knowledge corresponds quite adequately with the pragmatic approach defended by Thoenig and others (Thoenig, 2000).

From this perspective, evaluation is considered to be more credible if it is adjusted to the reality of the decision-making process. Like corporate executives, public decision-makers give priority to practical or qualitative information obtained by speaking to individuals they trust. Therefore, evaluation should be limited in scope; focused on clearly defined problems; use language that policy makers and the society at large can understand; and obtain data that are available or can be obtained rapidly at a low cost.

In accordance with these characteristics, the basis for this type of pragmatic evaluation is that evaluators should not embark on making judgments and assessments (particularly when they must evaluate ongoing reforms). As expressed by its advocates, evaluation should be decentralized and participatory, done concurrently by networks of professionals directly involved in the implementation of reforms and it should aim at describing a state of affairs rather than analyzing it. As a consequence, evaluation will more likely provide performance proxies rather than assess external impacts. For BO, this approach may produce the kind of evaluative knowledge that can be easily shared and exchanged. It also allows BO to continue to play a monitoring role.

This evaluation approach is attractive for its simplicity. It assumes that knowledge will be quite explicit and relatively easy to handle. It also assumes that people have defined roles and that the flow of information is mainly bottom-up. However, innovative public policies often require understanding how it is possible to induce change through non-standardized processes. Often this will require a lot of dialog and the flow of information to be interactive.

*Theory-Based Evaluation: Theoretical Assumptions*

Theory-based evaluation was a response to the questions raised on the view of programs as black boxes (Chen, 1990; Weiss, 1995). In a recent article of Birckmayer and Weiss (2000), we found a brief and precise description of this approach. According to them, the basic idea is to surface the assumptions on which the program is based in considerable details. The evaluation will have to review what activities are being conducted, what effect each particular activity is meant to have, what are the following steps in the program, what the expected response is and so on, so as to find out whether the process matches the expected outcomes. The evaluation then follows each step in the sequence to see whether the expected steps actually materialize.

Following the same authors, an evaluation that investigates the theories underlying a program will, thus, have to collect data at many points along the course of the program so as to answer various questions, such as: Does the program succeed in getting the attention of target groups? Do the activities bring about a sense of trust? Does the program provide the planned activities? And this series of questions would end with a question on the outcome of the program. Therefore, what TBE does is to track the stream of steps along the road so as to find out whether the theories on which the program is based are realized in action.

The benefits that advocates of TBE claim for this approach [Birckmayer and Weiss (2000)] are of three kinds:

1. TBE provides information about the mechanisms that intervene between program activities and the achievement (or nonachievement) of expected results. The evaluation can track each link in the chain of assumptions. As a consequence, the results of such an evaluation will show which chains of assumptions are well supported by data collected, which chains break down.
2. TBE is supposed to provide better knowledge about the mechanisms of change that will not only benefit the specific program under study. The hope is that the knowledge will generalize to a wider array of change efforts. In this way, it enables the results from the evaluations to be fed into a wider knowledge of such programs.
3. TBE also highlights the elements of program activity that deserve attention in the evaluation, and it requires the operational staff to be explicit about their assumptions.

TBE is particularly adequate to know more about the actual effects of policies. Too much research and evaluation are focused on implementation and participation, but not enough on the actual processes leading to outcomes of policies. The potential of TBE is there but so, too, is the risk of confusion in the collective sense of what is finally secure knowledge. Focusing on the theories of action gives evaluation a deeper sense that may be also conflicting with the time pressure and the need for quick answers of both managers and budgeters.

For BO, this approach may allow them to go beyond the straightforward evaluation of programs by agencies, producing the kind of evaluative knowledge that deals with the complex interactions that exist between various types of interventions and effects.

*Participatory Evaluation: Stakeholders Constructions*

Evaluation as a participatory process is based on the identification and involvement of stakeholders, the surfacing of claims, concerns, and issues to facilitate consensus in negotiations. From this perspective, evaluation is seen as a political act. According to Stake (1975), the participatory evaluation is constructivist in the sense that perceptions on program activities and effectiveness are social constructions. It is also considered to be a responsive approach since parameters and boundaries for the evaluation are to be determined through an interactive and negotiated process involving stakeholders.

One of the main arenas for participatory evaluation is in international co-operation. According to Jackson 2000: "Participatory evaluation can be defined as the production of collective knowledge and cooperative action in which the stakeholders in development interventions participate substantively in identifying evaluating issues, designing evaluation, collecting and analysing data, and acting on the results of evaluation findings." This type of community-based participatory evaluations can play an important role as a leverage that might reorient public sector bureaucracy (Feinstein and Puetz, 2000).

Other similar well-known approaches, such as Patton's utilization-focused evaluation (1986), reduce the scope of participation by doing evaluations that provide information decision makers view as necessary. This approach is, thus, based on the principle of usefulness and actual use of the evaluation. In this case, there is a need to identify the intended users of the evaluation, who are brought together and organized into an evaluation task force, to work with the evaluator and take part in the decision making of the evaluation. The evaluator together with the intended users decides the focus of the evaluation, reviews the options, and selects the approaches. The evaluator helps the intended users to decide whether the evaluation is worth doing. If they decide to proceed, next stages embrace discussions about methods, measurement, and design. Further on, data are collected and analyzed and the intended users actively participate in interpreting findings, forming judgments, and making recommendations. In the light of findings, it is then decided whether the evaluation results are to be disseminated.

This type of evaluation approach does not foresee the participation of all stakeholders since it is considered that participants have to be enthusiastic, committed, competent, and interested. The idea is that the primary participants are lower down in the hierarchy and that participation is bottom-up. Therefore, not all the participants are motivated enough nor have the ability to support their involvement. Nevertheless, Patton considers that ability is not an impediment as such and that the project might have a low level of participation.

Participation is widely believed to be positive. Participation gives explicit consideration to social, political, and cultural factors since it is based on a need to include, discover, and understand. From a philosophical point of view, participation is also viewed as necessary given the interdependence to create knowledge. That is, each actor depends on others to provide information and to understand its own position.

For BO, this approach to evaluation will be difficult given the uncertainty associated, not only with the policies but also with the evaluation process itself. According to Gregory (2000), there may be an imbalance of knowledge between stakeholders; fundamental conflicts may arise that are not easily resolved; and the free flow of information between stakeholders may be an ideal that is rarely achieved. Still, BO can play a role in the diffusion of those experiences that appear to be successful from the perspective of stakeholders.

## Building Trust for Evaluation Knowledge Utilization

Before we get carried away by evaluation being integrated with decision making (by being more pragmatic) or more theoretical (in looking at theories of action) or more diverse and interdependent (because of its participatory nature), we need to think about the deficit of trust between policy actors.

As it has been pointed out above, a long bureaucratic and incremental tradition has created a deeply rooted culture of control and budgeting based on inspection of spending behavior. As a consequence, in order to reinforce the shift from traditional to strategic budgeting, there is a need to break the vicious circle originating in the inherent criticism from controllers, and the defensive attitudes from public managers. Only if relations among them become constructive instead of competitive will sharing evaluation knowledge be feasible. Public managers should perceive reports and constructive criticism as a normal step towards organizational learning (OECD, 1996).

The renewed focus on social capital provides a framework for evaluation knowledge management. For the majority of writers (Bourdieu 1986, Coleman, 1988, Putnam, 2000, OECD 2001) social capital is defined in terms of networks, norms, and trust and the way these allow agents and institutions to be more effective. Reciprocity and mutual support norms are basic for the construction of social capital. Historical personal experiences are as influential as the set of formal rules in determining the potential for interaction and validation of knowledge.

Building trust in the budget procedure depends on long-lasting and continuous relations of conditional and reciprocal nature. Cooperation should be oriented towards a common objective: the flow and use of evaluative knowledge. Trust development should facilitate the perception and awareness of interdependence in the network of managers, budgeters, and evaluators. These would reduce strategic uncertainty, risk levels, and the possibility of undisciplined budget behavior.

Institutional structures for evaluation knowledge management require the existence of well-functioning forums and organisms that facilitate the connection and integration among budgeters, managers, and evaluators. This organizational mechanisms should be coherent with the context. For instance, in a decentralized and uncertain context, horizontal interaction could be more effective than hierarchical channels.

Building trust is a slow and a costly process whereas its destruction can be quick. This long process of generating mutual trust among all the actors involved could be led by the department of the budget, or any other unit, but should count on the support from other departments. Some concrete initiatives for developing social capital among evaluators, managers, and budgeters are the following:

- Strengthening evaluation and budgeting units
- Job mobility, resource sharing, and training programs
- Joined formal and informal activities for evaluators, budgeters, and managers
- Explicit declarations of willingness to encourage innovation, to risk failure, and to learn from experience
- Accepting a diversity of evaluation models and approaches
- Forums for policy discussion

Social capital is essential for organizational learning and innovation in the public sector. A substantial increase of evaluation knowledge could be ineffective and even an obstacle disorienting budgeters if it does not go along with a corresponding development of trust and social capital in the budget process. Transforming evaluation information into knowledge, ready for decision making and resource allocation, demands a balance between information produced and existing collective trust in an organization. The availability of data, figures, and information on results is insufficient if it is not accompanied by the necessary capacity (technical and social) for collectively selecting and transforming this information into knowledge.

### Positive-Oriented Accountability

Another important aspect of the new role for the budget office is related to spending control and accountability systems. The traditional aim of financial control is to fight fraud. As Metcalfe and Richards suggest, this aim should be complemented with a more positive perspective of encouraging the desired overall budget performance (Metcalfe and Richards, 1990). Because of recent spending decentralization trends, initiatives to improve financial accountability systems need to be reinforced to ensure that delegated spending authority is being applied properly and results have reached anticipated standards. This reinforcement does not mean just increasing the capacity to identify culpability or to enforce punishment.

To be successful in the improving of accountability, it is necessary to change the commonly held but false assumption that accountability and spending performance are inherently in conflict. Accountability is usually reduced to issuing and applying legal and financial regulations to constrain the efficient performance of public servants. Although difficult to achieve, a well-designed accountability system may encourage good spending results without damaging public service ethics. There is not necessarily a tradeoff between accountability and performance. What is needed is to overcome the widespread negative view of accountability. This applies to both those in charge of running budget accountability institutions and budget holders. The objective of financial control should not only be to prevent irregularities in the use of public resources but also to motivate desired spending behavior. And vice versa, performance management control may be useful to find out and correct irregularities.

A positive perception of accountability might encourage desired budget decisions rather than just prevent undesired ones. In other words, the two faces of the budgetary accountability coin should be taken into account. On the one hand, there is the constraining aspect of checking poor spending performance or the misuse of power (accountability institutions reacting negatively to correct unacceptable budget nondiscipline). On the other hand, there is the guiding approach that requires the provision of a proactive and continuous feedback by setting values and norms from which policy and standards are derived.

Budget reforms since the 1980s prescribe budget targets and performance standards. However, solving the deficiencies of current accountability institutions is not just a question of finding ideal criteria (performance measures) for success. The effectiveness of accountability systems has been diluted to mere answerability, making it only necessary to justify and explain what has been done and to respond to questions raised by Parliament (Metcalfe and Richards,1990).

One of the difficulties lies in recognizing and capturing the multiple and conflicting pressures coming from different groups (managers, professionals, clients, peers, constituencies, etc.) claiming a need for modifications to spending targets. Ideally, priorities need to be established according to the relevance of such groups—as sources of legitimacy—to construct a framework of performance reference that synthesizes all relevant criteria of success. Appropriate accountability regimes should be taken into account and be coherent with the existing sources of influence.

Accountability and budget performance assessment in the public sector should also be oriented towards adapting spending values and beliefs rather than just applying rational criteria (such as the Three Es) and enforcing compliance. Negative accountability should be compensated with positively oriented assessments and organizational-program learning. Inspection and rigid control on undesired spending do not guarantee improvement in spending performance. On the contrary, at a certain point accountability can actually begin to encourage dysfunctional behavior ("creative" accounting, biased or fictitious budgeting, concealing information, nonproductive internal competition, etc.). In contrast, positive accountability facilitates the internalization of sound performance values and provides guidance for sound spending behavior.

In short, another role of the evaluation for strategic budgeting should be to facilitate a balanced functioning of the two faces of spending accountability systems. This means avoiding monopolising accountability efforts on inspection and negative performance in which the only concern of the central budget unit is to keep the control and stability of the budget system. The traditional accountability system only functions when reacting to nondisciplined budget behavior. A new accountability approach that is more proactive and continuous needs to be developed if capacity to change is considered a priority. The central budget unit and financial management units in spending departments should encourage a more strategic budgeting by explicitly or tacitly rewarding adaptive behavior, that is, taking risks and experimenting. In a context of instability, a positive perception of accountability as guidance rather than inspection is more appropriate since an overemphasis on inspection of nondesired budget behavior may mean blockage and incapacity to adapt. In this respect, a continuous guiding role played by the central budget offices facilitates adaptation (Mayne and Zapico, 1997).

## Conclusioins

For some years now, in most OECD countries, it has been claimed that budgeting decisions should be supported by performance information and that results management was needed to promote a change in the culture of government. Despite some progress in performance measurement and assessment, budgeters and managers have rather focused on technical aspects of designing measurement indicators. Depending on the kind of services and programs, indicators have been valued or simply considered a bureaucratic response to the demand of evaluative knowledge. Single evaluation studies have also been considered at times useful to clarify issues, but more often a formal response to an obligatory requirement.

The need for change and innovation in performance measurement and evaluation is particularly intense if we take into account the increasing tendency towards a decentralized agency model and the existence of a complex public policy environment. In a decentralized system, the traditional type of budgeting control and "negative" accountability needs to be put into doubt. Decentralization calls for a more flexible type of spending control based on the understanding of problems and contextual factors. This is even more the case in those instances of public service that operate in an unstructured context where there is uncertainty, instability, diversity, and interdependence.

In this chapter, strategic leadership from BO has been defined as contributing to develop the kinds of evaluative knowledge that are most relevant to budgeters, managers, and stakeholders. A pragmatic decision rule for BO can be whether evaluation should be based on the traditional Three Es or on the ideas behind Metcalf's Three Ds. The basic distinction is that the more traditional Three Es approach assumes that predefined and stable objectives are available that presuppose a well-known cause-effect relationship between organization activities and outcomes. However, the capacity of managers to be Economic, Efficient, and Effective is insufficient when goals are changing or when outcomes cannot be readily anticipated.

In a more complex environment where public managers work in a context of change and uncertainty, the Three Ds approach is better equipped to capture the innovating capacity of public managers. That is the capacity to carry out the Diagnosis of new problems and the Design of new solutions, and to Develop their implementation.

When turning to evaluation theories and approaches in a context of uncertainty, we conclude that there is not one single formula or model but a variety of avenues and sources of information. The key issue is that the information is available and that it is conducive to learning since learning through evaluation is building social capital among budgeters, managers, and stakeholders. Learning may require practical information, limited in scope, focused on clearly defined aspects of a problem, rapidly available, and at a low cost. It may also be the compensation for efforts to disentangle the underlying—"theoretical"—assumptions on which a program is based. Learning can also come as the sudden understanding of processes through information produced by stakeholders as a response to their questions and concerns.

But the production of information is not enough. For actors to play a role or act in a knowledgeable manner, they need to change their interaction patterns. The BO has a role to develop in the creation of structures, rules, and incentives that may facilitate a better balance between competition for resources and cooperation and mutual understanding. In particular the change in the nature of the relations among budgeters, managers, evaluators, and other stakeholders would be encouraged by a change in the accountability systems, from the traditional inspection role that reacts to non-disciplined budget behavior, to a proactive role that explicitly encourages and supports strategic spending behavior.

Learning and social trust benefit from exchange and participation. It is crucial to realize that other actors can see things in different ways. Very often, what seems non-rational or inadmissible at a first glance will later find its place and show its potential.

## References

Birckmayer, Johanna D., and Carol H. Weiss (2000). "Theory-Based Evaluation in Practice: What Do We Learn?" *Evaluation Review,* Vol. 24 (4): 407–431.

Bourdieu, P. (1986). "The Forms of Capital" in J. E. Richardson, (ed.) *A Handbook of Theory and Research for the Sociology of Education*, New York: Greenwood.

Carter, N. (1989). "Performance Indicators: Backseat Driving or Hands off Control?" *Policy and Politics.* XVII(2): 131–138.

Carter, N. 1991. " Learning to Measure Performance: The Use of Indicators in Organizations," *Public Administration* 69.

Chen, H. (1990) *Theory-Driven Evaluation* Newbury Park, CA: Sage.

Coleman, J. (1988) "Social Capital in the Creation of Human Capital" *American Journal of Sociology*, Vol. 94. Supplement 95–120.

European Group of Public Administration (1996). "Strategic Spending Management A new role for the Budget Centre," Budapest meeting 1996.
Feinstein, O., and Puetz, D. (2000). "Synthesis and Overview" in O. Feinstein and R. Picciotto "Evaluation and Poverty Reduction," The World Bank, Washington DC.
Gregory, Amanda (2000). "Problematizing Participation," *Evaluation*, Vol 6 (2): 179-199
Gunther, R. 1980. *Public Policy in a No-Party State Spanish Planning and Budgeting in the Twilight of the Francoist Era*, p. 51. Berkeley, CA: University of California Press.
Hugues, M. and T. Traynor (2000) "Reconciling Process and Outcomes in Evaluating Community Initiatives" in *Evaluation*, Vol 6 (1): 37-49.
Jackson, E. (2000) "The Front-End Costs and Downstream Benefits of Participatory Evaluation", in O. Feinstein and R. Picciotto "Evaluation and Poverty Reduction," The World Bank, Washington DC.
Leeuw, F. L., R. C. Rist, et al. (1994). *Can Governments Learn? Comparative Perspectives on Evaluation & Organizational Learning*. New Brunswick, N. J.: Transaction Publishers.
Mayne, J. and Zapico E. (1997), *Performance Monitoring in the Public Sector*, London: Transaction Publishers.
Metcalfe, L. and S. Richards (1990). *Improving Public Management*. 2nd edition. London: Sage, pags. 210, 96, 40, 44.
Metcalfe, L. (1991). "Public Management: From Imitation to Innovation." Paper presented at the Annual Conference of the International Association of Schools and Institutes of Administration (IASIA), Kota Kinabalu, Sabah, Malaysia, 28 July 2 August. 910.
Metcalfe, L. (1993) "Public Management: From Imititation to Innovation" in J. Kooiman *Modern Governance*. Londres: Sage Publications.
OECD. (1996). Performance Auditing and the Modernization of Government, PUMA, Paris.
OECD. (2001). "The Well-Being of Nations: The role of Human and Social Capital," Paris.
Office of Management and Budget (1995). *Making Government Work: Budget of the United States Government, Fiscal Year 1996*. Washington DC.
Patton, M.Q. (1986) *Utilization-Focussed Evaluation*, London, Sage.
Putnam, R. (2000) *Bowling Alone: The Collapse and revival of American Community*. Simon Schuster, New York.
Schick, A. (1990) Budget for Results: Recent Developments in Five Industrialized Countries." *Public Administration Review*. Vol. 50, No. 1 January-February.
Stake, R.E. (1975). "An Interview with Robert Stake on Responsive Evaluation." in R.E. Stake (Ed.), *Evaluating the Arts in Education: A Responsive Approach* (p. 33-38). Columbus, OH: Merrill.
Thoenig, Jean-Claude, (2000) "Evaluation as Usable Knowledge for Public Management Reforms," *Evaluation*, Vol. 6 (2) 217-229.

Weiss, Carol, H. (1995) "Nothing as Practical as Good Theory: Exploring Theory-Based Evaluation for Comprehensive Community Initiatives for Children and Families" in J. P. Connell, A.C. Kubich, L. Schorr, and C. Weiss, *New Approaches to Evaluating Community Initiatives: concepts, methods and contexts*. Washington, DC: Aspen Institute.

# Part 5

# Multi-Study Evaluation and the Learning Organization

# 13

# Evaluation, Knowledge Management, and Learning: Caught between Order and Disorder

*Kim Forss and Claus C. Rebien*

### Introduction

There are many who practice the art of evaluation, and there is no doubt that ours is a growing profession. But since the beginning, evaluation research has had problems with learning and with how the products of our profession come to be used. These two concepts—learning and use—form the "soft core" of evaluation research. As evaluators we would all like to see evaluations put to use, and would hope that many learn from our efforts. But alas, the evidence suggests that learning and utility are not outstanding attributes of evaluation. It is an area where much is said, but where much still remains to be done. This chapter focuses on the connection between organizational learning and evaluation; that is, we are interested in how evaluations are used within systems of knowledge management.

Why are people interested in learning and knowledge management? The prevailing perspective in the theory of organizational learning is to view learning as an intentional process directed at improving effectiveness. The prominence of this instrumental perspective in the prestigious management literature (Porter, 1980; Sammon, Kurland, and Spitalnic, 1984) undoubtedly contributes to its pervasiveness. Some authors (Argyris and Schön, 1978; Fiol and Lyles, 1985) have gone so far as to imply that organizational effectiveness must be enhanced in order to claim that organizational learning has occurred.

## The Purpose of this Chapter

We have over the years found that the tradition of evaluation research is deeply embedded in the experiences and expectations of bureaucratic organizations. The focus is on governments and their agencies, and their collaboration in multilateral agencies (Leeuw, Rist, and Sonnichsen, 1994; Forss, Cracknell, and Stromquist, 1998). Organization theory, on the other hand, often fetches its inspiration and its normative ideals from self-organizing systems, such as jazz ensembles, entrepreneurial firms, high-tech companies, and the like (Schon, 1983; Hedberg, 1981; Weick, 1977; Åman, 2003). There is much in the theory of organizational learning that appears quite revolutionary compared to the standard rhetoric of learning from evaluation. We would like to introduce and test some of these ideas. In particular, we take our starting point in the contradiction between the long-term need for learning and the short-term need for efficiency. What are the lessons in terms of evaluation design, and could the complexity of evaluation be extended by design elements that combine the planned approach in evaluation with a measure of uncertainty that fosters learning?

## Methods

We chose a case study approach to the subject. Each case is a narrative of an evaluation process in which one of us took part. Following a brief account of the evaluation process, we explore the roles played by humor, improvisation, and small wins. It should not come as a surprise that these are not outstanding features of the cases. However, we turn back to the stories, and analyze them to see whether the design could have been done differently, so as to increase opportunities for learning. This leads to an introduction of more complex design features, but also to a directly normative hypothesis concerning how learning could have been increased in these particular cases.

## Knowledge Structures

So as to avoid confusion at a later stage, we have to set out what we mean by learning. For us, learning can be defined as changes in knowledge structures.[1] The definition immediately raises two questions: for the practically minded, "How do we define change?" and for the more theoretically minded, "What are knowledge structures?" Starting with the latter, knowledge structures are complex patterns that arise as the human brain receives stimulus from life experiences. These stimuli are received, interpreted, processed, and stored. So knowledge structures are at the root of learning; they are the result of learning and at the same time they shape learning.

But do organizations possess knowledge structures? An underlying assumption in most of the literature on organizational learning is that it is individuals who learn. Organizations can facilitate or obstruct learning, but it is individuals who actually do the learning—whose knowledge structures change. But there are also those who argue that it is possible to assess organizational knowledge structures (Björkegren, 1989; Forss, Cracknell, and Samset, 1994), or who focus on organizational units as the basis of learning (Senge, 1990).

Let us return to the practical question of change. If learning is defined as change in knowledge structures, it becomes obvious that this could be for better and for worse. Any change in knowledge structures would hence be seen as learning, which means that de-learning, forgetting "learning mistakes," is as much learning as aspects of change that have more positive connotations. Hence, learning as such does not automatically enhance the efficiency of the organization. Stacey (1996) repeatedly shows how learning can improve the long-run performance of an organization by increasing its intelligence, creativity, and innovativeness—but it does so through processes that often seem costly and unnecessary in the short run. An intelligent organization cannot be built while maintaining efficiency (McMaster, 1996). At least in the short run, resources spent on learning add to the cost side in a cost-efficiency calculation.

## Components of Knowledge Management

Let us assume that organizations can possess knowledge structures, and that these change. What kind of change would be desirable? Some systems properties come to mind. Good knowledge structures would presumably tend to be broad; that is, to cover a wide variety of stimulus. They would be elaborate; that is, they would hold more complexity and would be able to organize and make sense of contradictory stimulus. Furthermore, it is likely that organizational learning would be supported by the emergence of dominant knowledge structures.[2] As for the organization of the processes that create learning, Huber (1991) proposed a distinction that links the elements of knowledge management:

1. Knowledge acquisition, for example, through recruitment, takeover of new companies, research, training, and downright purchase of information.
2. Knowledge distribution, for example, by systems design, personnel management, seminars and training, databases.
3. Knowledge interpretation, the processes through which information is given meaning.
4. Organizational memory, storing information so that it can be retrieved and put to use—if not before, then at the exact point in time when it is needed.

These aspects of knowledge management all suggest slightly different roles for evaluation. However, before we proceed to the role of evaluation in knowledge management, we would like to explore the issue of organizational learning a bit further. Learning cannot be seen as an isolated event following, for example, reading an evaluation report. In order to be a meaningful concept in the management sciences, it has to be seen as something expressed in structures, processes, as well as in organizational culture. This is also widely recognized in management literature (Forss, Cracknell and Stromquist, 1998).

## A Contradiction in Terms

Weick and Westley (1996) note that organizational learning is actually an oxymoron.[3] Organization and learning, as they say, are essentially antithetical processes. To learn is to disorganize and increase variety. To organize is to forget and decrease variety. In the rush to embrace learning, evaluation research has often overlooked this tension. The reluctance to grapple with the antithesis has led to derivative ideas and unrealized potential.

The relationship between learning and organization has sometimes been treated as a choice of structure. It has been suggested that certain forms, such as self-designing organizations and adhocracies, are particularly good at adapting to changing environments. In terms of creativity and original thinking, these seem to be recommended forms (Morgan, 1986). Other structures, such as bureaucracies, are dedicated to efficiencies and associated with mechanical division of labor, rigid chains of command, clear distinctions, and technical rationality. These are qualities to repress or forget confusing and contradictory knowledge. In the practice of evaluation, we meet bureaucracies more often than we meet self-designing systems, and hence there could be a bias in how we connect evaluation to organizational learning.

The dichotomy suggests that self-designing organizations learn while bureaucracies organize. However, on closer examination the picture seems more complex. March (1991) suggests that each form learns, but the learning is of a different order. Self-designing organizations have a tendency to explore, bureaucracies to exploit. Both are forms of learning, and resilient organizations do a little bit of both. We will now illustrate the discussion with the help of two case studies: one of a health management project and the other in the field of research cooperation.

## The First Case Study: Healthy City

*Context and Evaluation Design*

The World Health Organization (WHO) led network of healthy cities all over the world is designed to tackle health problems in big cities in a cross-disciplinary and holistic way. Rather than treating symptoms of poor health conditions, the healthy city project is designed to strengthen preventive measures and to work actively with health promotion. There is widespread evidence that preventive care and health promotion reduce a number of health problems, for instance, as they relate to malnutrition of infants, children care in general, hygiene, smoking, and alcohol consumption. But the scope of healthy city projects is broader than that. Quality of life aspects are targeted for prevention of loneliness and stress depressions. Promotion of better quality of life is hence seen as integral with good health, and as part of the prevention of physical diseases.

This case concerns an evaluation of the healthy city project in one of the capitals of northern Europe. The city has had a healthy city project during the last fifteen years. The scope of the evaluation was to demonstrate to politicians and other stakeholders that the healthy city concept is "healthy" and effective. The evaluation was at the same time charged with investigating the delivery mechanisms for the various activities under the project, and investigate the soundness of the way resources were prioritized. The evaluation was designed including a series of workshops with staff of the healthy city project and with self-evaluation elements where the evaluator would tutor staff in conducting self-evaluations of project activities. Hence, there was a deliberate attempt to introduce participatory elements. The design also included evaluator-led case studies of specific activities, statistical analysis of large health statistics, interviews with all staff, and interviews and focus-group interviews with staff from organizations that cooperated with the healthy city project.

*From Information to Knowledge Management*

Can the evaluation be understood as a process of knowledge management? First, was there any *acquisition of new information*? As is the case of most evaluations, they rarely come up with entirely new information. They rather combine existing information in new ways, making stakeholders see new connections, new angles. The same was the case with the evaluation of the healthy city project. While for many years it had been an ambition to open fifteen healthy city offices across the city, the evaluation delivered the financial information in a new way, which made stakeholders realize that this would never be financially sustainable. The costs would simply be too high—and rather the current number of offices should be reduced from nine to four in order to create greater critical mass in each of the remaining offices.

New information was also generated in relation to target group coverage. Again, the information—statistical data—had been with the project for many years. But the analysis of the data within the framework of the evaluation revealed that the healthy city project in fact spent the most resources in the best of neighborhoods while spending no or very few resources in the poorest neighborhoods. This is obviously a problem given the fact that most lifestyle-generated health problems are linked to social status: drinking, smoking, eating habits, physical exercise, etc. The project spent fewest resources in the parts of the cities with the greatest problems. This was information surfacing during the evaluation.

A third example of new information generated is the management of the project. The project staff members were very enthusiastic and knowledgeable and worked relatively independently in each of the nine offices. This had been a good mode of operation during the initial years of the project. New ideas, activities, and ways of doing things constantly developed. After ten years it became increasingly difficult to manage the decentralized, independent approach. There was too little networking between the offices, knowledge sharing was poor, and the project was running literally hundreds of activities with little coordination and learning between them—and a lack of strategic direction. This information was readily available when the evaluation started—and management had already begun to tackle the problem by creating common action plans, inter-office networking, etc. But centralizing and trying to coordinate after ten years of independence is not easy, and often meets with resistance. The evaluation was able to put this information into a framework. It showed that the mode of operation was actually detrimental to the whole purpose of the project since it meant that the project—because resources were not pooled and coordinated, and learning and experience not shared—had less impact with less people than would a more coordinated effort.

To what extent was this *information distributed* during the evaluation process? A workshop was held at the beginning with all project staff where evaluation questions and indicators were discussed and sharpened. Later in the process, a mid-term workshop and a final workshop were held with staff. Here preliminary and final results, respectively, were presented and discussed. In addition, meetings were held in each of the nine offices where staff were instructed in self-evaluating techniques—and where results from the self-evaluations were later analyzed and discussed with them. Steering group meetings with project management were held three times during the process, which also accommodated distribution of information. And finally, a presentation was made to the politicians in the city council after the mid-term workshop. The politicians had called for the evaluation—and its use would depend on their ownership of the information in it.

Finally, to what extent was the *information used and hence knowledge created*? Knowledge was created to a large extent. Not that everybody agreed to the interpretation of information, its new packaging, and the frame of reference into which it was placed. But the new knowledge was there, and most staff, management, and politicians actually turned the information into knowledge by re-designing the healthy city project: pooling of resources in fewer offices, targeting the poorer neighborhoods, coordinating activities, and reducing their number to concentrate resources on fewer well-defined activities.

## Evaluation, Knowledge Management, and Learning 241

*What Could Have Been Done Differently?*

What were some of the reasons behind this evaluation leading to transformation of information into knowledge, achieving actual learning? In this case, there were at least three reasons related to chaos, humor, and improvisation, respectively.

One of the first reasons was a certain element and level of *chaos*. The city council had for a few years made attempts to reform the whole preventive care activities of the city administration. With a newly elected city council and with ever-declining funds, the political climate for making changes was there. The administration management and staff thus at the outset were aware that this would be a last call. Their own active participation and willingness to change would be a prerequisite for achieving influence on the changes that politicians would make in any case. This "threat" thus acted both as a stick (politicians will make changes in any case) and a carrot (let us try to influence the changes) for participation. The chaos and insecurity provided a fertile ground for the learning mechanisms of the evaluation, and for the translation of information—which, in many cases, had been available for many years—into new knowledge. During the evaluation process, the whole health administration—and not only the sections dealing with prevention—started a major reorganization, which further added to the chaos—and the willingness to learn.

In the overall climate of chaos, *humor* could be used as a mechanism for "seeing things in a different light." Most staff members had been working with health issues for ten, fifteen, or twenty years. They were—and are—very dedicated and skilled. But they also develop interpretations of reality that they need in their daily practice in order to survive. Interpretations that are necessary when day after day you work against the tide to benefit people that are at the bottom of the social pyramid: alcoholics, drug addicts, lonely people, unemployed, elderly left with no or little care, etc. Sometimes it may seem hopeless, and you develop your own interpretations: any cut, any change will be to the detriment of these people that you try to help. After a while, your interpretation becomes a barrier to change!

The use of anecdotes, self-irony, and humor on the part of the evaluators made staff relax and, in glimpses, see a way out of their interpretations, see ways that would allow for changes while at the same time allowing them to help the disadvantaged. Ways that would often—through prioritizing resources—even allow them to do more than before.

Finally, *improvisation* was part of the reason why knowledge generation and learning took place. At one stage during the process, the winds from the city council seemed to indicate that politicians were prepared to shut down the healthy city project entirely. The pressure from the political level had created the climate of chaos that allowed for learning. Should staff and management come to believe that closure would be the most likely outcome of the evaluation, it would mean an end to the climate of knowledge generation and learning. If you are about to be shut down you are not exactly inspired to think creatively. At the same time, the evaluation was showing evidence that although resources in many ways were managed and prioritized in a less than optimal manner the project was, in fact, showing good results. With better management and prioritizing, there was every reason to believe that the project would benefit the population of the city for many years to come. Improvisation and creativity were necessary. The evaluator suggested to the health administration managing the evaluation that a presentation be made before the city council of intermediate evaluation results. The idea was that presented with the facts concerning the many positive results and the dialogue with politicians, they would work more constructively with the future of the healthy city project—both during the evaluation process and after. It was agreed that the unorthodox presentation before the city council should be made. The improvisation had the desired effect. It put the healthy city project back on the agenda as something a number of councilors were dissatisfied with—but which at least was on the agenda for discussion on how best to make use of the funds.

## The Second Case Study: Research Cooperation

*Context and Evaluation Design*

For more than twenty years, Sweden has been engaged in a program of research cooperation with Vietnam. A number of Swedish universities have taken on Ph.D. students from Vietnamese universities, and Swedish professors have conducted courses in Vietnam. Funds from the bilateral aid program have helped strengthen university libraries, build and supply laboratories, establish computer networks and Internet access. Several joint research projects have been concluded in diverse areas such as forestry, tropical agricultural systems, marine biology, and health systems.

The program consists of some ten to fifteen research projects. Some of these have been ongoing for more than ten years; others have started recently. Each program cycle lasts for four years, and at the end of a cycle there is usually some form of review. The most recent program came to an end in 2002, and therefore Sida (the Swedish bilateral aid agency) commissioned an external evaluation of the program. The purpose of the evaluation was to assess results and analyze how the program could be made more focused and better coordinated.

The evaluation was designed to be participatory, meaning that the Vietnamese researchers, as well as the Ministry of Science and Technology in Vietnam, would be closely involved—in particular to:

- Define the criteria of successful projects,
- Engage in a dialogue on methods of evaluation research,

- Supply basic data for the evaluation,
- Contribute to the analysis of data, and
- Develop the recommendations for the future program.

An evaluator would coordinate the process, but in so doing would work closely with Sida and with the Vietnamese authorities. The process was divided into three phases:

1. All the Vietnamese researchers were invited to a three-day workshop in Hanoi, where the subject of the evaluation was introduced, and where the criteria for success were set, together with the methods of research.
2. Subsequently, the Vietnamese universities gathered the data, for example, on research publications, training, impact of research findings, and so on, and towards the end of this phase, the evaluator visited all the universities and reviewed the data. In the meantime, he had also interviewed the Swedish universities that took part in the program.
3. A draft evaluation report was written and circulated to all stakeholders, then a final three-day workshop was convened in Hanoi. Again all the universities took part, as well as the Ministry and Sida. During the meeting, recommendations were elaborated, and some of the findings were discussed in depth by all the universities.

A final evaluation report was written and presented to Sida and to the Vietnamese authorities. It was expected to be used in negotiations for the next four-year program, which was to start in 2003. The evaluation did start as planned in September 2002, when the first workshop in Hanoi took place. The Vietnamese universities gathered data in October and November, and the evaluator visited them in early December. The draft report was presented in early January, and the final workshop took place in mid-January. The whole process was completed by February.

One of the reasons to engage the Vietnamese counterparts so heavily in the process was their profession. They are, indeed, researchers, and hence it would be easy to get them engaged in data collection, methodological discussions, as well as in the analysis. Did it work out that way? To some extent yes, but perhaps not as generally and wholeheartedly as the evaluator had expected. Yet another reason to suggest a participatory approach was that the Vietnamese Ministry of Science and Technology had strong views on the program, and Sida thought it would be an advantage if the Ministry shared the same understanding of the basic realities of which were good projects and which were bad. It was believed that participation in the evaluation would help generate such a shared understanding.

It was also quite obvious from the outset that some projects would have to be phased out. Even if the program as a whole could expand, there would have to be some form of redesign that could make management less cumbersome, and that meant fewer projects. The evaluator, as well as Sida, wanted to make sure that the focus of a new program built on the most outstanding achievements in the present program, and that the decisions on new priorities were understood by all—and were seen as legitimate. Did it work out that way? Partly, as those programs that were to continue clearly saw the logic of that, but those who were phased out did not find the process any more acceptable for having seen the axe falling—and were manipulated to have a hold on the handle.

*From Information to Knowledge Management*

How can the evaluation be understood as a process of knowledge management? First of all, was there any *acquisition of new information*? As for Sida, it is not likely that the evaluation brought up any information that the organization did not possess before. Of course, there were details, in terms of how many research papers were produced on the different projects, the nature and impact of capacity building, the application of research and its impact. But the general thrust of the findings, the recommendations, the identification of best performing projects, held few surprises. The same applied to the Vietnamese authorities. The universities, on the other hand, did learn. Those who took part got an introduction to evaluation methodology, they learned to know each other, and they came to understand their own projects as part of a whole program.

Second, to what extent was *information distributed* in the process? Apart from the two workshops, at the beginning and at the end of the evaluation, the only other venue for knowledge distribution was the personal interactions between the evaluator and those he interviewed when visiting the universities. The draft report (and later the final) was spread to the universities, but that is part of the workshop process.

Third, to what extent was *information used and hence knowledge created*? The first step in knowledge interpretation was when the universities provided information to the evaluator, and he tried to make sense out of that. The second was when his efforts were fed back to the universities, and they tried to make sense of that, Finally, in the last workshop, everybody tried to make sense of the whole process.

There is, indeed, a report, but the question is whether that means there is a memory. Evaluation reports in Sida tend to be forgotten relatively quickly,[4] and the fact that a publication has a number in a series is no guarantee that anybody will find it, let alone use it. The Vietnamese organizations do not have any systems to store and retrieve evaluation reports that were commissioned in development cooperation. Any memories of this exercise, whether fond or sad, rest with individuals and would be of a private nature.

## Evaluation, Knowledge Management, and Learning 245

*What Could Have Been Done Differently?*

So, in hindsight, what could have been done to better strengthen organizational learning? The evaluation was of a short duration and it was rather focused in terms of reference. But we will not suggest that it had to be made longer and more comprehensive. We assume that there are things to do within the budget frame that did exist. Let us see whether the design features proposed by Weick and Westley figured at all in the process.

Humor? No, not to any great extent. The workshops were rather somber activities. Vietnam is a hierarchical society, and there is not much room for laughter when a ministry calls its subordinated authorities to an evaluation meeting. Nor does the ministry treat its relation to a major bilateral donor as a joke. The report does not make for amusing reading; there are no elements of surprise, amusing stories, or rhetorical devices to liven up the text. Going through the report, and rethinking the workshops, it seems clear that these could make better use of humor, but there are inherent limitations—not least because of the strong control element in the task.

Improvisation? Yes, to some extent. Within the overall structure of the process, the main improvisations were (1) to define success criteria in plenum, with all stakeholders, and (2) to come up with research methods and a plan to gather data. This would have been impossible with another audience, but with a research community it was feasible. But once the criteria were set, and methods decided, there were no changes. It was implemented as planned, with no changes along the way.

Small wins? Yes, one could argue that the slow build-up of common knowledge, and the identification of patterns of success and failure on projects, represented small wins. Perhaps one could have arrived at more novel findings, but what the evaluation did come up with was shared knowledge. Though it was not new for some of the actors, it was for others. In retrospect, the evaluation must be seen as a rather orderly process. There was little chaos in it, and also few great surprises. It was a fairly conventional, although reasonably successful, evaluation. It is an open question whether it could have brought higher gains in learning. If the evaluation were to accomplish more, it would have to be more fun (not hard to imagine), somewhat more open as a process (quite possible, but then probably requiring more resources). It did build on small wins, so there is not much to add in respect of that. To add humor and to plan less would mean to invite a bit of disorder, if not necessarily chaos.

*Analyzing the Cases: From Dilemma to Complexity*

To move beyond the oxymoron, the practice of designing learning and systems of knowledge management will have to be both about establishing routines and accepting disruptive, non-routine behavior. Too much of either ultimately destroys the organization. This suggests that the problem of learning should be viewed not as a choice between order and disorder, but rather as an optimal juxtaposition of the two. The optimal learning point would be when both conditions exist simultaneously. Weick and Westley (1997) suggest that the optimal juxtaposition between order and disorder is created not through alternation, but through the intimate and continuing connection between the two.

This would be the moment when the sciences of complexity need to be introduced. Complex systems develop on the border between chaos and order. There are, of course, many aspects of complex systems, but one of the most essential is non-linearity, that is, the relations between the elements in the system are non-linear (Mainzer, 1994). The idea of evaluation as a more or less good, accurate, and well-written study, which is read, digested, and acted upon, is rather simple. It is definitely a linear concept. But evaluation seen as an emerging process, where different forces act upon stakeholders that all have more or less clearly understood, contradictory, overlapping, and complementary objectives, is definitely a non-linear concept. It shows evaluation as part of a stream of information, to be understood and managed through complex structures and processes, and to be developed into organizational knowledge. The case studies clearly outline such processes.

First, the evaluation reports as such play rather marginal roles. The important learning events occur in preparatory meetings, in procedures of data collection, through joint analysis of achievements, and in the search for data from other sources, benchmarking, and comparative analysis, etc. We have treated the process use of evaluation elsewhere (Forss and Rebien, 2002), so this is familiar ground. The point is that the extended evaluation process itself can be viewed as a stream of information, which is gradually—through many processes—converted into knowledge.

Second, the evaluation processes themselves are part of larger organizational processes. In terms of knowledge management, the information gathered through the particular evaluation efforts that we focused on, was supplemented by other information of substantive (health and research, respectively), social, political, and economic nature. The outcome of the evaluations and how they were used could only be understood as part of larger organizational processes, where information was managed by multiple stakeholders inside and outside of the organization.

The actual expression of complexity may occur in situations that go beyond the ordinary, for example, in moments of humor, improvisation, and small wins, or even in combinations of these. And this may promote learning among individuals in an organization. The case studies would seem to support this. The Vietnam evaluation was fairly conventional—and produced little new knowledge and almost no learning. The healthy city evaluation was chaotic and it was necessary to improvise several times during the evaluation process. But this did generate some new knowledge, and it definitely created learning.

## Conclusion

It has been said about the so-called *information age* that we have too much information—but not enough knowledge, that is, knowledge meaning information transformed into learning, action, and change. Evaluations are part of the information industry. But evaluations do not necessarily produce knowledge. In fact, it is a criticism raised against our industry that the studies and the information we produce often do not lead to significant change and learning.

In this chapter, we have explored the balance between knowledge management systems, evaluation systems, organizational change, and learning. A dilemma has been identified between rationally planned evaluations and knowledge management systems on the one side—and change processes and learning on the other. The basic question raised was: Can learning and change be facilitated through rationally planned, logical evaluation processes that feed into systematic knowledge management systems?

In answering the rhetorical question with a "no, not to any great extent," we have instead asked how evaluations and knowledge management systems could be designed in order to optimize the potentials for learning and change.

The answer to the latter question is—based on literature research and case studies—that evaluations and knowledge management systems need to strike a careful balance between order and disorder in order to facilitate learning and change. Too much order, systems, logic, and too many rules and regulations promote rigidity. Too much disorder causes confusion and action paralysis. Neither the one nor the other is facilitative to learning and change. The dilemma has to be addressed through a "both-and" approach.

There are a number of strategies to choose to promote learning and change from evaluations, both during planning, and implementation, and when reporting back information from the evaluation.

1. During planning, evaluators and evaluation commissioners must acknowledge the nature of learning and change, that is, its incremental and disorderly patterns, and the need to balance order and disorder. The evaluation process must allow time to pass, must organize arenas for confrontation and reflection, and must leave room for improvisation.
2. During the evaluation process, evaluators and evaluation commissioners should acknowledge the importance of process use and facilitate and promote its strengthening. There are four distinct forms of process use: improving ongoing activities/interventions; strengthening the organizational culture; form and enhance professional and organizational networks; and learning how to learn. Through an explicit focus on one or more forms of process use from the outset, learning and change will be facilitated. Evaluation processes can be examples of how order and disorder are balanced,

how rationally planned processes are inevitably interrupted by unforeseen circumstances, and how the balance between order and disorder leads to constant adaptation.
3. In the feedback phase, it must be acknowledged that evaluations are but one "stream of knowledge" entering the knowledge management system of any organization. In total, the system has to handle several streams, making a virtual river of knowledge. To ensure feedback from evaluations, organizations will have to link evaluation knowledge to other knowledge streams in new ways. Single evaluation reports, with conclusions and recommendations, have to be coupled with information generated from the budgeting and accounting systems, customer surveys, user surveys, and the management information systems in general. Knowledge has to be blended across organizational, sector, and professional boundaries in order to see new linkages and opportunities. The "garbage can" model offers one metaphor for how decisions are taken in large organizations.

Evaluators and evaluation commissioners need to acknowledge this fact when planning evaluations. They need to be innovative in pointing to new ways of analyzng and using the plethora of knowledge—and in the process they should pay attention to the use of, for example, improvisation and humor in facilitating learning and change. The point is to manage the information processes in a way that ensures a certain measure of disorder. This, in turn, takes courage and self-confidence, confidence that reducing their complete control of the exercise—introducing disorder and improvisation—leads to better results. This is a subject for further investigation. For now it suffices to compare the challenge to the one faced by a manager in an organization who can increase staff productivity and innovations by delegating authority and relaxing the formal controls on staff that are so characteristic of traditional hierarchical bureaucracies. Only a balance between order and disorder will facilitate the transformation of information into knowledge, that is, learning, action, and change.

## Notes

1. It would take us too long to cover the literature on learning. Our definition stems from the work of Bateson, 1972; Piaget, 1976; Perris, 1986.
2. This is a very condensed summary of an ongoing debate in management studies, social psychology, and organization theory, and fuller discussion can be found in Beer, 1990; Douglas, 1986; Morgan, 1986; Sandelands and Stablein, 1987.
3. A contradiction in terms, such as flexible blueprint, a victorious defeat, or military intelligence.
4. For a discussion of evaluation and learning in Swedish development cooperation, see, for example, Forss, 1985; Riksrevisionsverket, 1989; Carlsson et al., 1999)

## References

Åman, P. (2003). "Revolution by Evolution: Transforming International Management in the Established MNC." Ph.D. diss., Stockholm: Institute of International Business.

Argyris, C., and D. Schon. (1978). *Organisational Learning.* San Francisco: Jossey Bass.
Bateson, G. (1972). *Steps to an Ecology of Mind.* New York: Ballantine Books.
Beer, S. (1990). *The Critical Path to Corporate Renewal.* Boston: Harvard Business School Press.
Björkegren, D. (1989). *Hur organisationer lär.* Lund: Studentlitteratur.
Carlsson, J., M. Eriksson-Baaz, A-M Fallenius, and E. Lövgren. (1999). *Are Evaluations Useful? Cases from Swedish Development Cooperation.* Stockholm: Sida.
Douglas, M. (1986). *How Institutions Think.* London: Routledge and Kegan Paul.
Fiol, C. M., and M. A. Lyles. "Organisational Learning." *Academy of Management Review* 10 (1985): 803–813.
Forss, K. (1985). "Planning and Evaluation in Aid Organisations." Ph.D. diss. Stockholm: EFI/IIB.
Forss, K., B. Cracknell, and K. Samset. "Can Evaluation Help an Organisation to Learn?" *Evaluation Review* 18(5) (1994).
Forss, K., B. Cracknell, and N. Stromquist. (1998). Towards Better Development Cooperation: Organisational Learning, External Pressure and Complex Networks. A report commissioned by the Ministry for Foreign Affairs, Stockholm.
Forss, K., and C. Rebien. "Process Use of Evaluations." *Evaluation* 8(1) (2002): 29–45.
Hedberg, B. (1981). "How Organisations Learn and Un-learn." In P. C. Nyström and W. H. Starbuck, eds., *Handbook of Organisational Design*, vol 1. New York: Oxford University Press.
Huber, G. P. "Organisational Learning: The Contributing Processes and the Literatures." *Organisation Science* 2(1) (1991).
Leeuw, F. L., R. C. Rist, and R. C. Sonnichsen. (1994). *Can Governments Learn? Comparative Perspectives on Evaluation and Organisational Learning.* New Brunswick, NJ, and London: Transaction Publishers.
Mainzer, K. (1994) *Thinking in Complexity: The Complex Dynamics of Matter, Mind and Mankind.* Berlin: Springer Verlag.
March, J. G. "Exploration and Exploitation in Organisational Learning." *Organisation Science* 2(1) (1991).
McMaster, M. D. (1996). *The Intelligence Advantage. Organising for Complexity.* Boston: Butterworth-Heinemann.
Morgan, G. (1986). *Images of Organisation.* Beverly Hills: Sage.
Perris, C. (1986). *Kognitiv Teori i Praktik och Teori.* Lund: Natur och Kultur.
Piaget, J. (1976). *The Essential Piaget.* Ed. Howard Gruber and Jacques Voneche. New York: Basic Books.
Porter, M. E. (1980). *Competitive Strategy: Techniques for Analysing Industries and Competitors.* New York: Free Press.
Riksrevisionsverket. (1989). *Lär sig Sida?* Stockholm: Riksrevisionsverket.
Sandelands, L. E., and R. E. Stablein. "The Concept of Organisation Mind." *Research in the Sociology of Organisations* 5 (1987): 136-162.
Sammon, W. L., M. A. Kurland, and R. Spitalnic. "A Social Information Processing Approach to Job Attitudes and Task Design." *Administrative Sciences Quarterly* 23 (1984): 224–253.
Schon, D. (1983). *The Reflective Practitioner.* New York: Basic Books.
Senge, P. M. (1990). *The Fifth Discipline, The Art and Practice of the Learning Organisation.* New York: Doubleday.
Stacey, R. D. (1996). *Complexity and Creativity in Organisations.* San Franscisco: Berrett-Koehler.
Weick, K. "Organisations as Self-Designing Systems." *Organisational Dynamics* 6(2) (1977): 30–46.

Weick, K., and F. Westley. (1996). "Organisational Learning: Affirming an Oxymoron." In S. Clegg, C. Hardy, and W. Nord, eds., *Handbook of Organisation Studies*. London: Sage.

# 14

# Patterns of Evaluative Knowledge Creation and Utilization within the World Bank

*Mita Marra*

### Introduction

This chapter examines what and how evaluative knowledge is generated and used by managers and decision makers within an organizational setting. We aim here to fill a gap in the analysis of the use of evaluation within organizations by bringing the notion of organizational knowledge to the *forefront*. Organizations, in fact, continuously create knowledge by reconstructing existing perspectives, frameworks, or premises on a day-to-day basis (Nonaka, 1994). Evaluation is part of this organizational knowledge, which evaluators, program designers, and program managers share within and outside the organization. The challenge then is not only to detect the use of discrete pieces of evaluation studies, but rather to explore how and to what extent streams of evaluative knowledge reinforce organizational knowledge-creating processes over time. We aim to put forward a new viewpoint on evaluation use, shifting the attention from evaluation studies to streams of evaluative knowledge, which contain a judgment or help managers make a judgment.

We consider the specific instance of the World Bank, where managers attempt to realize development policy objectives. We begin with the analysis of core features of the World Bank evaluation studies—most notably, participatory, theory-driven, and ex-post cost-benefit analyses—and we integrate them with considerations on patterns of conversion of tacit into explicit evaluative knowledge. Tacit knowledge is the patrimony of formal and informal networks, normative values and beliefs, which organizations share in their everyday dealings (Nonaka, 1994). Explicit or codified knowledge draws on the cumulative, scientific discoveries, and theories about how society works. Within an organization, for instance, planners can design programs on an explicit theoretical basis, and evaluation can investigate whether their assumptions of a theory hold in practice (Weiss, 2000). Yet, the knowledge that people use in authoritative positions is largely tacit: many programs are the product of experience, intuition, and professional rules of thumb and evaluation can uncover the implicit assumptions underlying the programs (Weiss, 2000), contributing to organizational evaluative knowledge creation.

This chapter is organized as follows. In the first three sections, the analysis highlights the tacit nature of evaluative knowledge, which is mobilized across the organization through continuous interaction between evaluators and program managers. Case study findings suggest that evaluation participatory processes help socialize streams of evaluative knowledge beyond specific studies and formal reporting. Yet, to facilitate the sharing of work practices, experiences, and social and individual perspectives among different actors within and outside the organization, organizational, financial, and time resources may put severe constraints to accommodate the work of organizational communities engaged in evaluative knowledge creation for strategic planning. In the following two sections, the analysis illustrates how theory-driven approaches and figurative language codify evaluative concepts that combined with other knowledge sources come to be accepted by organizational actors. In section six, we report evidence of use of evaluative knowledge translating into work practice change and policy reformulation. Finally, we draw a number of conclusions and implications for public management on such issues as: (a) management styles and relations with evaluative streams; (b) value orientation embedded within evaluative streams; (c) properties and components of evaluative knowledge that managers value for strategic planning; and (d) standards that managers apply to justify and internalize evaluative knowledge in work practices and policy making.

## Research Design

We chose a case study approach focused on four evaluation studies (see Table 14.1). Through in-depth interviewing of high-level decision makers (six), program managers (twenty-four), experts (fourteen), and evaluators (six), we traced the evaluative information contained within these reports to understand how it became evaluative knowledge shared within the organizational setting of the World Bank. Between June 2000 and May 2001, we completed fifty semi-structured interviews in addition to researcher's participant observation, and document analysis of public records, and evaluation reports.

## The Tacit Nature of Evaluative Knowledge

The tacit knowledge that develops in highly complex tasks—for example, the formulation of a global forestry policy for sustainable development, the conception of new training courses against corruption, or the revision of dam

## Table 14.1
## Key Features of Evaluation Studies Examined

|  | Forestry Study | Public Expenditure Review | Large Dam Evaluation | Anti-corruption Mid-term Evaluation |
|---|---|---|---|---|
| Policy/ Program evaluated | Implementation of the 1991 World Bank's Forest Strategy | Process, content, and technique of Public Expenditure Review | 50 Bank-financed large dams construction on economic, social, and environmental development vis-à-vis Bank's standards and safeguard policies. | Training offerings on investigative journalism |
| Policy/ Program's outcomes of interest | The Bank's role in forest-rich and forest-poor countries in the forest sector, and on poverty alleviation within developmental objectives. Bank support experiments in logging | Quality, timeliness, cost efficiency and impacts on external assistance and public expenditure reform in developing countries | Improvement and expansion of power generation, irrigation, domestic and industrial water supplies | Anti-corruption outcomes and institutional development |
| Date of final report | 6/23/00 – FY2000 | 11/13/98 – FY1999 | 8/15/96 – FY1997 | FY 1998 |
| Location of the evaluation sites | World Bank Headquarters, and Brazil; Cameroon; China; Costa Rica; India; Indonesia | Internal process evaluation | Desk review of 50 large dams | Tanzania, Uganda |
| Methods | 1) Case study fieldwork; 2) extensive consultation with stakeholders; 3) global policy review and six regional portfolio reviews. | 1) Application of OED's evaluation methodology to a stratified sample of PERs by a panel of experts; 2) an independent survey of PER task managers; 3) interviews of senior developing country officials; and 4) consultations with officials from the IMF and other partners. | 1) Content analysis of documents on large dams projects financed by the Bank; 2) survey questionnaire to implementing agencies; 3) informal interviews of operational staff. This information was reviewed to identify those projects that have been successful, overall, in supporting the objective of sustainable development as well as those instances where adverse impacts are unacceptable. | 1) Theory-driven approach; 2) case study fieldwork; 3) In depth-interviewing; 4) content analysis of documents; 5) social science empirical literature review. |
| Major findings | The Bank has implemented the 1991 Forest Strategy only partially, and through an increased number of forest-related components in its environmental lending. The effectiveness of the strategy has been modest, as well as the sustainability of its impact. | PER quality has shown some improvement in recent years, yet some PERs show dated analyses of spending policies with little concern for cost efficiency or the quality of public services. PERs had only a modest impact on Bank lending strategies, client expenditure policies, and aid coordination. | 74 percent of the 50 dams reviewed contributed to energy production, flood control, water supply for urban and industrial uses, and irrigation. Resettlement was inadequately managed in half the projects. The 50 dams have a mixed record on the management of environmental consequences. | The awareness raising approach to change the cognition and mindset of officials and journalists does not guarantee empowerment at the societal level. |

safeguards—is hard to capture in formal organizational procedures. Tacit knowledge relies on the sharing of experiences and expertise over time between senior employees and novices (mentoring and master-apprentice relationships), stakeholders outside the organization, and among a fairly stable group of professionals—such as the community of environmental engineers, ecologists, macroeconomists, or public sector specialists (Nonaka et al., 1994, 2000).

According to our case study findings, much of the evaluative knowledge mobilized within the organization was tacit; it was tied to personal relations, shared habits, and intuition, all of which was not previously documented. For instance, the dam evaluation shed light on the issue of resettlement and the failure of the costly compensation schemes for indigenous populations. The forestry study pointed to the Bank managers' resistance to undertake forestry projects due to their high risk of failure. Uncovering this behavioral pattern implicitly shared among the community of ecologists and environmental managers was crucial to understanding the implementation problems of forestry projects. The anticorruption evaluation found that the educational materials and case studies needed to be more suited to the situation in the countries and that the workshops were directed solely at print reporters and did not address the specific needs of radio and TV journalist-participants, while in the rural areas of both Tanzania and Uganda, radio is the most important and effective medium to reach out to local communities.[1]

This tacit knowledge—both social and individual—could not be found in previous reports and manuals; it drew on field research and country case studies accounting for diversity in socioeconomic, political, and institutional circumstances, and built on country experts' perspectives and country workshops' proceedings that encouraged representatives from government, NGOs, the private sector, and academia to provide their feedback outside the organization. Within the Bank, evaluation processes (i.e., systematic data collection and monitoring, surveys and in-depth interviewing, peer review, and formal and informal dissemination procedures) rather than single studies made it possible to elicit specific information held exclusively by different departments, and a range of different stakeholders, generating unique evaluative knowledge, much beyond the formal reporting. Next, we turn to analyze how World Bank managers and decision makers shared this tacit evaluative knowledge to trigger organizational action and strategic decisions.

**Interaction and Participation Help Socialize Evaluative Knowledge**

According to Nonaka (Nonaka et al., 1994, 2000), tacit knowledge is shared through the deep socialization of a project team, or what he calls a microcommunity of knowledge. Socialization means that members of the community not only come to understand each other's definition of shared situations but also agree on a common definition and "justified true belief" about how to act in that situation. Knowledge then is created in the process of working together, benefiting largely from the mutual insight of organizational members to formulate an organizational advancement strategy (Nonaka et al., 1994, 2000).

Case study findings suggest that interaction among evaluators, program managers, and decisions makers is one of the most effective ways to create and transfer streams of evaluative knowledge across the organization. For instance, in the case of the World Bank anticorruption evaluation, program managers pointed out that collaborative interactions with the evaluation team helped clarify aspects of program design and implementation. Although the evaluation study attempted to conceptualize and systematize all information acquired, program managers reported that informal, direct, and systematic interaction with the evaluation team was the fastest and easiest way of learning the results while the study was ongoing (Marra, 2000). Program managers got engaged in the evaluation process as joint players to uncover the premises of the program logic to improve the design and performance of the anticorruption training offerings.² Evaluators involved program managers not only as key institutional informants, but as members of the evaluation process to share beliefs about which actions work and which do not. This evaluative information is basically interactive, flows when the evaluation process is under way, and is not tightly linked to the specific study at hand (Weiss, 1980; Vedung, 1997; Kirkhart, 2000). Thus, we can talk about an evaluative stream generated interactively within the organization rather than a single evaluation study on anticorruption.

In the case of the large dam evaluation, both program managers and high-level decision makers recognized that evaluators catalyzed major international stakeholders' attention on the issues related to dam building in an international event held in Gland in 1998 jointly organized with the World Conservation Union—IUCN. By socializing evaluative information on the social and environmental indirect costs associated with dam building, the Gland workshop provided a space for public debate and created the conditions for stakeholders from governments, NGOs, and multilateral and bilateral agencies to begin an international dialogue, as one respondent noted:

> It is useful to have an international public debate so as people from governments, and NGOs, and multilateral and bilateral agencies come together to discuss future policies.

The dam evaluation team organized the Gland workshop not only to disseminate the study findings, but to provide an opportunity for addressing the fundamental questions regarding dams in an open space before thirty-seven holders, representing diverse interests from around the world (IUCN, 1997). The cost-benefit desk review of fifty Bank-financed large dams, revealed the basic issues—resettlement and environmental damage—underlying the controversial aspects associated with dam projects. Initiated by evaluators, the Gland workshop became the place for decision makers to set new dam safety priorities and begin to address resettlement problems. In this case, interaction between evaluators and decision makers occurred at the end of the evaluation process, when the study was completed and the report already issued. But, through interaction, evaluative knowledge became available to support discussion and future strategy, calling for a subsequent evaluation effort to address more in depth the costs of resettlement and the development impact of dams.³

Also the evaluation of the Bank's 1991 forest protection strategy promoted a highly participatory process contributing to the broader forest policy review launched by the environmental department heads to change the Bank's global forestry policy. Different units and organizations across the Bank were involved in a comprehensive consultative effort to spur reflection around the core theme of forestry sustainable management. While evaluators looked back to evaluate the Bank's 1991 forest strategy, a Bank working group began to draw up a new strategy in mid-1998. Later the working group formed a technical advisory group of stakeholders at all levels to monitor the openness of the process and ensure that the voices of all relevant stakeholders were heard in regional, global, and issues-based meetings.

Unlike the other two evaluation processes, the forestry evaluation team did not exclusively initiate the consultation and the analysis. Nevertheless the evaluative stream of information upgraded the debate not only within the Bank, but also among the major stakeholders in the development community and beyond—reaching as far as the Republic of China.[4] All interviewees valued the independent analysis and research.[5] The distinctive feature of the evaluation process was its participatory nature, able to triangulate different viewpoints to reach robust conclusions. Program managers, as well as the decision makers and NGO members interviewed, acknowledged their own active participation in the study design phase, noting that they provided feedback on the findings while the study was under way, and reviewed the official final draft, as reported below:

> With the forestry study, the evaluation team has really made an effort to bring people around the table and talk this issue through not only Bank staff, but also NGOs, and the regions, and the borrowing countries.

Specifically, the forestry evaluation process involved people in government, development agencies, NGOs, and the private sector.[6] The evaluation design paper was translated into Balahasa, French, Mandarin, Portuguese, and Spanish (languages spoken in five of the six case study countries). From the outset, a four-member advisory committee counseled the evaluation team on the design paper, the selection of country case studies, the preliminary findings, the consultation plan, and the final report. Dissemination was also broadly widespread, beginning well before the report was officially issued and publicized outside the Bank. Besides discussing the preliminary report with Bank managers and shareholders in 1999 in Washington, DC, evaluators held multi-stakeholder country workshops in Brazil, China, India, and Indonesia (between November 1999 and April 2000).[7]

The cases illustrated thus far show that managers value broad-based participatory studies, which, in turn, guarantee triangulation and more robust conclusions. Furthermore, interaction and participation may occur in different points in time, at the outset, during, or at the end the study; yet, interactive processes enhance evaluative knowledge creation and dissemination, detached from specific studies and reports. In fact, evaluative knowledge survives long beyond the life-shelf of formal reports, as shown by the dam-related evaluative stream. In this specific case, the report was issued in 1997 while its own findings continued to feed the subsequent evaluation and research effort of the World Commission on Dams and were still discussed at the Board of World

Bank Executive Directors in 2001 vis-à-vis the changed international development conditions and priorities.[8]

Yet, the sharing of tacit evaluative knowledge required new organizational arrangements, financial, human, and time resources, different kinds of evaluation project schedules, and new physical space to accommodate the work of micro-communities involved in evaluative knowledge creation. Both the forestry and the anticorruption evaluation mobilized considerable financial resources to conduct the fieldwork, specific technical capacity and expertise to analyze the data, and time consuming coordination among the different team members. Given the systematic time and budgetary constraints, the question is whether to employ human, organizational, and financial resources to perform participatory evaluations of such scope. Next section seeks to address this issue.

## Solving the Trade-offs of Time and Money Vis-à-Vis Strategic Planning Needs

In line with Nonaka's conclusions (2000), case study findings suggest that the extent of interaction and participation within evaluation studies is a choice that has to be considered in an organization's advancement strategy—and is closely connected to establishing an overall enabling context. As emerged specifically from the forestry evaluation case study, when organizational informational needs are explicitly related to the intention to reformulate the organizational strategy, there is a clear and articulated demand for evaluation to inform organizational actions and decisions.

The relevance of the forestry policy review called for a major knowledge sharing effort to address the global problems related to forests. As the principal evaluator reported, from the very outset, the forestry evaluation was expected to inform not only Bank decision makers but also whoever could be interested in the issues the evaluation addressed. The intended audience included program managers and members of civil society, who, as civic volunteers and opinion leaders in their communities, may have strategic interest in such issues as deforestation, sustainable management vs. illegal logging, poverty reduction, and preservation of the livelihood of local people. The evaluation effort involved not only human, and financial resources, but also a continuous process triggering dynamic cooperative relations among various functions and organizational departments as well as stakeholders outside the Bank. No one major department or group of experts had the exclusive responsibility for creating new knowledge, but evaluators facilitated the parallel knowledge creation process, taking place simultaneously at the top, middle, and lower management as well as beyond the organizational boundaries. In this context, redundant information sped up concept creation around key evaluative issues leading to the reformulation of the World Bank forestry policy, as shown later on. By design the forestry study was instrumental to the broad-based review of the organizational strategy, as most respondents reported, as follows:

People writing the new forestry strategy have taken OED recommendations into account...

In the other two cases considered, there was no awareness of informational gaps to address existing organizational weaknesses. There was no intention to change the strategy for dam building or for anticorruption, nor was there any explicit demand for evaluation. Yet, evaluative knowledge sharing was key to strategizing and reflecting upon organizational action, all the more when global issues were involved. Through socialization, unique knowledge became valuable to take action, to apply it to value-creating tasks and competence, and to capitalize such evaluative knowledge on existing corporate opportunities for strategic planning.

For instance, most interviewees agreed that the dams evaluation was the catalyst for the constitution of the World Commission on Dams (WCD), which conducted the second phase of the review of the impact and performance of large dams throughout the world to set global standards for dam-building and large infrastructure projects.[9] Likewise, interviews suggested that the anticorruption evaluation paved the way for the complete restructuring of the anticorruption strategy with the introduction of new training courses addressing the weakness of the awareness raising approach as the only mechanism to fight corruption.[10]

In both the dams and anticorruption studies, the evaluation team took the initiative and bore the costs to open up the space for sharing evaluative information and debating its implications during the study process and at the end of the process. By contrast, the forestry study sought participation from the outset, in the research design phase and all along the implementation of the study until the report was issued, building upon the conscious overlapping of the organizational information, the different departments' activities, and the management responsibilities. Through a cross-fertilization process, the forestry study benefited from the policy review, where the evaluation, in turn, provided the opportunity to reflect on past experience and share lessons throughout the organization.

The analysis therefore suggests that across all three case studies presented thus far evaluators were left with the choice to create the conditions for processes of evaluative knowledge generation and sharing across the organization. Yet, the forestry case study particularly highlights the implication for the organization to proactively mobilize financial, physical, and technical resources for broad-based participatory evaluation efforts to feed major organizational advancement strategies. There is a need, though, to strike a balance between efficient organizational information processing and creative and redundant evaluative streams tapping into the existing pools of tacit knowledge, seeking effectiveness and competitiveness, and reinvigorating the quality of conversations taking place within and outside its organizational borders.

Next, we turn to analyze how tacit evaluative knowledge becomes explicit and codified to be used within and outside the organization.

## Metaphors and Theory-Based Approaches Make Evaluative Knowledge Explicit

To externalize evaluative knowledge means to express concepts and judgments through language. This is obviously a crucial step of the evaluation knowledge creation process, one that may ultimately result in the advancement of a program or policy through a new product, process, or service, such as the reformulated forestry policy, the revised dam safety standards, or the new anticorruption training courses.

The use of figurative language through metaphors and the systematic reconstruction of the logic underlying World Bank anticorruption initiatives and the 1991 forestry strategy allowed evaluators to externalize the knowledge managers possess in their day-to-day work, making this tacit evaluative knowledge explicit. Concepts like "chilling effect" or "awareness raising" embodied evaluative judgments and organizational knowledge shared by different actors within the Bank. With awareness raising, the anticorruption evaluation distinctively featured the Bank's first approach to fighting corruption through sensitizing journalists and other public officials. With "chilling effect," the forestry study identified Bank staff's increasing disengagement in forest-related projects because of the high risk of being associated (in the minds of NGOs, environmental groups, and the general public) with environmental degradation and ecological disasters.

In this regard, the metaphor of chilling effect served to conceptualize program managers' reluctance for forestry lending. The awareness raising was expediently used to denote the flaws of the anticorruption training initiatives, helping convey the judgment on their likely weak societal impact and organize internal discussion and debate (Vedung, 1997). Such evaluative concepts acquired their own life far from the specific evaluation studies and reports. They captured the blend of experience and imagination of organizational members that could mentally visualize them and catalyze evaluative knowledge for thinking differently of their own work practices and effects.

Furthermore, by eliciting program designers' own theories about how programs were expected to work, evaluators "disaggregated the assumptions into the mini-steps that are implied and confronted the leaps of faith and questionable reasoning that are (often) involved" (Weiss, 1980; p. 25). Uncovering the implicit theoretical premises embedded in anticorruption and forestry programs favored thinking and reflection upon program design and implementation. This analytic decomposition of the Bank's program logic helped program managers clarify and systematize their implicit thinking, facilitating understanding of program outcomes and aiding the decision-making process.

Our case study findings indicate that the evaluative knowledge produced through the theory-based approach contained both prescriptive and descriptive components. Prescriptive theory encapsulated the structure of the program in countries requesting World Bank assistance against corruption or for forestry protection, and the ways to implement the program so as to understand whether failures resulted from program design or from implementation. Descriptive theory instead, unveiled the underlying causal mechanisms that linked inputs, implementation processes, and outcomes, specifying how the program works and identifying the conditions under which certain processes arise and their likely consequences. It provided an understanding of the program's potential by highlighting the intervening variables; diagnosing potential problems; and uncovering causal processes to understand why, for example, anticorruption activities did or did not work.

For instance, in the anticorruption case, the prescriptive theory reassembled the various components of the Bank's strategy in dealing with the corruption problem by clarifying the goals and outcomes of the intervention. The descriptive theory looked into the assumptions about the causal relationships between the mechanism of raising awareness on corrupt practices among journalists and the desired outcome of corruption reduction. According to the evaluation findings, the focus on awareness raising to change the cognition and mindset of officials and journalists was the weaker point in the program logic, relying on the assumed "automatic progression" from awareness of an unjust situation to intervening to bring it to an end.

Furthermore, the empirical evidence did not justify the emphasis on empowerment as an effective mechanism to fight corruption. Even when individuals are empowered, the evaluation pointed out, it is not certain that empowerment at the social or organizational levels will follow. In addition, special attention was paid to identifying elements of the program's underlying logic with evidence from the social and economic sciences. As the principal evaluator pointed out, "such an assessment is necessary, because no evidence exists that a policymaker's (or practitioner, change agent, or Bank official's) assumptions are scientifically grounded. However, by the same token, no a priori assumption can be made to the contrary" (Leeuw et al., 1999; 30).

In the forestry study, the evaluation team followed a similar approach, highlighting weaknesses in the design and in the implementation process. The first design flaw was the Bank's assumption that developing countries would borrow Bank resources to conserve forests. Forests being global public goods that are likely to be under-produced, forest conservation involves major positive externalities for forest-poor countries, while forest-rich developing countries bear its high costs. The 1991 policy assumed forest-rich countries would borrow from the Bank to finance the "production" of such a global asset, whereas demand for forestry lending remained low, particularly in Brazil. Drawing the implications for the Bank and developing countries, the evaluation made this logical inconsistency clear and explicit (OED, 2000).

Another major flaw was found in the logging ban applied to all forests. The logging ban, in halting forestry production in any circumstances, underestimated the importance of forest products to the livelihood of indigenous people. The study revealed the missing link between the Bank's 1991 forest strategy and the Bank's mission to reduce poverty, and questioned the unconditional logging ban enforced since 1991. The evaluation acknowledged its symbolic importance, keeping the Bank from being associated with deforestation and with commercial and illegal practices, but also pointed out the policy's unintended effect of indirectly contributing to deforestation, and management's "chilling effect," that is, managers steered away from forestry lending (OED, 2000).

What is worth noting here is that creating evaluative concepts and making them explicit beyond the specific studies contributes to strategic decisions, hence this process is itself a strategic concern. As shown in the two case studies, the externalization process led to reformulation of the premises underlying the original policy or program in order to make it more effective. Yet indifference and even preconceived judgments against evaluation may hamper the implementation of an advancement strategy. Next we turn to analyze how evaluative knowledge is accepted and justified across the organization.

## The Expectations of Users: Combining Different Sources of Evaluative Knowledge

After an evaluative concept has been created, the assessment of its need will follow. It is here that "a well-formulated advancement strategy—which should include certain organizational objectives—can be directly applied to the group process" (Nonaka et al., 2000; 348). In other words, while organizational evaluative knowledge creation is a continuous process, an organization needs to orient this process at some point in order to accelerate the sharing of evaluative streams within and beyond the boundary of the organization for further knowledge creation. This convergence process needs to be based on the "justification" or truthfulness of evaluative concepts. Justification is the process of final convergence and screening, which determines the extent to which the evaluative knowledge created within the organization is truly worthwhile for the organization and society. What matters here are the "standards" for judging truthfulness.

What standards do World Bank managers and decision makers use to justify the truthfulness of evaluative knowledge? As the Public Expenditure Reviews evaluation case study showed, high-level decision makers focused on consistency with the current organizational strategy, to verify whether those evaluation concepts were compatible with the existing priorities and operations of the Bank. Given the centrality of public expenditure review related to countries' budgeting and spending, evaluation was perceived as a performance assessment of not only PERs per se, but also of all the activities associated with public expenditure analysis and support.[11] In analyzing the content, process, quality, timeliness, cost efficiency, and impact on external assistance and public expenditure reform in developing countries, evaluators concluded that PERs were inadequate in quality, in usefulness for decision making, in cost efficiency, and in credibility for developing countries. The evaluation pinpointed major areas for improvement, focusing specifically on the need for shifting attention to public sector performance and outcomes rather than inputs, and promoting in-countries broadly participatory processes to increase the usefulness of these analyses (OED, 1998a).

The second standard to justify the PER evaluation conclusions was the consistency of the evaluative knowledge with future values and strategies of the World Bank. Drawing on the study findings, public sector specialists and experts on the advisory board of the Bank formulated new PER guidelines providing a framework for country-based programs of assistance.[12] The guidelines aimed to articulate the purpose of the PER and guide program managers in undertaking the exercise. The goal was to combine and integrate the analytical process for country-based aid programs with governance concerns, such as, for instance, the assessment of the countries' budgetary system, its performance in delivering public services, identifying broad knowledge and information gaps to be addressed in the country assistance strategy.

The community of experts (i.e., public sector specialists and macroeconomists) looked more at the analytical content of the evaluation and felt that shifting to a focus on results required rethinking the role and functions of the public sector and the analytical instruments available to improve it. "The public expenditure review (PER) should become the Public Sector Performance Review (PSPR)"—commented a public sector specialist, recognizing the need for change from a bureaucratic command-and-control culture with arbitrary and oppressive rules to a culture that is focused on serving citizens, earning trust, achieving results, and working better while costing less. And the PER evaluation helped contextualize this broadly shared knowledge on public sector reform to the day-to-day work of the Bank public expenditure analyses.

What is worth noting is that the evaluative knowledge was the product of a combination of explicit knowledge related to public sector reform tenets with some other already-existing-explicit knowledge, specifically related to Bank strategic planning and governance quality assessment. Through sorting, adding, re-categorizing, and re-contextualizing, evaluators reframed the goals of public expenditure reviews, drawing upon scholarly research on results-oriented management existing within and outside the organization. In this case, the justification of evaluative knowledge relied on the analytical and technical components of evaluation.

# Evaluative Knowledge Creation and Utilization within the World Bank 263

The third standard to judge the evaluation truthfulness was the reaction of program managers directly or indirectly targeted by evaluation recommendations. Despite the initial resistance to evaluation findings, the basic message was received:[13]

> What counts is not just reviewing public expenditure—one interviewee said—but measuring public sector performance and changing its culture.

As interviews suggested, program managers began gradually to replace PERs with another analytical and planning tool, that is, the Poverty Reduction Strategy Paper (PRSP), as the latter became mandatory for debt relief initiatives. The PRSP integrated the PER analytical aspects, adding explicit governance concerns to the poverty reduction strategies. Full-fledged PRSPs currently describe the country's plan for macroeconomic, budgetary, and social policies to foster growth and reduce poverty, and are prepared by the member country with support from Bank and IMF staff, as well as civil society and other development partners.

Case study findings show that middle and lower program managers began to play with evaluative information, making it compatible with their mandatory tasks and operations in a very creative fashion. The evaluative knowledge produced translated into a management tool, which helped orient and redress the day-to-day organizational operations. In short, convergence around PER-related evaluative concepts proved that the kind of evaluative knowledge created was truly worthwhile for program managers. Evaluation findings and recommendations were consistent with the organization's advancement strategy and thus used to persuade organizational members to apply them, and build the competences needed to further develop them in the future.

Overall, findings highlight that evaluative streams cut across the middle, upper, and lower management, mediating and facilitating information processing. Yet, evaluative knowledge needs to be accepted, and that the role of top or middle management is key to determine the standard of acceptance and trigger convergence. This is a knowledge creation process, which is highly strategic and influenced by the "aspiration" of the leaders of the organization. The ability of leaders to maintain continuous self-reflection in a wider perspective is indispensable when it comes to accepting the evaluative knowledge created. Next, the analysis turns to considering the change in work practices and policies resulting from the acceptance and internalization of evaluative knowledge.

## The Uses of Evaluative Streams: Change in Work Practices and Development Policies

After searching for, socializing, categorizing, documenting, and justifying evaluative information, organizational members are involved with a tangible form of knowledge, achieved by combining existing knowledge, products, procedures, and components with the new evaluative concepts. As shown above in the case of PER, program managers began to assemble the concepts on governance and public sector performance drawn from the evaluation with the mandatory concerns for poverty reduction strategies. The experts engaged in the ex ante quality assessment of Bank analytical documents and adopted the evaluation criteria the PER evaluators had applied (World Bank, 2000b; semi-structured interviews). In other words, the evaluation's main recommendations were shared and applied. Currently, Bank PERs have become more focused, more selective, and more participatory, as well as less costly, according to those interviewed.

In the field of anticorruption activities, efforts to reengineer the first generation of media workshops included a series of electronic seminars for radio and TV journalists, allowing for better targeting both by geographical area and education level, decentralization in training delivery, and greater involvement of local organizations to produce more specific materials. At the same time, a whole new set of training and policy dialogues was launched to integrate the awareness raising approach with a more broad-based participatory effort bringing public officials, politicians, and civil society to discuss about corruption.

As far as the dam evaluation, interviewees reported greater awareness of critical issues associated with dams as a result of evaluation, and more emphasis on resettlement plans, environmental assessments, and safety issues. Especially in Europe and Central Asia, where most dam safety projects are under way, attention shifted towards minimizing the adverse technical and environmental effects produced by obsolescence, and degradation of the dam infrastructure. In the Africa and East Asian Pacific regions, an ever increasing demand for hydropower energy presented Bank staff with a daunting trade-off: whether to apply the costly Bank's safeguards or let the private sector take over. Those interviewed acknowledged that the Bank's involvement would help ensure better social, technical, and environmental standards but Bank involvement might come at too high a price in terms of finance and damage to the Bank's reputation.

Regarding the forestry evaluation, the recently reformulated strategy endorsed global and local partnerships; established concessional resources to supplement the regular Bank budget for study and analyses in this field; set up funding mechanisms to internalize global externalities; promoted sustainable forestry production, where appropriate, but ensured conservation in tropical moist forests; and strengthened the emphasis on poverty reduction and measures to improve the livelihood of indigenous people. Such changes were in line with evaluative suggestions and recommendations.

In all four case studies presented thus far, at the level of both work practices and policy formulation, evaluative knowledge was incorporated into organizational action and strategic planning. As shown above, the outcome of the four steps of the evaluative knowledge creation process—sharing tacit knowledge, creating concepts, justifying concepts, and applying them in the day-to-day work—resulted in a possible project/activity innovation, an organization's advancement strategy, or just raw knowledge.

Such findings suggest that the use of streams of evaluative knowledge as opposed to discrete evaluation studies consists of a feedback loop, in which the knowledge created circles back to strategic efforts, continually altering or adapting the organizational advancement strategy as well as its vision, and action. This feedback loop may call for a new way of structuring the organization, point to new areas to exploit, identify new knowledge-creation projects, or suggest new barriers to dismantle in order to create future competitive advantages.

## Implications for Public Management

### a) Management Styles and Relations with Evaluative Streams

The process of building evaluative knowledge is not encapsulated in specific studies but takes place when organizational members reflect on their actions, and the evaluation-based information is more than the specific information required immediately by each individual. The sharing of the extra information between individuals promotes the sharing of individual tacit knowledge and members share overlapping information, reducing the impact of managerial hierarchy and promoting mutual trust. In fact, the channels through which senior and lower managers acquire evaluative knowledge are basically informal through socialization processes that go beyond the typical "top-down" or "bottom-up" management styles. Socialization of research design, data collection, analysis, and finding-reporting democratizes the processes of evaluative knowledge creation. As shown above, the participatory evaluation approach of the forestry study made it possible to socialize unique information held exclusively by different departments at different management levels within and outside the Bank.

Indeed, participatory processes of evaluative knowledge generation and sharing pave the way to substantive innovation in public management. In fact, the essence of a traditional bureaucratic machine is top-down information processing using division of labor and hierarchy. Top managers create basic managerial concepts (the premises of decision making) and break them down hierarchically, in terms of objectives and means, so that subordinates can implement them (Nonaka, 1994). Conversely, moving in the reverse direction, information is processed and transformed from the particular to the general. Frontline managers are immersed in the day-to-day details of particular technologies, products, and markets. No one is more expert in the realities of an organization's business than they are. But, while these employees are deluged with highly specific information, they often find it extremely difficult to turn that information into useful knowledge (Nonaka, 1994).

Evaluative knowledge creation occurs at both management levels, orienting chaotic information toward purposeful vision and strategy, and socializing it across lower layers within the day-to-day program managers' experience. The forestry evaluation process particularly promoted the parallel evaluative knowledge creation through extensive participation inside and outside the Bank at all levels, and meaningful concepts creation: that is, the chilling effect, the logging ban with their country-specific variations. The PER study, conversely, channeled the practice and interests of program managers towards PERs more strategic used for lending programming and more focused on public expenditure outcomes than inputs, and participatory in-country analyses rather than formal comprehensive reports.

*b) Value-orientation of Evaluative Streams*

Besides influencing management styles, evaluative knowledge promotes certain values and preferences for organizational actions over others. The systematic focus on the countries' development needs, priorities, problems, and gaps endorsed not only the perspective of the Bank, the corporate culture of the organization, but the genuine interest of aid recipients, through the independent analysis and research. The dam evaluation revealed explicitly the general interest for development, pointing to the environmental and social downsides of dams, and calling for stricter safety standards in Bank-funded operations to avoid social and environmental dumping. Also the forestry study made the point for reconciling the illegal logging ban with the need for sustainable forestry management services. In brief, evaluative streams continuously bring inside the organization outside perspectives, making managers keener on different opinions and practices, while the mix between internal and external evaluation sources adds to the methodological strengths and reliability of information.

*c) Properties and Components of Evaluative Streams that Managers Value for Strategic Planning*

Managers seem to value those properties and components of the evaluative knowledge associated with (a) firsthand data collection within country case studies, and (b) theory-driven analyses, externalizing those tacit insights coming from the field. Uncovering the tacit knowledge from the field and the day-to-day practice of development operations, the forestry and the anticorruption evaluations provided evidence of how well those policies and programs "worked" in different circumstances. Looking at the premises of program design, the prescriptive aspects of strategies, and the causal mechanisms of program activities both in Uganda and Tanzania, the anticorruption evaluation externalized the program managers' implicit thinking and their leaps of faith.

The externalization of this mostly tacit organizational knowledge helps organizational members to reflect critically upon their action and vision. Field-research coupled with the uncovering of theories embedded implicitly in program designs contributes to clarifying the tacit premises of organizational action and validates them against empirical evidence. The knowledge thus produced promotes *improvement* through better-informed policies and more targeted programs.

*d) Managers' Standards for Acceptance and Application of Evaluative Knowledge*

Finally, managers' justification of the evaluative knowledge produced within the organization revolves around the criteria and standards that govern their attention. As in the case of the PER evaluation, for top managers, evaluation was equivalent to a performance indicator to enforce organizational accountability; for experts, it was an analytical contribution to better design organizational programs, while for project managers it was a tool to handle implementation problems and deficiencies.

Overall, the analysis suggests that the evaluative knowledge creation process builds on the organization's strategic ability to acquire, create, exploit, and accumulate evaluative information continuously and repeatedly in a circular process, where individuals can link related concepts and areas of knowledge to allow problems to be viewed from many angles, and draw relationships between different sets of information, far from the episodic event of an evaluation study.

## Notes

1. Based on the evaluation report.
2. Based on semi-structured interviews.
3. Based on semi-structured interviews with program managers.
4. The principal evaluator currently sits on the Chinese committee in charge of formulating a sustainable policy of forestry management in China (based on interview with the principal evaluator).
5. Based on semi-structured interviews with program managers.
6. Based on semi-structured interview with the principal evaluator.
7. Based on semi-structured interview with the principal evaluator.
8. Based on semi-structured interviews and the researcher's participant observation.
9. After a broad-based two-year investigation and analysis, in November 2000 the Commission released its report, entitled "Dams and Development:" A New Framework for Decision-Making."
10. The new so-called "core courses" go beyond the awareness raising approach for an integrated framework. This key component of the courses is to provide the partici-

pants with the necessary tool kit to unable them to design a coherent anticorruption strategy and discuss the challenges of integrating participatory and awareness raising processes with concrete institutional reforms.
11. Based on semi-structured interviews with program managers.
12. Based on semi-structured interviews with experts.
13. Based on semi-structured interviews with program managers.

## References

Argyris, C. (1994), *On Organizational Learning*, Malden, MA: Blackwell.

Argyris, C. and Schön, D.A. (1978), *Organizational Learning*, Reading, MA: Addison Wesley Publishing Company.

Bolman, L.G., and Deal, T.E., (1997), *Reframing Organizations,* Jossey-Bass Publishers-San Francisco.

Chelimsky, E., Shadish, W., (1997), *Evaluation for the 21th Century*, Sage Publications, Thousands Oaks, London, New Delhi.

Henry, G. (2000), "Why Not Use?," *New Directions for Evaluation,* Number 88, winter, Jossey-Bass Publishers.

Hertz, R. and Imber, J.B. [Eds.] (1995), *Studying Elites Using Qualitative Methods,* SAGE Publications.

House, E. (1986), 'Internal Evaluation,' *Evaluation Practice,* 7(1):12-47'

House, E. H. and Howe, K. R. (1999), *Values in Evaluation and Social Science Research,* Sage Publications.

IUCN – World Conservation Union, World Bank (1997), *Large Dams: Learning from the Past, Looking at the Future,* Workshop Proceedings, Gland, Switzerland, April 12-13, 1997, Gland: IUCN; Washington, DC: World Bank.

Jackson, E., (1999), *Knowledge Shared: Participatory Evaluation in Development Cooperation*, West Hartford, Conn.: Kumarian Press; Ottawa:IDRC.

Kirkhart, K.E. (2000), 'Reconceptualizing Evaluation Use: An Integrated Theory of Influence,' *New Directions for Evaluation,* Number 88, winter, Jossey-Bass Publishers.

Leeuw, F., Rist, R., Sonnichsen, R. (1994), *Can Government Learn?,* Transaction Publishers.

Leeuw, F., Van Gils, G.H., and Kreft, C. (1999), " Evaluating Anti-Corruption Initiatives: Underlying Logic and Mid-term Impact of a World Bank Program," *Evaluation* 5(2):194-219.

Lindblom, C. E. and Cohen, D. K. (1979), *Usable Knowledge. Social Science and Social Problem Solving,* Yale University Press.

Litterer, J. A., (1980), 'Elements of Control in Organizations,' in Jelinek, M., Litterer, J.A., Miles, R. E. (Eds.), *Organizations by Design: Theory and Practice,* Plano, TX: Business Publications.

March, J. G., and Simon, H. A. (1958), *Organizations,* New York: John Wiley.

Marcus, G. E., (1998), *Ethnography through Thick and Thin*, Princeton University Press, Princeton, New Jersey.

Marra, M., (2000), 'How Much Does Evaluation Matter? Some Example of Utilization of the Evaluation of World Bank's Anticorruption Activities,' in *Evaluation*, Vo. 6(1): 22-39.

Mayne, J. (1994), 'Utilizing Evaluation in Organizations: The Balancing Act,' in Leeuw, F.L., Rist, R.C., and Sonnichsen, R.C., [Eds.] (1994), *Can Governments Learn? Comparative Perspectives on Evaluation and Organizational Learning,* New Brunswick, NJ: Transaction Publishers.

Nonaka, I. (1994), 'A Dynamic Theory of Organizational Knowledge Creation,' *Organization Science,* Vol. 5, No. 1.

Nonaka, I., Von Krogh, G., Kazuo, I. (2000), *Enabling Knowledge Creation. How to Unlock the Mistery of Tacit Knowledge and Release the Power of Innovation,* Oxford University Press.

Operations Evaluation Department (1996), *The World Bank's Experience with Large Dams – A Preliminary Review of Impacts,* World Bank, Washington DC.

Operations Evaluation Department, (1998a), *Public Sector Performance – The Critical Role of Evaluation,* Selected Proceedings from a World Bank Seminar, World Bank, Washington DC.

Operations Evaluation Department, (1998b), *Recent Experience With Involuntary Resettlement. Thailand – Pak Mun,* Report No. 17541, World Bank, Washington DC.

Operations Evaluation Department (1998c), *The Impact of Public Expenditure Review,* World Bank, Washington DC.

Operations Evaluation Department, (2000), 'Involuntary Resettlement: The Large Dam Experience,' *Precis,* No. 194, World Bank, Washington DC.

Operations Evaluation Department, (2000), 'A Review of the World Bank's 1991 Forest Strategy and its Implementation,' Volume I, Main Report, World Bank, Washington DC.

Operations Evaluation Department (2000), *The World Bank Forestry Strategy – Striking the Right Balance,* World Bank, Washington DC.

Park, P.(1999), "People, Knowledge, and Change in Participatory Research," in *Management Learning,* Vol. 30, n.2, pp.: 141-157.

Patton, M. Q. (1997), *Utilization-Focused Evaluation: The New Century Text,* Sage Publications.

Patton, M.Q., (1990), *Qualitative Evaluation and Research Methods,* Sage Publications, London.

Picciotto, R., (1997), 'Evaluation in the World Bank: Antecedents, Instruments, and Concepts,' in Chelimsky, E., and Shadish, W. (1997) [Eds.], *Evaluation for the 21$^{st}$ Century,* SAGE Publications, Thousands Oaks, London, New Delhi.

Picciotto, R., and Wiesner, E., (1998), *Evaluation and Development,* The Institutional Dimension, Transaction Publishers, New Brusnwick (USA) and London (UK).

Rist, R., (1999), *Program Evaluation and the Management of Government,* Transaction Publishers.

Svensson, K. (1997), 'The Analysis and Evaluation of Foreign Aid,' in Chelimsky, E., and Shadish, W. (1997) [Eds.], *Evaluation for the 21$^{st}$ Century,* SAGE Publications, Thousands Oaks, London, New Delhi.

Vedung, E., (1997), *Public Policy and Program Evaluation,* Transaction Publishers.

Weiss, C. (1980), 'Knowledge Creep and Decision Accretion,' *Knowledge: Creation, Diffusion, and Utilization,* Vol. 1, No. 3: 381-404.

Weiss, C. (2000), 'Which Links in Which Theories Shall We Evaluate?,' *New Directions for Evaluation,* No.87, Fall.

Weiss, C., and Bucuvalas, M. (1980c), 'Truth Tests and Utility Tests: Decision makers' Frames of Reference for social science research,' *American Sociological Review,* Vol. 45, (1):302-313.

World Bank, (1998), *Assessing Development Effectiveness,* Operations Evaluation Department of the World Bank, Washington, DC.

World Bank, (2000a), *Glossary of Evaluation Terms,* Operations Evaluation Department, internal methodology paper.

World Bank, (2000b), Statistics on the World Bank's Dam Portfolio.

World Commission on Dams, (2000b), *Dams and Development: A New Framework for Decision-making,* EarthScan Publications Ltd., London and Sterling, VA.

Yin, R. K. (1994), *Case Study Research: Design and Methods,* Second Edition, Applied Social Research Methods Series, Volume 5, SAGE Publications, Thousand Oaks London, New Delhi.

# Postscript

## Theory of Knowledge and Use of Evaluation: Popper's Relevance for the Concept of Streams of Evaluation Knowledge

*Olaf Rieper*

The relevance of Karl R. Popper to the discussion on streams of evaluation knowledge is illustrated through references to Popper in selected works of Donald T. Campbell and Charles C. Lindblom. The two authors hold different positions in regard to theory of knowledge in evaluations, which help to deepen the understanding and clarify points in the actual debate within the evaluation community. The thoughts of Campbell and Lindblom are enriching the discussion of the various points of views in relation to streams of evaluative knowledge and individual evaluation studies that are dealt with through out this book. The relevance of Popper for evaluation is visible on the issue of evaluative knowledge, on use of evaluation, and on unintended consequences of interventions.

### Introduction

Karl R. Popper seems to encompass both the "monitoring" and the "evaluation" component in the concept of streams of evaluation knowledge. These two aspects are in this chapter represented by Donald T. Campbell and Charles E. Lindblom, both of whom are used as prisms for an exploration of the intellectual relevance of Popper for the discussion in this book on evaluation knowledge based on individual evaluation studies and on streams of information. I attempt to limit the focus to two dimensions: theory of knowledge and use of evaluation. Campbell and Lindblom differ on both dimensions, but both are using Popper to consolidate their points of view. Examples from references to Popper by Campbell and Lindblom and by evaluators of today are used to illuminate the discussion of the chapters in this book by relating to the questions on managing streams of evaluation knowledge and individual evaluation studies.

Campbell is well known for his writings on quasi-experimental design in evaluation (Campbell, 1957, 1969). Charles C. Lindblom's well-known key concept, "muddling through," in decision-making and policy processes is relevant for use of evaluation. The reason for having chosen these two authors, beyond their obvious relevance for theory of evaluation knowledge and use, is that they represent divergent positions as to what constitutes valid scientific knowledge as well as what is characteristic for the policy and decision-making processes in which evaluation knowledge is supposed to be used. Thus, the evaluation aspect and the monitoring aspect of M&E systems are hopefully deepened and made more clear to the readers by taking some points of the discussion in the field of evaluation and in social science more generally back to its historical roots. In a few words, Campbell represents the means-ends rational view on society and a belief in the superiority and validity of scientific knowledge, whereas Lindblom represents a less rational view and has less faith in the status of scientific knowledge to be used for improvements in society.

Both authors even with such different positions have been associated with Popper. How can it be? What issues in relation to the theory of knowledge and to the use of knowledge in Popper's writings have been referred to by Campbell and Lindblom, and what issues have others associated with Campbell and Popper? What questions and issues have been paths and food for further discussion in this book?

The chapter is explorative because it would be an enormous task to read through even the major part of the works of Popper, Campbell, and Lindblom. I have taken a few examples from their writings to demonstrate Popper's contribution to evaluation today.

The structure of the chapter is as follows. First, the main issues in Popper's writings will be outlined. Second, the relevance of Popper on issues within the theory of knowledge in evaluation will be explored. Third, the relevance of Popper on issues within the theory of use of M&E systems will be sketched out.

## Main Issues in Popper's Writings

Popper's contribution to the social sciences is in two fields: One is in the theory of scientific knowledge, the other is in his anti-historiscism and its implications for how we use knowledge of society in designing social institutions.

*Popper's theory of scientific knowledge* emerges from his criticism of the Vienna Circle of Logical Positivists. He contributed to the debate within the philosophy of science through his critical rationalism, which is in opposition to the positivistic belief in verification of social regularities or laws. His formulation of the principle of falsifiability became famous, and is clearly of relevance to the concept of "evidence based" evaluation:

## Theory of Knowledge and Use of Evaluation 273

... I shall not require of a scientific system that it shall be capable of being singled out, once and for all, in a positive sense; but I shall require that its logical form shall be such that it can be singled out, by means of empirical tests, in a negative sense: *it must be possible for an empirical scientific system to be refuted by experience.* [(Popper, 1972a (1959), pp. 40-41)].

I suppose that today every evaluator would agree on this statement. But if we take it a little further disagreement arises. Take the issue of how to select evaluation studies for use in synthesizing reviews that are part of streams of knowledge even if they build on individual evaluation studies. Should the studies selected all be based on experiment design and should, e.g., case studies be included as well? What are the criteria for internal validity of data? And how is external validity secured, that is, how do we know that findings and results of evaluation studies can be transferred to other contexts and interventions?

Popper's *criticism of historicism* has one central implication for the use of social science (evaluation included) in designing and changing society, namely his concept "piecemeal social engineering," according to which social change takes place by small adjustments and readjustments rather than by trying to redesign major parts of society. Society is improved not by formulating grand objectives for high politics, but rather by avoiding evils (risks) that most of the actors agree about.

One has to remember that Popper was thinking and writing in the context of the intellectual and political Marxist debate of the "law of history." Popper was from his youth debating against the totalitarian ideologies and regimes of his time, that is, the fascist and the communist ideologies. Popper's point of view was that the social sciences do not allow us to make historical prophecies, but they may give an idea of and provide reason for what can and what cannot be done in the political field.

How does the concept of "*piecemeal social engineering*" relate to his critique of historicism? Motivated by his belief that totalitarian ideologies typically justify themselves by referring to general laws of the overall development of history (and society), Popper worked with the aim of refuting that thinking, which he describes as "historicism." He regards history as a descriptive and explanatory discipline, not a generalizing one. History does not set up general laws, but tries to give a coherent narrative in which events are explained and inferred with the assistance of laws supplied by the social sciences. Popper argues against the possibility of large-scale, unconditional prediction about the course of history in general.

From Popper's critique of the historicism in the totalitarian regimes of his time to his opposition to a design of a utopian society in the future the road is logical. No social science is capable of having a theory that legitimizes sacrifices for a major redesign of social institutions (a revolution) to a communist paradise (or other ideal future state of society). The doctrine of historicism states that the task of social sciences is to propound historical prophecies and that historical prophecies are needed if we wish to conduct politics in a rational way (Popper, 1972b, p. 336). Popper argues against the doctrine of historicism by saying, first that predictions in science are conditional, and second that historical prophecies can only be derived from scientific predictions if they apply to systems that have isolated, stationary, and recurrent characteristics. This is certainly not the case of social systems.

Again, few if any evaluators would probably disagree on this point of view. The connection to evaluation use can be made if one descends from Popper's macro perspective on society to the middle range level of programs and institutions. At the middle range level of society Popper's statement can be translated into scepticism of the fruitfulness of huge individual ex-post evaluation studies to be used as information base for redesigning policy and program at one point in time. This supports the argument that evaluation studies should not stand alone.

One response to these implications is summed up in Popper's notion of "piecemeal engineering." This concept he formulates in contrast to the "utopian engineering" that can be regarded as an extreme version of management by objectives. Popper describes it as the formulation of the final objective for the society, a master plan, with which all the intermediary objectives have to comply. The overall objectives have to be established first, and then the underlying ones are to be established. Piecemeal engineering, in contrast, focuses on identifying and fighting the problems and evils of present society instead of trying to attain the highest objectives.

> ...by using the piecemeal method we may get over the very greatest practical difficulty of all reasonable political reform, namely the use of reason, instead of passion and violence, in executing the programme. There will be a possibility of reaching a reasonable compromise and therefore of achieving the improvement by democratic methods. [(Popper, 1969 (1945), p. 159)].

Another issue of relevance for evaluation is Popper's focus on *negative side effects of interventions* and of human behavior in general. In several of his works Popper stated that the main task of the theoretical social sciences is to trace the unintended social repercussions of intentional human actions (Popper, 1972, p. 342; Popper, 1992, p. 80). In fact, unanticipated consequences of human actions are regarded as an important field of study in social sciences, such as sociology. Robert K. Merton devotes several pages that subject in his classical book: *Social Theory and Social Structure* (Merton 1964, pp 51ff).

Vedung has been aware of Popper's contribution on that issue to evaluation, and relates the discussion of unintended consequences to criticism of the goal-attainment evaluation model and to the strength of side-effects evaluation (Vedung, 1997, pp. 45–59). The side effects might be difficult to identify in M&E systems that are designed as goal attainment models of evaluation, but are most likely to be identified in carefully designed comprehensive evaluation studies that are theory driven.

### The Relevance of Popper to the Theory of Knowledge in Evaluation

The term "theory of knowledge" in evaluation is drawn from Shadish, Cook, and Leviton (1991) meaning what counts as acceptable knowledge about the object being evaluated. Which methods produce credible evidence? And which philosophical assumptions are behind the valued concept of knowledge?

*Examples of Popper's References to Campbell and Vice Versa:*

An example of Campbell referring to Popper is his article on "Reforms as Experiments" from 1969 referring to Popper's *Conjectures and Refutations* (1969) to justify that competitive scrutiny (the social experimentation) is the main source of objectivity in sciences. Campbell states that it epitomizes an ideal of democratic practice in both juridical and legislative procedures (Campbell, 1969, p. 416). The increasing use of the concept of "evidence" in the evaluation literature indicates a growing interest for legitimizing evaluation based on (quasi) experimental designs. Also the establishment of the Campbell Collaboration within social and educational policies and practices (as well as the Cochrane Collaboration within medicine) mirrors a concern for basing evaluation methods on a specific scientific paradigm.

This tendency in fact favours individual evaluation studies based on experiment design with the strength of obtaining highly internal validity of findings, but with the weaknesses of risking low external validity and of leaving out the learning potential of process evaluation because teachings for program managers and decision makers are contextual specific. However streams of information based on experiment design may well be suitable for less complex interventions with well-defined goals and measurable indicators of success.

The reverse example of Popper's reference to Campbell is in Schilpp (1974). Here, Popper responds to Campbell (as part of a discussion) and states:

> Professor Campbell's remarkable contribution is perhaps the one which shows the greatest agreement with my epistemology, and (what he cannot know) an astonishing anticipation of some things which I had not yet published when he wrote his paper. In addition it is a treatise of prodigious historical learning: there is scarcely anything in the whole of modern epistemology to compare with it; certainly not in my own work. His historical references are all highly relevant; they are a real treasure house; and they often surprised me greatly.

> For me the most striking thing about Campbell's essay is the almost complete agreement, down even to minute details, between Campbell's views and my own. I shall try to develop one or two of these points a little further still, and shall then turn to the very rare and comparatively minor points where there may be some difference of opinion. (Popper cited in Schilpp, 1974, pp. 1059–1065)

It is obvious that Popper experiences a high degree of agreement between Campbell's view and his own.

Examples of Lindblom referring to Popper is Lindblom (1990, chapter 10), where the issue is the professional dependence on lay probing. Lindblom is using Popper as support to the statement that all science is enlightened common sense and that testing for empirical "truth" becomes a social process.

Also Lindblom and Campbell have referred to each other. In his discussion of social science knowledge in relation to ordinary inquiry, Lindblom rejects the idea of a scientifically guided society, and argues for a model of a self-guided society. Lindblom regards an important dimension in the self-guided society to be learning from error and from action.

> In the model of scientific guidance, problem solving is entirely cerebral. In the alternative model, the acknowledged impossibility of anyone's ever achieving a full grasp of the relevant complexities of society compels action in ignorance. Hence the model counts on strategies like trial and error, in which the trial serves not simply as an action to attempt a solution but provides feedback information to illuminate subsequent attempts. In this model, citizens, functionaries, social scientists, and other experts do what they have learned and then learn what they have done ..." (Lindblom, 1990, p. 219)

Lindblom is referring to Campbell's Reforms as Experiments and seems to consider the controlled experiment design as an extreme version of the trial and error strategy.

Lindblom's position on trial and error in his vision of the self-guided society seems to be familiar with the positions on streams of evaluation knowledge put forward in this book.

By an "extreme version" I refer to the meaning that one extreme of the trial and error strategy is the controlled scientific experiment. The other extreme is the practice of trying different interventions and by experience finding out which one is a good one providing expected results. The practice might be the practice of program staff or of professional service providers. For the evaluation field the two extremes might be exemplified by the controlled experiment design (once again) and self-evaluation based on case studies.

*Examples of Other Authors Associating Views of Campbell or Lindblom with Popper's*

Hoffstetter and Alkin in their summary and synthesis of studies of evaluation utilization are citing another author for having references to Popper (as well as to Campbell) in relation to the argument that ordinary knowledge is not fundamentally different from policy (social) science knowledge and that the two are intrinsically bound together (Hofstetter and Alkin 2002, p 11). The issue here is in the field of theory of knowledge. The author is making the point that what differentiates the two types of knowledge is how they are verified. Ordinary knowledge is field-tested by those who hold such knowledge (that is, by trial and error in practice settings) whereas policy science (and evaluative) knowledge is, at best, verified via quasi-experimental research design or other design and methods of empirical research.

Shadish, Cook, and Leviton (1991) are relating Campbell to Popper; six out of seven references to Popper in their book are to be found in the chapter on Campbell. In particular, Shadish, Cook and Leviton stress the parallel between Campbell and Popper in their emphasis on the experiment design to obtain valid knowledge. According to Campbell internal validity is foremost obtained by random assignment of control and treatment groups, because this design allows the falsifying of many competing interpretations. Rating out alternative explanations is the crucial issue, like in Popper's principle of falsifiability. Like Popper, Campbell also stresses the importance of variation (as in biological and social evolution) and he regards evaluation as a means to select that variant (of an intervention or social program) that reduces the severity of a social problem (Shadish, Cook, and Leviton, 1991, pp. 122–147).

The discussion of strengths and weaknesses of the experimental designs in social science in general and in evaluation in particular is ongoing. Oakley (2000) has made a plea for the randomized experiment design. In the field of meta evaluation or systematic reviews, the Cochrane center within medicine and the Campbell Collaboration in social, behavioral and educational arenas have as objectives to produce and disseminate systematic reviews of studies of interventions. As criteria for selecting the individual studies to be reviewed, the studies in which experiment designs are used have a high priority. Evaluators and social researchers have proposed alternatives to experimental design for systematic reviews; e.g., Pawson, 2002 has recommended narrative reviews with a "configurational" approach to causality, as well as realist reviews that utilize a "generative" approach to causation (Pawson, 2002).

## The Relevance of Popper to the Theory of Use in Evaluation

The theory of use of evaluation concerns how social science information can be used in social policy and programming. It deals with different kinds of use and what evaluators can do to increase use (Shadish, Cook, and Leviton, 1991, p. 36). The use of evaluation is also related to the evaluators' perception of policy processes and decision making in designing and implementing programs and interventions to reduce social problems.

*Examples of Other Authors Associating Campbell or Lindblom with Popper*

Fitz-Gibbon (2002) is referring to Popper when arguing for a democratic/professional scientific approach to design of monitoring and evaluation systems, in contrast to a hierarchical/controlling managerial approach with targets, rewards, and punishment.

> We can contrast Popper's "scientific" approach, involving participative, democratic, organic, interacting systems and acknowledging that the future is un-predictable, with a "totally planned" "managerial" society in which procedures are dictated and prescribed by hierarchical systems. It seems likely that two fundamental differences between these approaches are (1) a belief in being able to control and predict the future, and (2) a lack of trust and respect for those most closely involved: "the people" (Fitz-Gibbon, 2002, p. 141).

According to Fitz-Gibbon, Popper is arguing for the fundamental value not being to enable people to seek happiness, but to minimize avoidable suffering. This implies to locate problems and to take steps to improve the system to remove problems. Thus, this issue relates to Popper's concept of "piecemeal social engineering." In this way Fitz-Gibbon is using Popper more in the spirit of Lindblom than of Campbell by stressing the participative and democratic visions of Popper as well as Popper's argument against the planned means-ends rational society. As such the echo of the thoughts behind the M&E systems is heard; see the chapter of Rist in this book.

In the evaluation literature on utilization there are several references to Lindblom's thinking. Patton (1977, p. 148) has noted that evaluation is used as one piece of information that feeds into a slow, evolutionary process of program development. Program development is considered as a process of muddling through and evaluation is part of the muddling (Hofstetter and Alkin, 2002, p. 15). Again the similarity with the concept of streams of knowledge is obvious.

Albæk 1995 discusses the linkages between science and politics in a non-rational decision-making perspective, and draws heavily on Lindblom's theories. According to Albæk, Lindblom's concept on "muddling through" is a frontal attack on rational planning and its notions of the potential for implementing large-scale reforms. The basic view of this incrementalism is that decision makers choose to act cautiously when they are faced with great uncertainty because of lack of information on causes and effects, the actions of others, and the consequences of their choices. (Albæk, 1995, p. 87) observes that Lindblom's position resembles that of Popper when the latter recommends "piecemeal social engineering."

Let us take a closer look at Lindblom's notion of incremental social change or "muddling through" in order to see its connection to Popper's notion of piecemeal engineering and to M&E systems. Lindblom has authored two books on use of knowledge in the tradition of sociology of knowledge. The most recent one is from 1990 in which he argues that social science only has, and only should have, a limited role in policy and public administration. Social scientific analysis cannot demonstrate empirically the efficiency of one intervention over several others. Social science cannot be conclusive, other sources of knowledge are most valuable to policy-making. Social science knowledge is no alternative to ordinary inquiry, but an aid, refiner, extender, and, sometimes, tester of it (Lindblom, 1990, p. 216). Lindblom rejects the idea of a scientifically guided society, and is considering mutual adjustment as a general primary mechanism for development (p. 247), just as mutual adjustment in organization theory is regarded as a coordinating mechanism in complex systems with a high degree of uncertainty (Scott, 1998, p. 231ff).

The debate of rational versus non-rational processes has a long history in the social sciences and in organization theory in particular. This is described in the literature on evaluation use. Less known is the related discussion on strong versus weak causal reasoning. From a rational perception one should deal with a particular social problem by determining its particular causes and then develop politics that are directed at these causes. This type of reasoning Rein and Winship (1999) call strong causal reasoning. An approach to this problem will only work if the causes strongly affect the symptoms. Rein and Winship put up a number of good reasons for the impossibility of basing social policy on this type of thinking, e.g., social science has only been able to provide "weak" causal theories, essential normative questions cannot be answered by social scientists, social science models have almost always weak explanatory power and are sensitive to the model specification used (Rein and Winship, 1999, pp. 40–42).

This line of reasoning is very much in accordance with the logic of M&E systems, namely, that implementation studies should complement outcome evaluations.

## Conclusion and Discussion

I have used Campbell and Lindblom as prisms for discussing the possible relevance of Popper for the evaluation community in general and for the discussion in this book on streams of knowledge from M&E systems. I have selected examples showing that Popper has been used in evaluation literature primarily on the issue of what constitutes credible knowledge in evaluation, and on the issue of the nature of change in policy and public programs and the use of evaluation in these processes. The issue of negative side effects of interventions is important, but only modestly dealt with in relation to Popper.

Related to his epistemology of knowledge and his principle of falsifiability, Popper has been closely associated with experimental designs in evaluation, mainly via Campbell. Related to Popper's concept of piecemeal social engineering, Popper has been used to argue for incremental change in policy and programs and for a more modest role for social science knowledge and a more influence from practical knowledge by professionals and citizens.

How could both Campbell and Lindblom with rather different positions be associated with Popper? The closest link is to Campbell and his reasoning on experimental designs. This goes very well with the epistemology of Popper. The link between piecemeal engineering and incremental change is much looser because Popper is reasoning at a societal level against theories (and practice) of revolution (at macro level), whereas Lindblom's focus is on policy processes, that is, a middle range level of society.

I have tried to illustrate how Popper's work is seen through selected works of Campbell and Lindblom and other more recent authors within the evaluation field, and is relevant for the discussion in this book on evaluation knowledge. As for the use of evaluation I have drawn parallels between incremental change, muddling through, and piecemeal social engineering on the one hand, and "streams of evaluation knowledge" on the other hand. As for the theory of knowledge it has been demonstrated how Popper has been referred to in the tension between ordinary knowledge and scientific knowledge based on experiment design. The discussion of valid methods and criteria for selection of studies used in meta evaluations or systematic reviews is highly relevant, because such reviews are to become a major part of future streams of evaluation information and knowledge.

## References

Albæk, Erik (1995) 'Between knowledge and power: Utilization of social science in public policy making'. *Policy Sciences* 28:79-100.

Campbell, Donald T. (1957) 'Factors relevant to the validity of experiments in social settings'. *Psychological Bulletin* 54(4):297-312.

Campbell, Donald T. (1969) 'Reforms as experiments'. *American psychologist* 24(4): 409-429.

Fitz-Gibbon, Carol Taylor (2002) 'Evaluation in an Age of Indicators. Challenges for Public Sector Management'. *Evaluation* 8(1):140-148.

Hofstetter, Carolyn Huie and Marvin C. Alkin (2002) 'Evaluation Use Revisited' in D. Nevo and D. Stufflebeam (eds.) *International Handbook of Educational Evaluation.* Kluwer Academic Press. Dordrecht.

Lindblom, Charles E. (1959) The Science of 'Muddling Through'. *Public Administration Review* XIX: 79-88. Springer.

Lindblom, Charles E. (1990) *Inquiry and Change. The Troubled Attempt to Under-stand and Change Society.* Yale University Press.

Lindblom, Charles E. and David K. Cohen (1979) *Usable Knowledge. Social Science and Social Problem Solving.* Yale University Press.

Lindblom, Charles E. and E.J. Woodhouse (1993) *The policy-making process* (3rd ed.). Englewood Cliffs, NJ: Prentice Hall.

Merton, Robert K. (1964) *Social Theory and Social Structure – Revised and enlarged edition* (p 51ff). London: Collier-Macmillan Limited.

Oakley, Ann (2000) 'Experiments in Knowing – Gender and Method in the Social Sciences'. *Polity Press.* Oxford.

Patton, Mikael Q. (1977) 'In search of impact: An analysis of utilization of the federal health evaluation research' in C.H. Weiss (ed.) *Using social research in public policy making,* pp 141-164. Lexington, MA.

Pawson, Ray (2002) Evidence-based Policy. The Promise of "Realist Synthesis". *Evaluation* Vol 8(3):340-358.

Popper, Karl R. (1969) *The Open Society and Its Enemies.* Volume I. London: Routledge (original 1945).

Popper, Karl R. (1972) *Conjectures and Refutations. The Growth of Scientific Knowledge.* London and Henley: Routledge and Kegan Paul.

Popper, Karl R. (1972b) *The Logic of Scientific Discovery*. London: Hutchinson.
Popper, Karl R. (1992) *In Search of a Better World. Lectures and essays from thirty years*. London and New York: Routledge.
Rein, Martin and Christopher Winship (1999) 'The Dangers of "Strong" Causal Reasoning in Social Policy'. *Society* 36(5):38-46.
Schilpp, Paul Arthur (ed.) (1974) *The Philosophy of Karl Popper*. La Salle, Illinois: Open Court Publishing Company.
Scott, Richard W. (1998) *Organizations: rational, natural, and open systems*. Upper Saddle River, N.J.: Prentice-Hall.
Shadish, William R. Jr., Thomas D. Cook and Laura C. Leviton (1991) *Foundations of Program Evaluation. Theories of Practices*. London: Sage Publications.
Vedung, Evert (1997) *Public Policy and Program Evaluation*. London: Transaction Publishers.
Weiss, Carol Hirschon (2000): 'The Experimenting Society in a Political World' in Leonard Bickman (ed.): *Validity and social experimentation: Donald Campbell's legacy*. Thousand Oaks, California: Sage Publications.

# Conclusion

# A Brief Critique

*Ray C. Rist*

Nearly 400 yeas ago, Francis Bacon wrote that knowledge is power. That maxim still holds true today. Indeed, as the breath and depth of knowledge in the world has grown exponentially in these last centuries, so, too, has the means by which this knowledge can be used as a form of power that shapes our lives. Whether it is the green revolution that now feeds millions or biological and nuclear weapons that can destroy millions, the scale of the impacts of new knowledge is immense. This continuous production of new knowledge available surely outpaces our ability to mediate and codify it.

This volume addresses this emergence of new knowledge in one delimited arena, albeit an important one—that of contemporary organization life. The focus on knowledge creation here is on that to be learned from the ways in which organizations design themselves, their behaviors, their intended objectives, and the results of their actions. Organizations are one (if not the most) dominant characteristic of contemporary life. They structure how we arrange our lives in profound, and not so profound, ways. They help define our definitions of ourselves, give more or less status to the work we do, and shape our activities and actions for most of our waking hours.

And so, how do organizations create, mediate, and distribute new knowledge? They do it in multiple ways, for example, by systematically learning from pilot initiatives, by fostering research and development, by bringing in new talent and perspectives from outside, by being open to what may be trial and error of new innovations, by listening to their environment and their clients, by keeping extensive records and documents, by monitoring their own performance, and, central to the thesis of this book, by evaluation.

Organizations learn more or less quickly, more or less systematically, and more or less comprehensively. History is replete with evidence of organizational learning—or the lack of it. Military strategies that worked at one time do not at a later time; business practices that were successful once were later no more; medical procedures and crime prevention, the same. Evaluation has become a central management tool for learning about the consequences (intended and unintended) of organizational action.

What this book posits is that the evaluation community is lagging behind in its understandings of the learning needs of increasingly large numbers of organizations that view themselves as learning organizations. These high performance organizations embrace learning and knowledge as fundamental to their own existence and success. They are continually working to enhance their means of knowledge management so that they can draw on their own organizational knowledge to improve their performance. The strategies for building effective and accessible knowledge management systems require bringing together information and knowledge from multiple sources and then codifying it in ways appropriate to the information needs of the organization.

The evaluation community, on the other hand, takes as the norm for how to relate to organizations those that continue to behave in conventional ways, maintain conventional structures, have low investments in both knowledge and performance management, and presume they can function in a status quo environment. These organizations ask for individual evaluation studies and the evaluation community is happy to comply. Whether the organizations are asking the right questions, whether they can use the evaluative information produced, and whether the evaluation is timely and relevant to management needs are of concern to some evaluators, but not to the degree that the relation breaks down. The evaluators are hired to produce studies and it is studies they produce. The scale and scope of evaluation work is overwhelmingly limited in this approach, both in terms of knowledge produced and in the validity of the findings.

Stretching the thesis still further, the proposition by Furubo and others in this volume is that the evaluation community, itself, consequently behaves in ways that are increasingly irrelevant (if not dysfunctional) to the learning needs of more and more organizations. There is a downward spiral and the evaluation community seems either unaware or unwilling to do anything about it.

### How and Why is This So?

Succinctly, the evaluation community overwhelmingly continues to define evaluation work as the production of individual, discrete studies for individual, discrete users. Studies pile up over time; evaluation amnesia means the same questions are asked time and again; the time lags have all sorts of adverse consequences; and careers are built on how many studies one has done as well as how large the study budgets have become. The evaluation community perpetuates an approach to its craft with which it is comfortable, where it has set up its own incentive and reward structures, and where it socializes new recruits with training on how to design, manage, and report on yet more individual evaluation studies. And all this goes on as the growing disillusionment about the ability of evaluation to contribute to organizational knowledge management gains strength.

The other side of this coin also needs to be noted. Many evaluators continue in this approach because many organizations ask it of them. Individual studies are requested and funded for the study of discrete activities and interventions. Not all organizations think of becoming high performance or do they think they are currently under-performing. They can also be using evaluations for reasons other than organizational improvement. Thus, the present set of arrangements is quite acceptable. This is the world, more or less, of single studies for single users. It is a minuet both groups seem ready to dance.

But all around them the world is changing and the music is quite different. Whether it is the New York City Police Department; the health observatories of Canada, France, Germany, the Netherlands, or Switzerland; international development banks; Italy's policy of regularization for the shadow economy; or systematically assessing policy tools in Canada (all of these examples in this book), the reality of new forms of evaluative knowledge creation in organizations is happening outside the traditional bounds of producing more and more single evaluation studies. As the volume makes clear, what is emerging is the expectation, indeed, the demand, for streams of real-time evaluative knowledge within high performance organizations as a tool for managing successfully.

Perhaps the evaluation community will begin to make this transition from producing individual, single evaluation studies to contributing to streams of evaluative knowledge. The tools to do so are already available as the chapters here by Perrin, Marra, Spinstasch, and Dalher-Larsen, among others, document. And the production of individual studies need not cease. These studies can feed into the creation of streams if appropriately done so. Perrin, in his chapter, describes two approaches—that of the synthesis and the identification of good practices. Others are noted elsewhere. But the point is fundamental. Piling up more and more discrete studies has significant limitations in generating new knowledge or providing useful guidance for managers.

There is a subtext here to be noted as well. High performance organizations moving to the development of streams of evaluative knowledge are not waiting for evaluators to get the message. They are hiring others to do the work. The analytic skills to do evaluation syntheses or continually aggregate and distill evaluative evidence are available in many social science disciplines. Thus, the following syllogism: If evaluators focus on conducting single studies, and if single studies are increasingly marginalized and irrelevant to the information needs of organizational managers, then evaluators are increasingly marginalized and irrelevant to these same managers. This is the message the evaluation community seems unwilling to acknowledge.

## A Final thought

Individual evaluation studies will be part of the organizational landscape for some time to come. Many organizations think they need them and many evaluators think it is their responsibility to produce them. New evaluative knowledge that is useful to organizational leadership may or may not emanate from all this work. The evidence to date is not encouraging.

But there are new realities that are challenging the status quo and comfort level of the evaluation community. High performance organizations are drastically changing the paradigm of presuming that good evaluative knowledge will come from providing single studies for single users—or even single studies for multiple users. A quite different approach to evaluative knowledge has emerged where the creation and sustaining of streams of such knowledge is now a fundamental requirement. This book has sought to describe this new approach and its ramifications with a number of case examples. It has also given examples of organizations that are aware of this new approach and are struggling to find their way into it. The evaluation community can acknowledge this shift in the creation of knowledge systems and respond accordingly, or not. Either way, the evaluation community will have shaped its own future.

# List of Contributors

Xavier Ballart is Professor of Political and Administrative Sciences, Universidad Autónoma de Barcelona. He is also the Vice Dean of the School of Political Science and Sociology. He is the former editor of Revista Española de Ciencia Política. His research interests include: program evaluation, innovation in Public Management, public administration in Spain and in Europe, and most currently, on symbolic policies where he is writing a book.

Per Oyvind Bastoe, a sociologist has held various senior positions in the Norwegian Government administration, in Nordic consulting companies and in Multilateral Development Banks. He has published several books, articles and reports on results management and organizational change issues. He is currently Principal Results Management Specialist in the Asian Development Bank in Manila.

Peter Dahler-Larsen, Ph.D., is professor at the Department of Political Science and Public Management, University of Southern Denmark. His main research interest is in institutional and constructivist approaches to evaluation. He is also interested in theory-based evaluation. He is currently the President of European Evaluation Society.

Pearl Eliadis is a lawyer who specializes in public policy, with a focus on governance, social justice, and community development. She is Chief Knowledge Officer at the J.W. McConnell Family Foundation in Montreal where her responsibilities include strategy and evaluation. Before that she was Senior Research Director of the Policy Research Initiative of the Privy Council Office (Canada). Ms. Eliadis is a member of the Ministerial Advisory Group of the federal Minister of Justice and the Banff Policy Forum.

Kim Forss graduated from the Stockholm School of Economics, but now works as an independent researcher and consultant out of his company Andante—tools for thinking AB. He works with the design of evaluation systems, development of evaluation methodologies, and he undertakes the conducting of evaluations—sometimes as an external evaluator, at other times to facilitate internal evaluation.

Jan-Eric Furubo is an experienced evaluator since the 1970s. Since the mid-1980s he has been with the National Audit Office in Sweden. He is the author of many articles and publications in the field of evaluation and the relation between budgeting, auditing and evaluation. He is co-editor of the International Atlas of Evaluation published 2002. He has been member of the board and Secretary General of European Evaluation Society.

Yoon-Shik Lee is a professor of the Department of Public Administration at Soongsil University in Seoul, Korea. His major field is Program Evaluation. He is now interested in not only program evaluation but also information management. He served as President of the Korean Association for Policy Analysis and Evaluation in 2000 and President of the Korean Association for Policy Studies in 2003. He is now serving as Chairman of the Professional Committee on Innovation and Decentralization Evaluation in the Presidential Committee on Government Innovation and Decentralization.

Frans L. Leeuw is currently Director, Research, Statistics and Documentation Center (WODC), Ministry of Justice, the Netherlands. He is also Professor, Evaluation Studies, Faculty of Social Sciences, Utrecht University. He was President of the European Evaluation Society (1999-2002). As of September 2003, he is President of the Dutch Evaluation Society. He has authored numerous articles, reports, and books in the areas of program evaluation, theory-based evaluations, educational evaluations, and performance monitoring.

Donald Lemaire has degrees in both economics and law. A member of the Quebec Bar, he has extensive experience and considerable expertise in public administration. He began his career with the federal public service in September 1981 as an economist with Agriculture Canada. After fulfilling various functions with the Social Sciences and Humanities Research Council and Correctional Service Canada, in the early 1990s. In April 2003, he took on top executive roles, such as Special Advisor to the Deputy Minister and Acting Assistant Deputy Minister at Justice Canada. He has recently been appointed Vice-President with the Public Service Commission.

Mita Marra is assistant professor of public policy at Maastricht University and research fellow within Italy's National Research Council. Since 1998, Mita Marra has consulted with the World Bank Institute and the Operations Evaluation Department of the World Bank. She is interested in the role of evaluation within the public sector.

Ragnhild Øvrelid's research practice and publications are mainly within the field of Sociology of Law. She has conducted evaluation projects and worked as a counselor organizing the use of research-based knowledge in the Ministry of Justice and The Ministry of Social Affairs. She is currently senior adviser at Statskonsult, conducting projects concerning public management.

## List of Contributors

Burt Perrin, an independent consultant based in France, has over thirty years' practical experience internationally in evaluation, policy and program development, and strategic planning on behalf of governments at all levels, international organizations, non-governmental organizations (NGOs), and the private sector. He places strong emphasis on taking a practical approach so that evaluation is most likely to result in action. He is particularly known for his ability to identify and synthesize information that cuts across topic areas, jurisdictions, and discrete program boundaries.

Claus C. Rebien is Head of Department for Public Administration & Law at the Danish consultancy company COWI. He has undertaken numerous evaluation assignments, developed evaluation manuals, guidelines and systems and done research internationally on evaluation tools and methods. Presently, he is involved in evaluation projects for the European Commission, and in developing an evaluation guide for the Ministry of Finance in Denmark

Olaf Rieper is director of research at the Institute of Local Government Studies, Denmark (AKF). He has been a visiting scholar at the University of Michigan and expert at the Centre for European Evaluation Expertice, Lyon, France. He has written on evaluation research methods and conducted evaluation on research programs for the Norwegian Research Council. He has been on assignments for the EU Commission.

Ray C. Rist is a Senior Evaluation Officer in the World Bank. Prior to coming to the World Bank in 1996, his career has included fifteen years in the United States government with appointments in both the executive and legislative branches. He has served as a university professor with positions at Johns Hopkins University, Cornell University, and George Washington University. Dr. Rist was the Senior Fulbright Fellow at the Max Planck Institute in Berlin, Germany in 1976 and 1977. He has authored, edited, or co-edited twenty-four books, written more than 125 articles, and has lectured in more than sixty countries. He serves on the editorial boards of nine professional journals.

Markus Spinatsch has worked in the areas of fundamental and applied research, first in international development, then in the field of health behavior and addictions. From 1991 to 1996, he was head of the Administration Control Unit of the Swiss Parliament. Since 1997, Dr. Spinatsch has been an independent consultant for public policies and administration in Bern, Switzerland.

Nicoletta Stame is professor of Social Policy at the University of Roma "La Sapienza." She has been the first president of the Italian Evaluation Society and is currently president of the European Evaluation Society. She is associate editor of *Evaluation*. She has worked on the theories and methodologies of evaluation, and has been involved in the evaluation of programs of local development, regularization of irregular work, social welfare and public administration reform. She is author of "L'esperienza della valutazione" (Rome, 1998), and of many articles and essays.

Marit Stadler Waerness works as management consult in the Norwegian Statskonsult, a state-owned company that deals with public management development. Previously she has worked for the Swedish National Audit Office and National Agency for Higher Education. She has a broad experience in the areas of performance management, evaluation and organizational development in the public sector.

Eduardo Zapico is now working as adviser in the Evaluation Unit of the DG Budget of the European Commission. Previously he worked as a Deputy Director of Policy Analysis, in the DG Budget at the Ministry of Finances in Spain. He has worked in the National Audit Office of Spanish central Government, in the fields of public expenditure control and program evaluation. He has collaborated on Budgeting and PEM capacity development projects with the OECD/SIGMA department, for Central and Eastern Europe, and with the World Bank/FM team for Latin America. Before, he worked at the European Institute of Public Administration (EIPA) in Maastricht (The Netherlands), teaching and researching on public management and budgeting.

# Index

African Development Bank xvi,
  Experience in implementing results-based management, 98-108, 102-105
  Vision, 101

Budgeting
  Links to evaluation, xix, 20, 215-229
  Strategic leadership from central budget office, 216-218

Canada
  Audit General, 132, 133
  Economic Council, 130
  Institute for Health Information, 53, 55, 56
  International Development Agency, 130
  Justice Canada, 135, 138
  Non-legislative policy instruments, xvii, 131, 136, 285,
  Statistics Canada, 53
  Treasury Board, 133
Cochrane Collaboration 57, 59, 60, 61, 275, 277
Contribution Theory 8

Denmark
  National indicator project, 74-75

England
  Health development agency (HAD), 58, 61'
  Health observatories, 53, 55, 56, 59
  National Audit Office, 84

Evaluation
  Amnesia, 156, 284
  Attribution, 11, 116, 117
  Cluster 27-29
  Contribution to knowledge management, xiv, 24, 25, 171-183, 246, 248
  Ex-post, 12
  Good practice system 34-40, 60
    Cultural factors, 38-40
    Leadership and Strategy, 40-41
    Measurement, 41
    Technology, 37-38
    Three levels, 36-37
  Information systems, 13, 65
  Limitations of single studies, viii, 23, 25, 97, 115-118, 283-286
  Links to strategic budgeting, 215-229
  Links to strategic planning, 266-267
  Meta-analysis, 32-33
  Participatory, 223-224
  Streams of evaluative knowledge
    Synthesis, x, 25-27, 29-30, 30-33, 62, 285
    Information systems, x
    Mandated evaluations, x
    Multi-study evaluations, xi
  Systematic reviews, 118-119
  Thematic, 29, 119
  Theory-based, xiii, 83-94, 118-119, 222-223, 229, 259-261
  Types of evaluative knowledge, 83-84
  Uses in decision-making, 13, 15-19, 113-126, 147-162, 169, 173, 225-226, 229

France
  Health observatory, 53, 55, 56

Germany
  Federal health monitoring system, 53, 55, 56

291

Health Observatories xv, 285
  Broker approach, 55
  Monitoring public health, 52-54
  Role in knowledge management, 60-63
  Synthesizer approach, 54-55
Health statistics 50-52, 63

Information systems
  Bounded rationality, 67
  Construction, 66, 67-72
  Criteria-setting, 76
  Evidence-based, 65, 66, 67, 71
  Organization, 66-67
  Political construction, 66, 68, 72, 75
  Social construction, 68-69
  Technological infrastructure, 76-77
International Evaluation Research Group (IERG) 98
Italian shadow economy 122-125, 285

Knowledge management xiv, xvi, 24, 43, 57, 85-92, 170-183,
  Contribution of evaluation, 24, 42-43, 62, 171-172, 235-248
  Links to organizational learning, 235-248
  Use of evaluation synthesis, 25-33
  Use of internet, 169-183
Knowledge processing 57, 60
Knowledge societies 190-193
Korea
  Board of Audit and Inspection, 178
  Evaluation use of ICT, 175-183
  Law on evaluation of government affairs, 175
  Ministry of Planning and Budget, 175, 177
  Office for Policy Coordination, 175

Millennium Development Goals (MDG) xvii, 115, 119-122

Netherlands
  Audit Office, 81-83, 84-87, 929-9
  Central Bureau for Statistics, 83, 89
  Education Inspectorate, 88-91
  Ministry of Education, xvi
  Ministry of Justice, xvi, 84, 88, 91-92
New Public Management 49, 160, 189, 265-267
  Line of sight, 10
New York City
  Use of performance data, 14, 285
Norway
  Budget process, xviii, 193
  Evaluation information in ministries, 187-211
  Ministry of Education, 197-201, 205
  Ministry of Foreign Affairs, 194-197, 205, 206, 208, 209-210
  Ministry of Social Affairs, 201-204, 205-206
  Office of the Auditor General, 204, 207, 209

Organizational knowledge 236-238, 248, 251-267, 283-286
Organization for Economic Cooperation and Development (OECD) 54, 105, 109, 129, 131, 148, 189, 228
Organizational learning 83, 235-248

Performance audits 84
Performance-based management
  Performance indicators, 8, 11
Performance-based monitoring and evaluation 6, 9, 12, 13
  Use as a management tool, 12, 19, 97
Performance budgeting 216-229
Performance evaluation 8
Performance monitoring 7, 220
Program cycle xiii, 13
Program theory 81-94, 148, 229
Project cycle 13

Results-based management (RBM) xvi, 4, 97
  Managing evaluative knowledge, 98-99
Results-based monitoring and evaluation (See also, "Performance-based monitoring and evaluation,") 4, 5

Social capital 225-226
Sweden
  Evaluation culture, 149-152

National Audit Office, 153
Switzerland
   Health observatory, 54, 56, 61
   Knowledge needs in national health service, 50

United Nations Development Program (UNDP) 99
United States
   Agency for Healthcare Research and Quality (AHRQ) 58, 59, 61
   Agency for International Development (USAID) 99
   Government Accountability Office (GAO) 26, 31, 99
   Government Performance and Results ACT (GPRA) 4, 82
   Joint Commission on Hospital Accreditation, 72-74
   Office of Management and Budget (OMB) 216

World Bank xix, 99, 121, 148, 189, 251-267

World Health Organization (WHO) 54, 238